always up to date

The law changes, but Nolo is always on top of it! We offer several ways to make sure you and your Nolo products are always up to date:

 Nolo's Legal Updater

We'll send you an email whenever a new edition of your book is published! Sign up at **www.nolo.com/legalupdater**.

 Updates @ Nolo.com

Check **www.nolo.com/update** to find recent changes in the law that affect the current edition of your book.

 Nolo Customer Service

To make sure that this edition of the book is the most recent one, call us at **800-728-3555** and ask one of our friendly customer service representatives. Or find out at **www.nolo.com**.

4th edition

The
Small Business
Start-Up Kit

By Peri Pakroo

Edited by Barbara Kate Repa

Fourth Edition	FEBRUARY 2006
Editor	BARBARA KATE REPA
Cover Design	SUSAN PUTNEY
Illustrations	ALEXIS MOLLOMO
Book Design	TERRI HEARSH
Production	MARGARET LIVINGSTON
Proofreading	ROBERT WELLS
CD-ROM Preparation	ANDRÉ ZIVKOVICH & DOUG VARN
Indexer	MICHAEL FERREIRA
Printing	CONSOLIDATED PRINTERS, INC.

Pakroo, Peri.
   The small business start-up kit / by Peri Pakroo ; edited by Barbara Kate Repa.--4th ed.
     p. cm
   Includes index.
   ISBN 1-4133-0412-5 (alk. paper)
   1. Small business--Law and legislation--United States--Popular works. 2. New business enterprises–Law and legislation–United States–Popular works. I. Repa, Barbara Kate. II. Title.

KF1659.Z9P35 2006
346.73'0652--dc22

2005055490

Acknowledgments for the First Edition

Many thanks to Beth Laurence, for her sharp editing as well as her encouragement and understanding as I finished the first edition of this book in the middle of a cross-country move. Thanks also to Jake Warner for his helpful input and suggestions, and his unwavering sparkling energy. Thanks are also due to Janet Portman for her review of the material on commercial leases; Patti Gima and Steve Elias for lending their expertise in domain names and trademark law; and James Judd for assistance with the information on Internet sales taxes. As always, I was helped immensely by the support of all the Nolo editors, and I will miss all of you.

Alexis Mollomo provided the lovely illustrations within these pages, for which I'm happy and grateful—thanks, Ali. Thanks also to Terri Hearsh for making the information in this book clear and attractive, as well as to Ely Newman and André Zivkovich for creating the forms CD-ROM. And a big thank you goes to the Nolo marketing folks for their smart and creative style in getting the word out about this book.

Without my partner in crime this last year might have squashed me. Showers of thanks and love to Turtle.

PHP 2000

Dedication

I dedicate this book to my grandmother Eunice Michaelson Jones—a spitfire if ever there was one.

About the Author

Peri Pakroo is a media developer and consultant, specializing in legal and start-up issues for businesses and nonprofits. She owns and runs p-brain media (www.pbrainmedia.com), a media and communications firm that develops informational content for print, Web, video, and other media. She received her law degree from the University of New Mexico School of Law in 1995, and a year later began editing and writing for Nolo, specializing in small business and intellectual property issues. She has edited such titles as Nolo's *Starting & Running a Successful Newsletter or Magazine*; *Getting Permission: How to License & Clear Copyrighted Materials Online & Off*; *Music Law*; and *How to Write a Business Plan*. Besides working with legal and business issues, Peri has also headed the editorial departments of two arts and entertainment weeklies and a monthly food and lifestyle magazine. She lives with Juno, Kitty B, and Turtle in New Mexico.

Table of Contents

5 Drafting an Effective Business Plan

6 Pricing, Bidding, and Billing Projects

7 Federal, State, and Local Start-Up Requirements

8 Risk Management

9 Paying Your Taxes

10 Laws, Taxes, and Other Issues for Home Businesses

11 Entering Into Contracts and Agreements

12 Bookkeeping, Accounting, and Financial Management

13 Websites and E-Business

14 Planning for Changes in Ownership

15 Building Your Business and Hiring Workers

16 Getting Professional Help

Appendixes

A State Contact Information

B How to Use the CD-ROM

C Tear-Out Forms

Partnership Agreement

Application for Employer Identification Number (Form SS-4)

Determination of Worker Status for Purposes of Federal Employment Taxes and Income Tax Withholding (Form SS-8)

Election To Have a Tax Year Other Than a Required Tax Year (Form 8716)

Entity Classification Election (Form 8832)

This book includes the following icons to help you find the information you need more quickly and easily.

 Tip. A commonsense tip to help you understand or comply with legal requirements.

 Warning. A caution to slow down and consider potential problems.

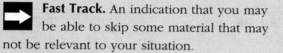 **See an Expert.** A suggestion to seek the advice of an attorney or tax expert.

Fast Track. An indication that you may be able to skip some material that may not be relevant to your situation.

 Recommended Reading. A suggestion to consult another Nolo book or legal or tax resource.

 Checklist. A quick summary of the start-up steps included in each chapter.

 Cross-Reference. Refers you to related information in another chapter of the book.

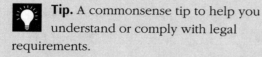 **Worksheet.** Links you to the interactive worksheet you can find on the CD-ROM accompanying this book.

CHAPTER 1

Working for Yourself

You don't have an MBA. Hell, you've never taken a business class. You spent your college years studying literature and art history, and periodically dropping out to travel the world. And now you find yourself thinking about going into business for yourself—maybe restoring antiques, illustrating books, running a café, or selling software. "Me, a businessperson?" you skeptically wonder. You keep trudging to work each morning, but as the hours tick by you find yourself fantasizing more and more about kissing your 9-to-5 job goodbye. You jot down some notes, work out some kinks in your plan and continue to wonder whether it just might fly ….

Unfortunately, most people who have toyed with business ideas this way never get to find out whether they would have worked or not. For a variety of practical, financial, and psychological reasons, most folks just don't take the leap from idea to reality. This is really a shame, since there's nothing that complex or difficult about turning a business idea into an actual working business. Most prospective entrepreneurs would be surprised —and encouraged—to know that they can get most of the way across the line between "I'm thinking about starting my own business" and "I own and run my own business!" simply by completing a short list of bureaucratic tasks. This book will explain what those tasks are and how to complete them.

Stephen Parr, owner and director of Oddball Film and Video, a stock film and video footage company in San Francisco, California:

I started making video art in the 1970s. After a while I started collecting all these weird bits of film because it was cheaper than shooting it myself. I gathered all kinds of old, found footage like military training films, educational films, home movies, and all kinds of other images and put them together into montages, which I screened in nightclubs as background visuals. I was showing them all over—nightclubs in New York, Chicago, San Francisco—and I made some money by selling the tapes to the clubs.

Then I started getting calls from these companies in Silicon Valley that produce industrial videos, like training films and promotional programs for corporate trade shows. Video game companies were calling, too. Companies like Sega, Sun Microsystems, and Silicon Graphics wanted to pay me for my footage. The guy I lived with at the time thought I should go into business selling the stock footage I had collected, but I didn't know if I could make a living doing it. I didn't know anything about the stock footage business. There were a few companies doing it, but they were in New York or L.A., and they seemed really huge.

But since I liked working with images and since the business had already started to take off on its own, I finally decided to formalize it. I started by picking a company name. I wanted something interesting that conveyed what I did. We came up with Oddball. It's a word that people don't really use anymore, more of a '40s or '50s expression—an oddball is someone kind of weird, unbalanced, or unusual, you know? Well, from there, I just kept compiling more footage, and over the years I started logging it, and buying more.

At the most basic level, my business involves finding, organizing, and preserving historical footage. And then distributing it. Our clients include ad agencies; news organizations; documentary and feature film makers; industrial, corporate, and music video producers; educational filmmakers; and anyone who needs offbeat and unusual images. In one way, we're like a library: We archive and license historical visual information.

These days, I spend most of my time trying to organize and publicize my business. We just launched our website, and that takes time to maintain. And I spend a lot more time trying to obtain films than actually looking at them. Still, what I do at Oddball is an extension of the work I've been doing since the 1970s. I guess it became a business the day I decided I wasn't going to do anything else.

A. Getting On With Your Business

You undoubtedly already know that getting a business off the ground isn't easy. You've got a million different details to work out—how you'll produce your product or service, how much you'll charge, what marketing strategies to use, how to manage your cash flow—and you need to nail all of this down before you stand to make a dime. You'll likely find that very few, if any, other businesspeople have done exactly what you're setting out to do, so you'll have to answer a lot of questions on your own (or with your partners). It can be scary and lonely—and while exhilarating, it's almost always stressful.

But compared to working out the details of how your business will run and become successful, clearing the bureaucratic hurdles isn't a big deal at all. Dealing with governmental start-up requirements has been done millions of times before by all types of different businesses. While the bureaucracy governing small business often seems like a convoluted maze, you can take comfort in the fact that the procedures are standard—they apply more or less the same to everybody. The answers *are* out there. Unlike your unique business strategy that you'll need your best creative wits to devise, conquering the bureaucracy is essentially a no-brainer. Yes, it requires some patience and fortitude, but by no means do you need any special skill, education, or experience. As long as you do a bit of homework and arm yourself with an overview of the process (as you're doing by reading this book), you'll be able to meet all the small business registration requirements without breaking a sweat.

You can usually start a sole proprietorship (the legal term for a one-owner business) or a partnership (a business with more than one owner) by registering with just one government office. And for business owners who want protection from personal liability for business debts—often referred to by the legal jargon "limited liability"—the simplest corporations or limited liability companies (LLCs) require only a couple more registration tasks to

complete. In other words, once you've got your business idea developed to a certain degree, all you need to do is visit a few government offices, fill out some forms, and pay some fees—and suddenly your idea will have become an actual, legitimate business.

Keep in mind that there's certainly a lot more to launching a successful small business than dealing with bureaucratic requirements. For starters, you'll need to have a sound business idea, and you'll need to be able to develop good management skills to guide it to success. This book, however, largely leaves these issues for other resources to cover. Unlike many other small business guides, this one doesn't require you to spend your precious time quizzing you on whether you have the right personality to be your own boss, evaluating your business idea, or helping you to identify the personal goals that you hope to achieve by starting a business. If you need more help deciding whether or not you want to start a business or what kind of business you should start, you should probably buy a different book. If, on the other hand, you want a book that cuts to the chase and explains systematically what you need to do to launch a business officially and legally, this book is for you.

Online resources for small business startups. If you need more guidance on other aspects of starting a small business, consult the Business & Human Resources section of Nolo's website at www.nolo.com. You'll find several articles on business start-up issues, including tips for getting a business off to a smooth start.

But this book is also for those of you who are somewhere in between: fairly certain you want to give your idea a try but not quite ready to march down to city hall to register your business. In addition to explaining the start-up requirements that apply to most small businesses, this book also outlines the preliminary work you should do before heading out to file all your official forms. Chapters

2 through 5 discuss fundamental tasks such as choosing the right legal structure for your business (sole proprietorship, partnership, LLC, or corporation), coming up with a catchy and legally sound business name, and finding a location that's good for business. The book also explains how to draft a business plan that will help you define your business, plan for profitability, and attract lenders and investors. It goes through strategies for pricing your goods and services, and helps you understand how to put together bids and proposals. If you've already taken care of some or all of these tasks, you can either skip these chapters or use them as a guide to evaluate what you've already done.

Finally, to help you all the way through your start-up days, later chapters introduce you to a number of basic issues facing every ongoing business. These include insurance, taxes, contracts and agreements, and bookkeeping and accounting. Though they're not exactly start-up requirements, they're important to understand in the dawning days of your business so that you'll be able to handle them later when business is fast and furious.

Finally, keep in mind that businesses with employees have significant additional responsibilities. Chapter 15 offers a general overview of the laws and regulations that govern businesses with employees. If you're thinking about hiring employees, that chapter will help you figure out if you're ready to tackle the many requirements that come with your first hire. Chapter 15, Section A, also explains the difference between employees and independent contractors—an important distinction, because using independent contractors does not subject you to most of the laws that apply when you hire employees.

More help with employee issues. If you decide that you need to hire any employees, you'll probably need to do further reading. An excellent and exhaustive resource is *The Employer's Legal Handbook*, by Fred S. Steingold (Nolo).

B. Deciding Whether to Go Official

Some of you may be facing a different question. Instead of wondering whether or not to start a business, you may be trying to decide whether or not to formalize your business—to go the official route and register your business with the appropriate agencies in your state. For instance, maybe you've been doing freelance graphics work on the side for a number of years, but now you're thinking of quitting your 9-to-5 job to take on graphics work full time. If you're not sure whether you want to register your business and open it up to the world of government regulations, the information about registration requirements in this book will put you in a better position to make a decision. Chapter 7 walks you through the many governmental requirements that apply to all new businesses, and explains how to go about finding and satisfying any additional requirements that may apply to your specific business.

Stephen Parr, owner and director of Oddball Film and Video, a stock footage company in San Francisco, California:

What a business really is, is you deciding you have a business. It's really nothing more than that.

Generally speaking, anyone with a good-sized or otherwise visible business should bite the bullet and complete all of the necessary registration tasks to become official. Operating under the table can all too easily be exposed, and the government can come after you for fines and penalties—and might even shut down your business—simply for conducting business without first completing the necessary paperwork. And if you're making a profit, ignoring the IRS is definitely a bad idea. In addition to fines and back taxes, you could even face criminal charges and jail time.

On the other hand, tiny, home-based, hobby-type businesses can often operate for quite some time without meeting registration requirements. If you're braiding hair or holding an occasional junk sale out of your garage, for instance, you can probably get by without formal business registration—at least for a while. Keep in mind, however, that just because it may be possible doesn't mean it's the best option. Often, formally registering your business can benefit you as well, since you can then write off business expenses and reduce your personal taxes. Chapter 9, Section A3, discusses hobby businesses in more depth, including how tax laws deal with businesses that continually lose money.

You'll need to learn to trust yourself, both when you feel optimistic and when you suspect that one of your ideas is less than brilliant. You'll also have to develop a sense for when you need help, and to be judicious in taking the advice of people around you. Part of the art of controlling your own destiny is accepting the wisdom of others while maintaining your own focus and direction. It's not always an easy balance to maintain, but you'll undoubtedly get better at it as you gain experience in running your own show. The bottom line: Think hard, keep your mind open—and fight like hell to make your ideas a reality.

Take the leap.

C. Getting Ready for the Ride

One of the main ideas to take away from this book is that there's nothing mysterious or even terribly complex about the process of starting your own business. Whether you've drafted a highly specific business plan with the help of accountants and consultants or you've scratched it out on a cocktail napkin, the process of turning that idea into a legitimate business is the same. That process is covered in this book.

How you build and run your business, on the other hand, is where the real challenge comes in. You'll need confidence to get your business rolling—and you'll need guts, too. You may well find that some of the questions burning in your mind have no defined answer, because no one has asked that question or tried that idea before. You probably wanted to start a business in the first place so that you could make your own decisions—but this can often be quite a heavy burden. You may not believe it now, but some days you'll probably find yourself wishing you had a boss.

Business Plans

Business Plan Pro 2006
by Palo Alto Software

A fast, easy way to generate the plan you need to launch or expand your business.

How to Write a Business Plan
by Mike McKeever

Explains how to write a business plan, whether for your own purposes or to attract money from lenders or investors—including how to evaluate the profitability of your business idea; estimate operating expenses; determine assets, liabilities, and net worth; and find potential sources of financing.

Business Operations

How to Run a Thriving Business: Strategies for Success & Satisfaction
by Ralph Warner

Packed with the ideas, strategies, and lessons that have kept a successful entrepreneur in business for more than 30 years.

Negotiate the Best Least for Your Business
by Janet Portman and Fred S. Steingold

A guide to the ins and outs of finding a space for your business, negotiating a lease, and solving problems that arise from it.

Legal Forms for Starting & Running a Small Business
by Fred S. Steingold

Dozens of legal forms and documents crucial for the success of a small business.

Legal Guide for Starting & Running a Small Business
by Fred S. Steingold

All the legal info you need to get your business off the ground and running—including how to raise start-up money, attract the best help, buy or sell a business or franchise, negotiate a favorable lease, insure your business, and resolve legal disputes.

Quicken Legal Business Pro 2006

A software package containing more than 140 legal forms and the complete text of five of Nolo's bestselling business titles—including *Legal Guide for Starting & Running a Small Business, Tax Savvy for Small Business, Everyday Employment Law: The Basics, Marketing Without Advertising,* and *Leasing Space for Your Small Business.*

Whoops! I'm in Business: A Crash Course in Business Basics
by Richard Stim and Lisa Guerin

Have the drive, but need the "know-how" to start and run a business? Find answers to your business questions in this book.

E-Business

How to Get Your Business on the Web
by Fred S. Steingold

All the information, instructions, and forms you need to get your business on the Internet—and make it a success.

Forms of Ownership

Business Buyout Agreements: A Step-by-Step Guide for Co-Owners
by Anthony Mancuso and Bethany K. Laurence

Explains how to protect your business interests by drawing up a "premarital" agreement between you and your business co-owners that sets out a plan for what happens if you or a co-owner leaves the company. A must for any new business with more than one owner.

Form Your Own Limited Liability Company
by Anthony Mancuso

Offers instructions and forms to create an LLC in your state, as well as a full explanation of LLCs and how they work.

More Small Business Products From Nolo   (continued)

Incorporate Your Business: A Legal Guide to Forming a Corporation in Your State

by Anthony Mancuso

Ready to incorporate your business? This do-it-yourself guide provides everything you need to get the job done—without a lawyer.

Incorporator Pro

by Anthony Mancuso

If you're ready to incorporate your business, this software will save you thousands.

LLC Maker

by Anthony Mancuso

Windows software that assembles LLC articles of organization according to state legal requirements, plus an operating agreement and other LLC formation paperwork.

Nolo's Quick LLC: All You Need to Know About Limited Liability Companies

by Anthony Mancuso

Explains the basics of limited liability companies, and helps you figure out whether structuring your business as an LLC is the right way to go.

The Partnership Book: How to Write a Partnership Agreement

by Ralph Warner and Denis Clifford

Describes the legal and practical issues of creating a partnership—including financial and tax liabilities, contributions and distributions, and changes in ownership.

Intellectual Property

Trademark: Legal Care for Your Business & Product Name

by Stephen R. Elias

The information and forms you need to choose a distinctive trademark, register it, and fight infringers.

Marketing

Marketing Without Advertising: Inspire Customers to Rave About Your Business & Create Lasting Success

by Michael Phillips and Salli Rasberry

Explains the secret of attracting customers without pricey ads—including how to build trust with potential customers, encourage customer recommendations, improve customer service, list products and services widely and inexpensively, and use the Internet to market services and products.

Protecting Business Assets

Nondisclosure Agreements: Protect Your Trade Secrets & More

by Richard Stim and Stephen Fishman

This book, with forms on CD-ROM, explains how to protect your trade secrets with a nondisclosure agreement (or "confidentiality agreement") before sharing them with potential partners and employees, and includes 19 different legal forms.

Tax

Deduct It! Lower Your Small Business Taxes

by Stephen Fishman

Take all the business deductions you're due—travel expenses, meals, and more.

Home Business Tax Deduction: Keep What You Earn

by Stephen Fishman

The complete guide to the tax deductions your home office can claim.

Tax Savvy for Small Business

by Frederick W. Daily

Offers plain-English tax laws and rules on business deductions, plus tax info on LLCs, partnerships, corporations, and more.

More Small Business Products From Nolo
(continued)

Workplace Laws

The Employer's Legal Handbook
by Fred S. Steingold

All the basics of employment law in one place. It covers safe hiring and firing practices, wages, hours, employee benefits, taxes and liability, discrimination, and sexual harassment.

Everyday Employment Law: The Basics
by Lisa Guerin and Amy DelPo

A quick reference to employment law, combining legal information and practical ideas.

Working With Independent Contractors
by Stephen Fishman

This book explains all the tricky IRS rules and provides forms and instructions for hiring ICs.

☑ Chapter 1 Checklist

☐ Decide whether to formalize your business.

☐ Research business start-up steps.

☐ Brace yourself for start-up fun and mayhem.

Choosing a Legal Structure

You probably already have a rough idea of the type of legal structure your business will take, whether you know it or not. That's because, in large part, the ownership structure that's right for your business—a sole proprietorship, partnership, LLC, or corporation—depends on how many people will own the business and what type of services or products it will provide, things you've undoubtedly thought about quite a bit.

For instance, if you know that you will be the only owner, then a partnership is obviously not your thing. (A partnership by definition has more than one owner.) And if your business will engage in risky activities (for example, trading stocks or repairing roofs), you'll want not only to buy insurance, but also to consider forming an entity that provides personal liability protection (a corporation or a limited liability company), which can shield your personal assets from business debts and claims. If you plan to raise capital by selling stock to the public or want to give your employees stock options, then you should form a corporation.

If you've considered these issues, then you'll be ahead of the game in choosing a legal structure that's right for your business. Still, you'll need to consider the benefits and drawbacks of each type of business structure before you make your final decision.

In all states, the basic types of business structures are:

- sole proprietorships
- partnerships (general and limited)
- limited liability companies (LLCs), and
- corporations.

To help you pick the best structure for your business, this chapter explains the basic attributes of each type. And it will also help you answer the most common question new entrepreneurs ask about choosing a business form: Should I choose a business structure that offers protection from personal liability—a corporation or an LLC? Here's a hint as to what the best advice will be: If you focus energy and money into getting your business off the ground as a sole proprietorship or a partnership, you can always incorporate or form an LLC later. *make sure franchise allows this change*

Limited Liability

One basic distinction that you'll probably hear mentioned lots of times is the difference between businesses that provide their owners with "limited liability" and those that don't. Corporations and LLCs both provide their owners with limited personal liability. Sole proprietorships and general partnerships do not.

So what does limited liability mean? Basically, that the creditors of the business cannot normally go after the owners' personal assets to pay for business debts and claims arising from lawsuits. (Liability for business debts is discussed in detail later in this chapter.)

As you read about specific business types in this chapter, you'll see how a decision to form a limited liability entity (a corporation or an LLC, mainly) can dramatically affect how you run your business. On the other hand, while sole proprietorships and partnerships are somewhat simpler to run than corporations and LLCs, they may leave an owner personally vulnerable to business lawsuits and debts.

A. Sole Proprietorships

Sole proprietorships are one-owner businesses. Any business with two or more owners cannot, by definition, be a sole proprietorship. If you know that there will be two or more owners of your business, you can skip ahead to Section B, below.

Technically, a sole proprietorship is simply a business that is owned by one person and that hasn't filed papers to become a corporation or an LLC. Sole proprietorships are easy to set up and to maintain—so easy that many people own sole proprietorships and don't even know it. For instance, if you are a freelance photographer or writer, a craftsperson who takes jobs on a contract basis, a salesperson who receives only commissions, or an independent contractor who isn't on an employer's regular payroll, you are automatically a sole proprietor. This is true whether or not you've registered your business with your city or obtained any licenses or permits. And it makes no difference whether you also have a regular day job. As long as you do for-profit work on your own (or sometimes with your spouse—see "Running a Business With Your Spouse," below) and have not filed papers to become a corporation or a limited liability company, you are a sole proprietor.

⚠ **Don't ignore local registration requirements.** If you've started a business without quite realizing it—for example, you do a little freelance computer programming, which classifies you as a sole proprietor by default—don't let the fact that you're technically already a sole proprietor fool you into thinking that you've satisfied the governmental requirements for starting a business. Most cities and many counties require businesses—even tiny home-based sole proprietorships—to register with them and pay at least a minimum tax. And if you do business under a name different from your own, such as Custom Coding, you usually must register that name—known as a fictitious business name—with your county. In practice, lots of businesses are small enough to get away with ignoring these requirements. But if you are caught, you may be subject to back taxes and other penalties. (See Chapter 7 for an explanation of how to make the necessary filings with the appropriate government offices.)

Running a Business With Your Spouse

If you plan to start a sole proprietorship and expect that your spouse may occasionally help out with business tasks, you should be aware of a fuzzy area in federal tax law that you can use to your advantage. The IRS typically allows a spouse to pitch in without pay without risking being classified as an owner or as an employee of the other spouse's business. This situation is sometimes erroneously called a "husband-wife sole proprietorship."

The normal rule is that someone who does work for a business must be one of three things from a legal standpoint: a co-owner, an employee, or an independent contractor. But when that someone is your spouse, this rule is softened somewhat. Your spouse can volunteer—that is, work without pay—for your sole proprietorship without being classified as an employee, freeing the business from paying payroll tax.

That saves you money—and, if you have no other employees, also allows you to avoid the time-consuming record keeping involved in being an employer. Similarly, a spouse who is not classified as a partner or an independent contractor won't have to pay self-employment taxes, and your business won't have to file a partnership tax return.

Also consider that under marital property laws that vary from state to state, if a business is started or significantly changed when a couple is married, both spouses may have an ownership interest in the business regardless of whose name is on the ownership document.

If you are concerned about the possible consequences of divorce, read Chapter 14, "Planning for Changes in Ownership." It discusses how divorce and other life events such as retirement and death can affect ownership of a business, and explains how to plan in advance to accommodate the possibilities. You may also want to check with a lawyer who is experienced in handling marital property issues to see how your business could be affected in the event of a divorce in your particular state.

Finally, if you and your spouse both want to be active partners in a co-owned business—each with an official say in management—you should create a partnership or an LLC or corporation, even though this will mean filing somewhat more complicated tax returns and other business paperwork. If your spouse tries to squeak by as a volunteer in a so-called husband-wife sole proprietorship when you're really working together as a partnership, you run the risk of being audited and having the IRS declare you're a partnership—and sock your spouse with back self-employment taxes.

---

1. Pass-Through Taxation

In the eyes of the law, a sole proprietorship is not legally separate from the person who owns it. This is one of the fundamental differences between a sole proprietorship and a corporation or LLC, and it has two major effects: one related to taxation (explained in this section), and the other to personal liability (explained in the next).

At income tax time, a sole proprietor simply reports all business income or losses on his or her individual income tax return. The business itself is not taxed. The IRS calls this "pass-through" taxation, because business profits pass through the business to be taxed on the business owner's tax return. You report income from a business just like wages from a job, except that, along with Form 1040, you'll need to include Schedule C, on which you'll provide your business's profit and loss information. One helpful aspect of this arrangement is that if your business loses money—and, of course, many start-ups do in the first year or two—you can use the business losses to offset any taxable income you have earned from other sources.

> **EXAMPLE:** Rob has a day job at a coffee shop, where he earns a modest salary. His hobby is collecting obscure records at thrift stores and rummage sales. Contemplating the sad fact that he has no extra money to spend at the flea market on Saturday morning, he decides to start selling some of the vinyl gems he's found. Still working his day job, he starts a small business that he calls Rob's Revolving Records.
>
> During his first full year in business, he sees that a key to consistently selling his records is developing connections and trust among record collectors. Unfortunately, while he is concentrating on getting to know potential buyers and others in the business, sales are slow. At year end he closes out his books and sees that his website, marketing items such as business cards, and other incidental supplies have cost him nearly $9,000, while he made only $3,000 in sales. But there is some good news: Rob's loss of $6,000 can be counted against his income from his day job, reducing his taxes and translating into a nice refund check, which he'll put right back into his record business.

⚠️ **Your business can't lose money forever.** See the discussion of tax rules for money-losing businesses in Chapter 9, Section A3.

📖 **Be ready for the day you'll owe taxes.** Once your business is underway and turning a profit, you'll have to start paying taxes. (See Chapter 9 for an overview of the taxes that small businesses face.) Taxes can get fairly complicated, however, and you may need more in-depth guidance. For detailed information on taxes for the various types of small businesses, read *Tax Savvy for Small Business*, by Frederick W. Daily (Nolo).

This book gives exhaustive information on deductions, record keeping, and audits that will help you reduce your tax bill and stay out of trouble with the IRS.

2. Personal Liability for Business Debts

Another crucial thing to know about operating your business as a sole proprietor is that you, as the owner of the business, can be held personally liable for business-related obligations. This means that if your business doesn't pay a supplier, defaults on a debt, loses a lawsuit, or otherwise finds itself in financial hot water, you, personally, can be forced to pay up. This can be a sobering possibility, especially if you own (or soon hope to own) a cool house, a car, or other treasures. Personal liability for business obligations stems from the fundamental legal attribute of being a sole proprietor: You and your business are legally one and the same.

As explained in more detail in Sections C and D of this chapter, below, the law provides owners of corporations and LLCs with "limited personal liability" for business obligations. This means that, unlike sole proprietors and general partners, owners of corporations and LLCs can normally keep their houses, investments, and other personal property even if their business fails. In short, if you are engaged in a risky business, you may want to consider forming a corporation or an LLC (although a thorough insurance policy can protect you from most lawsuits and claims against the business if your company is a sole proprietorship or partnership).

⚠️ **Commercial insurance doesn't cover business debts.** While commercial insurance can protect a business and its owners from some types of liability (for instance, slip-and-fall lawsuits), insurance never covers business debts. The only way to limit your personal liability for business debts is to use a limited liability business structure such as an LLC or a corporation (or a limited partnership or limited liability partnership).

3. Creating a Sole Proprietorship

Setting up a sole proprietorship is incredibly easy. Unlike starting requirement for an LLC or a corporation, you generally don't have to file any special forms or pay any special fees to start working as a sole proprietor. You'll simply declare your business to be a sole proprietorship when completing the general registration requirements that apply to all new businesses, such as getting a business license from your county or city or a seller's permit from your state.

For example, when filing for a business tax registration certificate with your city, you'll often be asked to declare what kind of business you're starting. Some cities require only that you check a "sole proprietorship" box on a form, while other cities have separate tax registration forms for sole proprietorships. Similarly, other forms you'll file, such as those to register a fictitious business name and to obtain a seller's permit, will also ask for this information. (These and other start-up requirements are discussed in detail in Chapter 7.)

B. Partnerships

Bring two or more entrepreneurs together into a business venture, stir gently, and—poof!—you've got a partnership. By definition, a partnership is a business that has more than one owner and that has not filed papers with the state to become a corporation or an LLC (or a limited partnership or limited liability partnership).

⚠ Partnerships and registration requirements.
While businesses with two or more owners are partnerships by default, they still must satisfy various governmental requirements for starting a business. Most cities and many counties require all businesses to register with them and pay at least a minimum tax. And if you do business under a name other than the partners' names, you usually must register that name—known as a fictitious business name—with your county. (See Chapter 7 for an explanation of how to make the necessary filings with the appropriate government offices.)

1. General vs. Limited Partnerships

Usually, when you hear the term "partnership," it means a general partnership. As discussed in more detail below, general partners are personally liable for all business debts, including court judgments. In addition, each individual partner can be sued for the full amount of any business debt (though that partner can turn around and sue the other partners for their share of the debt).

Another very important aspect of general partnerships is that any individual partner can bind the whole business to a contract or business deal—in other words, each partner has "agency authority" for the partnership. And remember, each of the partners is fully personally liable for a business deal gone sour, no matter which partner signed the contract. So choose your partners carefully.

There are also a couple of special kinds of partnerships, called limited partnerships and limited liability partnerships. They operate under very different rules and are relatively uncommon, so are only briefly described here.

A limited partnership requires at least one general partner and at least one limited partner. The general partner has the same role as in a general partnership: He or she controls the company's day-to-day operations and is personally liable for business debts. The limited partner contributes financially to the business (for example, invests $100,000 in a real estate partnership) but has minimal control over business decisions or operations, and normally cannot bind the partnership to business deals. In return for giving up management power, a limited partner gets the benefit of protection from personal liability. This means that a limited partner can't be forced to pay off business debts or claims with personal assets, but can lose an investment in the business. But beware: A limited partner who tires of being passive and starts tinkering under the hood of the business should understand that his or her liability can quickly become unlimited that way. If a creditor can prove that the limited partner took acts that led the creditor to believe that he or she was a general partner, the limited partner can be held fully and personally liable for the creditor's claims.

More on limited partnerships. See *The Partnership Book: How to Write a Partnership Agreement*, by Ralph Warner and Denis Clifford (Nolo).

Another kind of partnership, called a limited liability partnership (LLP) or sometimes a registered limited liability partnership (RLLP), provides all of its owners with limited personal liability. In some states, these partnerships are only available to professionals, such as lawyers and accountants, and are particularly well suited to them. Most professionals aren't keen on general partnerships, because they don't want to be personally liable for another partner's problems—particularly those involving malpractice claims. Forming a corporation to protect personal assets may be too much trouble, and some states won't allow these professionals to form an LLC. The solution is often a limited liability partnership. This business structure protects each partner from debts against the partnership arising from professional malpractice lawsuits against another partner. (A partner who loses a malpractice suit because of personal mistakes, however, doesn't escape liability.)

2. Pass-Through Taxation

Similar to a sole proprietorship, a partnership (general or limited) is not a separate tax entity from its owners; instead, it's what the IRS calls a "pass-through entity." This means the partnership itself does not pay any income taxes; rather, income passes through the business to each partner, who pays taxes on a share of profit (or deducts a share of losses) on an individual income tax return (Form 1040, with Schedule E attached). However, the partnership must also file what the IRS calls an "informational return"—Form 1065—to let the government know how much the business earned or lost that year. No tax is paid with this return—just think of it as the feds' way of letting you know they're watching.

3. Personal Liability for Business Debts

Since a partnership is legally inseparable from its owners, just like a sole proprietorship, general partners are personally liable for business-related obligations. What's more, in a general partnership, the business actions of any one partner bind the other partners, who can be held personally liable for those actions. So if your business partner takes out an ill-advised high-interest loan on behalf of the partnership, makes a terrible business deal, or gets in some other business mischief without your knowledge, you could be held personally responsible for any debts that result.

EXAMPLE: Jamie and Kent are partners in a profitable landscape gardening company. They've been in business for five years and have earned healthy profits, allowing them each to buy a house, decent wheels, and even a few luxuries—including Jamie's collection of garden sculptures and Kent's roomful of vintage musical instruments. One day Jamie, without telling Kent, orders a shipment of exotic poppy plants that he is sure will be a big hit with customers. But when the shipment arrives, so do agents of the federal drug enforcement agency, who confiscate the plants, claiming they could be turned into narcotics. Soon thereafter, criminal charges are filed against Jamie and Kent, resulting in several newspaper stories. Though the partners are ultimately cleared, their attorney fees come to $50,000 and they lose several key accounts, with the result that the business runs up hefty debts. As a general partner, Kent is personally liable for these debts even though he had nothing to do with the ill-fated poppy purchase.

Before you get too worried about personal liability, keep in mind that many small businesses don't face much of a risk of racking up large debts. For instance, if you're engaged in a low-risk enterprise such as freelance editing, landscaping, or running a small band that plays weddings and other social events, your risk of facing massive debt or a huge lawsuit is pretty small. For these types of small, low-risk businesses, a good business insurance policy that covers most liability risks is almost always enough to protect owners from a catastrophe like a lawsuit or fire. Insurance won't cover regular business debts, however. If you have significant personal assets like fat bank accounts or real estate and plan to rack up some business debt, you may want to limit your personal liability with a different business structure, such as an LLC or a corporation.

4. Partnership Agreements

By drafting a partnership agreement, you can structure your relationship with your partners pretty much however you want. You and your partners can establish the shares of profits (or losses) each partner will receive, what the responsibilities of each partner will be, what should happen to the partnership if a partner leaves, and how a number of other issues will be handled. It is not legally necessary for a partnership to have a written agreement; the simple act of two or more people doing business together creates a partnership. But only with a clear written agreement will all partners be sure of the important—and sometimes touchy—details of their business arrangement.

In the absence of a partnership agreement, your state's version of the Uniform Partnership Act (UPA) or Revised Uniform Partnership Act (RUPA) kicks in as a standard, bottom-line guide to the rights and responsibilities of each partner. Most states have adopted the UPA or RUPA in some form. In California, for example, if you don't have a partnership agreement, then California's RUPA states that each partner has an equal share in the business's profits, losses, and management power. Similarly, unless you provide otherwise in a written agreement, a California partnership won't be able to add a new partner without the unanimous consent of all partners. (Cal. Corp. Code § 16401.)

In short, it's important to understand that you can override many of the legal provisions contained in the UPA or RUPA if you and your partners have your own written agreement.

 **Businesses with more than one owner should address potential changes in ownership.** The partnership agreement provisions discussed in this chapter cover the very basics. Chapter 14, Section B, covers what is known as a buysell agreement, which establishes rules for what will happen if an owner retires, becomes disabled, dies, gets divorced, or otherwise faces a situation that brings business ownership into question. Buysell provisions can exist in a separate document or may be included in partnership agreements or other organizational documents depending on the company structure: operating agreements for LLCs, or bylaws for corporations. Read Chapter 14 to become familiar with the ownership issues that can arise when your business is owned by more than one person—and how best to head off problems with a solid agreement.

What a Partnership Agreement Can't Do

Although a general partnership agreement is an incredibly flexible tool for defining the ownership interests, work responsibilities, and other rights of partners, there are some things it can't do. These include:

- freeing the partners from personal liability for business debts
- restricting any partner's right to inspect the business books and records
- affecting the rights of third parties in relation to the partnership—for example, a partnership agreement that says a partner has no right to sign contracts won't affect the rights of an outsider who signs a contract with that partner, and
- eliminating or weakening the duty of trust (the fiduciary duty) each partner owes to the other partners.

There's nothing terribly complex about drafting partnership agreements. They're usually only a few pages long and cover basic issues that you've probably thought over to some degree already. Partnership agreements typically include at least the following information:

- name of partnership and partnership business
- date of partnership creation
- purpose of partnership
- contributions (cash, property, and work) of each partner to the partnership
- each partner's share of profits and losses
- provisions for taking profits out of the company (often called partners' draws)
- each partner's management power and duties

- how the partnership will handle departure of a partner, including buy-out terms
- provisions for adding or expelling a partner, and
- dispute resolution procedures.

These and any other terms you include in a partnership agreement can be dealt with in more or less detail. Some partnership agreements cover each topic with a sentence or two; others spend up to a few pages on each provision. Of course, you need an agreement that's appropriate for the size and formality of your business, but it's not a good idea to skimp on your partnership agreement.

For more on partnerships. *The Partnership Book: How to Write a Partnership Agreement,* by Ralph Warner and Denis Clifford (Nolo), is an excellent step-by-step guide to putting together a solid, comprehensive partnership agreement. Also, *Business Buyout Agreement: A Step-by-Step Guide for Co-Owners,* by Anthony Mancuso and Bethany Laurence (Nolo), explains how to draft terms that will enable you to deal with business ownership transitions. If you think you may want more than the simple partnership agreements in this book but don't want to spend a lot of time on it, there are more detailed partnership agreement forms on CD (as well as many other resources for running your small business) in *Quicken Legal Business Pro 2006* (Nolo). You can learn more about these resources at www .nolo.com.

Take a look at the short sample partnership agreements on the following pages to see how a very basic partnership agreement can be put together. (You'll also find a blank partnership agreement in Appendix C and on the CD-ROM that comes with this book.) These samples are about as basic as it gets—the bare minimum—and you'll almost surely want to use something more detailed for your business.

Partnership Agreement #1

Alison Shanley and Peder Johnson make the following partnership agreement.

Name and Purpose of Partnership

As of September 22, 20xx, Alison and Peder are the sole owners and partners of the Vermont Fly-Fishing Company. The Vermont Fly-Fishing Company shall be headquartered in Rutland, Vermont, and will sell fly-fishing equipment by mail order.

Contributions to the Partnership

Alison and Peder will make the following contributions to the partnership:

Alison Shanley	cash	$10,000
	desk, miscellaneous office furniture	1,000
	Total contribution:	$11,000
Peder Johnson	cash	$7,000
	computer system	$2,000
	Total contribution:	$9,000

Profit and Loss Allocation

Alison and Peder will share business profits and losses in the same proportions as their contributions to the business.

Management of Partnership Business

Alison and Peder will have equal management powers and responsibilities.

Departure of a Partner

If either Alison or Peder leaves the partnership for any reason, including voluntary withdrawal, expulsion, or death, the remaining partner will become the sole owner of the Vermont Fly-Fishing Company, which will become a sole proprietorship. The remaining owner will pay the departing partner, or the deceased departing partner's estate, the fair market value of the departing partner's share of the business as of the date of his or her departure. The partnership's accountant will determine the fair market value of the departing partner's share of the business according to the partnership's book value.

Mediation of Disputes

Alison and Peder agree to mediate any dispute arising under this agreement with a mutually acceptable mediator.

Amendment of Agreement

This agreement may not be amended without the written consent of both partners.

Alison Shanley	Peder Johnson
Signature _____	Signature _____
Date _____	Date _____
Address _____	Address _____
_____	_____
Social Security # _____	Social Security # _____

Partnership Agreement #2

Christine Wenc, Simon Romero, and Brendan Doherty agree to the terms of the following agreement.

1. **Name of Partnership.** Christine, Simon, and Brendan are partners in the Wenc & Romero Partnership. They created the partnership on July 12, 20xx.

2. **Partnership Purpose.** The Wenc & Romero Partnership will provide newspaper clipping services to clients.

3. **Contributions to the Partnership.** Christine, Simon, and Brendan will contribute the following to the partnership:

   Christine: $1,000 cash; one Macintosh computer (value $1,500), and one monitor (value $500).

   Simon: $1,000 cash; one fax machine (value $400); one laser printer (value $1,200).

   Brendan: $500 cash; various office equipment (value $500).

4. **Profits and Losses.** Christine, Simon, and Brendan will share profits and losses as follows:

Christine	40%
Simon	40%
Brendan	20%

5. **Partnership Decisions.** Christine, Simon, and Brendan will have the following management authority:

Christine	2 votes
Simon	2 votes
Brendan	1 vote

   No partner may accept a new client without the agreement of the others.

6. **Additional Terms to Be Drafted.** Christine, Simon, and Brendan agree that in six months they will sign a formal partnership agreement that covers the items in this agreement in more detail, and the additional following items:
   • each partner's work contributions
   • provisions for adding a partner
   • provisions for the departure of a partner, and
   • provisions for selling the business.

7. **Amendments.** This agreement may not be amended without the written consent of all partners.

Christine Wenc
Signature_____ Date _____

Simon Romero
Signature_____ Date _____

Brendan Doherty
Signature_____ Date _____

C. Limited Liability Companies (LLCs)

Like many business owners just starting out, you might find yourself in this common quandary: On one hand, having to cope with the risk of personal liability for business misfortunes scares you; on the other, you would rather not deal with the red tape of starting and operating a corporation. Fortunately for you and many other entrepreneurs, you can avoid these problems by taking advantage of a relatively new form of business called the limited liability company, commonly known as an LLC. LLCs combine the pass-through taxation of a sole proprietorship or partnership (taxes on business income are paid on each owner's individual income tax returns) with the same protection against personal liability that corporations offer.

Beware of special state rules. For example, California prohibits licensed professionals from organizing as an LLC (but not as a professional corporation or limited partnership). Some other states have extra LLC formalities for licensed professionals, which you can discover by asking your state licensing board.

1. Limited Personal Liability

Generally speaking, owners of an LLC are not personally liable for the LLC's debts. (There are some exceptions to this rule, discussed below.) This protects the owners from legal and financial liability in case their business fails, or loses a lawsuit, and can't pay its debts. In those situations, creditors can take all of the LLC's assets, but they generally can't get at the personal assets of the LLC's owners. Losing your business is no picnic, but it's a lot better to lose only what you put into the business than to say goodbye to everything you own.

> **EXAMPLE:** Callie forms her own one-person mail-order business, using most of her $25,000 in savings to establish a professional website and buy mailing lists. Callie realizes that she'll have to buy a significant portion of her sales inventory up front to be able to ship goods to her customers on time, so she plans to buy those items on credit. While she is willing to risk her $25,000 investment to pursue her dream, she is worried that if her mail-order business fails, she will be buried under a pile of debt. Callie decides to form an LLC so that, if her business should fail, she'll only lose the $25,000; no one will be able to sue her personally for the business debt that she owes. She feels more secure going into business knowing that even if her business fails, she can walk away without the risk of losing her house or her car.

Keep in mind that, like a general partner in a partnership, any member of a member-managed LLC can legally bind the entire LLC to a contract or business transaction. In other words, each member can act as an agent of the LLC. (Some LLCs are managed by managers, instead of by members. In manager-managed LLCs, any *manager* can bind the LLC to a business contract or deal.)

While LLC owners enjoy limited personal liability for many of their business debts, this protection is not absolute. There are several situations in which an LLC owner may become personally liable for business debts or claims. However, this drawback is not unique to LLCs—the limited liability protection given to LLC members is just as strong as (if not stronger than) that enjoyed by the corporate shareholders of small corporations. Here are the main situations where LLC owners can still be held personally liable for debts:

- **Personal guarantees.** If you give a personal guarantee on a loan to the LLC, then you are personally liable for repaying that loan. Since personal guarantees are often required by banks and other lenders, this is a good reason to be a conservative borrower. Of course, if no personal guarantee is made, then only the LLC—not the members—is liable for the debt.

- **Taxes.** The IRS or the state tax agency may go after the personal assets of LLC owners for overdue corporate federal and state tax debts, particularly overdue payroll taxes. This is most likely to happen to members of small LLCs who have an active hand in managing the business, rather than to passive members.
- **Negligent or intentional acts.** An LLC owner who intentionally or even carelessly hurts someone will usually face personal liability. For example, if an LLC owner takes a client to lunch, has a few martinis, and injures the client in a car accident on the way home, the LLC owner can be held personally liable for the client's injuries.
- **Breach of fiduciary duty.** LLC owners have a legal duty to act in the best interest of their company and its members. This legal obligation is known as a "fiduciary duty," or is sometimes simply called a "duty of care." An LLC owner who violates this duty can be held personally liable for any damages that result from the owner's actions (or inactions). Fortunately for LLC owners, they normally will not be held personally responsible for any honest mistakes or acts of poor judgment they commit in doing their jobs. Most often, breach of duty is found only for serious indiscretions such as fraud or other illegal behavior.
- **Blurring the boundaries between the LLC and its owners.** When owners fail to respect the separate legal existence of their LLC, but instead treat it as an extension of their personal affairs, a court may ignore the existence of the LLC and rule that the owners are personally liable for business debts and liabilities. Generally, this is more likely to occur in one-member LLCs; in reality, it only happens in extreme cases. You can easily avoid it by opening a separate LLC checking account, getting a federal employer identification number, keeping separate accounting books for your LLC, and funding your LLC

adequately enough to be able to meet foreseeable expenses.

2. LLC Taxation

Like a sole proprietorship or a partnership, an LLC is not a separate tax entity from its owners; instead, it's what the IRS calls a "pass-through entity." This means the LLC itself does not pay any income taxes; instead, income passes through the business to each LLC owner, who pays taxes on the share of profit (or deducts the share of losses) on the owner's individual income tax return (for the feds, Form 1040 with Schedule E attached). But a multiowned LLC, like a partnership, does have to file Form 1065—an "informational return"—to let the government know how much the business earned or lost that year. No tax is paid with this return.

LLCs give members the flexibility to choose to have the company taxed like a corporation rather than as a pass-through entity. In fact, partnerships now have this option as well. (See Chapter 9, Section C.) You may wonder why LLC owners would choose to be taxed as a corporation. After all, pass-through taxation is one of the most popular features of an LLC. The answer is that, because of the income-splitting strategy of corporations (discussed in Section D2a, below), LLC members can sometimes come out ahead by having their business taxed as a separate entity at corporate tax rates.

For example, if the owners of an LLC become successful enough to keep some profits in the business at the end of the year (or regularly need to keep significant profits in the business for upcoming expenses), paying tax at corporate tax rates can save them money. That's because federal income tax rates for corporations start at a lower rate than the rates for individuals. For this reason, many LLCs start out being taxed as partnerships, and when they make enough profit to justify keeping some in the business (rather than doling them out as salaries and bonuses), they opt for corporate-style taxation.

3. LLCs vs. S Corporations

Before LLCs came along, the only way all owners of a business could get limited personal liability was to form a corporation. Problem was, many entrepreneurs didn't want the hassle and expense of incorporating, not to mention the headache of dealing with corporate taxation. One easier option was to form a special type of corporation known as an S corporation, which is like a normal corporation in most respects, except that business profits pass through to the owner (as in a sole proprietorship or partnership), rather than being taxed to the corporation at corporate tax rates. In other words, S corporations offered the limited liability of a corporation with the pass-through taxation of a sole proprietorship or partnership. For a long time, this was an okay compromise for small-to-medium-sized businesses, though they still had to deal with many of the corporate aspects that S corporations retained. (Discussed in more detail below.)

Now, however, LLCs offer a better option. LLCs are indeed similar to S corporations in that they combine limited personal liability with pass-through tax status. But a significant difference between these two types of businesses is that LLCs are not bound by the many regulations that govern S corporations.

Here's a quick rundown of the major areas of difference between S corporations and LLCs. (Keep in mind that corporations, including S corporations, are explained in more detail in the next section.)

- **Ownership restrictions.** An S corporation may not have more than 75 shareholders, all of whom must be U.S. citizens or residents. This means that some of the C corporation's main benefits—namely, the ability to set up stock option and bonus plans and to bring in public capital—are pretty much out of the question for S corporations. And even if an S corporation initially meets the U.S. citizen or resident requirement, its shareholders can't sell shares to another company (like a corporation or an LLC) or a foreign citizen, on pain of losing S corporation tax status. In an LLC, any type of person or entity can become a member—a U.S. citizen, a citizen of a foreign country, another LLC, a corporation, or a limited partnership.

- **Allocation of profits and losses.** Shareholders of an S corporation must allocate profits according to the percentage of stock each owner has. For example, a 25% owner has to receive 25% of the profits (or losses), even if the other owners want a different division. Owners of an LLC, on the other hand, may distribute profits (and the tax burden that goes with them) however they see fit, without regard to each member's ownership share in the company. For instance, a member of an LLC who owns 25% of the business can receive 50% of the profits if the other members agree (subject to a few IRS rules).

- **Corporate meeting and record-keeping rules.** For S corporation shareholders to keep their limited liability protection, they have to follow the corporate rules: issuing stock, electing officers, holding regular board of directors' and shareholders' meetings, keeping corporate minutes of all meetings, and following the mandatory rules found in their state's corporation code. By contrast, LLC owners don't need to jump through most of these legal hoops—they just have to make sure their management team is in agreement on major decisions and go about their business.

- **Tax treatment of losses.** S corporation shareholders are at a disadvantage if their company goes into substantial debt—for instance, if it borrows money to open the business or buy real estate. That's because an S corporation's business debt cannot be passed along to its shareholders unless they have personally cosigned and guaranteed the debt. LLC owners, on the other hand, normally can reap the tax benefits of any business debt, cosigned or not. This can translate into a nice tax break for owners of LLCs that carry debt.

4. Forming an LLC

Before you decide the LLC is the best thing since easy cheese, you should be aware that an LLC might not be as cheap to start as a partnership or sole proprietorship. To form an LLC, you must file Articles of Organization with your Secretary of State or other LLC filing office. A few states charge significant filing fees, plus annual dues (alternately called minimum taxes, annual fees, or renewal fees). These fees can push the costs of starting an LLC into the several-hundred-dollar range. Illinois, for instance, charges a $500 filing fee, and California requires that you pay a minimum annual LLC tax of $800 when you start your LLC—on top of its $70 filing fee.

Many brand-new business owners aren't in a position to pay this kind of money right out of the starting gate, so they start out as partnerships until they bring in enough income to cover these costs. And if you're thinking of forming a corporation instead, keep in mind that most states charge at least as much in fees for corporations. This plus the added expenses of running a corporation (legal and accounting fees, for example) will almost always make a corporation more expensive to run than an LLC.

⚠ Some LLCs must comply with securities laws. LLCs that have owners who do not actively participate in the business may have to register their membership interests as securities or, more likely, qualify for an exemption to the registration requirements. For information about exemptions to the federal securities laws, visit the Securities and Exchange Commission's website at www.sec.gov/smbus/qasbsec.htm#eod6.

📖 For more on LLCs. *Form Your Own Limited Liability Company*, by Anthony Mancuso (Nolo), gives detailed information on LLCs, including step-by-step instructions and forms for creating one. For a briefer treatment, consult *Nolo's Quick LLC: All You Need to Know About Limited Liability Companies*, also by Anthony Mancuso. It offers an overview of LLCs as well as comparisons to other business structures, but does not include any start-up forms.

D. Corporations

For many, the term "corporation" conjures up the image of a massive industrial empire more akin to a nation-state than a small business. In fact, a corporation doesn't have to be huge, and most aren't. Stripped to its essentials, a corporation is simply a specific legal structure that imposes certain legal and tax rules on its owners (also called shareholders). A corporation can be as large as IBM or, in many cases, as small as one person.

One fundamental legal characteristic of a corporation is that it's a separate legal entity from its owners. If you've already read this chapter's sections on sole proprietorships and partnerships, you'll recognize that this is a major difference between those unincorporated business types and corporations. Another important corporate feature is that shareholders are normally protected from personal liability for business debts. Finally, the corporation itself—not just the shareholders—is subject to income tax.

💼 Publicly traded corporations are a different ballgame. This section discusses privately held corporations owned by a small group of people who are actively involved in running the business. These corporations are much easier to manage than public corporations, whose shares are sold to the public at large. Any corporation that sells its stock to the general public is heavily regulated by state and federal securities laws, while corporations that sell shares, without advertising, only to a select group of people who meet specific state requirements are often exempt from many of these laws. If you plan to sell shares of a corporation to the general public, you should consult a lawyer.

1. Limited Personal Liability

Generally speaking, owners of a corporation are not personally liable for the corporation's debts. (There are some exceptions to this rule, discussed below.) Limited personal liability is a major reason why owners have traditionally chosen to incorporate their businesses: to protect themselves from legal and financial liability in case their business flounders or loses an expensive lawsuit and can't pay its debts. In those situations, creditors can take all of the corporation's assets (including the shareholders' investments), but they generally can't get at the personal assets of the shareholders.

> **EXAMPLE:** Tim and Chris publish *Tropics Tripping,* a monthly travel magazine with a focus on Latin America. Because they both have significant personal assets, and because they will have to borrow a lot of capital to start up their magazine, they form their business as a corporation to protect their personal assets in case their magazine fails. They do great for a few years, but suddenly their subscription and advertising revenue starts to suffer when a recession plus political unrest in several Latin American countries reduces interest in travel to that area. Hoping the situation will turn itself around, Tim and Chris forge ahead—and go deeper into debt as it proves impossible to pay printing and other bills on time. Finally, when their printer won't do any more print runs on credit, Tim and Chris are forced to call it quits. *Tropics Tripping*'s debts total $250,000, while business assets are valued at only $90,000—leaving a $160,000 debt to creditors. Thankfully for Tim and Chris, they won't have to use their personal assets to pay the $160,000, because, as owners of a corporation, they're shielded from personal liability.

Corporations aren't the only option. With the advent of limited liability companies, corporations aren't the only business entities that provide limited liability status for all owners. (See Section C on LLCs, above.)

Forming a corporation to shield yourself from personal liability for business obligations provides good, but not complete, protection for your personal assets. Here are the principal areas in which corporation owners still face personal liability:

- **Personal guarantees.** If you give a personal guarantee on a loan to the corporation, then you are personally liable for the repayment of that loan. Since lenders often require a personal guarantee, this is a good reason to be a conservative borrower. Of course, if no personal guarantee is made, then only the corporation—not the shareholders—is liable for the debt.
- **Taxes.** The IRS or the state's tax agency may go after the personal assets of corporate owners for overdue corporate federal and state tax debts, particularly overdue payroll taxes. This is most likely to happen to owners of small corporations who have an active hand in managing the business, rather than to passive shareholders.
- **Negligent or intentional acts.** A corporate owner who is negligent (that is, careless), or perhaps even intentional, and ends up hurting someone, can't hide behind the corporate barrier to escape personal liability. Shareholders are subject to personal liability for wrongs they commit—such as attacking a customer or leaving a wet floor in a store—that result in injury.
- **Breach of fiduciary duty.** Corporate owners have a legal duty to act in the best interest of the company and its shareholders. This legal obligation is known as a "fiduciary duty," sometimes simply called a "duty of care." If an owner violates this duty, the owner can be held personally liable for any damages that result from his or her actions (or inactions). Fortunately for corporate owners, run-of-the-mill mistakes or lapses in judgment aren't usually considered breaches of the duty of care. Most often, breach of duty is found only for serious indiscretions such as fraud or other illegal behavior. For

example, if a corporate officer falsified some financial data in order to seal a deal with a client, that officer may be held personally liable for any damages that result from that breach of duty to the company.

- **Blurring the boundaries between the corporation and its owners.** When corporate owners ignore corporate formalities and treat the corporation like an unincorporated business, a court may ignore the existence of the corporation (in legal slang, "pierce the corporate veil") and rule that the owners are personally liable for business debts and liabilities. To avoid this, it's important for corporate owners not to allow the legal boundary between the corporation and its owners to grow fuzzy. Owners need to scrupulously respect corporate formalities by holding shareholders' and directors' meetings, keeping attentive minutes, issuing stock certificates, and maintaining corporate accounts strictly separate from personal funds.

Don't be fooled into thinking that incorporating will solve all your liability problems. Limited personal liability can prevent you from losing your home, car, bank account, and other assets—but it won't protect you from losing your investment in your business. A business can quickly get wiped out if a customer, employee, or supplier wins a big lawsuit against it and the business has to be liquidated to cover the debt. In short, even if you incorporate to protect your personal assets, you should purchase appropriate insurance to protect your business assets. (Insurance is discussed in Chapter 8, "Risk Management.") But remember, insurance won't help if you simply can't pay your normal business debts.

2. Corporate Taxation

The words "corporate taxes" raise a lot of fear and loathing in the business world. Fortunately, the reality of corporate taxation is usually less depress-

ing than the hype. Here are the basics—think of it as Corporate Tax Lite. If you decide to incorporate, you'll likely want to consult an accountant or small business lawyer who can fill you in on the fine print. (See Chapter 16 for information on finding and hiring a lawyer.)

The first thing you need to know is that you'll be treated differently for tax purposes depending on whether you operate as a regular corporation (also called a C corporation) or you elect S corporation status for tax purposes. An S corporation is the same as a C corporation in most respects, but when it comes to taxes, C and S corporations are very different animals. A regular, or C, corporation must pay taxes, while an S corporation is treated like a partnership for tax purposes and doesn't pay any income taxes itself. Like partnership profits, S corporation profits (and losses) pass through to the shareholders, who report them on their individual returns. (In this respect, S corporations are very similar to LLCs, which also offer limited liability along with partnership-style tax treatment.) These two types of corporations are explained in more detail just below.

a. C Corporations

As a separate tax entity, a regular corporation must file and pay income taxes on its own tax return, much like an individual does. After deductions for such things as employee compensation, fringe benefits, and all other reasonable and necessary business expenses have been subtracted from its earnings, a corporation pays tax on whatever profit remains.

In small corporations in which all of the owners of the business are also employees, all of the corporation's profits are often paid out in tax-deductible salaries and fringe benefits—leaving no corporate profit and, thus, no corporate taxes due. (The owner/employees must, of course, pay income tax on their salaries on their individual returns.)

Fringes and Perks

Like employee salaries, corporations can deduct many fringe benefits as business expenses. If a corporation pays for benefits such as health and disability insurance for its employees and owner/employees, the cost can usually be deducted from the corporate income, reducing a possible tax bill. (There's one main exception: Benefits given to an owner/employee of an S corporation who owns 2% or more of the stock can't be deducted as business expenses.)

As a general rule, owners of sole proprietorships, partnerships, and LLCs can deduct the cost of providing these benefits for employees, but not for themselves. (These owners can, however, deduct a portion of their medical insurance premiums, though it's technically a deduction for the individuals, not a business expense.)

The fact that fringe benefits for owners are deductible for corporations may make incorporating a wise choice. But it's less likely to be a winning strategy for a capital-poor start-up that can't afford to underwrite a benefits package.

Marginal Tax Rates for Corporations

The following chart shows tax rates for corporations. For example, if a corporation's taxable income was $75,100, it would pay 15% of its first $50,000 of income, 25% of the next $25,000 and 34% on its remaining $100 in income. The corporation's marginal tax rate—the tax rate a corporation would pay on the last dollar of its income—would be 34%.

Taxable Income	Marginal Tax Rate
0 to $50,000	15%
$50,001 to $75,000	25%
$75,001 to $100,000	34%
$100,001 to $335,000	39%
$335,001 to $10,000,000	34%
$10,000,001 to $15,000,000	35%
$15,000,001 to $18,333,333	38%
Over $18,333,333	35%

Note: These corporate rates don't apply to professional corporations, which are subject to a flat tax of 35% on all corporate income.

Initial rates of corporate taxation are comparatively low (see "Marginal Tax Rates for Corporations," below). Corporations that keep some profits in the business from one year to the next—rather than paying out all profits as salaries and bonuses—can take advantage of 15%–25% tax brackets. This practice, sometimes called income-splitting, basically involves strategically setting salaries at a level so that money left in the business is taxable only at the 15% or 25% corporate tax rate (which applies to profits up to $50,000 or $75,000). Since any amount of "reasonable" compensation to employees is deductible, corporate owners have lots of leeway in setting salaries to accomplish this.

EXAMPLE: Alexis and Matt run Window to the Past, Inc., a glass manufacturing business that specializes in custom work for architectural renovations. Toward the end of the year, they calculate that year's profit to be approximately $145,000. They decide to give themselves each a $50,000 bonus out of the profit (on top of their $40,000 salaries). Because both salaries and bonuses are tax-deductible business expenses, this reduces Window to the Past's taxable income to $45,000. The resulting corporate profit of $45,000 will be taxed at only 15%, the lowest rate. (If Alexis and Matt had left all the profits in the business, the profits over $75,000 would have been taxed at 34%, and profits over $100,000 would have been taxed at a whopping 39%.) Of course, the bonuses Alexis and Matt give themselves increase their personal income, which will be taxed on their individual returns. Still, their personal tax rates are lower than the high corporate rates of 34% and 39%.

This income-splitting strategy is available only to shareholders who also work for the corporation. If they're not at least part-time employees, then shareholders won't be in a position to earn salaries or bonuses, and will be able to take money from the corporation only as dividends.

b.   Double Taxation

This brings us to the vexing problem of double taxation, routinely faced by larger corporations with shareholders who aren't active employees. Unlike salaries and bonuses, dividends paid to shareholders cannot be deducted as business expenses from corporate earnings. Since they're not deducted, any amounts paid as dividends are included in the total corporate profit and taxed. And when the shareholder receives the dividend, it is taxed at the shareholder's individual tax rate as part of personal income. As you can see, any money paid out as a dividend gets taxed twice: once at the corporate level, and once at the individual level.

You can avoid double taxation simply by not paying dividends. This is usually easy if all shareholders are employees, but probably more difficult if some shareholders are passive investors anxious for a reasonable return on their investments.

c.   S Corporations

Unlike a regular corporation, an S corporation does not pay taxes itself. Any profits pass through to the owners, who pay taxes on income as if the business were a sole proprietorship, a partnership, or an LLC. Yet the business is still a corporation. This means, of course, that its owners are protected from personal liability for business debts, just as

shareholders of C corporations and members (owners) of LLCs are.

Until the relatively recent arrival of the LLC (discussed in Section C, above), the S corporation was the business form of choice for those who wanted limited liability protection without the two-tiered tax structure of a C corporation. Today, relatively few businesses are organized as S corporations, since S corporations are subject to many regulations that do not apply to LLCs. (See Section C, above, for an outline of the differences between S corporations and LLCs.)

3.   Forming and Running a Corporation

In addition to tax complexity, a major drawback to forming a corporation—either a C or an S type—is time and expense. Unlike sole proprietorships and partnerships, you can't clap your hands twice and conjure up a corporation. To incorporate, you must file Articles of Incorporation with your Secretary of State or other corporate filing office, along with often hefty filing fees and minimum annual taxes. And if you decide to sell shares of the corporation to the public—as opposed to keeping them in the hands of a relatively small number of owners—you'll have to comply with lots of complex federal and state securities laws.

Finally, to protect your limited personal liability, you need to act like a corporation, which means adopting bylaws, issuing stock to shareholders, maintaining records of various meetings of directors and shareholders, and keeping records and transactions of the business separate from those of the owners.

Corporations must comply with securities laws. Corporations must either register their shares with the Securities and Exchange Commission or qualify for an exemption to securities registration requirements. For information about small business exemptions to the federal securities laws, visit the Securities and Exchange Commission's website at www.sec.gov.

To sum up, the protection afforded by incorporating comes at a price. Figure in the likelihood that you'll have to hire lawyers, accountants, and other professionals to keep your corporation in compliance, and it's easy to see how expensive running a corporation can be.

Recommended reading on corporations. For more information on the many complexities of running a corporation, read *The Corporate Records Handbook: Meetings, Minutes & Resolutions,* by Anthony Mancuso (Nolo).

E. Choosing the Best Structure for Your Business

Although there are many differences among the various types of business organizations, most business owners choose an operating structure based on one legal issue: the personal liability of owners for business debts. While the issue of personal liability can have a huge impact on successful small businesses a few years down the road, business owners who are just starting out on a shoestring often care most about spending as little money as possible on the legal structure of their business. This is certainly an understandable approach: Far more new businesses die painful deaths because they don't control costs than because they lose costly lawsuits. In short, for many new small businesses, incorporating or organizing as an LLC is as unnecessary an expense as a swank downtown office or a gleaming chrome espresso machine in the lunchroom.

That said, owners of any business that will engage in a high-risk activity, rack up large business debts, or have a significant number of investors should always insist on limited personal liability, either with an LLC or a corporation. This is even more true if the business can't find or afford appropriate insurance.

If you decide that limiting your personal liability is worth the extra cost, you still need to decide whether to form a corporation or an LLC. With the LLC's arrival, many business owners who want limited liability protection realize that incorporation normally only makes sense if a business needs to take advantage of the corporate stock structure to attract key employees and investment capital. No question, corporations may have an easier time attracting capital investment by issuing stock privately or publicly. And some businesses may find it easier to attract and retain key employees by issuing employee stock options. But for businesses that never go public, choosing to operate as LLCs rather than corporations normally makes the most sense, if limited liability is the main concern. If the corporate stock structure isn't something you want or need for your business, the simplicity and flexibility of LLCs offer a clear advantage over corporations.

Location matters. Another important consideration in choosing your business structure may be related to the state you choose to locate it in, especially if you are going into business with people who do not live in your state. This is because states differ widely in how they tax different business entities and nonresident business owners. There can be big state tax complications when a business either operates in more than one state or has owners in more than one state. A tax attorney can tell you whether you can reduce your taxes and increase profits by choosing one state over the other as your headquarters.

Analyzing Your Risks

Starting a business is always risky. In some businesses, however, the risks are particularly extreme. If you're planning to launch an investment firm or start a hazardous waste management company, there is little doubt that you'll need all the protection you can get, including limited personal liability as well as adequate insurance. Other businesses are not so obviously risk-laden, but still could land you in trouble if fate strikes you a blow. When analyzing your business, note that red flags for riskiness include:

- using hazardous materials, such as dry cleaning solvents or photographic chemicals, or hazardous processes, such as welding or operating heavy machinery
- manufacturing or selling edible goods
- driving as part of the job
- building or repairing structures or vehicles
- caring for children or animals
- providing or allowing access to alcohol
- allowing activities that may result in injury, such as weightlifting or skateboarding, and
- repairing or working on items of value, such as cars or antiques.

If you've identified one or more serious risks your business is likely to face, figure out whether business insurance might give you enough protection. Some risky activities, such as job-related driving, are good candidates for insurance and don't necessarily warrant incorporating. But if insurance can't cover all of the risks involved in your business, it may be time to form an LLC or a corporation.

Keep in mind that insurance will never insulate you from regular business debts. If you foresee your business going into serious debt, an LLC or corporation may be the best business structure for you.

Chapter 2 Checklist

- ☐ Identify the number of owners of your business.

- ☐ Analyze your business's risks and decide how much protection from personal liability you'll need.

- ☐ Determine how you'd like the business to be taxed (as a pass-through entity or as a corporation).

- ☐ Decide if your business would benefit from the stock structure of a corporation (by being able to distribute stock options and sell stock).

- ☐ Choose a business structure.

- ☐ If you will structure your business as a partnership, draft and sign a partnership agreement.

- ☐ If you will structure your business as an LLC or corporation, file articles with your state and draft bylaws (for corporations) or an operating agreement (for LLCs).

CHAPTER 3

Picking a Winning Business Name

There's a lot of room for personal and professional creativity when picking a business name, but there are also legal requirements and pitfalls that you absolutely need to understand. In particular, it's important for all business owners to understand the basics of trademark law, which establishes and protects the legal right to use a particular name for businesses, products, or services.

If you choose a business or product name that's too similar to a competitor's name, for instance, you could find yourself accused of violating the competitor's trademark (called "infringement" or "unfair competition"), and you could be forced to change your business name and possibly pay money damages. Having to change a business name can be a serious blow to a business that has worked hard to build name recognition among its customers—not to mention the cost of changing signs, stationery, preprinted invoices, and the like.

But suppose you plan to open a local business so small that you don't even expect to compete with businesses in the next county, much less in another state or country. You probably wonder if the arcane world of trademark law really affects you. Just 20 years ago the answer would have clearly been no—you didn't really have to worry too much about national or global name conflicts back then. As long as a quick search of your phone book didn't reveal any obvious local conflicts and you didn't call your business "Ford," "IBM," or some other famous name, you were fine. But in today's world of the Internet, mail order, and rapidly growing national chains, "local" obviously isn't what it used to be. Even if you're opening just a tiny bookstore in a small town, if you inadvertently choose the same name as an Internet store that sells books, you may very well be accused of infringing the online store's trademark—even if the online store's headquarters are on a different continent.

One good way to figure out how concerned you need to be about trademark law is to consider the consequences of having to change your business name. If a name change would be cheap and easy and wouldn't seriously confuse your customers, then don't lie awake nights worrying about picking a name that's absolutely bulletproof. However, if changing your name would be messy or expensive (changing signs, Yellow Pages ads, and business directory listings, to mention a few possibilities), take the time and trouble to be sure the name you plan to use doesn't already belong to someone else.

Are you convinced that paying attention to the law of business names is important? Good. Now you'll learn how to choose a name that won't land you in legal hot water and how to secure the maximum legal protection for it. This chapter will also cover some nonlegal aspects of naming your business, including tips and advice on how to choose the most effective name for your particular business.

Watch out for other legal issues. Besides watching out for trademark conflicts, business owners also need to comply with other legal rules. Many businesses must comply with their county's fictitious business name requirements. (See Chapter 7, Section C.) Typically this means you'll need to register a fictitious business name statement (or similar document) with your county clerk and possibly publish it in a local newspaper. And for corporations, LLCs, and limited partnerships, the state filing office (usually the Secretary or Department of State) must approve your business name before it will accept Articles of Incorporation, Articles of Organization, or a Statement of Limited Partnership.

Getting the Terms Straight

One reason the law of business names often seems confusing is that it is riddled with lots of arcane and often overlapping legal jargon. For example, local, state, and federal agencies often use different terms to describe the same or very similar legal concepts. Here's a brief rundown of the terms you need to know, all of which are discussed in greater detail in the rest of this chapter.

- The term **legal name** means the official name of the entity that owns a business. The legal name of a sole proprietorship is simply the full name of the owner—for example, John Potter. If a general partnership has a written partnership agreement that gives a name to the partnership, then that name is the legal name. Otherwise, the legal name of the general partnership is simply the last names of the owners. (Many sole proprietorships and partnerships present their business to the public under a name that's different from their legal name—see fictitious business name, below.) And for corporations, LLCs, and limited partnerships, the legal name is the name registered with the state filing office (usually the Department or Secretary of State).

- A **trade name** is simply the name that a business uses with the public, which may or may not be the same as the name of the business owner or the business's legal name. John O'Toole's Classic Cars, Amoeba Records, and Nolo are examples of trade names. You see trade names on business signs, in the telephone book, and on invoices. In many transactions, such as opening a bank account or applying for a loan, you'll need to provide the owners' names, the legal name of the business (if different), and the trade name of the business (if different).

- The term **fictitious business name** is used when the trade name of a business is different from its legal name. For instance, if John O'Toole named his sole proprietorship Turtle's Classic Cars, the name "Turtle's Classic Cars" would be a fictitious business name because it does not contain the owner's last name, "O'Toole." A fictitious business name is sometimes called a **DBA** name. DBA stands for "doing business as," as in: "John O'Toole, doing business as Turtle's Classic Cars." Corporations and LLCs may also have to file fictitious name statements if the name they hold out to the public differs from the legal name they registered with the state. For example, if the owners of Southern Colusa County Auto Mechanics Ltd. Liability Co. decide to operate a repair shop under the fictitious name "Grease Monkeys," they'll have to file a fictitious name statement.

- The legal name of a business that must register with the state to be legally created is called a **corporate name,** an **LLC name,** or a **limited partnership name.** If a corporation, LLC, or limited partnership operates under the same name that's registered with the Department or Secretary of State, then its corporate, LLC, or limited partnership name will be both its legal name and its trade name.

- A **trademark** (sometimes called simply a mark) is any word, phrase, design, or symbol used to market a product or service. Technically, a mark used to market a service, rather than a product, is called a service mark, though the term "trademark" is commonly used for both types of marks. Owners of trademarks have legal rights under both federal and state law, which give them the power in some cases to prevent others from using their trademark to market goods or services.

- **Business name** tends to be a catchall term that can refer to any of the names used by a business—the name of a business itself, a corporate name, a fictitious business name, or the names of a business's products and services.

Business Names and Trademarks Often Overlap

Many trade names double as trademarks and service marks for products and services of the business. For instance, when McDonald's (trade name) advertises McDonald's French fries, the trade name "McDonald's" also becomes a trademark, because it is used to identify the maker (or brand) of French fries. And when the company puts up a sign in front of its restaurant, the term "McDonald's" becomes a service mark, identifying who's providing the fast food service of that restaurant. In other words, any time you use your trade name to identify a product, service, or business location, you're using the trade name as a mark—either a trademark or a service mark. As you can see, a name can wear a bunch of different hats: It can be a trade name, a legal name, and a trademark (or service mark) all in one.

Legal Name	Trade Name	Trademarks/Service Marks
McDonald's Corporation	McDonald's	McDonald's French fries Big Mac Ronald McDonald Golden arches symbol
Microsoft Corporation	Microsoft	Microsoft Word Internet Explorer "Where do you want to go today?" slogan
Trader Joe's Company	Trader Joe's	Trader Joe's Baked Tortilla Chips Trader Giotto's Italian Roast coffee beans Trader Darwin's Vitamins
Ronco, Inc.	Ronco	Popeil Pocket Fisherman Dial-O-Matic Food Slicer
Kraft Foods, Inc.	Kraft	JELL-O Gelatin Cheez Whiz Tang Instant Breakfast Drink "It's the cheesiest" slogan for Kraft Macaroni & Cheese "Good to the last drop" slogan for Kraft Maxwell House Coffee

A. An Overview of Trademark Law

In a nutshell, trademark law—which is really a catchall term referring to a large body of statutes, regulations, and court decisions—prevents a business from using a name or logo that is likely to be confused with one that a competing business already uses. This general rule applies both to the name of a business and to the names of any of its products or services.

Trademark Protects More Than Names

This chapter focuses on how trademark applies to business names. But the rules discussed here apply to a lot more—logos, designs, slogans, and packaging features can also be protected by trademark. For example, Nike's slogan "Just Do It" and American Express's mantra "Don't leave home without it" are protected by the law of trademark. For more information on using trademarks in other aspects of your small business, read *Trademark: Legal Care for Your Business & Product Name*, by Stephen R. Elias (Nolo).

Allowing businesses to have exclusive use of certain names helps consumers to identify and recognize goods in the marketplace. When you buy Racafrax brand of wood glue, for instance, you'll know that it will be similar in quality to the Racafrax glue you bought last time. By contrast, if any company were allowed to call its glue "Racafrax Glue," customers would never know what they were getting. And because customers would never know when they were using the Racafrax company's glue, the Racafrax company wouldn't be able to build customer trust or goodwill, even if its glue was the best available. In this way, consumers and businesses alike benefit from trademark protection.

This section will give you a rundown of what's protected by trademark law and how to determine and protect your rights to the names you use. This will help you understand what steps you should take as part of forming your business to avoid infringing others' rights (and opening yourself up to lawsuits). And it will also give you the legal basics you'll need to protect your business name and to figure out whether your rights are being infringed by others down the road.

⚠️ **Pick a name that won't bring legal trouble.** The main reason to learn the basics of trademark law is not so you can successfully defend your name in court against another business that tries to use it. Even if you were to win a complex and expensive court fight, you'd be a huge loser when it comes to time, worry, and legal fees. Far better to avoid disputes in the first place by choosing a safe name that has a very low likelihood of leading to customer confusion and, therefore, an infringement lawsuit.

1. What Is a Trademark?

The definition of "trademark" is simple: Any word, phrase, logo, or other device used to identify products or services in the marketplace is a trademark. This includes the names of products or services themselves and often the name of the business that's selling them. Using a name in public commerce to identify goods or services for sale is enough to make it a trademark; there is no registration requirement. However, registration with the U.S. Patent and Trademark Office will greatly strengthen your power to enforce your rights to the trademark. For example, if you federally register your trademark, you can stop any subsequent user in your field from using the same or a confusingly similar mark anywhere in the United States. (Trademark registration is covered in Section E, below.)

Keep in mind, however, that a key part of the definition of a trademark is that it must be used in public to identify goods or services for sale. So if you don't use the name of your business or product or service in public in conjunction with something you're trying to sell, it isn't considered a trademark. For example, if a software company called ZZP Web Masters markets bookmarking software for the Internet called "WebWorm," then the name WebWorm is a trademark. If the only marketing done for WebWorm is an ad that reads, "Manage your bookmarks with WebWorm," then the business name ZZP Web Masters will not be a trademark, because it's not used in public to sell WebWorm. But an ad that reads, "WebWorm: The best bookmarking software on Earth, by ZZP Web Masters," includes two trademarks: the product name WebWorm and the trade name ZZP Web Masters.

By the same token, a name that appears only in nonpublic documents—such as an internal memo or a product sample that isn't available to the public—isn't a trademark.

For practical purposes, many if not most business names are also considered trademarks, since most businesses do use their names to promote or sell their product or service.

Trademarks vs. Service Marks

You've probably heard the term "trademark," which applies to names, logos, and slogans that identify products (such as Chia Pet), a whole lot more than the term "service mark," which is used when a name identifies a service (such as H&R Block Tax Preparation Services). Because the legal rules for trademarks and service marks are virtually identical, the term "trademark," or sometimes just "mark," is commonly used for both types of marks. But since the two terms do refer to technically different things, you should be aware of the distinction, especially if your business will primarily provide services.

---

a. Trademark Rights

The power of a trademark comes from the fact that you may be entitled to exclude others from using the same mark. If you were the first to use the trademark, then you own certain rights to it and can take legal action against others who use it illegally. In legal terms, if others "infringe your trademark" by using it in a way that's likely to confuse your customers or that has "diluted" your trademark, you can take them to court and force them to stop using it, and maybe even to pay damages.

For example, if ZZP Web Masters had been selling WebWorm for two years and then another company started selling a similar product called "WebWorm," ZZP Web Masters could sue the other company and force it to stop using the product name "WebWorm." If ZZP Web Masters could prove that its business suffered because of the infringement, it might also be entitled to some financial compensation (damages) from the other company. (See Sections 2 and 3, below, for a discussion of when use of a similar trademark can cause customer confusion or trademark dilution.)

So far, so good—you're probably even wondering why everyone says trademark issues are such a bear to deal with. Here's why: Just because you own a trademark doesn't mean you can always prevent someone else from using it (and, likewise, another owner of a trademark can't always prevent you from using that mark). Unlike a copyright, which generally gives the same level of protection to all owners, a trademark gives widely varying degrees of protection to the owner, depending on a variety of circumstances. So, as explained below, the key legal point isn't so much whether you own a trademark but whether it qualifies for trademark protection—and, if so, how much.

b. Strong vs. Weak Marks

The general rule is that distinctive business names such as Yahoo! and Mountain Dew receive the strongest legal trademark protection. What makes a mark "distinctive" is explained in more detail below, but, for the moment, it's important that you understand why distinctive names get more protection. The theory is that distinctive names such as Pepsi or Cisco make strong connections in the minds of consumers, and play a big role in consumers' buying choices. The opposite is considered to be true for names that aren't very distinctive, such as Quality Vitamins or Brite Paint.

Since distinctive names are thought to play such a big role in helping consumers choose among brands, it follows that the more distinctive a name is, the more likely it is that customers will be confused (in legal theory at least) by more than one business using the name. To avoid this confusion, the law gives more protection to distinctive names, and less or none to names that are merely ordinary and descriptive.

A truly distinctive trademark (also called a "strong trademark") is one that clearly distinguishes the product or service it represents from others. Memorable, unusual names such as Xerox or 3M are additional good examples of distinctive marks. While there's no magic formula for what makes a trademark distinctive, strong marks tend to be surprising or fanciful names that often have nothing to do with the business, product, or service. Still more examples of distinctive marks include Velcro and Comet, the cleanser.

On the flip side, a weak trademark consists of ordinary, descriptive words that merely describe aspects of the product or business, such as durability ("Sturdy Knapsacks"), location ("The Edge of Town Tavern"), or other qualities ("Speedy Dry Cleaners," "Tasty Vegetables"). Also, trademarks that include personal names are usually considered to be ordinary marks and, therefore, weak. (But, as explained below, weak trademarks can become stronger with use.)

An additional reason why ordinary, descriptive trademarks aren't strongly protected, at least at first, is to make sure that competitors aren't unfairly prevented from using common words to describe their own products. For example, a food delivery service company called "Galloping Gourmet" wouldn't be able to monopolize the word "gourmet" and stop a deli from using the name "Tom's Gourmet Sandwiches."

c. How Trademarks Can Grow Stronger

A weak trademark can eventually offer good protection if it becomes distinctive and therefore stronger through use. Called "acquiring a secondary meaning" in legalese, this is particularly likely to occur when a product or service with a weak mark becomes a lasting success, making it likely that the public will associate the mark with the product or service being sold. For example, as the designer clothing brand Tommy Hilfiger has become popular nationwide, its previously weak trademark grows stronger as customers come to associate the ordinary name with a particular company. Other examples of the weak-to-strong phenomenon include Burger King, Tom's Natural Toothpaste, Ben & Jerry's Ice Cream, and The Yellow Pages.

d. Unfair Competition Laws

What if your weak trademark never becomes strong? Just because you have a weak trademark doesn't mean that others are free to use your business name. Because of a legal doctrine called "unfair competition," you may be able to prevent others from using your descriptive name, so long as you used it first. While unfair competition law is a separate body of law from trademark law, it can have the same effect. It comes from the same basic idea that it's not fair for another business to rip off your business's good reputation.

For example, if you've been selling dry cleaning services in Bakersfield under the name Jean's Quick Cleaners, and someone else in the same city opens Jeanne's Quick Cleaners, you could claim unfair competition and convince a court to prevent the newcomer from using that name. As you can see, unfair competition law can have the same result as trademark law: It can prevent another business from using a name identical or confusingly similar to yours, if you used the name first. Keep in mind, however, that your right to stop trademark infringement is stronger than your right to stop unfair competition, so it will be easier to prevent someone from using your business name if it's trademarked.

2. When Do Trademarks Conflict?

As you surely know, plenty of businesses share the same name, or at least part of the same name, without violating each other's trademark rights. Examples include United Airlines and United Van Lines, Ford Motor Company and Ford Modeling Agency, and Scott Paper Products and Scott Sunglasses. This is perfectly legal, because trademark infringement occurs only when the use of a mark by two different businesses is likely to cause customer confusion. (An exception to this rule, called the "dilution" doctrine, is explained in Section 3, below.) If customers aren't likely to be confused, then both businesses may legally use the same mark. But if customer confusion is likely, then the rightful owner of the mark can prohibit the other businesses from using it, and can sue for damages (financial compensation) for any unauthorized use.

Dual uses of the same or similar mark can cause customer confusion if it's unclear which company actually makes a product or provides a service, or if customers will be misled as to the source of the product. Customer confusion can happen in a number of different ways. Sometimes dual uses of a mark lead customers to believe that a certain company made a product when it actually did not. Or a customer may see trademarks being used in two different places and think that the companies are jointly owned or somehow affiliated, which may not be true.

Determining whether two marks legally conflict (in other words, whether customer confusion is likely) is one of the trickiest bits of trademark law.

In making this determination, courts deem the following factors to be particularly important:
- how strong (distinctive or well known) the original trademark is
- how much the products or services really compete against one another, and
- how similar the trademarks are in appearance, sound, or meaning.

We'll look at each of these in more depth in the next few sections. As you read on, keep in mind that trademark conflict is a legal question—which means that legal rules, as opposed to common sense, will dictate the outcome.

a. How "Strong" Is the Mark?

As discussed above, distinctive ("strong") marks receive the most protection, because, in legal theory, they are more likely to stick in consumers' minds and play a role in their buying choices. Since strong trademarks tend to stick in customers' minds, so the theory goes, customer confusion is likely if more than one company uses a strong trademark. To protect consumers from such confusion, courts will typically prohibit more than one company from using a strong trademark. Besides protecting consumers, prohibiting multiple uses of a strong trademark prevents businesses from stealing customers or getting a free ride off another business's good reputation by using an established business's trademark.

For example, the very strong and well-known trademark Microsoft is firmly implanted in millions of people's minds. If a company called itself Microsoft Consulting, plenty of people would be confused about whether Bill Gates had anything to do with that consulting company. If Bill Gates sued Microsoft Consulting for trademark infringement, he would have a very good chance of winning.

Trademark law doesn't give much, if any, protection to weak trademarks, because they don't trigger a strong association in customers' minds between the mark and a particular product or service (or so the legal thinking goes). For that reason, courts are less inclined to find that customer confusion is likely when more than one business uses a weak trademark. Note that this is true even if customer confusion does in fact exist.

For example, if Smith Jewelry and Smith Hardware exist in the same town, customers may wonder if they're owned by the same family. Nevertheless, trademark law won't protect the name of either business, since the name Smith is so common. (However, unfair competition law may protect the hardware store Smiths if the jewelry store Smiths started getting into the hardware business, making the businesses direct competitors.)

b. Do the Products or Services Actually Compete?

If the products or services that share the same trademarks are in completely unrelated fields or industries, or if they're sold in different geographical regions (and not on the Internet), there's obviously far less chance that customers will be confused. In other words, the less products or services actually compete, the less likely it is that there will be a trademark violation.

For example, a pizza joint named Rocket Pizza probably won't be confused with a record store named Rocket Records, even if they exist in the same city. And an auto shop named Armadillo Repairs in Portland, Maine, most likely won't run into any trademark conflicts with Armadillo Auto Repairs in San Diego. Because they are so far apart and serve purely local customers, chances are slim that customers would confuse the two companies.

EXAMPLE: You open a coffee shop in Austin, Texas, and name it Pam's Coffee Stop. A year later, you're driving through Albuquerque, New Mexico, and notice a small café also named Pam's Coffee Stop. After thinking about it, you decide that there's little chance of a trademark violation by either business. The trademark is ordinary and descriptive and therefore weak, plus the shops are so far away

from each other that they're not competitors. But this gets you wondering what you'd do if a big national chain started using the name and moved into your area. The answer is, you would retain the right to use the name because you were the first to use it in your area (as long as the national chain hadn't registered the name with the U.S. Patent and Trademark Office before you first used it). But the chain could prevent you from expanding into other areas of the country if this ever became your goal.

⚠ **New marketing techniques, new competitors.** As mentioned at the beginning of this chapter, with the arrival and widespread use of the Web, the fast expansion of mail order catalogue businesses, and ever more frequent travel, the old rule that small, local businesses don't have to worry about trademarks from other geographical regions has largely gone out the window. Today even small, local businesses commonly establish websites; hundreds of thousands of businesses send out catalogues; and some local restaurants and hotels seek to reach a national (or even worldwide) pool of tourists. The upshot is that many formerly local businesses that just a few years ago never would have been confused with each other are now competitors, which of course increases the likelihood of customer confusion and trademark infringement if their names are the same. (Be sure to read Section B, below, on new trademark issues and considerations in today's ever-shrinking world.)

Of course, there are plenty of gray areas in which two businesses aren't in head-to-head competition but use the same marks for products that are similar enough to make a customer stop and think, for example, "Is a Parker calendar made by the same company as Parker pens?" Even though a company with the same name may not be stealing business from a competitor, it may be unintentionally taking advantage of that company's goodwill and getting a free ride from its advertising.

Whether infringement exists in these gray areas often depends on how strong the original trademark is (as discussed above). If the original trademark is weak, there's probably not much goodwill or reputation to rip off (few customers would be confused by the similar name), so a court wouldn't be likely to find there was infringement. But if the original trademark is strong, there's a greater likelihood that the newer trademark will rip off the older one's reputation, making it likely for the court to agree that there's been an infringement.

> **EXAMPLE:** Your pet products company begins selling a toy that looks like a cross between a dog and a weasel, which you name the Garden Weasel. Soon after your toy hits the market, the makers of the nationally marketed Garden Weasel 5-in-1 garden tool contact you, claiming that you are infringing their trademark. Since you feel that the products are unrelated enough to minimize the chance of customer confusion (the products don't compete with one another), your first thought is to stick with the Garden Weasel name.
>
> Think again. The Garden Weasel trademark is distinctive (memorable and unusual) and, therefore, strong. If you are sued—and you may well be—defending the lawsuit is likely to cost you tens or possibly even hundreds of thousands of dollars that you almost surely can't afford. And if the Garden Weasel mark is strong enough, you may lose the suit, even though the products don't compete. A better approach would probably be to tweak your name a bit, to something like the Lawn Weasel or the Garden Ferret, for instance.

c. Sight, Sound, and Meaning Test

Obviously, dual use of identical trademarks can cause customer confusion, as discussed above. But what about merely similar trademarks? If two marks look alike, sound alike, or have the same meaning, a court could decide that they conflict with each other, just as if they were identical. Small or superficial differences between two trademarks may not be enough to prevent customer confusion. The difference in spelling, for example, does not make the name "Ekzon" sufficiently different from "Exxon" to avoid trademark problems. And even though they're expressed in two different languages, the names "Le Petit Fleur" and "The Little Flower" have the same meaning, which increases the likelihood that some customers could confuse the two.

> **EXAMPLE:** You open an auto lubrication business and name it Jiffy Oil. A few weeks later, you receive a stern letter from the attorneys of Jiffy Lube, a national chain of auto lubrication businesses. The letter informs you that the name "Jiffy Oil" infringes on their rights to the trademark "Jiffy Lube," since customer confusion is likely because the names are very similar, are used to describe an almost identical service, and mean pretty much the same thing. They demand that you change your business's name or be taken to court. You'd be wise to comply with their demand. Their "Jiffy Lube" trademark, though a descriptive term (for fast lubrication), has become a very strong mark over time—customers have come to recognize it as a specific brand of service. And because your shop is a direct competitor of Jiffy Lube, the chance of customer confusion is high.

Christopher Johnson, publisher of the *Weekly Alibi* (formerly *NuCity*), a free weekly newspaper in Albuquerque, New Mexico:

When you are starting a small business, there are so many things to think about—important things like financing, initial marketing, etc. For many people (myself included), the last thing to cross your mind is whether the use of your business name is legal. About three years after I started my weekly newspaper, NuCity, *right when the company was finally stable, a weekly newspaper with a similar name* (New City) *in a different state took note of us and threatened litigation for trademark infringement. So, just at the time that my newspaper was really taking off, I had to decide between fighting a weak lawsuit or changing the name of the paper altogether. Of course, we came up with a much better name, and though it was an expensive process to change all our printed and marketing materials, in the end it was well worth it. Rest assured that the first thing that we did prior to making a final decision on our new name was to verify that no one else had a trademark on that name. I now own the national and international trademark rights to* Weekly Alibi, *and can't wait to act like a moron and threaten other newspapers with lawsuits.*

In the future, I will check to see if a name is available before I start any business. If you are starting a business where your name has significant marketing value, it is well worth your time to check to see if your chosen name is available to use and then to complete the process to secure your trademark rights to it.

3. The Dilution Exception

As mentioned several times, there is a big exception to the rule that one trademark infringes another only where there is the likelihood of customer confusion: Even when customer confusion is improbable, courts will stop a business from using a trademark that's the same as or similar to some-

one else's if the use has diminished—or "diluted"—its distinctiveness. This legal protection kicks in only when a mark is so well known that even if you were to use it in a different context from the original trademark, lots of people would think of the original trademark. For example, a court might stop an athletic shoe manufacturer from using the trademark Exxon or a gas station from calling itself Nike. Even though customers would not be likely to confuse an oil company with a shoe maker, this sort of copying is a legal no-no, since allowing others to use the very famous trademark can chip away at its distinctiveness and slowly reduce its legal strength.

B. Trademark Issues Online

As in many other legal areas, the traditional principles of trademark law are scrambling to keep up with the fast clip of technological change. The Internet has changed many of the rules regarding trademark issues, just as it has created some entirely new ones. This section outlines a number of Internet-related concerns regarding trademarks and business names.

1. The Web Has Changed the Rules

As described in the previous section, one of the touchstones of trademark infringement is whether or not the two trademarks in question are likely to cause customer confusion. In the pre-Internet world, small, local businesses didn't have to worry too much about name conflicts as long as no one in their area had a similar name. But geographic distance is irrelevant in cyberspace.

Particularly if you plan to put your business online, you'll have to consider not only the trademarks of businesses already on the Web, but also those of businesses located anywhere the Web reaches—which, of course, is just about everywhere. If you create a Web page for a small home-based business, your business is no longer local in character—you're essentially launching a national or worldwide business that can compete with businesses everywhere, whether or not those businesses are online.

For example, if you create a website for your antique restoration business, Dalliance Designs, you could be competing with every antique restoration business in the country. If one of these owns the trademark "Dalliance Designs," your effort to share the market with that business opens a potentially ugly can of legal worms.

The Web has changed trademark rules for everybody—even businesses that don't go digital. As more and more small businesses launch websites introducing themselves in a keystroke to consumers all over the globe, your purely local, offline business might find itself in competition with businesses several time zones—or even continents—away. Although courts are still chewing over many trademark issues raised by online commerce, it is already clear that, in some circumstances at least, a Web business with the same name as yours poses just as great a threat of a trademark lawsuit as does a real-life, bricks-and-steel business across the street.

> **EXAMPLE:** Jarrod is a mechanic who opens a small machine shop in a rural area of California. He's lived in the area for 30 years, and knows every business for miles around. Nevertheless, as part of choosing a name for his business, Jarrod carefully checks the phone book and the county register for fictitious business names. He ultimately settles on his first choice, Checkers Tool and Die.
>
> All goes smoothly for a few months, until a customer compliments Jarrod on his slick-looking website. This leaves Jarrod totally confused, since he hates computers and has only a vague notion of what the Web is. But in talking with his customer about this mysterious website, Jarrod realizes that a machine shop in Florida is also using the name "Checkers Tool and Die," and sells a number of specialized parts via an online catalogue. This doesn't par-

ticularly worry Jarrod until his customer (a lawyer, naturally) goes on to explain that if the distant business can prove it owns the trademark to "Checkers Tool and Die" and convince a court that it shares the same market as Jarrod, it might be able to force Jarrod to stop using the name.

Although at least one customer has been confused, Jarrod doesn't really expect the Florida outfit to go after him—after all, his business is small and local, provides primarily repair services (with parts as a sideline), and doesn't sell on the Web. Nevertheless, even the possibility of legal trouble worries him—especially because he'd like to open a retail machine parts shop next to his repair shop. After learning that the Florida outfit has been using the name Checkers Tool and Die for years and seems to be putting lots of energy into expanding its website, Jarrod decides to be safe and spend the time and money necessary to change the name of his business to White Mountain Tool & Die before he expands.

2. Domain Name Conflicts and Cybersquatting

Besides making sure that your business name won't create trademark trouble, if you plan to create a website for your business, you'll also need to choose a domain name that's legally safe. A domain name (such as nolo.com) is part of a website's URL (such as http://www.nolo.com/index.html), which functions as its Internet "address" online. Later sections of this chapter discuss the process of choosing and registering a domain name; for now, the focus is on the trademark issues that can arise regarding domain names.

The first thing you should understand is that, generally speaking, your domain name will function as a trademark if you conduct business at your site—that is, if you offer products or services for sale. This is true whether or not you register it with the U.S. Patent and Trademark Office (PTO). As discussed in Section E, registering your domain name with the PTO will strengthen your power to enforce your trademark rights to it, but using it for a commercial purpose is all that's technically necessary to establish your trademark rights. For instance, amazon.com is the domain name for a huge website that sells books, videos, and other products—and the name amazon.com also serves as a trademark. This means that trademark law prohibits anyone else from using the name amazon.com for their business.

Keep in mind, however, that if your domain name is generic, such as software.com or books.com, it won't qualify for much trademark protection. This rule applies to generic business or product names such as *lawyer, building supplies,* or *pet food*—the law will generally not allow you to establish any trademark rights to these generic terms. But as discussed earlier (in talking about weak trademarks), even generic domain names can grow stronger with use. Consider etrade.com, which has become almost synonymous with online stock trading. Originally, the name wouldn't have deserved much trademark protection since it wasn't distinctive at all—anyone can slap an "e" on the beginning of a word. Now, however, the mark has acquired "secondary meaning" and is entitled to trademark protection.

For most business owners, the best way to make sure their customers will find them online is simply to tack ".com" onto their regular business names. However, while trademark law will allow two or more companies to use the same name as long as it won't confuse customers, the technical limitations of the Web won't allow for two identical domain names. In other words, Ford Trucks and the Ford Modeling Agency won't both be able to use ford.com as a domain name. Since each website must have its own unique address, you may be out of luck if someone is already using your business name, plus .com, as a domain name. As you can imagine, this is where things can get sticky.

a. Dealing With Domain Name Conflicts

If you're starting a brand-new business that you haven't named yet, choose a name that also can be used as a domain name. That way, you can register it as a domain name right away and sidestep the whole issue of what to do if your domain name is already taken. You'll need to decide for yourself how important it is to you to have a domain name that's the same as your business name. If it's really important, then you may have to work hard to come up with a business name that's good for business, available as a domain name, and available as a trademark. If it's not that important, then your naming process will be somewhat easier—but you may regret it down the road when your business name can't be registered as a domain name.

A few possible scenarios may arise when someone is using your business name as a domain name. One is that you may simply have missed your chance to get that domain name yourself—even though you have trademark rights to it—and will either have to choose a different name or buy it from whoever registered it first. These are likely to be your only options if your mark isn't nationally famous and if customers aren't likely to be confused by another business using your name.

> **EXAMPLE:** Gene and Beth run a bookstore in New Orleans called Lexicon. After about a year of planning, they decide to launch a website—but are disappointed to find out that the domain name lexicon.com is already taken. By doing a search on the Web, and by going to the lexicon.com website, Gene and Beth discover that the owner of lexicon.com is a freelance editor in Chicago. Since Gene and Beth's bookstore doesn't have any national exposure, they probably won't be able to force the editor in Chicago to give up the name, because the editor's site probably would not confuse customers into thinking there was some association with their bookstore.

On the other hand, you may be able to assert your trademark rights against someone using your trademark as a domain name if:

- his or her use of the trademark is likely to cause customer confusion, or
- your trademark is distinctive and nationally known—even if the other party's use of it is not likely to cause customer confusion. (Recall from Section A, above, that laws against trademark dilution protect famous marks from use by others, even if customer confusion is not likely.)

EXAMPLE: Assume that Gene and Beth's bookstore, Lexicon, already had a well-established national mail-order catalogue business and the name Lexicon was familiar to a national audience. In this situation, they might be able to assert their trademark rights in court and force the Chicago editor to give up the lexicon.com domain name.

You will have to weigh carefully the pros and cons of attempting to force someone to give up a domain name based on a potential trademark infringement. On the one hand, the possibility of prevailing and getting the domain name you want may make this course worth it, depending on your business model. On the other hand, remember that lawsuits cost time and money; they can easily exceed $10,000 in legal and court fees (and can sometimes cost ten or 20 times that amount). If your case is a marginal one, you may be better off simply choosing a different domain name or even buying the name from the other party, who might prefer to sell rather than to fight a losing battle.

⚠ Come to your own defense. Your trademark rights can become weakened if you fail to defend your trademark when you know or should know that it's being infringed. For this reason, it's probably a good idea to go after a website or any other business or individual that infringes your trademark. For more in-depth information on defending your trademark and dealing with infringers, see *Trademark: Legal Care for Your Business & Product Name*, by Stephen R. Elias (Nolo).

b. Dealing With Cybersquatters

You may find that the domain name you want has already been registered by someone who wants to sell it back to you at a profit. For instance, say you own a well-known car racing magazine called *Auto Racing Today*. When you are ready to launch a website, you discover that the domain name autoracingtoday.com is already registered by another business, which offers to sell the name back to you for $250,000 (actually a modest amount compared to similar sales). This practice, known as "cybersquatting," became a real problem in the late '90s before businesses realized the importance of reserving domain names as early as possible.

A 1999 federal law known as the Anti-Cybersquatting Consumer Protection Act makes cybersquatting illegal and provides remedies for those injured, including getting the domain name back and possibly receiving money damages. To win a cybersquatting lawsuit, you'll have to sue the cybersquatter in federal court and prove that:

- the domain name registrant (the cybersquatter) acted in bad faith by registering the name solely to make a profit by selling it back to you
- your mark was distinctive at the time the domain name was registered
- the domain name is identical or confusingly similar to your trademark, and
- you were the first to use the trademark in commerce.

An alternative to a lawsuit is to use a procedure set forth by ICANN (short for International Corporation for Assigned Names and Numbers), the international group now in charge of Internet domain name policy. ICANN's process for resolving cybersquatting disputes is known as the Uniform Domain Name Dispute Resolution Policy (UDRP), and typically will cost far less and take less time than a lawsuit. The case you'll have to prove is similar to what would be involved in a federal lawsuit. You will have to show that:

- the domain name is identical or confusingly similar to your trademark
- the registrant has no legitimate interests in or rights to the domain name, and
- the domain name was registered or is being used in bad faith.

Another advantage of the ICANN procedure is that it can be used in international domain name disputes, while a lawsuit based on the Anti-Cybersquatting Act can only be brought against domain name registrants in the United States. For more information, visit ICANN's website at www.icann.org.

3. Using Meta Tags That Conflict With Trademarks

Meta tags are keywords, embedded in the HTML source code of Web pages, that search engines such as Yahoo! or Excite look for when conducting a search. For instance, if you did a Yahoo! search for the term "digital video," the search engine would check the meta tags of all the pages on the Web, and return to you the ones that contained the key words "digital video" in their source codes. Assuming that sites such as *DV Magazine* and Sony Electronics would have included the term "digital video" in their meta tags, your search would bring up those sites and those of whoever else used that meta tag.

When choosing meta tags for your site, be careful not to use someone else's trademark without their permission—doing so may subject you to a trademark infringement lawsuit. It's becoming common for trademark owners to sue others who use their trademarks as meta tags to deceptively lure browsers to their sites. For example, a site called Calvin Designer Label used the words "Playboy" and "Playmate" as meta tags so that anyone searching for those words would be directed to the Calvin page. When *Playboy* magazine sued, a federal court found Calvin Designer Label liable for infringement and ordered it to stop using *Playboy's* trademarks as meta tags.

On the other hand, there may be instances in which it is legal to use someone else's trademark in your meta tags—even without permission. Generally speaking, this is more likely if the use is for a legitimate descriptive purpose. For example, in another *Playboy* case, the famous magazine sued Terri Welles, a former Playmate, for using the terms "Playmate of the Year" and its abbreviation "PMOY" at her website, www.terriwelles.com, and within the site's meta tags. Welles had won the title Playmate of the Year in 1981, and was using her site to promote herself for her modeling career. A court found that her use of "Playmate of the Year" and "PMOY" was permissible, since she had earned the title and was using it legitimately to describe herself. Her case was also strengthened by the fact that her site offered numerous disclaimers that it was not endorsed by or affiliated with *Playboy* magazine.

Remember also that an owner of a weak, descriptive trademark doesn't have much, if any, power to stop you from using part or all of that trademark. For instance, you could safely include the words "house" and "garden" in the meta tags of your home design website without being afraid that *House & Garden* magazine would sue you. The same goes for using the word "news" for your hiking site, without fear of a lawsuit from *U.S. News & World Report* magazine. Of course, using actual trademarked phrases such as "U.S. News & World Report" or "House & Garden" as meta tags would probably get you into trouble.

Unfortunately, there's no clear test for determining whether it's permissible to use someone else's trademark as a meta tag. The only way to get a definitive answer may be through a lawsuit, something you probably don't want to risk. Proceed with caution when using any trademarks owned by others in your website or in its meta tags, and definitely avoid any deceptive use of trademarks to lure browsers to your site.

C. Name Searches

By now you get the picture that a dispute over business names can be thorny. To avoid potential trademark hassles later on, you need to do some early digging before you finally settle on a name for your business. The main way to accomplish this is to conduct a name search to find out whether another business is already using a name that's identical or similar to the one you want to use. The information in this section will help you figure out how to go about researching your chosen name, and what to do once you've found one that you'll be able to use—and protect—as a trademark.

Searching domain name availability. To find out if a domain name is available, simply go to one of the many domain name registrars online (a good list is available at www.internic.com). The registrars typically allow you to enter the name you want, and will tell you whether it's available and, if not, who has registered it. Doing a name search for trademark purposes, on the other hand, requires consulting more sources, as described in this section.

The scope of your search will depend largely on the size and geographical scope of your business and your plans for its future. If you plan from day one to sell a product nationally—whether via catalogue, through retailers, or online—you'll obviously need to worry about trademarks across the country. If, on the other hand, you're starting a small home-based service business, don't plan to advertise, and are relatively certain you won't expand geographically, a search of names in your county, and perhaps state, may be all you need—though it's always wise to search widely so that you at least know what's out there.

Keep in mind that the extent of your search encompasses not only how widely you search geographically, but also how deeply you search—in terms of looking not only for identical names, but also for those that are merely similar or have a slight resemblance to yours. Searching for the exact name (also called a "direct hit" search) is quick and cheap, but risks missing look- and sound-alikes. A more in-depth search, such as one that looks for names with slight variations in spelling, is safer, but can get quite complicated and expensive.

1. Sources of Name Information

Domain name research can be difficult because there is no one place to look. In large part, this is because a business can—and millions do—establish a trademark simply by using it. Since millions of marks aren't registered with the government, in addition to checking federal and state trademark databases you'll want to check many other sources of information, such as business directories and phone books, for unregistered trademarks. You should check some or preferably all of the following resources for name conflicts, depending on how extensive a search you need (methods for searching these databases are discussed below in Section 2).

a. The World Wide Web

It is probably best to start with the Internet because this resource is huge, fast, and free. By using several of the Web's search engines, such as Yahoo!, Lycos, or Google, you can quickly see whether someone else on the Web is using a specific term and how he or she is using it. Search engines are easy to use: Simply enter the terms you're looking for (often called a "query"), and the engine will scan the Web and retrieve any sites that contain the terms in your query. Consult the "help" area of the particular search engine you're using for more detailed instructions on how to construct your queries.

Another easy way to check trademarks online is to go to a domain name registrar online and put in variations of the name you want to use. (Go to www.internic.com for a list of registrars.) If another company has reserved a domain name that contains your trademark, chances are you won't be able to use it. If the domain name qualifies as a trademark—which essentially means that the other company is using it to sell a product or service online—then, as described earlier in this chapter, you won't be able to use it as a trademark if your use would be likely to confuse customers.

b. Phone Directories

Don't overlook the phone book as a valuable source of local name information. If you find someone who's using the name you want in your local area and your businesses are similar, there's no reason to waste money further searching the federal trademark register or other databases. However, if your businesses are different enough, you might still be able to use the name.

c. Industry Sources

Trade publications and business directories can be great sources of business name information (and they can also give you good ideas for names). You can also call trade associations and chambers of commerce to ask if they can provide lists or directories of businesses in the area.

d. Federal Trademark Database

All those starting a business, no matter how tiny and local, should search the federal trademark database to determine whether the name they want to use has already been registered by a similar business in the United States. The most important reason to do this is to avoid being sued for "willful infringement." If you use a trademark already registered at the federal level (even if yours is a tiny, local business), you can be sued for knowingly violating someone else's trademark—even if you didn't actually check the federal database and had no idea it was there. Searching the federal database can be complicated, and there are a few different ways to go about it—including hiring a trademark search firm to do the work for you. (Search options for the federal trademark database are discussed below in Section 2.)

e. State Databases

Many state corporation and LLC filing offices (usually the Secretary of State) maintain databases of registered names of corporations, limited partnerships, and LLCs. To find out whether a name appears in your state's corporate, LLC, or limited partnership database, contact your state corporate filing office to determine its process for name searches. You may be able to search for names by phone, by mail, or online.

In addition, check your state's trademark registry. This registry is often part of the Secretary of State's department, though sometimes it has its own department. Find out the trademark office's rules for searching, or you can hire a trademark search firm to do the work for you. (Search firms are discussed below in Section 2.)

f. County Fictitious Business Name Databases

Many counties maintain a database of fictitious business names (FBNs) that have been registered in that county. Even if you won't be using a fictitious business name—because you'll use your own name or your corporate, limited partnership, or LLC name—it's a good idea to check the FBNs used by other businesses in your county or state. Depending on how widely you're planning to search, you may want to search nearby counties or every county in the state.

Keep in mind that the free or relatively cheap searches offered by state and county agencies usually check only for exact matches—and won't tell you whether a similar name is included in that database. If, for example, the county clerk's office tells you that "The Dog House" does not appear in its fictitious name database, you might be surprised later to find that "The Dawg Haus" has been in business for years. In short, you may have to do a more extensive search than the one provided by the state or county office.

⚠️ **County and state databases have limits.** Just because a name doesn't appear in any county or state name databases, that doesn't mean another business doesn't already own that trademark. Use of the name, not registration, is what creates trademark ownership. Plenty of businesses own trademarks that they have never registered, so it's important to check for unregistered trademarks using the resources discussed above. And many businesses won't bother registering at the state level, but will register a federal trademark. If you plan to invest time and money in establishing your trademark, it's essential that you do a federal trademark search, too.

EXAMPLE: Tom and Jen, both veterinarians in California, search their county's fictitious business name database for the name "Critter Care," which they want to use for the animal hospital they're planning to open. They don't find anyone else using the name in their area, so they believe they can use it. But just to be safe, Jen decides to check the California state trademark directory for the name. She finds out that a California corporation has already obtained state trademark protection for the name "Critter Care." Since that corporation was doing business under its own name and not a

fictitious one, it didn't have to register with any county fictitious name databases—so even if Tom and Jen had checked fictitious names statewide they wouldn't have found it. (Tom and Jen also would have found the name by checking the Secretary of State's corporate name database.)

2. Searching the Federal Trademark Database

As discussed above, to avoid a charge of willful infringement, it's a very good idea to check the federal trademark registry, maintained by the U.S. Patent and Trademark Office (PTO). While tiny microbusinesses might get away without a federal search, most businesses should accept the fact that the Internet and other communication technologies have simply created too many potential trademark conflicts, even for small businesses. They need to search the PTO's database of federally registered trademarks.

If possible, begin your search with the free trademark database on the PTO's website. The PTO's database consists of all federally registered marks and all marks for which registration is pending. To start, go to the PTO's Trademark Electronic Business Center at www.uspto.gov/web/menu/tmebc/index.html and choose "Search." Then follow the instructions you see on the screen.

If using the Internet isn't feasible for you, visit your local Patent and Trademark Depository Library (PTDL)—there's at least one in every state—and use its research materials. (The PTO maintains a list of PTDLs nationwide. The list is posted at the PTO website at www.uspto.gov/go/ptdl/ptdlib_l.html.) If a PTDL isn't convenient, a large public library or special business and government library near you should carry the federal trademark register, which contains all federal trademarks and service marks arranged by categories of goods and services.

Another option is to hire a professional search firm to do the work for you. You can order a complete search of registered and unregistered marks through Trademark Express, Thompson and Thompson, CCH Trademark Research Corporation, or one of the PTDLs that offer electronic search services for very reasonable fees (for example, see the Sc[i]3 website at www.sci3.com).

If you decide to hire a search firm, the cheapest and easiest type of national search is a direct-hit search, which will reveal whether another business has registered an identical name with the federal Patent and Trademark Office. You can often hire one of the companies mentioned above to do a direct-hit search for you for less than $50. But while direct-hit searches are quick and cheap, they usually won't turn up trademarks that are similar, but not identical, to the name you're considering. For example, if you want to name your softball training center "The Strike Zone," a direct-hit search may not turn up a trademark for "The S. Zone." And, as discussed above, any mark that looks like, sounds like, or means the same as your name could present a trademark conflict.

More extensive national searches take a lot more time and money but may be necessary if you plan for your business to reach a wide audience and want to eliminate any risk of infringing someone else's existing trademark. For an in-depth search, it may make the most sense to hire a search firm; expect a fee of roughly $200 to $350 for a professional, comprehensive search. If you do decide to hire search services, you're likely to save money if you do some quick, preliminary searches on the Internet yourself—to rule out some of your choices. For more information on national trademark searches, see *Trademark: Legal Care for Your Business & Product Name,* by Stephen R. Elias (Nolo).

3. Analyzing Your Search Results

If, after your search, you determine that the name you've chosen does not already belong to someone else (or that someone else isn't using a similar name), you can go ahead and use it. Assuming you really are the first user of the name, you'll own the trademark, which will give you the right to stop others from using it in certain situations. But since registering a trademark conveys important additional rights and protections, you may want to register your name with the federal and state governments. The basics of trademark registration are discussed in Section E, below.

But what if your search (or a search done by a professional firm) turns up an identical or similar name to the one you want to use? If the name is a famous trademark, it's probably time to pick a new name. Remember that if using your business name diminishes a famous trademark's distinctiveness or disparages its reputation for quality, the owner of the famous trademark may stop you from using your name even if its customers aren't likely to be confused between its products and yours.

Be sure to check domain names. If your Internet business will be important to you, pick a name that can also be used as a domain name. You can check whether a domain name is available at any domain name registrar, listed at www.internic.com.

If the name has been registered for official trademark protection, especially at the federal level, consider that a huge "No Trespassing" sign that should be taken seriously. Owners of federally registered trademarks have the right to use their trademarks anywhere in the country, and it is easy for them to sue and recover damages. If your search shows that the name is being used but isn't registered at the federal or state level, then you might have a bit more leeway—but not much more. Since use, not registration, conveys trademark rights, you still need to be very careful not to infringe that owner's rights.

That said, there are a few instances when taking a name that is already being used by someone else is okay. As mentioned, if the name is being used for a company that provides a very different product or service from the one you plan to sell, then you may have good reason to move forward with your plans to use the name. This is especially true if the two businesses serve only local markets and are hundreds of miles apart.

For example, just because a tiny clothing store in Boston calls itself Nature's Calling doesn't mean that you, in Aspen, Colorado, can't use Nature's Calling for your plumbing business. But if you wanted to start a clothing store in your town called Nature's Calling, and one already exists in Boston, then you should at the very least do more research before using it. If a federal trademark register search indicates that the Boston store has registered the mark "Nature's Calling," your subsequent use is a clear legal no-no. But even if the name is not registered and the Boston store seems like a local outfit, it could have plans to expand its territory or—even more likely—to create a website. Neither of these actions would necessarily prohibit your use of the name on your original store, but they could prevent you from using it more widely. The bottom line is that even if you feel certain that your business is different enough from that of the trademark owner to allow you to use the name, you should proceed only with lots and lots of caution.

How would you feel? If you are uncertain as to whether your proposed trademark would infringe an existing trademark, use a variant of the Golden Rule: How would you feel if you owned the existing trademark and someone started to use it? Ask a few friends the same question. If any of the answers are "Pissed off," consider choosing a different name, or at least invest a few hundred dollars in a consultation with an experienced trademark lawyer.

Other resources on name and trademark issues. For more help understanding the nuances of different types of trademarks, picking a bulletproof name, and searching and registering trademarks, see *Trademark: Legal Care for Your Business & Product Name,* by Stephen R. Elias (Nolo). And you'll find lots of free information on trademarks and business names in the Patents, Copyright, and Art area of Nolo's website at www.nolo.com.

D. Choosing a Domain Name

Assuming that your business will create a website—usually recommended—you'll need to choose a domain name and register it. (See Chapter 13 for more on creating a website and doing business on the Internet.)

A great domain name should be memorable, clever, and easily spelled. But keep in mind that names that are ordinary and descriptive won't qualify for much trademark protection. Many good domain names—for instance, coffee.com, drugs.com, and business.com—are not eligible for trademark protection because they are the names of whole categories of products or services. Besides, virtually every such generic domain name is undoubtedly already registered by someone else. Likewise, domain names that use surnames or geographic names are unlikely to get trademark protection. (Of course, it's possible for a generic name, such as etrade, to become famous and develop "secondary meaning," as we discussed in Section A3, above.)

You may want to register several domain names. In addition to your business name, you may want to register the names of your products or services, or other related names. Remember, names of your products or services may be as important as your business name from a marketing perspective. It's also a good idea to register common misspellings of your primary domain name and names that reflect the nature of your products or services. For example, if you design and sell gourmet aprons, and your primary domain name is kitchenstuff.com, you might also want to register aprons.com so that customers who are looking for aprons and enter "aprons.com" into their browser will land at your site. It will, of course, cost more for multiple registrations, but the increased traffic may be worth it.

One potential problem in picking a domain name is that millions of names are already taken. For example, if your business name is Flaky Cakes, you may find that FlakyCakes.com already belongs to someone else, so you'll have to use a different domain name, or change your business name if it's important to you that your business name and domain name are the same.

If you do find a domain name that's available, make sure the domain name you pick doesn't conflict with someone else's trademark. Even if you come up with a domain name that is brilliant from a marketing standpoint, beware that your domain name is at risk if it legally conflicts with any of the millions of commercial trademarks that already exist. Remember, your domain name will probably function as a trademark just as your regular business name will—assuming you conduct business at your site. (This is true whether or not you register it with the U.S. Patent and Trademark Office—registering your domain name with the PTO will strengthen your enforcement rights, but using it for a commercial purpose is all that's technically necessary to establish your rights to it.) It follows that you are not allowed to use a domain name that's likely to cause customer confusion between your company and another, whether that company is online or off. (See Chapter 13, Section E, for detailed information on choosing and registering domain names.)

Apply for federal trademark registration. In addition to applying for protection for your business name, you should also try to register your domain name with the PTO. While you don't need

to register to establish your rights to your domain name, registering it will strengthen your power to enforce your rights to it against infringers. It will also prevent someone else from registering the same name—which could save a lot of headaches in the future.

For more information on domain names. Check out Nolo's website at www.nolo.com under the Business & Human Resources tab for more on choosing a domain name for your business. Also see *Trademark: Legal Care for Your Business & Product Name,* by Stephen R. Elias (Nolo).

E. Trademark Registration

By now you understand that registering your trademark will strengthen your rights to it and make it easier to protect the name in case of a dispute. Registration is simply the process of notifying the state or, more commonly, the U.S. government that you're using a particular trademark.

State vs. Federal Trademark Registration

State registration doesn't give as many benefits as federal registration, so it generally makes most sense to register federally for the widest scope of protection. Some trademarks, however, don't qualify for federal registration, because they aren't used in national, international, or territorial commerce—in other words, they're only used within the state. These marks can only be registered at the state level. Although use of a trademark on the Internet almost guarantees the right to apply for federal registration, if you truly are only using the mark within your state, state registration may be the only option.

When registration is complete, the trademark gets placed on an official list of registered names commonly called a trademark register. The U.S. Patent and Trademark Office (PTO) maintains two registers, the Principal Register and the Supplemental Register. State trademark offices have their own systems.

When people refer to a federally registered trademark, they're generally talking about marks on the Principal Register. Trademarks that appear on the Principal Register get the most protection, and the penalties can be harsh for those who improperly use a name that appears on it. The Supplemental Register, on the other hand, is reserved for weaker, less distinctive trademarks that don't qualify for the Principal Register. The main function of the Supplemental Register is to provide notice of a mark's current use to anyone who does a trademark search. After five years on the Supplemental Register, a mark may qualify to be moved to the Principal Register if it's been in continuous use during that period. Most states maintain just one register for all trademarks.

The PTO provides registration forms and instructions, which are available from a number of sources, including the PTO's website at www.uspto.gov. For simple trademarks such as business names (as opposed to trademarks for special packaging or product design —called "trade dress" in the biz), the instructions will probably be easy enough to follow. (You can also fill in and submit the form online at the PTO's Trademark Electronic Business Center—for detailed instructions on filing online see "Registering a Trademark Online," below.)

Beware of potential tricks and traps. For more information on federally registering your trademark, see *Trademark: Legal Care for Your Business & Product Name*, by Stephen R. Elias (Nolo).

State registration processes are generally similar to the federal system's procedure. Contact your state's trademark office for more information.

Registering a Trademark Online

If you haven't yet used your trademark. Go to the PTO's Trademark Electronic Business Center at www.uspto.gov/web/menu/tmebc/index.html and choose "Filing." To file electronically (you'll need to pay with a credit card), click eTEAS. Or to complete the application online, print it out, and send it in, click printTEAS (you'll need to print out your completed application and mail it to the PTO with a check). Then follow the instructions provided. Choose the "intent-to-use" (ITU) option, since you haven't yet used your trademark in commerce, and provide a drawing or image of the mark. Be prepared to respond to the trademark examiner's questions and concerns within the deadlines assigned to you.

If you have already used your trademark commercially. Go to the PTO's Trademark Electronic Business Center at www.uspto.gov/web/menu/tmebc/index.html and choose "Filing." To file electronically (you'll need to pay with a credit card), click eTEAS. Or to complete the application online, print it out, and send it in, click printTEAS (you'll need to print out your completed application and mail it to the PTO with a check). Then follow the instructions provided. Choose the "actual use" option, since you are already commercially using the mark. Provide the information as requested: a drawing or image of the trademark, samples of how the trademark is actually being used, the first date the trademark was commercially used anywhere, and the first date the trademark was used outside your state. Be prepared to respond to the trademark examiner's questions and concerns within the deadlines assigned to you.

F. Winning Names for Your Business, Products, and Services

Now that you have a general idea of the legal hurdles you need to clear and the snags and traps to watch out for, let the naming begin! Despite the trademark hassles involved, choosing names for your business and its products or services remains one of the fun parts of starting your business. It gives you a chance to use your creative juices to come up with a name that is both marketable and infused with your individual personality (or the collective personalities of all the business partners). A business name can help you establish the overall vibe of your business, from strictly professional to downright funky to a dozen things in between.

In addition to legal restrictions and personal preferences, the traditions and realities of your particular industry or business will probably have a lot to do with what kind of business name you choose. Good, memorable business and product names range from the clever (SuperFantastic Bubble Plastic, Garden Weasel, Liquid Paper) to the straightforward (24-Hour Fitness, Fruit Roll-Ups, Jenny Craig Weight Loss Centres) to sometimes even the cryptic (Yahoo!, Chia Pet, Floam). In part because there really are so many different kinds of businesses and so many approaches to choosing a distinctive name, it's impossible to give any kind of specific advice on choosing a great name. There are, however, a few things that are helpful to keep in mind when choosing your business names.

- Especially for small local businesses that don't plan to expand geographically, straightforward, informative names often work better than fancy ones. For example, if you plan to open a shop selling aquarium supplies and tropical fish in Seattle, "Seattle Aquariums & Fish" may be a far more effective name than "The Lure of the Ocean." Also, since humble, descriptive names qualify for less trademark protection (unless they are already famous; see Section A2, above), choosing an ordinary name—especially one

with a geographic identifier—will make you less likely to infringe on someone else's trademark.

- Think about how your customers will locate your business and your products. If you don't expect customers to seek out or remember your company as a whole, but only its products, it's silly to focus much attention on the business name (which you may never use as a trademark). For instance, while millions of people know the product The Clapper and its commercial jingle ("Clap on! Clap off! The Clapper!"), few know or care who its makers are.

- Before you finally commit to a name, get some feedback from potential customers, suppliers, and others in your support network. They may come up with a downside to a potential name or suggest an improvement you haven't considered. Doing this type of homework is especially important if you will market your goods or services to customers who are members of several different ethnic groups. You obviously don't want to choose a name or symbol and learn later that it offends or turns off a key group of customers. For example, one organization we know couldn't figure out why it got such a cold shoulder from Mexican-Americans. The answer turned out to be that the shape, size, and typeface used on its signs was similar to a "No Trespassers—Keep Out" sign widely used in Mexico. And virtually everyone with email has by now seen a widely circulated humor piece on a number of advertising translation blunders—such as Kentucky Fried Chicken's "fingerlickin' good" slogan, translated in China as "eat your fingers off."

- Niche businesses are often identified by their trade names, even when the focus is on the products. This means that it is wise to pay particular attention to picking a memorable name if you will try to capture a particular, small field. The publisher of this book, Nolo, is a good example. Even though book buyers in other fields usually identify books they want by title or author, Nolo customers have come to recognize its name, often going into a bookstore and asking where the Nolo books are. In other words, Nolo has come to mean "self-help law" to many customers familiar with it, in contrast to the name HarperCollins—a large publisher of books on many topics—that might not evoke anything particular in most book customers' minds.

- In certain service businesses in which an owner's personal attention and savvy is important (for example, architecture or accounting), it is common to use the owner's name, as in Charles Schwab. In other service and retail businesses, it is more common to use creative names—Kinko's and Fuddrucker's come to mind—not only for the business itself, but sometimes for its products, too.

  EXAMPLE: Jerri and Orlando operate a car wash named Storm, which develops a good deal of name recognition in the city. Besides relying on the reputation of their trade name, they come up with clever names for various service packages (such as Sunday Shower, Typhoon Tuesday, and the Everyday Squall Special) in hopes that those names will catch on as well.

- Be sure your trade or business name will still be appropriate if and when your business grows. For example, if you open Miami Surf Shop, will it be a problem (or an advantage) if you want to open a second store in Orlando? Especially if you plan to sell products on the Internet, you should think twice about giving your business a geographical identifier. Similarly, if you start a business selling and installing canvas awnings using the name Sturdy Canvas Awnings, your name might be a burden if you decide to also start making other products such as canvas signs. On the other hand, the name Sturdy Canvas would let you move into all sorts of canvas products, such as duffel bags, canvas signs, and drop cloths.

Think nationally even if you act locally. As discussed throughout this chapter, even though you may plan to open just one local office or store, it's a good idea to be sure your name is safe from trademark conflicts on a statewide or even national basis (and, if appropriate, from domain name conflicts). Then, if your business takes off, you won't bump into someone else who already uses the name online or in another area.

☑ Chapter 3 Checklist

- ☐ Become familiar with the basics of trademark law, including what types of trademarks qualify for maximum legal protection.

- ☐ Draft lists of business, product, and domain names that could work.

- ☐ If you plan to do business online, check to see whether your proposed business names are available as domain names. (Ideally, your domain name(s) will be the same as your business or product names.)

- ☐ If the online aspect of your business will be important to you, narrow your list to those names that are available as domain names.

- ☐ Do a trademark search of the names on your list.

- ☐ If any names are already being used as trademarks, eliminate the ones that either are already famous trademarks or would lead to customer confusion if you also used them.

- ☐ Choose among the names that are still on your list.

- ☐ Register your business and product names as domain names whenever possible.

- ☐ Register your business and product names as trademarks.

■

Choosing a Business Location

For many types of businesses, location can mean the difference between feast or famine. Other enterprises will do more or less the same whether they're located in downtown Manhattan or in a deep crevasse on Mars. Not only does the importance of location vary greatly from business to business, but what makes a location desirable for one business might not work for another. Since there's no universal definition of what makes a location good for business, it's important for every business owner to figure out how location will (or will not) contribute to the success of the business—and to choose a spot accordingly.

That said, there are some basic issues to consider when choosing a business location. For starters, make sure the location makes economic sense. You won't want to spend a fortune for a spot on an exclusive commercial strip unless it's really going to pay off. It's obviously important that the rent for your business space fits into your overall budget. But don't be too frugal in this area—even the best-run business will fail if its customers can't find it or don't want to go to an unsafe neighborhood. And, of course, the location that you choose needs to be legally acceptable for whatever you plan to do there. Especially if you are planning to work from home or in a nonbusiness area, you'll need to check zoning laws to see if they prohibit your type of business. This chapter will help you figure out how to find a suitable place that meets all the needs of your business and complies with your local laws.

➡ Planning to work from home? If you've already decided that you want to run your business from home, you can skip most—but not all—of this chapter. Section B, below, provides a good introduction to zoning rules in general. And Section B3, below, outlines zoning issues specifically for home businesses. Read this material, then turn to Chapter 10, "Laws, Taxes, and Other Issues for Home Businesses" for a more in-depth treatment. That chapter is devoted to the special issues facing home business owners—including zoning, the home business tax deduction, and risk management.

A. Picking the Right Spot

Your first task is to figure out how important location is to your business. For some businesses, the classic "location, location, location" advice definitely applies. But for others, location may be a lot less important than getting affordable rental space. And for plenty of businesses, location is practically irrelevant: wholesalers, service businesses that do all their work at the customer's location (like roofers or plumbers), mail-order companies, and Internet-based businesses, for example. Especially if you can pass on your rent savings to your customers, picking a spot in an out-of-the-way area might be to your advantage. In other words, if location isn't that crucial to your business, don't blow all your start-up money on an expensive space in a thriving location.

If, on the other hand, you determine that location will be important to your business success, you'll need to figure out the best place to locate so that lots of customers can find you. It's one thing to know that you need a good location, but it can be harder to figure out what makes a location good. Ask yourself these questions:

- Will customers come on foot?
- Will customers drive, and, if so, where will they park?
- Will more customers come if you locate near other similar businesses?
- Will the reputation of the neighborhood or even of a particular building help draw customers?

As you ponder these and similar questions, here are a few things you'll want to consider.

1. Planting Yourself in Rich Soil

The key to picking a profitable location is to figure out what factors will increase customer volume for your unique business, and then to concentrate on finding a location that achieves as many of them as possible. For example, if you're opening a coffee shop, you may assume your customer volume will be highest if there's lots of pedestrian traffic nearby during the hours you plan to be open. Furthermore, if you envision your café to be a mellow place to sit and read, you'd probably prefer a university area or shopping district full of people with time to kill, rather than an area buzzing with busy business-people. If, on the other hand, you plan to open a small coffee shop with no tables—just fast, high-volume service—a busy downtown office district might be the right spot.

Audrey Wackerley, owner of RetroFit, a vintage clothing store in San Francisco, California:

> *When we first opened we got a space in the perfect neighborhood, with lots of thrift stores, coffee shops, and other walk-in type businesses on a strip with lots of foot traffic (plus, it was only a few blocks from my apartment). But we were on a cross street a few doors around the corner from Valencia Street, the main strip. We did okay, but nothing like the shops on Valencia itself. Finally we got a good deal on a storefront on Valencia Street, and we moved. Our business practically tripled! We do pay a bit more for the better space, but our boost in sales more than makes up for it.*

Keep in mind that different types of businesses attract customers in different ways. One key distinction is foot traffic versus automobile traffic. An auto repair shop, for example, will obviously draw customers in radically different ways from the coffee shop. For the auto shop, the choicest locale is a well-traveled street, where it will be seen by many drivers who will easily be able to pull into the lot. For an urban coffee shop, on the other hand, a popular location might be in an area where there are lots of people passing on foot. But of course no rule is absolute, and even some coffee shops thrive because commuters stop for "to go" coffee and baked goods every morning.

Also think about whether it would benefit your business to be around similar businesses that are already drawing the type of customers that you want. A women's clothing store, for example, would no doubt profit from being near other clothing shops, since many women shopping for clothes tend to spend at least a few hours in a particular area. The point is, the perfect location for any business is a very individual matter. Spend some time figuring out the habits of the customers you want to attract, then choose a location that fits.

2. Keeping Rent Within Your Budget

One obvious and important factor in finding a business space is how much you can afford. Chances are that you have found or will find a fabulous spot that you can only dream about because the monthly rent is so high. While it's okay to dream, don't be foolish enough to overpay for a space that you can't afford. As part of your business planning (discussed in detail in Chapter 5), determine how much rent you can afford each month, and stick to it.

One good way to find out how much rent is reasonable for an area is to call a commercial broker or agent in your area and have a chat about how much space generally goes for in the areas you're considering. Brokers and agents will generally give you an average figure for what commercial space costs per square foot per year in a given area; once you have this figure, you can compare it to the costs of any potential spaces you're considering. But keep in mind that agents and brokers are self-interested professionals who may benefit from higher rents. In other words, don't necessarily accept the figures they give you at face value.

Square footage rates are generally given in cost per year, so once you multiply the rate by the square footage of a space, you'll need to divide it by 12 to determine the monthly rent.

EXAMPLE: Jennifer and Oliver are planning to open a theater in a certain neighborhood of their city. They call a few real estate brokers out of the phone book whose ads indicate they handle commercial space leasing. All the brokers say that commercial space in the area they like generally goes for $10 per square foot. (Jennifer and Oliver know that this is an annual figure, which works out to about 83 cents per square foot per month.) A few weeks later, Jennifer and Oliver notice a building for rent, and call the agent for more information. The agent tells them that the monthly rent is $1,800, and that the space is 2,400 square feet. Jennifer and Oliver do the math and see that the rent is slightly less than the going rate for the area:

$1,800 per month
x 12 months per year = $21,600 per year

$21,600 per year
÷ 2,400 square feet = $9 per year per square foot

They figure that if the space rented out for the going rate, $10 per square foot, they'd have to pay $2,000 per month for the space.

$10 per square foot per year
x 2,400 square feet = $24,000 per year

$24,000 per year
÷ 12 months per year = $2,000 per month

They're not quite ready to enter a lease, but the fact that this space is somewhat of a bargain puts it near the top of their list.

While being realistic about your rent is important, don't sabotage your business by picking a cheap, but bad, location. This may seem obvious, but sometimes new business owners become blind to common wisdom when presented with an opportunity to rent a super-cheap space. Even if they've already determined that location will play a key role in their success, they either believe that the savings in rent will make up for slow sales or convince themselves that they'll be the pioneers in a new area that is sure to swell into a hot business district by the middle of next week. While this does occasionally happen (bless those brave pioneers), it's generally a poor idea to move into a dead section of town, since it almost certainly won't bloom fast enough to support your business in its financially vulnerable start-up days.

Unless you have a sound reason to believe that you'll get enough customers in your oddball location, don't let the lure of low rent tempt you into a bad business decision. At least in popular urban areas, rent can be the highest overhead expense for many new businesses.

3. Getting the Right Physical Features

When picking your space, your biggest consideration might not be where it is but what it is. Ask yourself whether the building facilities are appropriate or adaptable for your business. For example, if you're planning to open a coffeehouse, you might fall in love with a beautiful brick warehouse space in a funky shopping district. But if the place doesn't have at least minimal kitchen facilities, you should probably forget it. Unless you can convince your landlord to put in the needed equipment—plumbing, electrical work, and the rest (discussed below)—it's highly unlikely that laying out the cash to do it yourself will be worth it.

Sure, some improvements might be relatively cheap, such as putting up a wall or two or adding new light fixtures. But if the building lacks something major that is essential to your business operation, take it as a sign that the place isn't right for you—even if it has loads of other great qualities. You'll have to decide for yourself which features your business absolutely can't live with or without.

EXAMPLE: Charlotte and Sandra plan to open an alternative health store that will offer products such as medicinal herbs, aromatherapy products, and yoga supplies. They also plan to offer services such as aromatherapy sessions and consultations with nutritionists and herbalists. Since they have high hopes for the service side of their business, Charlotte and Sandra know that their physical space needs to be comfortable and appealing to customers. After looking at a number of storefront spaces in their chosen neighborhood, they find one that seems just perfect—until they notice the lack of windows. Except for the glass front door, the place has almost no natural light. Even though not having windows doesn't absolutely prevent them from doing business, Charlotte and Sandra decide that, given their expected customer base and their own feelings, they need a brighter space.

Another consideration that's important for many businesses these days is having modern phone lines and broadband Internet access—through cable, DSL, or a T1 line. Anyone who spends much time on the Web knows that old, slow lines can seriously impact your productivity (and drive you crazy to boot). Outdated phone lines can also slow down your faxes and may even result in dropped telephone connections—not exactly a good thing for business. When you're considering a specific space, ask the agent or the landlord for any information on the phone and data lines into the space, such as whether it's connected to a fiber optic network or has broadband Internet access. Also, find out if the landlord has sold the rights to the risers (wire conduits) in the building to a single telecommunications provider such as MCI or AT&T; if so, you could be stuck with that provider.

In addition to dealing with concerns about high-tech communications wiring, don't overlook plain old electrical power as an important consideration in choosing a business space. Make sure that any space you're looking at has enough power for your needs, both in terms of the number of outlets and the capacity of the circuits. If you'll mostly be running computer equipment, a copier, a coffee machine, and the like, chances are that any reasonably equipped commercial space will have enough power for you. But if you'll be running machinery or other electricity-hungry equipment, make sure to find out from the landlord how much juice the circuits can handle and whether a generator is available during power outages. Also, if you'll keep sensitive computer equipment at your office, ask the landlord how many hours of air conditioning are included in the terms of your lease, and negotiate longer hours if necessary.

Another common need for many businesses is adequate parking. If a significant percentage of your customers will come by car and there isn't enough parking at your chosen spot, it's probably best to look elsewhere. In fact, the city might not allow you to operate there if parking isn't adequate. (See Section B, below, on zoning laws regarding parking.)

Check local planning and health department requirements. For instance, if you're starting a small food manufacturing business to produce energy bars, you may need to rent a space with a certain number of vents, a fire-resistant roof, and walls of proper material and adequate thickness. You may also need a safe place to park refrigerated delivery trucks. And your business may be subject to special waste disposal requirements, so you may need extra space for waste storage or equipment. Contact your city or county departments of planning, health, or fire or another appropriate agency to find out. You should also check out state and federal laws that apply to your business. (See Chapter 7 for a discussion of licenses and permits.)

B. Complying With Zoning Laws

A certain spot may be good for your business, but if it's not properly zoned for what you plan to do, forget it. Local zoning laws (often called "ordinances" or "land use regulations") prohibit certain activities from being conducted in particular areas. To use an obvious example, a nightclub wouldn't be allowed to operate in a district zoned for residential use. Sure, only a fool would try to open a disco on a quiet residential street—but there are less obvious zoning restrictions that you must observe.

Zoning ordinances typically allow certain categories of businesses to occupy different districts of a city or county. For example, mixed commercial and residential uses might be allowed in one district while another district allows heavy industry and warehouses. So if you open your small jewelry-making business in a space zoned for commercial use, you could be in for a real headache if zoning officials decide you're a light-industrial business that's not allowed to operate in a commercial district. Similarly, you may not be allowed to run a commercial business—particularly one that's open to the public—in an industrial zone.

In addition to regulating the types of businesses allowed in certain areas, zoning laws also regulate specific activities. Depending on your area, you might be subject to laws regulating parking, signs, water and air quality, waste management, noise, and the visual appearance of the business (especially in historic districts). In addition to these regulations, some cities restrict the number of a particular type of business in a certain area, such as allowing only three bookstores or one pet shop in a certain neighborhood. Finally, some zoning laws specifically regulate home businesses.

If you have a home business. Zoning rules for home businesses are explained in detail in Chapter 10, "Laws, Taxes, and Other Issues for Home Businesses." Refer to that chapter for a full discussion of several special issues facing home business owners—including zoning, the home business tax deduction, and risk management.

Expect Zoning Laws on Parking Spaces and Business Signs

Local zoning laws commonly require a business to provide parking, and they also may regulate the size and type of business signs. Be prepared for your city or county to look into both these issues. If there's already a parking problem in your proposed area, you may have to come up with a plan for how to deal with the increased traffic your business will attract.

Also, be ready for zoning officials to get really nitpicky about your business sign. Many local laws limit the size of business signs (no signs over five feet by three feet, for instance), their appearance (such as whether they're illuminated, flashing, colorful, or made of neon), and their placement (flat against the building, hanging over the sidewalk, or mounted on a pole). There are even some regulations attempting to limit the use of foreign language on signs. Be sure to find out what your local regulations are before spending money on having signs made.

Know your neighbors. More often than not, zoning laws are enforced for the sake of the other people and companies in the neighborhood (this is particularly true of home-based businesses). While some areas are strict about their zoning laws, most of the time you won't have a zoning official knocking unannounced on your door unless neighbors have complained or you're in flagrant violation of the laws. Since enforcement is often triggered by complaints, it's a good idea to get to know your neighbors and develop good relationships with them. And, if you plan to run your business from home, be sure to read Chapter 10, which covers special zoning issues for home businesses.

Never sign a lease for a business space without first knowing that you'll legally be able to do business there. However, it's okay to sign a contingent lease, with a clause stating that the lease won't be binding if you don't get zoning approval. Being forced to move your business is a headache enough, but not nearly as catastrophic as having to pay rent on a lease for a space that you can't use.

When determining whether you'll be able to do business at a potential location, never assume that you'll be allowed to do a certain activity simply because the previous tenants of the space did it. For all kinds of reasons, some businesses get away with zoning violations, even for long periods of time. But new occupants are sometimes scrutinized more carefully than already-existing businesses. It may not be fair, but a new business may be told it can't do what an old one had long been doing.

It's also possible that the previous tenants had an official okay to operate outside the zoning restrictions. For example, the previous occupants might have had a zoning variance (an exception to zoning laws) for their particular business—one that won't necessarily be extended to you. And lots of times when zoning laws change, businesses that are already in place are allowed to keep doing what they were doing, even if the activity violates the new zoning law (a system referred to as "grandfathering"). When a tenant with a grandfathered exception leaves and new occupants come in, however, the new business usually has to abide by the new, more restrictive zoning law.

1. Finding Out What Laws Apply

How do you find out whether a given location is properly zoned for your business and whether you need to get any approvals? The answer varies from area to area. In some cities and counties, zoning approval is part of the tax registration process (discussed in Chapter 7). In San Diego, for instance, when you apply for your business tax certificate, you must also pay a Zoning Use Clearance fee to have your business approved for the location listed on your application. The city of Albuquerque also requires businesses to get zoning approval before allowing them to obtain a tax registration certificate, though there is no fee for the zoning clearance. Other cities, such as Boston, don't require proof of zoning approval before issuing a tax registration certificate—but that doesn't mean you should take the zoning laws any less seriously. Whether or not you're required to deal with your local zoning department before starting your business, you'll still be subject to its monitoring and enforcement.

If your city doesn't include zoning approval as part of its start-up requirements for new businesses, you'll need to do some detective work. Generally this involves talking with your local zoning officials. Most zoning agencies are part of city or county planning departments. Look under "Planning" or "Zoning" in the government section of your phone book. If your business will be located in a city, you probably only need to worry about city zoning ordinances. Businesses in rural areas should contact the county zoning or planning offices.

Getting zoning approval typically begins with filling out a form issued by the city planning department in which you provide information about your proposed location and what you plan to do there. In some cities, you may be required to submit detailed building plans to show exactly how you intend to use the space in question. Your application may be evaluated simply on the information you provide in the form, or the zoning department may send out an inspector to more closely examine the potential business space. Once the zoning department has all the information it requires to make a decision, it will either approve your application without limitations, approve it with certain conditions, or deny it altogether.

How Vigilant Are Zoning Officials?

There's a world of difference in how strict zoning officials are from area to area. Many zoning departments aren't terribly rigid about enforcement, mostly responding to complaints from neighbors or other citizens about businesses that create a nuisance or other trouble. In a few areas, however, zoning agents relish sniffing out minor infractions and enforcing their zoning ordinances to the letter.

If you're considering going ahead with your business despite what you consider to be a minor zoning problem, you should do your best to find out how strict the zoning police are in your area. Start by asking other local business-people about their experiences. If they tell you that there's little enforcement other than re-sponding to complaints, you can breathe a little easier about what might be a minor infraction, such as including tennis-racket stringing (which officials might consider a light-industrial activity) at your sports shop in an area zoned only for commercial use. Even so, it never pays to engage in a prohibited activity that is fundamental to your business. While tennis rackets could be strung elsewhere, a health club wouldn't want to have to locate its juice bar two blocks away.

But no matter how mellow your zoning department, at the very least you need to know what the rules are for your proposed location. Ignoring the rules while counting on lax enforce-ment is just plain dumb.

---

2. Dealing With Zoning Snags

If your zoning board has a problem with any of the activities you plan to conduct at your chosen location, you have a few options, usually ranging from making appropriate changes to your business to giving up on that location and finding a new one. Obviously, some zoning conflicts are simply not fixable—for example, you'll never be allowed to open a nightclub on a quiet cul-de-sac. But a creative (and, when necessary, assertive) business owner can often persuade zoning officials or the zoning appeals board to work out an acceptable accommodation that will allow the business to use the desired location.

For borderline situations, one approach is sim-ply to advocate an interpretation of the zoning law that's favorable to you *before* you get an official "No." Communicate with zoning officials, and try to persuade them to give you their seal of ap-proval.

If the zoning officials have already denied your application, it's often possible to appeal their decision, usually to a higher authority such as a board of appeals within the zoning agency or the city council. If you're successful, the zoning board may grant you a "variance," which is basically a one-time exception to the local zoning laws. Or the board may give you a "conditional use permit," which essentially gives you approval to operate your business as long as certain conditions are met, such as restricting the maximum occupancy to a certain number or providing additional parking spaces.

When lobbying for an exemption from a zoning requirement, be aware that you're asking for spe-cial treatment, so make your case as persuasive as possible. If your business will be valuable to the community, present evidence of that fact. Proof can include demographic data about the area, testimony from community leaders, or statements from other local businesspeople. Your goal is to show that the value of allowing your business in the area is greater than the trivial zoning conflicts that may exist. If you can compromise in some other area, offer to do so.

EXAMPLE: Carolyn wants to open a small printing shop, Nelson's Press, on a commercial strip where storefront space is cheap and plentiful. Before signing a lease, she applies for zoning approval. The local zoning board rejects her application because Carolyn's proposed location is zoned commercial, while her print shop would technically be a light-industrial business. Carolyn decides to try to get an exception, because her printing operation will be small (only one small offset printing press) and would be an asset to the neighborhood, which has been struggling economically.

She submits detailed plans of her business to the zoning board, showing the business's small scope and including specific protocols for dealing with toxics such as ink. She also submits letters from other business owners in the neighborhood documenting how commerce in the area has languished for years and arguing that new businesses would help revitalize the strip. Many of the business owners also note that a local printer would be convenient for the existing area businesses, which currently have to go across town for their print jobs. A few weeks later, Carolyn gets a conditional use permit allowing her to proceed with her printing business, as long as she doesn't expand her business with additional presses and follows a number of standard rules governing the chemicals she'll use in printing.

3. Zoning Rules for Home Businesses

Similar to business owners who operate from commercial office spaces, those who run home businesses need to make sure they don't violate their local zoning rules. As home businesses have exploded in popularity, more local governments have adopted specific provisions in zoning laws controlling them. Mercifully, most of the rules are straightforward and fair—with some exceptions. If you're unlucky and find that you're subject to prohibitive municipal ordinances or private land use restrictions, take a hard look at whether you should set up shop in your home after all. But more often, you'll find that you'll need to jump through a simple hoop or two and pay a modest fee to run your business from home.

Dwellings in residential or mixed-use zones are often allowed to run businesses that have little likelihood of causing noise or pollution, creating traffic, or otherwise disturbing the neighbors. A few examples include freelance writers, artists, attorneys, accountants, architects, insurance brokers, and piano teachers.

To find out local rules, contact your city's planning or zoning department and ask for information on its rules for home businesses. Often, home business are allowed with some restrictions—such as limiting employees to residents, curbing the number of customers allowed, and prohibiting business signs posted outside. Also ask the local zoning authority whether any special rules exist for the specific type of business or activities you plan to conduct.

As to whether or not you need a permit to run a home business, local rules vary. If a permit is required, getting one is usually a simple matter of filling out a form provided by the planning department and paying a fee. You may also need to deal with other departments in addition to the zoning office. For example, depending on your business activities, you may need to get approvals from your county health or fire department.

For more on home office zoning. For more detail on permits for specific business activities, see Chapter 7 on start-up requirements. And see Chapter 10 for a full discussion of special issues facing home business owners—including zoning, the home business tax deduction, and risk management.

C. Commercial Leases

Chances are that you'll rent rather than buy a space for your business. After all, most small start-ups don't have the funds to purchase real estate, and it's usually not a good idea to saddle your business with high interest payments, anyway. But just because you've rented plenty of apartments or flats over the years, don't assume that you know the score when it comes to leasing business space.

Practically and legally speaking, there are significant differences between commercial leases and residential leases. Commercial leases are not subject to most consumer protection laws that govern residential leases—for example, there are no caps on deposits or rules protecting a tenant's privacy. Also, commercial leases are generally subject to much more negotiation between the business and the landlord, since businesses often need special features in their spaces, and landlords are often eager for tenants and willing to extend special offers. While a residential tenant will usually just take an apartment or flat more or less as-is, a business owner will often need to modify the existing space—for example, by adding cubicles, raising a loading dock, or rewiring for telephones, Internet access, and computers.

Since company owners must negotiate modifications suitable for their own operations, commercial leases are relatively flexible creatures. Of course, your bargaining power will vary a great deal from situation to situation. For example, getting a landlord to accept your demands would probably be a lot easier for a long-term lease in a largely vacant office building than for a six-month lease in a hot commercial area. Likewise, local independent landlords are often more willing to make concessions than huge property management companies or real estate investment trusts.

When negotiating a commercial lease, keep in mind that the success or failure of your business may ride on certain terms of the lease. The amount of the rent is an obvious concern, as is the length of the lease. (You probably don't want to tie yourself to a five- or ten-year lease if you can help it, in case your business grows faster than you expect or the location doesn't work out for you.) But other, less conspicuous items spelled out in the lease may be just as crucial to your business's success. For instance, if you expect your shoe repair business to depend largely on walk-in customers, be sure that your lease establishes your right to put up a sign that's visible from the street. Or, if you are counting on being the only sandwich shop inside a new commercial complex, make sure your lease prevents the landlord from leasing space to a competitor. If you are starting a new service company that you expect to grow quickly, make sure there's room for expansion.

The following checklist includes many items that are often addressed in commercial leases. Pay attention to terms regarding:

- rent, including allowable increases and method of computation
- whether the rent includes insurance, property taxes, and maintenance costs (called a gross lease), or whether you will be charged for these items separately (called a net lease)
- whether the rent includes heat, air conditioning, phone, garbage collection, water, and other utilities
- the security deposit and conditions for its return
- who is responsible for code compliance, security, and fire safety
- the length of the lease (also called the lease term) and when it begins
- whether there's an option to renew the lease or expand the space
- how the lease may be terminated, including notice requirements, and whether there are penalties for early termination
- exactly what space is being rented, including common areas such as hallways, rest rooms, and elevators, and how the space is measured (some measurement practices include the thickness of the walls)
- specifications for signs, including where they may be placed

- whether there will be improvements, modifications (called buildouts when new space is being finished to your specifications), or fixtures added to the space; who will pay for them; and who will own them after the lease ends (generally, the landlord)
- who will maintain the premises and provide janitorial services
- whether the lease may be assigned or subleased to another party, and
- whether disputes must be mediated or arbitrated as an alternative to court.

Beware the Americans With Disabilities Act. The Americans With Disabilities Act (ADA) requires all businesses that are open to the public or that employ more than 15 people to have premises that are accessible to people with disabilities. Make sure that you and your landlord are in agreement about who will pay for any needed modifications, such as adding a ramp or widening doorways to accommodate wheelchairs.

For more on leasing office spaces. For detailed information on finding a space and negotiating a lease, see *Negotiate the Best Lease for Your Business,* by Janet Portman and Fred S. Steingold (Nolo).

☑ Chapter 4 Checklist

☐ Determine how much rent you can afford.

☐ Decide what neighborhood best suits your business.

☐ Find out what the average rents are in the neighborhoods you're considering for your business office.

☐ Identify the features and fixtures your business space will need.

☐ Make sure spaces that you're considering are or can be properly zoned for your business.

☐ Examine all commercial leases carefully—and negotiate the best deal you can.

☐ If working from home, make sure your business activities will not violate any zoning restrictions on home offices.

Drafting an Effective Business Plan

If you think only Type A personalities compose business plans, think again. Talk to a random sample of successful business owners—even the most laid-back—and you'll be amazed at how many took the time to put their business plans into writing. If you're truly determined to succeed, you'll follow their example. Why? Because without a plan, you're leaving far too many things to chance. Just as a blueprint is used to ensure that a building will be structurally sound, a business plan will help you make sure that your business will be able to stay afloat.

The purpose of a business plan is simple: to bring together in one document the key elements of your business. These include the products or services you'll sell, what they'll cost to produce, and how much sales revenue you expect during your first months and years of operation. Most important, your plan will help you see how all the disparate elements of your business relate to one another, which will allow you to make any necessary alterations in order to maximize your business's potential to turn a profit.

Business plans are often written by business owners who want to borrow money or attract investment. This is good as far as it goes: Lenders and investors do want to understand as much as possible about how a business will work before deciding whether to back it financially. Unless you're prepared to show them a well-thought-out plan for making your business profitable, you won't have much chance of convincing them to finance your project.

But creating a business plan is a good idea even if you don't need to raise start-up money. The process of creating one often brings up issues and potential problems that you hadn't thought of before. And the discipline involved in developing financial projections such as a break-even analysis and a profit and loss forecast will help you decide whether your business is really worth starting, or whether you need to rethink some of your key assumptions. As any experienced businessperson will tell you, the business you decide not to start (often because its business plan doesn't pencil out) can

play a greater role in your long-term success than the one on which you bet your economic future.

This chapter explains how to create a thorough business plan, and describes basic types of business financing and lending sources. The approach to business planning here is simple and straightforward: It outlines a number of descriptive sections and a number of financial reports. When you have completed these sections, you will have the essential elements that will help guide you in running your business—and that will help attract funding if you need it.

For those who already have a plan. If you've already written a business plan, you may want to skip ahead to the financing discussion in Section I—although you might also want to review the sections on writing a business plan as a way of evaluating the work you've already done.

For more help on the business of business plans. Nolo offers a couple of resources for those in need of setting up or revising business plans. *How to Write a Business Plan,* by Mike McKeever, is a comprehensive guide explaining how to write a business plan—including how to evaluate the profitability of your business idea; estimate operating expenses; determine assets, liabilities, and net worth; and find potential sources of financing. And *Business Plan Pro 2006* is software that offers a fast, easy way to generate the plan you need to launch or expand your business.

A. Different Purposes Require Different Plans

All good business plans have two basic goals: to describe the fundamentals of the business idea, and to provide financial calculations to show that it will make good money. But, depending on how you intend to use it, a business plan can take somewhat different forms:

- If you will use your plan to borrow money or interest investors, write it with an eye toward selling your vision to skeptical people. Generally, you should include a persuasive introduction and a request for funds, in-depth market research information, an evaluation of your main competitors, your key marketing strategies, and a management plan. In addition, your plan should contain detailed financial information—including your best estimates of start-up costs, revenues, and expenses. Finally, since your plan will be submitted to people who don't know you well, the writing should be polished and the format clean and professional. (See Section I for a discussion of business financing basics.)

- If your plan will primarily be for your own use—that is, if you don't need to raise money—don't worry so much about making a sales pitch or slick presentation (although you'll probably want to do a quick market and competitive analysis). But don't skimp when it comes to doing your numbers. You'll need to include estimates of start-up costs, revenues, and expenses. The last thing you want is to experience the very real misery of realizing too late that your business never had a chance to make a solid profit.

Plan to get the help you need. Not all business-people are great writers. But excellent writing skills can be a big help in creating a compelling business plan. Consider paying a freelance writer with business savvy to help you polish your plan. Similarly, if you are challenged by numbers, find a bookkeeper or accountant to provide some help with the math.

B. Describing Your Business and Yourself

The first several sections of your plan should describe the beauty of your business idea. If you will show your plan to potential lenders, investors, or colleagues, you'll want to show them right up front that you've hit on a product or service that customers really want. In addition, you'll want to show that you are exactly the right person to make this fine idea a roaring success. Your goal is to have them say, "Wow! What a great business idea! And yes, I see exactly why Carlos Burns is the ideal person to make it a big success."

To accomplish these goals, you should include the following in your plan:

- a statement of the purpose of your business
- a detailed description of how the business will work
- an analysis of your market
- an analysis of your competitors
- a description of your marketing strategy, and
- a résumé setting out your business accomplishments.

Again, depending on how you intend to use your business plan, you may be able to skip some of these elements. For example, if you don't need to raise start-up money and are writing a plan mostly for your own use, you may decide to skip the résumé of your own business accomplishments. But think twice before you leave out too much. Any new business will need to be introduced to loads of people—suppliers, contractors, employees, and key customers, to name a few—and showing them part or all of your business plan can be a great way to do it.

1. State Your Business's Purpose

What will your product or service be? And why does the great big world—or your small town or narrow niche market—need the product or service you want to offer? The first paragraph of your plan should address this question as directly and compellingly as possible. For example, if you're planning to open a pet-grooming salon, you might start with the proposition that in today's increasingly busy world, pet owners need and want to keep their pets clean and groomed, but often don't have time to do it themselves. Similarly, if you want to start a sea kayaking guide service, you might start with the proposition that more and more people are participating in this exciting sport but need equipment, planning, training, and logistical help to do it in other parts of the world.

A statement of business purpose doesn't need to be complicated or lengthy. In fact, some of the best simply state the obvious. If the need for your business will be clear to lenders or investors (for example, a sandwich shop in a fast-growing office area), one paragraph may be all you need. But if the value of your business idea isn't so readily apparent (for example, an innovative software company), you will want to say more. Show how your business will solve a real problem or fill an actual need. And explain why customers will pay you to accomplish the task.

2. Describe Your Business

Once you've stated the need that your business will fill, describe exactly how you'll go about filling it. In this section, don't write a bunch of fluffy text about the brilliance of your entrepreneurial idea. Instead, outline in detail exactly how your business will operate. While the degree of detail may vary depending on what kind of business you're starting and who will be reading your business plan, your description should include specifics such as:

- how you will provide the product or service
- where you will buy key supplies
- how customers will pay you
- how many employees you will have, and what they will do
- your hours of operation, and
- your business location (if possible, include details about how your customers will find you).

Keep in mind that even the smallest, simplest business involves a swarm of pesky details. While you're writing your business description, don't assume there's anything obvious about your business, even if it's a tiny one-person operation. For example, if you plan to start a pet-grooming business, how many different types of services will you offer: Shampooing? Flea bathing? Nail cutting? Hair trimming? Teeth cleaning? Will you charge separately for each individual service, sell them in packages, or both? How will you attract customers and regularly stay in touch with the best ones? How will you accommodate animals with special needs such as allergies or behavioral problems such as aggressiveness? How will people drop off and pick up their pets? Will your business need insurance in case an animal is injured or dies while in your care?

A little repetition is okay. The description of how your business will operate is likely to be the longest section of your plan and will probably discuss topics that are also covered elsewhere. No problem. For example, you should discuss the key issue of how you will establish and keep a competitive edge in your big-picture business description as well as in the marketing strategy section. (See Section 5, below.)

Use the process of writing your business description as an opportunity to change or refine your business idea. When you write and rewrite this section, you'll probably come up with ideas and questions you haven't yet thought through. If so, great—this gives you an opportunity to fill in the gaps before you actually open for business. And even if you discover a flaw so big that you decide not to start the business after all, your business plan has done its job. While undoubtedly disappointing, it's far better for your business to fail on paper than in real life.

3. Define Your Market

Who will buy your product or service? Even the most innovative business will fail if it doesn't quickly find enough customers to make a profit. In this section, your task is to demonstrate to a potential investor or lender (or convince yourself) that there are indeed customers out there, ready and willing to buy your product or service. Use whatever data you can get your hands on to demonstrate this. And don't neglect your imagination—unconventional arguments are fine, as long as they are convincing. Here is a brief list of points you may wish to make.

- Similar businesses have been successful. For example, if several fitness clubs with Internet access are all the rage in L.A., you might explain why this is a good indication that your similar business would succeed in Chicago, where the market is currently dominated by less-cutting-edge gyms.
- Marketing surveys or demographic reports point to a growing need for your product or service. For instance, to buttress your contention that there will be a need for your new line of paralegal training materials, point to U.S. government reports listing paralegals as one of the fastest-growing occupations.
- Media reports confirm the popularity of and demand for your business. For example, include newspaper clips or transcripts of television news reports on the surge of demand for antibacterial air fresheners as evidence that your germ-killing Sani-Scent™ will sell.
- Your conversations with potential customers show a need for your business. It's often a good idea to carry out an informal survey of your most likely customers and include the results. For example, if you will run a business repairing and reconditioning acoustic guitars and similar stringed instruments, you might include results of a survey of guitarists and other musicians on what kind of repair services they need, as well as quotes from them saying that they'd use your services.

In addition to establishing that there is a solid market for your business, do your best to define and describe exactly who makes it up. If you're opening a bar with live entertainment, for instance, you might identify your market as primarily child-less, urban 21-to 35-year-olds who tend to have more disposable income and leisure time than others. Similarly, if you're planning an antique restoration service, you might identify your target market as professionals and others in the 40–70 age range with household incomes of $100,000 or more. The better you can show that you know exactly who your market is, the more confident lenders and investors will be that you can actually find these people and sell to them.

Include a profile of your target customer. Explain why and how a fictional person would need and use your product or service. Do your best to flesh out a believable person. Creating a typical customer gives a face to an otherwise abstract market definition and gives your market analysis more impact.

4. Analyze Your Competition

Just because you have a great business idea doesn't mean you'll be successful. Other businesses may have already cornered the market or be poised to do so. For example, lots of small business owners who ran successful video-rental businesses were wiped out when chains such as Blockbuster rolled out thousands of megastores. It's often all too easy for a bigger, better-capitalized outfit to copy your best features and pull the rug out from under your business. Use this section to explain why your business really will have few direct competitors— or, if competitors will abound (as is far more likely), to show how your business will develop and keep an edge. Don't be shy about detailing competitors' strengths as well as weaknesses as part of showing why your business will better meet customers' needs.

In discussing the competition, it's important to put yourself in the shoes of a customer who is comparing your business to a competitor's. From the customer's perspective, what factors are most important in choosing which business to patronize? Some obvious considerations are quality of products or services, convenience (access), reliability, and price. Your competitors will probably excel in some of these areas and be weaker in others. The same will probably be true of your business. The trick is for you to find a spot, or niche, among the competition, and offer a combination of elements —such as price and convenience—that no one else offers.

Think twice before competing on price. No matter how efficient your business is and how little you charge, someone will always charge less. Given the purchasing power and other efficiencies of big business, few small operators can successfully compete on pricing alone. Far better to look for another edge—quality, uniqueness, or customer convenience, to mention a few.

EXAMPLE: John wants to open a business to sell and service classic cars. In developing his business idea, he discovers that there are about a dozen existing companies within a 20-mile radius of his proposed location that already provide some or all of the services he envisions. Before finally committing to opening the business, he needs to identify and create a convincing competitive edge. One day, talking to a friend, he realizes that his edge could be a better system for finding parts. If he could locate new and used classic car parts nationwide, rather than just in his region, he would have a huge advantage over other shops. John begins by developing a database of websites that specialize in classic and reproduction car parts, organized by make and model. By using these online dealers—plus other dealers nationwide who aren't online, but whom John will get to know as he attends regional trade shows and does more national business—John

will be able to get parts faster than any of his competitors. Putting some extra energy into the parts aspect of his business gives John a key marketing hook to convince his knowledgeable (and often finicky) customers that his business really is a step ahead.

Businesses With Specialized Knowledge Are Hard to Copy

The business owner who knows the most about how to beat out competitors usually wins. But what is business knowledge, and how can you exploit it? In the broad sense, it's anything a business knows how to do that can give it a meaningful edge over competitors. Common examples include:

- the ability to buy products for resale cheaper than competitors
- a great location
- a unique, hard-to-duplicate product
- excellent customer service, and
- superior customer accessibility—for example, closer location, longer hours, or better parking.

Consider the example of Laura and Brad's import business. They were importing clothing from Guatemala, but, with competition from hundreds of other small importers, it was hard to make a dime. Leaving Brad to manage the business for a few weeks, Laura spent some time working with a dozen weavers in a small Guatemalan town. They focused on creating specially woven and dyed fabric suitable for luxury window coverings. Realizing that the high end of the import business was an underexploited niche, Laura quickly created a product with a hard-to-copy look and a solid profit margin. In short, she transformed a not particularly savvy, barely profitable import business into a highly intelligent, highly profitable one.

5. Describe Your Marketing Strategy

By now you've shown that there are people out there who will buy your product or service from you instead of from your competitors. Great, but your job isn't done. Investors and others interested in supporting your business will want to know how you'll reach your customers in a cost-effective way. The answer to this question is, in a nutshell: marketing strategy.

Any marketing strategy worthy of the name should be based on the particular characteristics of the market you're trying to reach, with the goal of reaching as many customers as possible for the least expense. For instance, if you're trying to reach a very tiny group of people, such as left-handed ophthalmologists, or even a slightly larger audience, such as digital video editors, it makes no sense to spend the big bucks required for television advertising. On the other hand, if your market consists of all children between the ages of six and ten, TV advertising at the right times and on the right channels might be an efficient way to reach them.

In describing your plan for reaching your customers, explain what methods you will use, such as radio or newspaper advertising, Web marketing, or directory listings such as trade directories or the Yellow Pages. If you plan to use nontraditional guerrilla marketing tactics such as putting up posters all around town or staging publicity stunts, explain exactly what you plan to do. And no matter what kind of marketing strategy you outline, be sure to explain why you think it will work.

Small businesses that don't have much of a marketing budget shouldn't be shy about their smaller-scale plans. Even if you don't plan to spend much (if any) money on marketing or advertising, you should have a plan for how you'll reach your first customers. In your business plan, simply explain what this strategy is. The following example shows how a small business with a minimal advertising and marketing budget might explain their strategy.

EXAMPLE: Turtlevision's marketing strategy. We plan to keep our marketing costs very low, at least for the first year or two. Rather than spending money on traditional advertising, our strategy will be to list our services in local video-related directories and use various online communities to promote ourselves. In addition, our plan for the early days of Turtlevision is to offer our services at a discount to various nonprofit organizations to develop our portfolio and to generate good word of mouth about our work. For example, Turtlevision is currently providing discounted services to the nonprofit Film Foundation to stream a monthly short film and video series on the Web. Our hope is that recommendations from our satisfied customers will give Turtlevision a start in the right direction.

Spam is bad. No matter how delectable you find the potted meat product, do not fool yourself into believing that sending out masses of unsolicited emails (a practice known as "spamming") will be good for your business. Most Web-savvy entrepreneurs already know what nutritionists have told us for years: Spam is bad for you. At the very least, it's bad for any goodwill that may exist for your business. No one likes getting junk email, no matter what fabulous deal it may offer. Be a good Net citizen and use more savory marketing tactics than spam.

Marketing without advertising can be successful. Especially in niche or local markets, people often make purchasing decisions based on the recommendations of people they respect, not on ads. If you doubt this, think about how you chose your dentist or plumber or the company that recently fixed your roof. Chances are good that you got a recommendation from someone you trusted. To be the beneficiary of positive word of mouth, you need to run an excellent business. Assuming you do, there are loads of cost-effective ways to let potential customers know about your great service. For a book full of great ideas, read *Marketing Without Advertising,* by Michael Phillips and Salli Rasberry (Nolo). Its subtitle, "Inspire Customers to Rave About Your Business & Create Lasting Success," explains exactly why every small businessperson should read it.

6. Describe Your Business Accomplishments

Above and beyond demonstrating the beauty of your business, you'll want to show that you're the right person to run it. Do this by creating a résumé showing your business accomplishments. Here you have the chance to highlight all of your relevant experience and training, as well as any other personal information likely to inspire confidence in you as a business person.

Prospective lenders and investors will want to know a number of things about you.

- **Do you understand the business?** Emphasize that you understand the basic tasks of the business inside and out. Surprisingly, lots of people start small businesses in areas where they are amateurs. For example, a person who isn't mechanically inclined but who loves German cars may want to open a VW repair shop. Lack of hands-on experience will likely be a red flag to investors, who know a nonexpert boss can't roll up his or her sleeves and help out in emergencies. Do your best to show them otherwise.

- **Can you manage people?** All sorts of organizations, including small businesses, fail because their leaders—no matter how technically competent—can't work well with others. Bad people-management is one of the surest ways to create a poor workplace atmosphere, one with low morale, mediocre productivity, and high turnover. If you have successfully worked with, and preferably led, people, you should emphasize this experience.

- **Do you understand money?** A surprising number of people who open small businesses don't know how to manage—or make—money. Even though their business idea is a good, competitive one and their employees are energetic, they make such poor financial decisions that their businesses don't prosper. Knowing this, people who will consider funding your business will want to see if you or another key person in your business has money management skills. If you do—even if your experience was in a very different business—emphasize it.

C. Making Financial Projections

In addition to describing how your business will work, including how it will reach plenty of customers and fend off competitors, you'll also need to do some number-crunching to show that your business will in fact turn a profit. All the rosy descriptions in the world won't make your business a success if the numbers turn up red.

Projecting the finances of your business may seem intimidating or difficult, but in reality it's not terribly complex. Basically, it consists of making educated guesses about how much money you'll need to spend and how much you'll take in, then using these estimates to calculate whether your business will be sufficiently profitable.

Predicting and planning the finances of your business is important not only to attract investors, but also to demonstrate to you and your family that your business idea will fly. If your first projections show your business losing money, you'll have an opportunity while still in the planning stage to make sensible adjustments, such as raising your prices or cutting costs. If your projections show your customer base growing gradually, you can plan for how you will get through the initial lean months. If you neglect to make financial projections, you won't realize your plan is a money-loser until you actually start losing money. At that point, it may be too late to turn things around.

Nonetheless, many new entrepreneurs avoid crunching their numbers, often due to fear that their estimates will be wildly off-base and yield useless results. This is a poor reason to avoid forecasting your finances. If you do your best to make realistic predictions of expenses and revenues and accept that your guestimates will not be absolutely correct, you can learn a great deal about what the financial side of your business is likely to look like in its early months and even years of operation. Even a somewhat inaccurate picture of your business's likely finances will be much more helpful than no picture at all.

Elissa Breitbard, owner of Betty's Bath & Day Spa in Albuquerque, New Mexico:

As time-consuming as it is to write a business plan, it is a critical factor to success—a symbolic security blanket. Our pre-start-up business plan bridged the chasm between the dream phase and a reality-based vision. In particular, churning out our first break-even analysis and cash flow statements was momentous, for the statements revealed the feasibility of our spa business. Even though the numbers weren't totally accurate (we have a lot more massage clients and fewer hot tub clients than projected), the important thing was to play with different scenarios and numbers and see that the business was, in fact, viable. The business plan helped us secure funding (not only from the bank, but also from family and friends) and provided me with a base of confidence—a concrete way to address some of the fears and issues that arise with taking a risk.

There's always talk about how many businesses fail; less discussed is the fact that the owners who have taken time to methodically set their business intentions in writing have a high rate of "making it." Now, two years into my business, I am rewriting and updating my business plan for our Phase II Expansion Stage.

For a basic understanding of your business's projected financial situation, you'll need to make the following estimates and calculations, all of which are discussed in detail in the rest of this chapter:

- **A break-even analysis.** Here you use income and expense estimates for a year or more to see whether, in theory at least, your business will be able to turn a profit. If you have trouble projecting a solid profit, you might need to consider abandoning your idea altogether.

- **A profit/loss forecast.** Here you'll refine the sales and expense estimates that you used for your break-even analysis into a formal, month-by-month projection of your business's net profit for at least the first year of operations.

- **A start-up cost estimate.** As the name suggests, this is simply the total of all the expenses you'll incur before your business opens. These costs should be included in your business plan to give a true picture of how much money you'll need to get your business off the ground.

- **A cash flow projection.** Even if your profit/loss forecast tells you that your business will have higher revenues than expenses, that doesn't mean that you'll always have enough cash available on key dates, such as when rent is due or when you need to buy more inventory. A cash flow projection lays out how much cash you'll have—or how much you'll be short—month by month. This lets you know if you'll need to get a credit line or set up other arrangements to make sure funds are available.

Get to Know Your Numbers

The calculations involved in accounting aren't terribly complex. The main reason people get confused is not that they're bad at math—it's that they don't understand what the numbers mean. It's important that you take a little time early on to learn what your key financial numbers are, and how they relate to one another. To help you keep the numbers straight, keep in mind this formula:

	sales revenue
−	costs of sale (variable costs)
=	gross profit
−	overhead (fixed costs)
=	net profit
−	taxes
=	after-tax profit

You'll have a much easier time understanding all the various financial calculations involved in accounting—including break-even, profit/loss, and cash flow analysis—once you're familiar and comfortable with this basic formula.

To make these financial forecasts, you could use accounting software, a simple spreadsheet program such as Excel, or even a calculator and some blank ledger sheets. With accounting software, most of your calculations can be done automatically with the click of a button, which can be very helpful when you're in the planning stages and trying out lots of different numbers.

If you plan to use software for bookkeeping and accounting once your business is started, you might as well also use it to prepare your financial projections. Accounting software is relatively easy to figure out and will definitely save you lots of time in the long run. *Quickbooks, Quicken Home & Business, MYOB Accounting,* and *Peachtree Accounting* are very popular and priced within reach of just about any budget. Magazines such as *Home Office Computing, MacWorld,* and *PC World* are good sources of information on other programs.

Once you start shopping for accounting and bookkeeping software, you'll probably also find special business plan software. Many of these programs, however, provide you with only a word processing function and some empty spreadsheets to fill in. Most real accounting software includes the same kinds of spreadsheets, and usually a lot more. Chances are the word processing program you already have is a lot more powerful than whatever is offered with a business plan program.

The rest of this chapter will walk you through each of these financial forecasts. When you're done, you should be able to tell whether your business will actually make enough money to pay the bills and turn a profit. Assuming the answer is yes, you'll also see whether you need to obtain start-up money from investors or lenders and, if so, how much. Finally, once your business is up and running, you can refer back to your forecasts to see how your performance is measuring up.

D. Break-Even Analysis

Your break-even point is the point at which the income you'll bring in just covers your expenses. Expenses include the costs of providing your product or service (also known as variable costs, since they change depending on how many products or services you provide), plus your overhead, like rent, salaries, and utility bills (commonly called fixed costs).

Break-Even Analysis Worksheet. On the CD-ROM that comes with this book, you'll find an interactive worksheet to help you calculate your break-even point. The file name of the worksheet is breakeven_worksheet.xls. For the automatic calculations in the worksheet to be active, you'll need to open the worksheet in a spreadsheet program such as Microsoft Excel.

To use the worksheet on the CD-ROM, follow the steps outlined below. Each step is explained in greater detail in this chapter. Enter figures only into white cells; do not enter anything in blue cells.

Step 1: Enter your estimated total annual revenues. This figure will not be used in the worksheet calculations, but will help you in the next step, in which you will break down your estimated revenues into categories.

Step 2: This step will result in an average gross profit percentage for your business as a whole, based on calculations for up to three categories of products or services your business will provide. First, enter the name for the category, then enter an average sales price, variable cost, and estimated revenues for each category. The total of your estimated revenues for all categories should equal your estimated total annual revenues from Step 1. If they do not, the worksheet will still calculate an average gross profit percentage based on the total of your category revenue estimates. However, you may want to evaluate why your category revenue estimates do not match the estimate for your business as a whole. Once you have entered numbers for all categories you plan to use (you do not need to use all three categories), your average gross profit percentage for your business as a whole will be displayed at the bottom of the section.

Step 3: Enter the type and amount of all fixed costs you anticipate for your business. Enter monthly figures; the worksheet will automatically calculate an annual amount.

Result: The worksheet will show you your break-even point, which is the amount of revenue you'll need to bring in before your business starts making any profits.

Because break-even analysis offers a glimpse of your ultimate profitability, it's a great tool for weeding out losing business ideas. For example, if you see that you'll need to achieve a highly optimistic sales number just to cover your costs, you should rethink your entire business plan. Maybe you'll figure out a way to adjust parts of your business so that you can realize a profit from lower sales. If not, it might be best to ditch your less-than-brilliant business idea.

To find your break-even point, first make a best-guess estimate of your sales revenue for the products or services you plan to sell. Then predict how much profit you'll make on each sale (by subtracting the costs of the sale from the revenue it generates) and figure out a "gross profit percentage," which tells you how much of each sales dollar exceeds the cost of the product or service itself. Finally, estimate what your fixed costs such as rent and insurance will be. After a few calculations, you'll see whether the profit you'll make on each individual sale (also called gross profit) will cover your fixed costs.

Before examining the details of calculating your break-even point, let's look at a simple example to illustrate the overall process. All the calculations are explained in more detail below; for now, just focus on the process as a whole.

EXAMPLE: Michele is starting a business selling her own handmade jewelry. To calculate her break-even point, she makes her very best estimate of how much jewelry she thinks she could sell in a year. She figures she could sell an average of 20 pieces a month at $20 apiece, making her yearly income $4,800. Then she figures out how much she'd make on each sale, above the cost of materials. (For this super-simplified example, let's leave the cost of her time out of the equation.) Since the materials for each piece cost Michele $5, she'd be making $15 on each sale. In other words, her gross profit would be $15 per piece. Next she calculates her gross profit percentage, which is her gross profit ($15) divided by her selling price ($20). This puts her gross profit percentage at 75%, which means that .75 of each sales dollar exceeds of the cost of the piece of jewelry itself. Next Michele would figure out what her fixed costs would be—say, the cost of her tools and the monthly fee for her booth at a local arts and crafts mall. She figures that these fixed costs total $50 per month, or $600 per year.

To calculate her break-even point, Michele will *divide* her annual fixed costs ($600) by her gross profit percentage (.75) to arrive at a break-even point of $800. This means that just to cover the costs of the materials and her tools and booth, Michele must bring in $800 per year. Anything above that amount will be her pretax profit. Since she earlier estimated that she could sell $4,800 worth of jewelry per year, Michele figures that she'll easily reach her break-even point—and make a $4,000 profit, as well.

Before explaining exactly how to do the calculations, this chapter quickly discusses two items that you need to understand before actually crunching your numbers: making financial estimates and categorizing your expenses.

1. Making Estimates

When you estimate your income and expenses, your estimates should extend over enough time to catch up with seasonal fluctuations. Depending on your type of business, your revenue and expenses may vary wildly from month to month. For example, if you plan to manufacture custom snowboards, most of your sales will be in the late fall and early winter months, while the opposite would be true if you made surfboards. A good way to account for this is to make estimates for each month of the year, then add them up to get a yearly figure. In making these estimates, it is wise to cover at least a one-year period, which is enough time to account for normal ups and downs, but not so long as to be overly speculative.

2. Categorizing Your Expenses

Your business expenses break down into two categories: fixed expenses (fixed costs) and variable expenses (variable costs). This division is not only important for your break-even analysis, it's also a standard method of categorizing expenses for accounting and tax reporting. The difference is explained here.

- **Fixed costs.** Commonly referred to as "overhead," these include all regular expenses not directly tied to the product or service you provide. Rent, utility bills, phone bills, payments for outside help such as bookkeeping services, postage, and most salaries (except in service businesses) are common fixed costs.

- **Variable costs.** These costs—sometimes also called product costs, costs of goods, or costs of sale—are directly related to the products or services you provide and include inventory, packaging, supplies, materials, and sometimes labor used in providing your product or service. They're called "variable" precisely because they go up or down depending on the volume of products or services you produce or sell. In the case of services, one of the biggest variable expenses is almost always the wages or salary of the service provider. (See "Salaries and Labor Costs—Fixed or Variable?" below, for a more complete explanation.)

Salaries and Labor Costs—Fixed or Variable?

Whether you'll categorize labor expenses as fixed or variable costs often depends on the type of workers you pay and the kinds of products or services you're selling. Salaries or wages of the managers and employees who are necessary to keep your business going (you or your bookkeeper, for example) are usually best seen as fixed costs. But salaries or wages for employees who create the products or provide the services you sell may be more appropriately treated as variable costs. For example, an ad agency that pays six freelance copywriters to service clients' accounts should treat the writers' paychecks as variable costs.

To figure out whether a labor cost should be designated as fixed or variable, ask yourself: If I sell one, ten, or 100 more products or services this week, will my labor costs go up? If not, you're probably looking at a fixed cost. For instance, suppose you're trying to decide whether your receptionist's salary should be categorized as a variable cost or a fixed cost. If you produce and sell 100 more Mr. Hankey dolls, will your reception costs go up? Probably not. So, your receptionist's salary should be part of your overhead. But if you have to hire five temporary employees to staff the phones at Christmastime to handle the spiking demand for Mr. Hankeys, their wages should be classified as variable costs. (Hint: Money paid to workers who are temps or independent contractors is usually categorized as variable costs, because those payments are usually tied to providing a product or service.) Of course, at some point of selling more products or services regularly, you'll probably decide to expand your business and increase your overhead, because you'll have to hire more support staff, managers, and other necessary employees just to get along. At that point, you should revisit your allocation of fixed and variable costs.

3. Estimate Your Sales Revenue

Start your break-even analysis by making your best estimate of annual sales revenues. Your estimate will obviously depend on several different variables, such as your type of business, what you plan to charge for each product or service you'll offer, and how successful you'll be at selling products and services.

Though at first it may seem overwhelming to project revenues based on so many untested variables, it is essential that you take the plunge and try out some numbers. Even though your estimates won't be anywhere near 100% accurate, they'll force you to focus and refine key elements of your business idea and may even help you spot big potholes in your plan. And besides, you need these estimates before you can move ahead with your break-even calculations, so get over it and start estimating.

Pricing help still to come. There are many issues to consider and various methods to use when figuring out how much to charge for your goods and services. Pricing issues are addressed separately, in Chapter 6, where you'll also find info on service billing options and how to put together solid bids and proposals.

One good way to estimate how much money you'll be bringing in is to compare your business with similar ones. Retail businesses, for example, often measure annual sales revenue per square foot of retail space. Thus, if you plan to open a pet supply store, you'll want to find out the annual sales revenue per square foot of other pet supply shops. While direct competitors probably won't share this information, industry trade publications almost always provide it. Attending industry trade shows where you can meet and talk with people who own similar businesses in other parts of the country is also another good way to gather valuable information.

EXAMPLE: Inga is planning to open a used bookstore in Milwaukee called Inga's Book Haus. She plans to sell mostly used books, which generally have a high profit margin, but she'll also stock a limited selection of new books at the front of the store to attract more customers. She'll sell some miscellaneous trinkets such as postcards and magnets as well.

To figure out how much sales revenue she can realistically expect for Inga's Book Haus, Inga calls up a couple of friends who are in the book business. One who works at a nearby used bookstore confides to Inga that the store sells approximately $450 worth of books per square foot per year. Another friend owns a new-and-used bookstore in Madison; she tells Inga that they bring in about $400 annually per square foot. Neither of these stores is exactly like the one Inga envisions; the one in Milwaukee doesn't sell any new books, and the one in Madison does a healthy trade in textbooks, which Inga doesn't expect at her store. To round out her information, Inga also looks into some trade publications and does a bit of sleuthing at local new-and-used bookstores, examining their prices and how busy they seem to be. Ultimately she decides that an annual income of $350 per square foot is realistic. She has her eye on a few storefronts, all around 1,200 square feet, so she estimates her annual revenues to be $420,000.

Basing your projected revenue on the numbers of similar companies also works for nonretail businesses such as wholesaling or manufacturing companies—but it can be somewhat tricky to find a solid basis for comparison. Unlike retail businesses, sales per square foot wouldn't really apply. If you're not already well-acquainted with your field, you'll have to do some research. Study similar businesses to find out how many employees they have, how wide their distribution is, and how much annual income they earn. Base your income projections on similarly sized businesses with a comparable range of distribution.

If yours is a service business, your estimate of sales revenue will depend on how many billable sales you'll be able to make each month. A big part of this calculation is how many hours you and any employees will work and how much you'll be paid per hour by your clients. But don't overlook the fact that all of your time won't be billable—you won't be providing services every hour you're at work. For example, if you run a landscaping business, a sizable portion of your time will be spent not performing landscaping work but managing your accounts, maintaining your equipment, and soliciting new clients. You'll need to make a realistic assessment of how much of your time will be taken up by these nonbillable activities and how much time you'll spend providing actual services to clients to get an accurate picture of how much money will be flowing in.

4. Calculate Your Average Gross Profit Percentage

Your next task is to figure your average gross profit percentage. It may sound complex, but basically it's just a figure that represents how much of each sales dollar will be left over after paying for the costs of the products or services themselves. There are a number of steps involved in calculating this figure, but none involves anything more than simple math: addition, subtraction, multiplication, and division. Once you know your average gross profit percentage, you'll easily be able to figure out how much money you'll need to bring in to cover all the costs of your business.

In a nutshell, to figure your average gross profit percentage you'll need to:

1. figure out your gross profit for each major category of your products or services

2. determine an average gross profit for your business overall, including all your products and services, and

3. divide your average gross profit by your average selling price.

In case you're wondering what the difference is between "gross profit" and "average gross profit," here's a quick explanation. (The details will be covered while going through the calculations below.) When you sell an individual product, the money that you earn above the cost of the item itself (called your variable cost, or sometimes cost of goods) is called gross profit. For instance, if your pet store sells a doghouse for $200, and you bought the doghouse for $110, then what's left over for you after the sale is $90: your gross profit. If your business sells more than one kind of product, you'll need to calculate an *average* gross profit for your total product line to get a realistic figure. The average gross profit for your pet store would include all of your products in the calculation—cat scratching posts, pet food, play toys, and so on—including their sales prices and what they cost you.

The next few subsections take you through the process of calculating your business's average gross profit.

a. Figure Your Gross Profit by Category

As described above, your gross profit is the amount of money you make on each sale, above what it costs you for the product or service itself—that is, the variable cost or cost of sale. Gross profit is determined simply by subtracting the variable cost of your product or service from its sales price.

Variable costs are generally fairly easy to estimate. If you're selling products bought from a wholesaler, your variable costs may be as simple as what you pay for the products themselves. If you'll assemble the products, then include your costs for the parts and labor needed to put them together. Also remember to include items such as packaging or freebies in your variable costs. If you only sell services, variable costs basically include what you pay to whomever provides the services (you or perhaps an employee), not including time spent on administrative tasks and managing accounts, which is generally considered to be a fixed, not variable, cost. It can sometimes be tricky

to figure out the variable costs of a service business. Do your best to separate out the costs that are not associated with individual projects—those are your fixed costs.

> **EXAMPLE:** Turtlevision, a digital video editing service, pays its staff editor $50 per hour for 80 hours per month of editing work. In addition, Turtlevision pays an office assistant $15 per hour for 100 hours per month of administrative work. Turtlevision's monthly variable costs would include the editor's salary of $4,000, but not the salary paid to the office assistant, which is not tied to any particular client or project.

One kink in figuring out your business's gross profit is that your selling prices and variable costs may vary a great deal from product to product (or service to service). For instance, say you buy cat collars for an average of $4, and sell them for an average price of $10 (your gross profit per cat collar would be $6). Doghouses, on the other hand, cost you an average of $110, and you sell them for an average price of $200 (your gross profit per doghouse would be $90).

To account for these differences, you should categorize your products or services and figure an average gross profit for each category. There are a few steps to follow, but hang in there—each one is pretty simple.

First, estimate the average selling price and average variable cost for products or services with roughly similar selling prices and variable costs. For instance, you might group all your animal collars together—for cats, dogs, and ferrets—since their selling prices ($9 to $13) and variable costs ($3 to $5) aren't too different. Don't lump together products or services with considerably different selling prices or variable costs. As a general rule, the more tightly you define your categories, the more accurate your estimates will be.

After you've estimated the average selling price and average variable cost for each category, subtract the average variable cost from the average selling price for each category, and you'll have an average gross profit dollar figure for each category.

	Animal collars	Bird- houses	Dog- houses
Average selling price	$11	$60	$200
− Average variable cost	$4	$30	$110
= Average gross profit	$7	$30	$90

The next step is to figure out a gross profit percentage for each category. A gross profit percentage tells you how much of each dollar of sales income is gross profit. To calculate each category's gross profit percentage, divide the average gross profit figure by the average selling price.

Animal collars category:

	Average gross profit	$ 7.00
÷	Average selling price	$ 11.00
=	Gross profit percentage	63.6%

Using the above example, it follows that if you sold $1,500 in cat collars, 63.6% of that—$954— would be gross profit, or the amount left over after paying costs of sale. As you can see, converting your gross profit into a percentage allows you to quickly figure out how much of your income will be left over after variable costs have been covered.

b. Calculate Your Average Gross Profit

After you've found the gross profit percentage for each category, you'll be able to determine your average gross profit for your business as a whole.

First, estimate your annual sales revenue per category. Earlier you estimated your total annual sales revenues; now divide that figure as best you can into your estimates for each category. For example, if you estimated total annual revenues of $100,000 for your pet supply business, divide that among your categories, such as collars, birdhouses, and doghouses—say $25,000 in collar sales, $40,000 in birdhouses, and $35,000 in doghouses. Base your division on your best sense of which categories

and products will make up a big part of your business, and which will have a smaller share. Then, for each product category, multiply the estimated sales revenue by the category's gross profit percentage (arrived at above) to figure out your total gross profit dollars per category.

Animal collars category:

	Estimated sales revenue	$ 25,000
x	Gross profit percentage	63.6%
=	Total gross dollars	$15,900

Finally, add together the gross profit dollar amounts for each category to arrive at a total annual gross profit for your business. Divide the total annual gross profit figure by the total annual sales that you estimated for all products or services. The result will be an average gross profit percentage for your business.

Let's look at how this process works with Inga's Book Haus.

EXAMPLE: As you may recall, Inga plans to sell new and used books, plus some peripheral items such as postcards and refrigerator magnets. Since the profit margins for new books, used books, and trinkets are different, Inga figures a gross profit percentage for each of these categories. (Inga might want to establish separate categories for hardback, paperback, and coffee-table books, but we'll keep things simple.)

To accomplish this, first Inga estimates an average variable cost for each category. In addition to the cost of the merchandise, she includes the cost of free bags, bookmarks, and wrapping paper for gifts. For instance, used books cost her an average of $3, and she figures the bookmarks and bags that go with each sale will cost her an average of 10¢. So her total average variable cost in the used book category is $3.10. She doesn't include fixed costs here, such as rent or salaries.

Next, Inga fills in an average selling price for each product category. Her average selling price for used books, for example, is $7. She then subtracts the average variable cost (arrived at above) from the average selling price to get an average gross profit figure for each product category. Subtracting her average variable cost for used books ($3.10) from her average selling price for used books ($7.00) leaves her with an average gross profit for used books of $3.90.

Used book category:

	Average sales price	$ 7.00
−	Average variable cost	$ 3.10
=	Average gross profit	$ 3.90

Inga does the same calculations for new books, which also shows an average gross profit of $3.90, and trinkets, which has an average gross profit of $1.40.

To determine the gross profit percentage, she'll simply divide the gross profit by the selling price in each category to get a gross profit percentage for each category. Dividing her average gross profit for used books ($3.90) by her average selling price ($7.00) gives Inga a gross profit percentage of 56% for used books, a good percentage. That means that for every dollar she'll bring in from used books, 44 cents per dollar will be eaten up on Inga's costs, leaving 56 cents per dollar to cover fixed costs and go toward a net profit. Her gross profit percentage for new books is 33%, and for trinkets it's an impressive 70%, as shown below.

New book category:

	Average gross profit	$ 3.90
÷	Average selling price	$12.00
=	Gross profit percentage	33%

Trinkets category:

	Average gross profit	$ 1.40
÷	Average selling price	$ 2.00
=	Gross profit percentage	70%

Using the gross profit percentages and estimated sales revenues for each category, Inga can calculate the gross profit dollar figure for each category. For example, her estimated annual sales of used books is $300,000. (Remember from Section 3, above, that Inga estimated her total annual sales revenue to be $420,000. She thinks used books will account for a little over ⅔ of her sales.) By multiplying $300,000 by the used book category's gross profit percentage (56%), she estimates an annual gross profit of $168,000. Adding up the gross profit figures for each category, Inga figures that her total gross profit will be $215,000. Finally, by dividing this amount by her annual estimated revenues of $420,000, she easily determines her total gross profit percentage, which is 51.2%.

	New books	Used books	Trinkets
Average variable cost per product	$ 8.00	$ 3.00	$ .50
+ bookmarks, bags	$ .10	$ .10	$ .10
= Average total cost	$ 8.10	$ 3.10	$ .60
Average selling price	$12.00	$ 7.00	$2.00
− Average total variable cost	$ 8.10	$ 3.10	$ .60
= Average gross profit	$ 3.90	$ 3.90	$1.40
Average gross profit	$ 3.90	$ 3.90	$1.40
÷ Average selling price	$12.00	$ 7.00	$2.00
= Gross profit percentage	33%	56%	70%
Average sales	$100,000	$300,000	$20,000
x Gross profit percentage	33%	56%	70%
= Annual gross profit	$ 33,000	$168,000	$14,000

Annual gross profit	
New books	$ 33,000
+ Used books	$ 168,000
+ Trinkets	$ 14,000
= Total annual gross profit	$ 215,000
÷ Total annual sales	$ 420,000
= Average gross profit percentage	51.2%

5. Estimate Your Fixed Costs

You're done with the hard part. Compared to calculating your gross profit percentage, fixed costs are a breeze. Simply estimate your monthly fixed expenses, including items such as rent, utility bills, postage, office supplies, uncollectable debts—basically, any anticipated costs that don't depend on the amount of the product or service you sell. Since many of these costs recur monthly, it's usually easiest to estimate them per month and total them for one year. It's also a good idea to throw in a little extra—say, 10% or so—to cover miscellaneous expenses that you can't predict. Once you've arrived at a total, you'll know that you'll need to make at least this much gross profit (and probably a healthy chunk more) to keep your business afloat.

> **EXAMPLE:** Here is a list of Inga's monthly estimates for fixed costs:
>
> | | |
> |---|---:|
> | Rent | $ 3,500 |
> | Wages for part-time clerks | 2,500 |
> | Utilities | 800 |
> | Telephone | 700 |
> | Office equipment | 700 |
> | Insurance | 500 |
> | Advertising | 700 |
> | Accounting | 300 |
> | Electronic payment system fees | 300 |
> | Misc. | 1,000 |
> | Total fixed expenses per month | 11,000 |
> | Annual total fixed expenses (monthly expenses x 12) | $132,000 |

Don't forget you have to eat. Notice that Inga has chosen not to list a salary here as an expense. She, like many sole proprietors, figures that her savings, help from friends and family, and some extra crumbs the business may produce should be enough to live on for the short term. Once she figures out how much profit the business will bring in regularly, she'll decide how much profit she can expect to take out of the business and add that number to her fixed costs. Leaving out payments for your own living expenses in your break-even analysis, however, can be dangerous, at least if you're planning to live off your business's profits from the get-go. If this is your plan, you should add to your fixed costs the minimum amount you'll need to take out of the business to cover your living expenses. Then, if you can't project your income to be higher than your fixed costs when the amount you'll need for living expenses is included, you'll know you can't plan on living off the company. This may be a clue that your business is not a good bet.

Keep fixed costs as low as reasonably possible. If your business is slow to get started—and lots of businesses take months or even years to become solidly profitable—high fixed costs can quickly eat up your savings. Rather than committing yourself to high overhead, it's usually better to keep expenses low, allowing increases only when your income justifies spending more. For example, few businesses really depend on a pricey physical location for their success. If your business won't depend on a big casual walk-in trade, don't overpay for a trendy zip code. Operating from a low-cost warehouse district, an older office building, or even your garage may work just fine, at least at the beginning.

6. Calculate Your Break-Even Point

Once you have estimated your fixed costs (from Section 5, above) and your average gross profit percentage (from Section 4, above), it's easy to figure out how much revenue you'll need to break even. Remember, your gross profit percentage represents how much of each dollar of revenue is actual profit, left over after paying for the product or service itself. To figure out your break-even point, you'll divide your estimated annual fixed costs by your gross profit percentage. The result will be the amount of sales revenue you'll need to bring in just to cover your costs.

EXAMPLE: The break-even point for Inga's Book Haus will equal her annual fixed expenses divided by her average gross profit percentage.

Annual fixed expenses	$132,000
÷ Average gross profit percentage	51.2%
= Break-even point	$257,813

If you're having trouble understanding how this equation works, you're not alone. Conceptually, it's a little tricky to see how dividing your fixed costs by your gross profit percentage yields your break-even point. Think of it this way: However much money your business brings in, some of it will be eaten up by the cost of the product or service itself (your variable costs), leaving you a reduced amount left over to pay your bills. How much is left over is determined by your gross profit percentage—this number tells you just how much will be left over, on average, from each dollar, after paying for your product or service itself (your variable costs). When you divide your estimated annual fixed costs by your gross profit percentage, the resulting number (the break-even point) is the exact amount that's enough to cover your fixed costs.

EXAMPLE: Another extra-simplified example should help illustrate this concept. Michele plans to go into business selling jewelry. Her gross profit percentage was .75, meaning that for every dollar she brought in, .25 would be eaten up by the cost of the jewelry materials, leaving Michele .75 to cover her fixed costs. Michele's fixed costs were $600 per year. So, you're wondering, why isn't Michele's break-even point $600? Because if Michele earned exactly $600 in a year, only 75% of that would be available to cover her fixed costs—the other 25% would have already been eaten up by the costs of her jewelry, leaving her unable to pay all of the $600 in fixed costs. To account for this, Michele needs to divide her fixed costs ($600) by her gross profit percentage (.75) to arrive at the higher amount that

she'll need to bring in to cover her fixed costs and her variable costs. Dividing $600 by .75 results in $800, her break-even point; if Michele brings in $800, .25 of it will go toward the cost of the product, and the rest ($600) is just enough to cover her fixed costs.

7. Analyze Your Result

If your estimated revenue exceeds your break-even point, great—but that's not the same thing as saying you are free to put the excess money in your pocket. Again, remember that every dollar you bring in doesn't come for free; you had to pay something for the cost of your product or service (variable costs). The portion of excess sales revenue that's really yours (ignoring taxes for the moment) is equivalent to your gross profit percentage of that excess revenue. To determine how much of the excess revenue is pretax profit, multiply the excess by your gross profit percentage. The result is your estimated net profit.

EXAMPLE: Earlier, Inga estimated her annual sales revenue to be $420,000—over $160,000 more than she needs to break even.

Estimated revenue	$420,000
− Break-even point	$257,813
= Excess revenues	$162,187

To figure out how much of her excess revenue will be actual pretax profit, Inga multiplies it by her gross profit percentage.

Excess revenues	$162,187
x Gross profit percentage	51.2%
= Net profit	$83,040

Inga is happy to see her projections show a profit. But she needs to remember that none of her estimates included any payments to herself, meaning she'll probably need to take some of that net profit just to meet her living expenses.

If, on the other hand, your break-even point is higher than your expected revenues, you'll have some decisions to make. For example, you'll have to decide whether certain aspects of your plan can be amended to come up with an achievable break-even point. For instance, perhaps you could find a less-expensive source of supplies, do without an employee, or save rent by working out of your home.

But don't change your numbers without a very good reason. When confronted by a break-even point that exceeds your estimated revenues, you may be tempted to tweak and squish your numbers into a profitable forecast, even if those numbers aren't realistic. Unless you really do have a good reason to think you can break even at a lower point, you'd be wise to guard again this temptation. For example, to have your plan pencil out in the black, you might boost your sales estimates in hopes that you'll somehow be able to pull it off. But can you really sell 50,000 Sausage Shooters™; 3,000 books on medieval dentistry; or 2,000 Tori Spelling mini-tees per month?

Generally speaking, when trying to pencil out a more profitable break-even point, it's best to focus on your costs. The most reliable way to tilt a business from the red to the black is to reduce what you will pay out, not to make a more optimistic projection of what you'll take in.

E. Profit/Loss Forecast

If your break-even analysis shows that, based on realistic estimates of revenue and expenses, your business will turn a profit, your next job is to use these figures to create the profit/loss forecast component of your business plan. Similar to a break-even analysis, a profit/loss forecast (sometimes called a P & L forecast) uses your estimates for sales revenue and variable costs to calculate your gross profit, then subtracts your fixed expenses from gross profit to arrive at net profit.

If you use accounting software, it will generate a P & L statement automatically once you enter monthly sales and expense estimates. You can also use the worksheet on the CD-ROM that comes with this book, as described below.

Profit/Loss Forecast Worksheet. On the CD-ROM that comes with this book, you'll find an interactive worksheet to help you do a profit/loss forecast. The file name of the worksheet is pl_worksheet.xls. For the automatic calculations in the worksheet to be active, you'll need to open the worksheet in a spreadsheet program such as Microsoft Excel.

To use the worksheet, follow the steps outlined below. Each step is explained in greater detail in the chapter. Enter figures only into white cells; do not enter anything in blue cells.

Step 1: Enter your estimated sales revenues for each month. If you will be starting a business in a month other than January, you may change the months to begin with your starting month.

Step 2: Enter the average gross profit percentage for your business as a whole. You need to enter this figure just once, in the first column under "January." The worksheet will automatically enter it for every other month.

Step 3: Enter your anticipated fixed expenses for each month. The worksheet uses common categories, and contains some rows you may customize for expenses specific to your business. If you do not anticipate a certain type of expense, you may leave cells blank.

Result: When you have entered estimated sales revenues, a gross profit percentage, and fixed costs for all months, the worksheet will display your estimated net profit or loss for each month.

The main difference between a P & L and a break-even analysis has to do with timing. A break-even analysis looks at profit and loss on a yearly basis, while your P & L forecast calculates monthly net profit. A P & L also differs from a cash flow projection, as discussed in Section G, below, in the kinds of income and expenses that it includes. A cash flow forecast looks at all sources of income and expenses, including loans, transfers of personal money into the business, start-up costs, and all other types of cash inflows and outflows. A P & L, on the other hand, is only concerned with money earned from normal business operations. For this reason, a P & L forecast will tell you whether your business operations are generating enough income to cover your expenses, something you can't glean from a cash flow forecast.

Here's how to translate your break-even figures into a profit/loss forecast: Start by breaking down your annual sales estimate into monthly amounts. If you expect significant seasonal fluctuations in sales, account for them here.

Next, figure your gross profit for each month. The easiest way to do this is to multiply each month's sales revenue by the gross profit percentage for your business as a whole, which you calculated earlier. (If you rounded off your gross profit percentage, you'll get a slightly different gross profit figure here than you did in your break-even analysis.)

Enter your monthly fixed expenses by category, and add them together to get monthly totals. Then, for each month, subtract your total fixed expenses from your gross profit and enter the result in the net profit row. If the result is a negative number, it means your expenses are more than your gross profit. Put parentheses around the result; in accounting symbols, a number in parentheses is a negative number.

⚠ **Your profit/loss statement doesn't include the whole picture.** Other income and costs such as loans and start-up expenses aren't included in your P & L statement, which reflects only money earned and spent as part of providing your products or services. For the full picture of all money that comes into and goes out from your business— including start-up costs, loans, taxes, and other money that isn't earned or spent as part of your core business operation—you'll need to do a cash flow analysis. (See Section G for a complete explanation of how to predict your cash flow.)

A completed P & L will outline your business's profitability month by month. If your expenses are higher than revenues for a month or two, don't panic—most start-up businesses lose money for at least a few months—but you will need to figure out how to make it through these lean months (for example, by getting a start-up loan). More important in the big picture is whether you can see a trend toward stable profitability. If not, you may need to revisit parts of your plan (or possibly scrap your idea altogether). But, as mentioned earlier, resist the temptation to inflate your sales estimates; a more realistic approach is to lower your costs. Once you have a P & L that shows consistent profits each month, based on realistic estimates, you're ready to move forward.

F. Start-Up Cost Estimate

If your profit/loss forecast shows your projected income will be higher than expenses each month, that's an optimistic sign. But beware that you haven't yet accounted for an important category of expenses: business start-up costs. The worst part about start-up costs is that you need to pay them before your business is actually making any money. That's why you should have a firm grasp on what you really need to spend to successfully start your business and a plan for where that money will come from. Of course, potential lenders or investors will want to see that you've accounted for these costs in your planning. But it's also important that you understand for yourself how high this initial financial hurdle will be so that you can figure out how to clear it. Obviously, you don't want to start a business with high start-up costs but low projected profits, since it will take you far too long to recover your initial investment.

⚠ **Buy only what your business really needs.** Too many new small business owners weigh down their new enterprises with unneeded start-up costs. Unless a particular item is absolutely necessary to generate revenue, don't buy it—or, if you

EXAMPLE: Inga's one-year profit/loss forecast for her bookstore is shown below.

Inga's Book Haus Profit/Loss Forecast: Year One Total

	Jan	Feb	Mar	April	May
Sales Revenues	$30,000	$35,000	$35,000	$35,000	$35,000
Gross Profit (51.2%)	**15,360**	**17,920**	**17,920**	**17,920**	**17,920**
Fixed Expenses					
Rent	3,500	3,500	3,500	3,500	3,500
Salaries & Payroll Taxes	2,500	2,500	2,500	2,500	2,500
Utilities	800	800	800	800	800
Telephone	700	700	700	700	700
Office Equipment	700	700	700	700	700
Insurance	500	500	500	500	500
Advertising	700	700	700	700	700
Accounting	300	300	300	300	300
Fees for Electronic Payment System (EPS)	300	300	300	300	300
Miscellaneous	1,000	1,000	1,000	1,000	1,000
Total Fixed Expenses	**11,000**	**11,000**	**11,000**	**11,000**	**11,000**
Net Profit (Loss)	**$4,360**	**$6,920**	**$6,920**	**$6,920**	**$6,920**

June	July	Aug	Sept	Oct	Nov	Dec	Year Total
$35,000	$35,000	$35,000	$35,000	$35,000	$35,000	$40,000	$420,000
17,920	**17,920**	**17,920**	**17,920**	**17,920**	**17,920**	**20,480**	**$215,040**
3,500	3,500	3,500	3,500	3,500	3,500	3,500	$42,000
2,500	2,500	2,500	2,500	2,500	2,500	2,500	$30,000
800	800	800	800	800	800	800	$9,600
700	700	700	700	700	700	700	$8,400
700	700	700	700	700	700	700	$8,400
500	500	500	500	500	500	500	$6,000
700	700	700	700	700	700	700	$8,400
300	300	300	300	300	300	300	$3,600
300	300	300	300	300	300	300	$3,600
1,000	1,000	1,000	1,000	1,000	1,000	1,000	$12,000
11,000	**11,000**	**11,000**	**11,000**	**11,000**	**11,000**	**11,000**	**$132,000**
$6,920	**$6,920**	**$6,920**	**$6,920**	**$6,920**	**$6,920**	**$9,480**	**$83,040**

do, spend as little as possible on it. Sure, you need a desk, but unless customers will see it (and sometimes even if they will), repainting a door and laying it across a couple of secondhand filing cabinets at a net cost of $40 makes a lot more sense than paying $800 for a new one.

Compared to the projections explained earlier, estimating your start-up costs is a breeze—just list them and add them up. Include items like business registration fees and tax deposits you need to pay up front; rent and security deposits you'll have to pay before business starts; and costs of any initial inventory, office supplies, equipment, and anything else you'll have to cover before your business starts bringing in money.

EXAMPLE: Inga makes a list of the start-up expenses she expects to pay before she'll start selling books:

Initial inventory	$20,000
Rent deposit (security deposit and last month's rent)	7,000
Office supplies, stationery	500
Cash register	500
Business registration fees	200
TOTAL	$28,200

If you don't have enough cash to pay all of your start-up costs out of pocket, you'll either need to come up with the money or figure out a way to spread the costs over the first few months of business, when you'll have at least some cash flowing in. For instance, maybe you could lease, rather than buy, needed equipment.

The next and final financial projection you'll need to do as part of your business plan—a cash flow projection—will help you plan and manage your incoming and outgoing cash so that you can cover needed expenses when they come due.

G. Cash Flow Projection

To round out the collection of financial information in your business plan, you should include a cash flow projection. While your profit/loss forecast may show that your business should make enough sales at a high enough price to cover your estimated expenses, a cash flow projection analyzes whether the cash from those sales, as well as from other sources such as loans or investments, will come in fast enough to pay your bills on time. Cash flow management is important once your business is up and running, especially if you plan to stock a good-sized inventory or extend credit to customers. A high sales volume won't be enough to cover your expenses if your customers are slow to pay you and your checking account is empty.

Cash Flow Forecast Worksheet. On the CD-ROM that comes with this book, you'll find an interactive worksheet to help you do a cash flow forecast. The file name of the worksheet is cashflow_worksheet.xls. For the automatic calculations in the worksheet to be active, you'll need to open the worksheet in a spreadsheet program such as Microsoft Excel.

To use the worksheet, follow the steps outlined below. Each step is explained in greater detail in the chapter. Enter figures only into white cells; do not enter anything in blue cells.

Step 1: Enter any cash you expect to have in the bank at the beginning of the period for which you are doing a cash flow forecast. You may change the months to begin with a month other than January. For most start-up businesses, the amount you enter here will be zero. Do not enter any amounts beyond the first month. The worksheet will automatically add any estimated cash available at the end of each month to your cash available for the next month.

Step 2: In the "Cash Ins" section, enter any estimated paid sales (not credit sales) you expect, plus any loans or other money you intend to put into the business.

Step 3: In the "Cash Outs" section, enter the amounts you expect to pay out from your business, in the month you expect to make the payments. The worksheet uses common categories, and contains some rows you may customize for expenses specific to your business. If you do not anticipate a certain type of expense, you may leave cells blank.

Result: When you have entered all anticipated cash ins and cash outs, the worksheet will display your projected cash flow.

Cash flow projection is also important in your planning stages to show how you intend to survive the first few lean months of business—particularly after you figure in your start-up expenses. If you'll have more than enough cash to cover your expenses for the first months of business, then you're one of the lucky few. More likely, you'll be pressed to figure out how to cover a cash deficit for at least the first few months, and maybe longer. One way to do this is to put off or cut some expenses. Another is to get a loan or sell part of your business to investors, or to hit up your family or friends for a loan. The important thing is to do your best to predict your cash needs in advance, both to give yourself ample time to come up with a plan for getting the cash and to inspire more confidence in lenders or investors.

Your cash flow projection will use many of the same figures you developed for your profit/loss forecast. The main difference is that you'll include all cash inflows and outflows, not just sales revenues and business expenses. Also, you'll record costs in the month that you expect to incur them, rather than simply spreading annual amounts equally over 12 months. Inflows and outflows of cash that belong in your cash flow analysis include loans, loan payments, and start-up costs. Once you're turning a profit, you'll also include income tax payments in your cash flow analysis, but, for now, assume that you'll be free from income taxes for your first year.

For each month, simply start your projection with the actual amount of cash your business will have on hand. Next, fill in your projected cash-ins for the month, which should include sales revenues, loans, transfers of personal money—basically, any money that goes into your business checking account. Add these together along with the cash you have at the beginning of the month to get your total cash-ins for the month.

Next, enter all your projected cash-outs for the month, such as your fixed expenses and any loan payments. Remember also to include costs of products and materials you use in your products or services—your variable costs. Add together all your cash-outs to obtain a total for the month. Subtract total monthly cash-outs from total monthly cash-ins, and the result will be your cash left at the end of the month. That figure is also your beginning cash balance at the start of the next month; transfer it to the top of the next month's column, and do the whole process over again.

EXAMPLE: Inga completes her cash flow projection for her first year in business, as shown above. She starts her projection one month early to account for the money she must spend before she opens her bookstore. In her cash-in section, she figures in $15,000 that she will put into the business: $10,000 of her own savings and an interest-free loan from her sister of $5,000. In her cash-out section, she includes what she'll pay for the initial set-up of the business, as well as that month's rent and a $500 allowance for unexpected expenses. Inga also includes in her cash-out section a $500 payment each month to her sister for the loan.

Notice that Inga's cash-outs look a bit different from her expenses in her profit/loss forecast, even though they add up to the same totals. The reason is that Inga's cash-out section of her cash flow projection reflects that some expenses are paid in lump sums rather than monthly, such as her insurance, which is paid twice a year. She also breaks up her estimates for office expenses into lump payments, as she doesn't expect to spend equal amounts each month.

Inga's Book Haus Cash Flow Projection: Year One

	Dec	Jan	Feb	Mar	Apr	May
Cash at Beginning of Month	$0	($17,200)	($16,540)	($8,920)	($3,400)	$4,220
Cash-ins						
Sales Paid	0	30,000	35,000	35,000	35,000	35,000
Loans and Transfers	15,000	0	0	0	0	0
Total Cash-ins	**15,000**	**12,800**	**18,460**	**26,080**	**31,600**	**39,220**
Cash-outs						
Start-up Costs	28,200	0	0	0	0	0
Books & Other Products	0	14,640	17,080	17,080	17,080	17,080
Rent	3,500	3,500	3,500	3,500	3,500	3,500
Salaries & Payroll Taxes	0	2,500	2,500	2,500	2,500	2,500
Utilities	0	800	800	800	800	800
Telephone	0	700	700	700	700	700
Office Equipment	0	1,400	0	2,100	0	0
Insurance	0	3,000	0	0	0	0
Advertising	0	700	700	700	700	700
Accounting	0	300	300	300	300	300
Electronic Payment System Fees	0	300	300	300	300	300
Loan Payments	0	500	500	500	500	500
Misc.	500	1,000	1,000	1,000	1,000	1,000
Total Cash-outs	**32,200**	**29,340**	**27,380**	**29,480**	**27,380**	**27,380**
Cash at End of Month	**($17,200)**	**($16,540)**	**($8,920)**	**($3,400)**	**$4,220**	**$11,840**

	June	July	Aug	Sept	Oct	Nov	Dec
	$11,840	**$17,360**	**$21,980**	**$29,600**	**$34,420**	**$42,040**	**$49,660**
	35,000	35,000	35,000	35,000	35,000	35,000	40,000
	0	0	0	0	0	0	0
	46,840	**52,360**	**56,980**	**64,600**	**69,420**	**77,040**	**89,660**
	0	0	0	0	0	0	0
	17,080	17,080	17,080	17,080	17,080	17,080	19,520
	3,500	3,500	3,500	3,500	3,500	3,500	3,500
	2,500	2,500	2,500	2,500	2,500	2,500	2,500
	800	800	800	800	800	800	800
	700	700	700	700	700	700	700
	2,100	0	0	2,800	0	0	0
	0	3,000	0	0	0	0	0
	700	700	700	700	700	700	700
	300	300	300	300	300	300	300
	300	300	300	300	300	300	300
	500	500	500	500	500	500	500
	1,000	1,000	1,000	1,000	1,000	1,000	1,000
	29,480	**30,380**	**27,380**	**30,180**	**27,380**	**27,380**	**29,820**
	$17,360	**$21,980**	**$29,600**	**$34,420**	**$42,040**	**$49,660**	**$59,840**

Also notice that Inga's estimated paid sales (as opposed to sales on credit) for the year come to the same total as her estimated annual sales revenue. That's because, for her first year, at least, Inga doesn't plan to take credit cards or checks, only cash and ATM purchases. That way all her sales will be paid immediately.

Inga's happy to see that by the end of April she should have cash left in the bank after all her expenses are paid (though she hasn't yet provided for money for her living expenses). Still, she needs to close the cash deficits that she predicts for her first three months in business. Based on her cash flow projection, an extra $17,200 up front would keep her cash flow (barely) in the black. She decides to apply for a loan of $15,000 and try to juggle expenses to cover the remaining $2,200 shortfall.

Once you've completed a year's worth (or more, if you want) of a cash flow projection, you'll have a blueprint for your business's financial situation from month to month. If any months are projected to have a cash deficit, you'll need to tweak your plan to make sure you can cover all of your important expenses. As usual, this means you'll have to juggle, reduce, or cut costs. A cash flow projection that shows difficulty in paying all your bills won't only scare investors away, it may mean that your plan needs serious revision. On the other hand, if your cash flow projection shows that you'll be in the black every month, then you'll be in a good position to show your numbers to potential sources of money—and to get your business underway.

! Credit transactions complicate the picture. Cash flow analysis is concerned with when your business receives or spends money, not when sales or purchases are made. This means that you'll need to account for delayed payments if you do any sales or purchases on credit.

For more on business plans. Mike McKeever's *How to Write a Business Plan* (Nolo), offers more detail on how to complete your cash flow analysis, including how to deal with credit transactions.

H. Putting It All Together

Congratulations! You've finished the descriptive and financial aspects of your business plan. While you kick back and enjoy a cold one, think about how you want to put all the information together. If you put the plan together for your own information, then you might want to simply review it, edit anything that needs fixing, print it out, and put it into a binder for your reference. If you plan to present the information as part of a loan request or as a package for investors to review, you might want to do some extra polishing. As mentioned earlier, consider hiring a writer to help develop the information into a well-written, persuasive document. The bottom line is to package the information as needed for your specific purposes. One of those purposes may be to raise start-up money, as described in Section I.

I. Using Your Plan to Raise Start-Up Money

With a solid business plan in place, you're well-positioned to seek start-up funds. Before you start your quest for cash, however, you'll need to understand the types and sources of financing generally available to start-up businesses. This section provides an overview of key concepts you need to know—and common lending sources to consider.

The reality is that it's much harder for start-up businesses to secure financing than for existing businesses, for the simple reason that start-ups lack any history of success or creditworthiness. And it's also tough for them to secure funds from conventional lenders such as banks. But your chances will be improved by understanding some basics about how financing works and by knowing where to look, beyond the traditional funding sources.

For more on business planning and start-up financing. See *How to Write a Business Plan,* by Mike McKeever (Nolo). It offers in-depth information on preparing a business plan to submit to financers and includes up-to-date information on funding sources.

1. Basic Types of Financing

An initial, fundamental distinction you should understand is the difference between debt financing and equity financing. The concepts are simple. With debt financing, you borrow money that needs to be repaid; equity financing involves receiving money in exchange for an ownership share, or equity, in your business. Debt financing involves a repayable loan; equity financing means acquiring new owners who invest cash in your business.

Unless you originally planned to get money by acquiring investors, chances are that a business loan is a more practical option for your business. Not only will bringing new owners into your business involve potentially complicated issues related to the legal structure of your business, but it will dilute the shares that you and any other original partners own. This means your share of business profits will be reduced, and—potentially even more troubling—you may have to share management control—and decision-making authority with the new owners, raising the distinct possibility of conflict.

One way to avoid this is to bring on investors as limited partners who will have no authority over business decisions. (See Chapter 2, Section B, for more on this arrangement.) But the bottom line is that equity financing involves more structural complexities than raising money via a loan.

2. What Attracts Funders

In addition to making sure you have a solid business plan that shows your business idea to be a winning one, funders will want to know other specific details of your financial situation. One of the most common measures that funders will examine is whether your business has a healthy balance between debt and equity—a relationship that is called a debt-to-equity ratio. Your debt-to-equity ratio is the extent to which your business is in debt to lenders, versus how much you and any other owners have invested in the business. The ratio calculated simply by dividing outstanding debt by the owners' equity in the business.

> **EXAMPLE:** Sara is considering financing options for her sole proprietorship, which has been in operation for about two years. So far, she has invested $50,000 of her own money into the business, and obtained one loan for $15,000, of which she has paid back $5,000. Her debt-to-equity ratio is calculated as follows:
> Outstanding debt: $10,000 ÷ owner's equity: $50,000
> Debt-to-equity ratio: 20%

In the most basic terms, lenders want to see a low ratio of debt to equity to make sure your business is not overextended and has sufficient assets to repay the loan. Commercially acceptable debt-to-equity ratios generally range from 50% to 150 percent—but since any ratios over 100% reflect more debt than equity, they should be viewed with caution. Conversely, if you have nearly no debt, lenders may take it as an indication that your business is not leveraging its assets to make the most of business opportunities.

Of course, when you're seeking a loan for the first time, your debt-to-equity ratio will be zero. The point is to understand the ratio and how lenders view it so that you can keep it in the right range as your business grows.

3. Sources of Funding

A fact that surprises many entrepreneurs is that the most popular source of start-up funding is the source closest to home: personal savings. A 2005 study by the United States Chamber of Commerce reports that 81% of the small businesses participating in the study used their personal savings to start their businesses. Contrast this with the 2% reporting receiving venture capital, or 3% receiving an SBA-guaranteed loan. (See "Sources of Start-Up Funding," below, for more results from this study.)

Statistics aside, start-ups need to be creative when looking for funds. Traditional funders such as commercial banks often won't consider your business until you have a successful track record. Happily, alternative sources of funds such as microlenders and small business incubators tend to be incredibly helpful, since they give not only money, but support and expertise to nurture your fledgling business. Of course, these sources may not be available in a certain region or may be overflowing with hopeful applicants. Possible sources for start-up funds are discussed below.

 **Establish a relationship with a bank.** It's smart to establish a relationship with a bank early in the life of your business, even if you don't need start-up funding. Open an account and use the services it offers to small business owners to establish your business as a trustworthy and reputable customer. With a solid relationship in place, you'll be in a better position to apply for funding down the road when your business is growing and needs money to expand.

Sources of Start-Up Funding

A 2005 report, "Access to Capital: What Funding Sources Work for You?" published by the U.S. Chamber of Commerce Statistics and Research Center, asked business owners to report where they obtained start-up funding. The figures below reflect the percentage of business owners that reported receiving start-up funds from that source.

- Venture capital: 2%
- Revolving credit: 3%
- SBA loan: 3%
- Home equity loan: 8%
- Friend/family loan: 15%
- Credit card: 15%
- Bank loan: 18%
- Personal savings: 81%

Source: "Access to Capital: What Funding Sources Work for You?" published by the U.S. Chamber of Commerce Statistics and Research Center, 2005. Available for download at www.uschamber.org.

a. Community Development Financial Institutions

It's a smart idea to start your search for start-up funding at alternative sources, such as community development financial institutions (CDFIs) in your community. CDFIs, which are certified by the U.S. Treasury, are a fast-growing segment of the business financing market specializing in loans to underserved communities and populations. Sometimes CDFIs are known in a community as a microlender or small business incubator. These funding organizations can be especially helpful for start-ups, businesses with poor credit, and businesses seeking relatively small loans, generally up to $100,000.

CDFIs usually, but not always, have a specific focus such as improving economic opportunities in blighted communities, or supporting businesses owned by women or minorities. But many of these organizations offer assistance broadly, not just to specific populations or communities. Even better, CDFIs often offer guidance and expertise to your business in addition to financing, which will help your chances of success.

For help in finding a CDFI. To find a certified CDFI in your area, go to the CDFI Fund website at www.cdfifund.gov and click on "Need a Loan?" at the left, then click on your state. You can download a guide to certified CDFIs in your area.

b. Bank Loans

As mentioned earlier, start-up businesses have a notoriously hard time getting financing from commercial banks. If, however, you are fortunate enough to find a bank willing to finance your start-up, you should understand the basics of how bank loans operate.

Loans can be secured or unsecured. When you obtain a secured loan, you give the creditor an interest in some kind of asset—such as business equipment, real estate, inventory, or receivables—in case you default on the loan. An asset used to secure a loan is called collateral. Lenders tend to be conservative when appraising the value of the collateral, and will only lend a percentage of that value. The loan amount compared to the value of the collateral is called a loan-to-value ratio. An unsecured loan is a loan that is not backed by any collateral.

Since a strong credit history or established cash flow will be essential in obtaining an unsecured loan, most start-ups aren't in a good position to obtain one. Also note that most start-up business owners will need to personally guarantee the loan, putting your personal assets at risk—even if you are incorporated. While a personal guarantee might be avoided if you put up sufficient collateral, the reality is that personal guarantees are a necessity for most loans to start-up businesses.

Certain details regarding your loan are obviously crucial, such as the length of time over which you'll pay it off—that is, the term, the interest rate, and any fees you'll need to pay. Most small business loans are short-term, from one to three years. And as with most other loans, the longer the loan, the higher the interest rate. Interest rates can be variable or fixed, usually a little higher for a fixed rate. In addition, you may have to pay points or other fees for various aspects of the application process, such as document reviews or credit checks. Find out if there will be any fees for prepayment of the loan.

Thinking Locally

Besides using the SBA programs to help secure funding from banks, start-up owners should be savvy about which banks offer the best chances of success. Local community banks that have a vested interest in the health of the local economy tend to be much more supportive of local businesses than big chain banks. And often, the application processes and criteria are softer at the smaller banks.

Similarly, be sure to look into credit unions, savings and loans, and other financial institutions in your area that may have financing programs for small businesses.

c. Small Business Administration

The Small Business Administration, or SBA, has developed programs to help solve the problem of banks being reluctant to lend to small businesses. The SBA does not provide loans itself, but helps businesses secure loans from banks by guaranteeing them—in other words, the SBA promises to repay the loan if the business defaults. To find out about the SBA's guarantee programs and the appli-

d. Family and Friends

Since start-ups are so commonly turned down by banks and other traditional funders, entrepreneurs often turn to friends and family for an injection of cash. But as you surely know, you must be careful when mixing money, blood, and friendship.

The best way to proceed is to be as businesslike as possible when getting money from family or friends. Draft a promissory note outlining the amount of the loan, the interest rate, and its repayment terms. Make it clear to the person who is lending you the money that you will treat the loan just like a commercial loan from a bank. And follow through with that promise by generating financial reports at least quarterly—and paying back the loan according to the agreed-upon terms.

e. Credit Cards and Personal Financing

Finally, if all other options have failed, many tenacious entrepreneurs turn to credit cards and home equity loans to get their ventures off the ground. This route may work, but you must watch for serious potential pitfalls. First, credit cards often charge much higher interest rates than business loans, and require minimum payments set at such a level that it could take decades to pay off your debt. If you keep high balances on the credit cards from month to month, paying just the minimum, your debt can quickly spiral out of control.

Another issue is that a business owner who resorts to credit cards to finance the business may not be as disciplined in managing the debt and spending. While bank lenders typically require financial reports and other proof of solid financial management, credit cards do not—potentially allowing you to get sloppy with your finances. Don't make this mistake. If you use credit cards as start-up funding, be just as serious about your book-keeping and financial management as if you had a big bank looking over your shoulder.

Home equity loans will usually offer better interest rates than credit cards, but of course, they require you to put your home at risk. If your business fails and you are unable to pay your home loan, you may face foreclosure. Be sure you evaluate this sobering possibility before taking out a loan against your home to finance your new business.

☑ **Chapter 5 Checklist**

☐ Decide how you will use your business plan: to attract investors or for your own use as a blueprint for your business.

☐ Draft sections of your business plan that describe your business in detail.

☐ Put together financial projections for your business, including a break-even analysis, a profit/loss forecast, and a cash flow analysis.

☐ Have a friend or business associate look over your plan—both the descriptive elements and the financial analysis—and make edits or suggestions.

☐ Edit your plan and prepare a final draft. Assemble the various sections of the plan into a final document, and package it as necessary for however you intend to use the plan.

☐ Evaluate your need for financing. If you decide to apply for a loan or to solicit investors, research the institutions in your area that offer potential sources of funds. Even if you decide not to seek financing right away, establish a relationship with a community bank to help your chances of obtaining a loan later.

■

CHAPTER 6

Pricing, Bidding, and Billing Projects

Pricing is a crucial factor in any business strategy, yet many fledgling business owners have little idea how to go about setting prices that are both competitive and profitable. This chapter explains how to develop your pricing strategy and introduces you to some standard methods for setting prices, whether your business sells services or products.

In addition, this chapter offers guidance for business owners who need to make bids to get work. Service businesses typically fall into this category, though sometimes product-based businesses also need to bid for jobs. This chapter also includes some general tips for the process and an outline for what typical proposals include.

On a cautionary note, be aware that antitrust laws forbid business competitors to fix, or even merely discuss, prices. For this reason, you won't find newsgroups or bulletin boards online where other businesses in a certain industry offer specific info on their pricing. Both online and off, pricing discussions among businesses in the same industry are not just taboo, they're illegal.

Directly sharing pricing info with competitors is illegal, but publishing general information about pricing guidelines is not. Good thing, since pricing is discussed first in this chapter.

Product sellers can skip ahead. Businesses that plan only to sell products don't need to deal with service-pricing or service-billing issues. If you don't plan to offer services, skip ahead to Section C, which discusses pricing for businesses that sell products.

A. Pricing and Billing for Service Businesses

Two major components of running a service-based business are setting prices and figuring out how to bill clients. Having rates that are well thought out is a key factor in soliciting clients confidently. And if you know the best way to bill them, you can manage your projects for maximum profitability and establish yourself as a true professional. This section explains these two essential tasks for service businesses. Once you understand what drives the pricing and billing processes, you'll find them much easier.

1. Setting Hourly Rates

Freelancers and service-based businesses often find it difficult to figure out what rates to use. Many can't understand how to assign value to their time. Bear in mind that your service rates are not just a measure of the value of your time—they also need to cover your overhead and yield your profits. There's no single formula to put a price on your services, but there are a couple of common approaches. One formula is based on adjusting the number of billable hours so that revenue equals salary, overhead, and profit. Some businesses base their rates on what the market will bear. Each of these approaches is described in more detail below.

a. Billable Hours Formula

Many service businesses use a fairly simple formula to calculate their hourly rate. To keep it simple, look at this formula as if you're a solo freelancer without any employees:

    Desired annual salary

+ Annual fixed costs (overhead)

+ Desired annual profit

÷ <u>Annual billable hour</u>

= Hourly rate

The gist of the formula is that it adds together all the money you want to bring in each year and divides that total by the number of hours you plan to work each year. The result is the hourly rate. This simple formula can be adjusted depending on the specifics of your business.

But first, it's a good idea to get a solid grasp on the concepts behind the formula.

- **Desired salary.** This is straightforward. How much would you like to earn annually? Include only salary here; desired profit comes later.
- **Fixed costs.** This is also a simple concept. How much will you spend each year on rent, utilities, office equipment, computers, and other items of overhead? As discussed in Chapter 5, fixed costs are independent of individual projects or services. You pay them regardless of how much business you're doing.
- **Desired profit.** You're in business to make a profit, not just to bring home a paycheck. A typical profit goal is 20% above salary and overhead (fixed costs).
- **Billable hours.** There's no single way to estimate this. Basically, the fewer billable hours you estimate, the higher your hourly rate will be; the more billable hours, the lower your hourly rate. A common way to approach this estimate is by calculating the number of potential billable hours in a year. With 52 weeks in the year and a 40-hour workweek, there are 2,080 potentially billable hours each year. Reduce that total by the number of nonbillable hours you expect to have—vacation, administrative work, or selling, for example. Just use your best estimate here. Very generally, the percentage of your time that is billable will probably be 50% to 80%. Much below that won't be very profitable, and higher than that usually isn't realistic. Use this percentage to determine how many billable hours you'll likely have each year. For instance, if 70% of your time will be billable, you will have 1,456 billable hours (2,080 hours x 70%).

Now add together your desired salary, fixed costs, and desired profit. Then divide that total by your billable hours. The result will be the hourly rate you'll need to charge to cover your fixed costs and bring in your desired salary and profit.

EXAMPLE: Samantha is starting a translation service and wants to figure out her hourly rate. She sets a salary for herself of $30,000 per year and estimates her annual fixed costs to be approximately $25,000. This totals $55,000 for salary and overhead. A 20% profit brings the total to $66,000. Samantha thinks she'll have to spend a good amount of time doing sales and getting her business off the ground, so she figures only about 60% of her time will be billable, resulting in 1,248 available billable hours. By dividing her salary, fixed expenses, and profit ($66,000) by 1,248 billable hours, Samantha sees that her hourly rate should be $52.88. She rounds that up to $55 per hour.

Salary:	$30,000
+ Fixed costs:	$25,000
Total salary & fixed costs:	$55,000
+ 20% profit:	$11,000
Total salary, fixed costs, & profit:	$66,000
÷ Billable hours:	1,248
Hourly rate:	$52.88

b. Setting Market-Based Rates

Another way to set your hourly rate is to throw the formula out the window and simply set your rate for what the market will bear. Beware that this might not yield a profitable hourly rate, because you're not basing your rate on the actual numbers you'll need to achieve. On the other hand, it may be more likely to deliver a rate that customers will accept.

If you base your rates on the market, use any market information you can get to guide you—including what competitors charge, industry standards, and your own experience of using various rates. If you constantly fail to snag clients once you provide a quote, that's a sign your rates may be too high. On the flip side, if you get every job you bid on, you could probably get away with nudging, or even shoving, your rates upward.

It is legal to research and use competitors' rates. The antitrust laws mentioned earlier are intended to protect consumers by maintaining competition in the marketplace. The laws are supposed to prevent anticompetitive agreements among competitors to set prices at a certain level. On the other hand, setting your rates to position your business among similar businesses is perfectly legal, so long as you obtained your competitors' pricing information from another source, not directly from them. After all, researching the market and setting prices accordingly is the essence of competition.

2. Billing Options

Service businesses and freelancers typically use a variety of billing options to accommodate different types of projects and clients. Common billing options include flat fees, hourly billing, and retainer arrangements. Each of these options is discussed below.

a. Flat Fees

With flat fee billing, you and your client agree to a total fee for a specific project. In the right situations, it is efficient and professional to charge your client a flat fee for your services. The fee should roughly reflect the number of hours you'll work multiplied by your hourly rate. Contractors typically discount their hourly rates for larger projects.

Billing per project usually makes clients happy because they know up front what their costs will be. Project-based billing can also benefit you. A flat fee encourages efficient project management and reduces the hassle of tracking and billing for your hours (though you should always keep track for your own records).

However, flat fees aren't the best idea for every project. You will feel underpaid if it takes much more work to finish a project than you expected, and the customer will feel overcharged if the project takes much less time than you estimated. If you want to bill per project, you and the client should both understand and agree on the project's exact scope. In fact, this agreement should be reached even before you quote a fee. Once the client accepts your fee, the project details should be outlined in a contract. Payment terms can vary, but contractors typically require a deposit up to one-half of the total fee on signing the project contract.

Sometimes it's not possible to pin down a project with specificity at the outset. Some clients simply don't want to hammer out all details. Other times, a short deadline makes it difficult or impossible to carefully consider all aspects of the project before you start work. In these cases, you ask for trouble if you set a flat fee.

Suppose, for instance, that a client calls and needs a new section developed for a website ASAP. The owners of the site desperately want you to start immediately, but you have only a vague idea of the work involved. A flat fee here would be a really bad idea—the project could take much longer than you expect, leaving you to do the work for an unfairly low flat rate.

If the project isn't carefully outlined before you start, forget the flat fee—hourly billing is probably the safest way to go.

b. Hourly Billing

Billing clients by the hour is pretty straightforward. You keep track of how many hours you work, and bill the client accordingly. As explained above, you should use this type of billing—also called "time and materials billing"—in situations in which the project isn't well defined.

While billing by the hour will protect you from being underpaid for a poorly defined project that takes more time than you thought it would, the client will never be happy if you present a huge, unexpected bill. Even when you choose hourly billing for a project without a clear scope, do your best to work efficiently, communicate with the client, and avoid handing over a surprising bill.

Keep in mind that it is up to you to demonstrate your value to the client, explaining why your hourly rate is justified and how you spent your hours. Even if you can't define the project specifically enough to set a flat rate, do your best to estimate how long the project will take, and try to keep your hours within your estimates.

 **Billable Rate Calculator.** On the CD-ROM that comes with this book, you'll find an interactive worksheet to help you calculate an hourly rate for your service business. The file name of the worksheet is billablerate_worksheet.xls. For the automatic calculations in the worksheet to be active, you'll need to open the worksheet in a spreadsheet program such as Microsoft Excel.

To use the worksheet, follow the steps outlined below. Each step is explained in greater detail in the chapter text. Enter figures only into white cells; do not enter anything in blue cells.

Step 1: Enter your desired annual salary. This is your take-home pay, not your overall business profit.

Step 2: Enter your estimated annual fixed costs. (For more on estimating fixed costs, see Chapter 5, "Drafting an Effective Business Plan.")

Step 3: Enter a profit goal for your business, as a percentage you want to exceed salary and fixed costs. A 20% profit goal is typical.

Step 4: If you know how many billable hours you plan to perform in a year, enter that amount. Or, if you're not sure how many billable hours you plan to work in a year, you can work backward by estimating the number of *nonbillable* hours you plan to spend—such as on vacation or doing administrative work—and subtracting those hours from the total number of possible billable hours in one year (2,080). The worksheet asks for your estimated nonbillable hours of various types for time periods that are easiest to estimate (for instance, vacation is estimated in weeks, while administrative work is estimated in hours per day), then converts those figures into annual hourly amounts. If you enter figures both for your estimated billable hours and estimated nonbillable hours, the calculator will use the first figure, estimated billable hours.

Result: The worksheet will show you what hourly rate you should charge in order to make your desired salary, cover your fixed costs, and make your desired profit, assuming you work the number of billable hours you estimated.

Charging for Outsourced Services

Sometimes service businesses need to hire another contractor (typically called a subcontractor) to get a job done for a client. You can charge your client for the subcontractor's work in different ways. You can simply charge your standard hourly rate for all work done for the client, whether your company did the work or a subcontractor did. This approach can work for or against you, depending on what you pay the subcontractor. Under the more common second approach, businesses mark up the cost of the subcontractors by 15% or 20% and bill the client accordingly.

Sometimes the client will hire and pay the sub directly, without a markup. This can work if that piece of the work is discrete, or distinct from the rest, and the client is responsible for supervising the sub's work and has appropriate liability insurance. However, many contractors prefer to choose and supervise all workers on the same project, for many reasons: They like to have total control over the project, they like to choose subcontractors whose work they trust, they usually make a fair profit on the subcontractor, and it

simplifies the project as well as the contractor's potential liability to the subcontractor and the client.

In any case, let your client know in advance whether you plan to use subcontractors on a project, especially if the subcontractor is a highly skilled specialist and the rate you bill for the subcontractor will be higher than your standard rate. Clients never like to be surprised with bills higher than they expected.

For example, Glenn is a construction contractor with a standard hourly rate of $55 per hour. When hired for a remodeling project, Glenn tells his client he will need to hire a few subcontractors over the course of the project who may have rates higher or lower than his. Glenn and the client agree that they'll mutually agree to each subcontractor and their rates before Glenn hires them. When it's nearly time to bring in a plumber, Glenn tells his client he'd like to hire Khalsa. Khalsa's own rate is $60 per hour, but Glenn marks up the rate by 15 percent to $69 so that he can make a reasonable profit for managing Khalsa on the project.

Set reasonable hourly increments when billing. For instance, will you bill the client a full hour for work that takes you 20 minutes to finish, or for a five-minute phone conversation? This approach is generally not recommended because clients see it as unfair. Many people use increments of 15 or 30 minutes for billing purposes. It can be good public relations to show some short phone calls on the bill with no charge attached. That makes the client feel better about the times you round up to the nearest 15 minutes for other tasks.

c. Retainer Arrangements

In a traditional retainer arrangement, the client pays an ongoing fee, usually monthly, to keep the contractor "on call" for certain services. Retainer arrangements are usually best for clients with regular and predictable needs—for example, maintaining a law firm's website, providing maintenance services for an apartment building, sewing and tailoring costumes for a theater, or doing public relations for a ski resort. As with flat-rate billing, you should always define the amount and scope of services expected of you under a retainer arrangement.

In some professional businesses, especially law offices, a "retainer" is requested at the outset that is really a deposit, or a prepayment of fees and costs, usually under a written fee agreement. Lawyers also sometimes use the traditional monthly-fee retainer described above.

B. Bidding and Creating Proposals

Sometimes it's not possible to sell a service or product just by offering it to the public for a certain price. Many service business (and some businesses selling products) must submit a bid or a proposal on a project to be considered for the job. (The terms "bid" and "proposal" are often used interchangeably.) If the client accepts the bid, then a contract is typically executed to confirm the sale.

Since bids can make or break a sale, you should take care when putting one together, both with the contents of the bid and its physical appearance. Often, the hardest part of bidding is breaking down the project into smaller parts so that you can make good estimates of how much work, time, and materials it will require. Once that's done, it's often quite easy to write the proposal. This section outlines how to put together a bid to increase your chances of success.

➡ When you don't need to get it in writing. If you don't need to learn about the bidding process, skip ahead to Section C, which discusses pricing for businesses selling products.

💡 When a proposal becomes a contract. A proposal usually becomes a contract once the client accepts your terms. In practice, however, you should suggest that you sign a separate contract to finalize the agreement with the client. This is partly because it's an opportunity to make sure the client truly understands what you said in your proposal. It's also a good idea because there are things you should cover in a contract that you wouldn't necessarily put in a proposal, such as

who provides the insurance, how you will handle extras or change orders, specifics of each side's remedies for breach of contract, which state's laws apply, and whether you will mediate or arbitrate any disagreements. (See Chapter 11 for an in-depth look at how to use contracts in your business.)

1. Get All the Information You Need

You won't be able to make an effective bid on a project until you thoroughly understand all the details involved. Ask the prospective client as many questions as necessary to flesh out the full scope of the project. A prospective client who's putting a project out to bid among competitors may already have a sheet of specifications, but if you have questions, ask them.

Often, the client will want to be involved in certain aspects of the project, so it's important you both agree who will take a primary role in various tasks or duties. You should hash out the breakdown of duties and workflow right at the beginning.

2. Break Down the Project and Make Estimates

In the next step, break down the project into manageable components and estimate how much time, labor, and materials you'll need for each one. This is generally the best way to make accurate estimates.

For instance, your head will spin if you try to estimate how long it will take you to complete an entire landscape design project. But once you break the project into parts—grading, spreading gravel, paving, planting trees, and so on—making estimates for the individual bits won't seem nearly as overwhelming.

Multiply the number of hours you expect the project to require by your hourly rate. It's common for freelancers to lower their hourly rates a bit if the project is a large one. This is reasonable, because it's usually more profitable for a freelancer to work consistently on one project than to work piecemeal on several smaller projects.

However, sometimes freelancers are tempted to lower their estimates out of fear. After adding up all the hours needed for a large project and multiplying this by their normal hourly rate, they think the fee looks too high and start slashing it to make it more acceptable to the client. Guard against this temptation. It's fine to reduce your hourly fee slightly when you anticipate efficiencies on a large-scale project, but don't sell yourself short just to get the job. Not only will you regret it after you've worked long hours on the project for an unreasonably low fee, but you'll fail to earn respect from clients if you don't ask for the compensation you are worth.

3. Consider Expenses

Who will be responsible for expenses incurred during the project? The answer varies from project to project; there are no hard and fast rules. Typically, contractors are responsible for covering their own normal expenses of doing business. (However, this is not always true. Attorneys, for example, commonly bill clients for copies and telephone calls.) Clients usually bear printing and production costs, as well as any costs that aren't typical to the contractor's business such as travel, international phone calls, or equipment rental fees.

In any case, you and the client should agree in advance who will cover which expenses. In addition, make sure to address whether there are any limits on reimbursable expenses or whether the client must approve expenses in advance. Also nail down how you will bill the client for expenses.

For example, travel expenses are quite often billed to clients. It's wise to make a specific breakdown of the expenses that will be covered, such as airfare, rental car, lodging, taxi, train, parking, and food.

Proposing reasonable limits on client expenses. Even if your client has deep pockets and seems willing to cover whatever expenses you incur, you should offer some limits on reimbursable expenses. This will help to head off any potential conflicts or unpleasant surprises over reimbursement bills. It also shows the client that you care about giving a good deal.

You can handle payments for expenses a number of different ways. A few possibilities are discussed below.

- Set an amount that the client will pay, regardless of the amount actually incurred. For instance, you and the client can agree that the client will pay $1,000 to cover all travel costs. If your actual costs are lower, the extra money will be yours; if higher, you'll eat the difference.
- Bill the client for actual expenses incurred. You can do this with or without a cap. For instance, you could agree that the client will reimburse you for all actual travel costs. Or, you could agree the client will reimburse you for actual travel costs up to $500.
- Set a per diem rate for certain expenses. "Per diem" simply means "per day." Food is typically billed at a set per diem rate—say, $35 or $50 per day.

EXAMPLE: Samantha is working on a bid for a translation project that will require her to travel to Brazil three times. Her client, Bahia Travel Company, says it will cover travel expenses and asks Samantha to draft a proposal specifying the terms. Samantha drafts the following terms regarding travel expenses that she will include in her proposal:

"Samantha will be responsible for all expenses involved in the project, except for travel-related expenses, which Samantha will bill to Bahia Travel Company monthly, as follows:

Airfare. Billed as actually accrued, including all taxes, not to exceed $1,500 per round-trip ticket. Tickets will be economy class.

Rental car. Billed as actually accrued, including insurance and taxes, not to exceed $50 per day.

Lodging. Billed as actually accrued, including all taxes, not to exceed $75 per night.

Food. Billed at $40 per day.

Taxi. Billed as actually accrued.

Parking. Billed as actually accrued."

4. Write Your Proposal

Once you've finalized the important details of the project, it's time to put together your proposal. Your goal is to present all important information clearly and to demonstrate you have a solid plan for getting the job done right. While proposals should always be professional and somewhat formal in tone, you should not be afraid to let your personality show. If you feel stiff, you won't usually have a better bid, just a more stilted one.

Most project proposals are two to three pages long, though there's no hard and fast rule here. You should use as much space as it takes to outline the project details with adequate—but not excruciating—detail. An outline for a project proposal might go something like this:

- **Project overview.** Describe the big picture, including relevant details about the client and an overview of the project.
- **Project objectives.** Include detailed information about the project, including all the different components of the project and how they fit together.
- **Proposed approach.** Describe how you would approach the project and how you would achieve the client's goals. Be specific, and don't assume that the client knows anything about how you do your work.
- **Specific responsibilities.** Outline what you understand your specific responsibilities would be.

- **Deliverables.** This is a term for the specific products that your work will yield. For instance, deliverables might include a 20-page written report, a set of tax documents, or a 100-page travel guide.
- **Timetable.** Scheduling is always an important part of project management, so you should always outline when you expect certain parts of the project will be completed.
- **Fee and payment terms.** In stating your fee, you don't have to explicitly state your hourly rate or how you arrived at your amount. Simply make it clear that your fee is based on your understanding of the project requirements as outlined in the rest of the proposal.
- **Expenses.** Outline whatever agreement you and the potential client have regarding who will cover which expenses.
- **Conclusion.** Wrap up the proposal. Strive for a professional tone that expresses your enthusiasm for the project. While some proposals serve as the project contract once the client has accepted them, you will usually say here that you expect to sign a separate formal contract.

C. Pricing for Businesses Selling Products

As with pricing services, there are different ways to figure out what to charge for the products that your business sells. Of course, your cost of acquiring or making the products will play a big part in your pricing decisions. But you may have difficulty deciding on an appropriate markup. This section will walk you through a few issues to consider when pricing goods.

Don't discuss your product pricing strategy with competitors. Antitrust laws forbid you to fix prices with your competitors and even to share price information or discuss prices with them. Steer clear of this potentially serious legal trouble.

1. Establish an Overall Pricing Strategy

Before deciding how much you'll charge for your widgets, you should think about and adopt an overall pricing strategy for your business. Keep in mind that the very same widget might be sold for 99¢ at your local 99¢ store, $5 at a chain retailer, and $25 at a swank boutique. The price can vary so much because each of these stores has its own pricing strategy—and you should, too.

The concept is simple: Will your business use a high-end, middle-end, or low-end strategy? Each strategy can be profitable if you work within its logic. Here's a quick description of how each strategy typically works.

- **High-end** shops can charge high prices so long as they offer something in return, such as a great selection of hard-to-find or highly specialized products, extraordinary customer service, an exclusive atmosphere, or simply top-notch quality.
- **Middle-end** shops charge average prices and succeed on the basis of other factors such as selection, customer service, and convenient hours and locations. None of these factors are exceptional enough to justify high-end prices, but they're attractive enough to draw customers who aren't necessarily looking for the very lowest price.
- **Low-end** shops succeed by forgoing some amenities such as a reliable selection or a convenient location. They attract customers by offering the lowest prices. Customers might have to paw through bins of merchandise or drive across town to a cold, cheerless warehouse store, but they'll do it because they know they'll get a bargain.

Whichever strategy you choose, it's important that you stick with it and use it consistently. You will confuse customers and push them to your competitors if you offer a confounding mix of high- and low-end items in the same store.

2. Research Markup Data

Once you've got your pricing strategy in place, you must decide how much you'll mark up your products for sale. You can set your prices appropriately after you do some research to figure out how much other similar businesses mark up their goods.

One easy source of markup information is simply the manufacturer's suggested retail price or MSRP, also called the suggested list price. If you buy a line of floor lamps that cost you $15 per unit and the MSRP is $45, then you know the manufacturer is recommending a markup of 200% of cost. You don't have to follow the recommendation (the days of adherence to MSRPs are over), but you'll get a good idea of what may be typical in the marketplace for that item.

In addition to using MSRPs, ask your manufacturers and suppliers for information they may have on average markup rates. Your suppliers can be a valuable source of this kind of information, beyond setting MSRPs for each product.

What's Up With Markup?

Markup is the amount that's tacked on to the cost of an item to arrive at its selling cost. For instance, a wristwatch that cost $25 to the re- tailer may be marked up by $37.50 for a selling price of $62.50. What can be confusing is that markup rates are sometimes expressed as a per- centage of cost, and other times as a percentage of selling price.

For example, the markup percentage for the wristwatch is 150% of cost or 60% of selling price. What does this mean? The percentage of cost calculation works like this: The cost of the watch ($25) is multiplied by 150%, resulting in a $37.50 markup, which is added to its original cost ($25) to arrive at the selling price of $62.50.

Here is the percentage of selling price calcu- lation: The selling price ($62.50) is multiplied by 60%, resulting in the same $37.50 markup ar- rived at with the percentage of cost calculation. As you can see, these two different ways of ex- pressing a markup percentage yield the same result.

When you search markup rates, be sure you know which type of percentage you're dealing with: percentage of cost or percentage of selling price. If you apply a percentage of selling price markup rate to the item cost, or use the percent- age of cost markup with the item's selling price, you'll end up with the wrong result. For in- stance, if you mistakenly calculate the wrist- watch markup by multiplying the item cost ($25) by the percentage of selling price markup rate (60%), you'll end up with a markup of $15, and a selling price of just $40.

You can find good information about industry standard markup rates in many sources. Trade as- sociations and journals may give you valuable data. Directories and guidebooks are available on many industries; these books tend to be expensive (easily $100 and up) but are often treasure troves of valuable industry info. Hoover's Inc. is a company that specializes in providing comprehen- sive market data—its website offers a wealth of information and publications for sale. Visit Hoover's Online at www.hoovers.com. Many of the titles offered at Hoover's are from Plunkett Research, another firm specializing in market data. Plunkett has its own website at www.plunkett research.com.

Don't stop there. Do your own research, and look specifically for info pertaining to your type of business. Search online, visit the library of a local business school, ask local trade associations, and generally do some sleuthing to turn up the data you need.

☑ Chapter 6 Checklist

☐ Never discuss the topic of pricing with competitors—basically, anyone in the same industry as you.

☐ If you're in a service business, set hourly rates carefully, either using a formula or basing the rates on market conditions. How- ever you set your rates, remember that you'll need not only to earn a salary but also to pay for your overhead and make a profit.

☐ If in a service business, you should also become familiar with various ways to bill clients and understand which methods are best for specific situations.

☐ If you will have to bid for work, learn how to put together a professional proposal.

☐ If you plan to sell products, develop an over- all pricing strategy to guide pricing decisions.

☐ And if you sell products, research the market to understand what typical markup rates are used by others in your industry.

■

Federal, State, and Local Start-Up Requirements

By now you've finished hammering out the details of how you plan to operate your business. In a perfect world, you could hang up your "open" sign and start selling your products or services at a nice profit. Sorry! In the real world of small business, things are not quite that easy. Before you can legally begin your business, you need to take care of a number of pesky requirements with government agencies from the city to the federal level. Although none of these requirements are difficult or even terribly time-consuming, lots of entrepreneurs get stymied at this point because it's so hard to find one centralized source of information that explains what to do. They're left to ferret out each bureaucratic requirement one by one and hope they've found all of them by the time they start doing business.

For example, your city tax office can tell you what forms you must file there but won't tell you how to obtain a permit in order to sell retail goods. And while your state sales tax agency may be able to tell you everything you need to know about getting a seller's permit, it won't explain how to obtain a federal employer identification number, which is required for most businesses. The process of finding out what you need to do and how to go about doing it can feel like putting together a jigsaw puzzle without knowing how many pieces it should have or how it should look when completed.

To help you figure out what you need to do and where you need to do it, all the basic start-up requirements are discussed here in one chapter. It guides you through the bureaucratic maze and explains the typical registration requirements that apply to most businesses. (Businesses with employees have to meet a few extra requirements, explained in Chapter 15.) There are far more specific regulations for specific small businesses, such as those relating to toxic waste disposal, than we could cover here—particularly at the state and city level. However, this chapter explains the basic regulatory structure that every businessperson will have to deal with and points out which agencies typically deal with certain types of requirements. By the time you finish reading this chapter, you'll know a number of registration requirements that you will have to meet, plus you'll have a good idea of where to check for other requirements that may apply to you, depending on what type of business you're starting and where you'll be conducting it.

Sure, dealing with city and state bureaucrats can be a mind-numbing endurance contest. But once the mystery is taken out of the registration process and you have a clear idea of which requirements may apply to you, you'll be able to tackle the bureaucracy with a minimum of time and stress.

Jennifer Mahoney, owner of an illustration service in Northern California:

I'm lucky enough to have a technical skill to combine with a regular drawing skill that puts me in a market niche among illustrators. Lacking any entrepreneurial "uncles," it took me a while to get a clue about the business world, like finding untapped markets, understanding agreements, getting paid, handling copyright issues, and finding out how many regulatory bodies need a portion of my modest income. It all felt like groping in the dark: Where are all the rules written down? I'm doing well for myself now, supporting my family, but I wish it hadn't taken me so long to figure out.

It may take more time to start a corporation, LLC, or limited partnership. Although starting up a company that offers limited liability—a corporation, LLC, or limited partnership—isn't rocket science, the process is more complex than starting a sole proprietorship or general partnership. While this chapter outlines the basic start-up requirements for businesses that offer limited liability, you will also need to understand some additional formalities and requirements. For example, if you plan to create one of these types of businesses, you may need to comply with federal and state securities laws. Section A, below, gives you a brief overview of the extra formation step (Step 1) you'll have to take to set up a business with limited liability. Once you have formed your corporation, LLC, or limited partnership, you'll be ready to use the information in this chapter on permits, licenses, and tax-filing requirements.

Here are the general start-up steps discussed in this chapter.

Step 1: File organizational documents with the Secretary of State or similar filing office (corporations, LLCs, and limited partnerships only).

Step 2: Obtain a federal employer identification number (FEIN).

Step 3: Register your fictitious business name with your county or state.

Step 4: Obtain a local tax registration certificate (also known as a business license).

Step 5: Obtain a permit to sell retail goods and collect state sales tax.

Step 6: Obtain specialized vocation-related licenses or environmental permits if necessary.

"Why Am I Filling Out All These Forms?"

Why do you have to sort your way through a tangled bureaucracy to start a small business? At the most basic level, there are three purposes to the various business permit and license requirements:

- **To identify you.** No matter what kind of business you run, society has an interest in making sure that you are accountable for your actions. That's why businesses that don't use their owners' names as part of their business names must often register a fictitious business name statement with the state or county. That way, a member of the public who has a problem with Racafrax Designs or Acme Sandblasting can easily find out who the owners are, complain to them, and, if necessary, sue them.

- **To protect the public.** Government agencies issue permits and licenses to ensure that your business offers safe products or services that won't harm people or the environment. For example, if you open a food service business, your city's department of health understandably wants to make sure that your kitchen is sanitary and will likely require that you obtain a permit, license, or other official approval before you can start serving snacks.

- **To keep track of your finances for tax purposes.** Several of the registration requirements are based on the government's nasty habit of taxing everything that moves (and lots of things that don't). To be sure that they collect every possible tax and fee, local, state, and federal governments use various registration requirements to keep tabs on your business.

A. Step 1: File Organizational Documents With Your State (Corporations, LLCs, and Limited Partnerships Only)

→ **Sole proprietors and partnerships can skip this step.** Only corporations, LLCs, and limited liability partnerships need to file organizational documents with the state. If you're starting a sole proprietorship or partnership, skip ahead to Step 2, discussed in Section B, below.

Unlike sole proprietorships or partnerships, businesses that offer limited liability don't just pop into existence as soon as their owners start selling products or services. If you want to create one of these types of businesses, you'll need to take the first step of filing registration papers with your state filing office, which typically is the Secretary or Department of State. (See Appendix A for contact information.) Since these business structures are regulated at the state level, each state has different rules for creating and managing them. For the most part, however, these laws are fairly similar. For corporations, the organizational document is usually called the Articles of Incorporation; for LLCs, it's generally called the Articles of Organization (although some states call it a Certificate of Organization or Formation). Limited partnerships also have to file registration documents with the state. To create any of these business structures, you'll need to do additional reading or consult other resources. (See "Additional resources from Nolo," below.)

When you file your organizational documents with your state, you will usually be registering your corporate, LLC, or limited partnership name at the same time. Typically, the agency in charge (most often the Secretary of State) must approve all names before they can be registered, otherwise your organizational papers will be rejected. Your name won't be approved if another business of the same legal structure (corporation, LLC, or limited partnership) in your state has already taken the business name you want to use. In other words, a California corporation may not use a name that's used by an existing California corporation, a New Mexico LLC may not use a name that is used by another New Mexico LLC, and so on. Some states check all of their name databases—LLC, corporate, and limited partnership—regardless of what form of business you're creating. To save time and headaches, do some research before you file your papers to make sure your proposed name is available. You can usually call or write to the state filing office to confirm availability. Quite a few states now also allow you to check for name availability online. Ask your state's filing office for its procedure.

💡 **Reserve your name.** Many states allow you to reserve a corporate, LLC, or limited partnership name once you've learned it's available. Doing so is a good idea, as it can't then be taken by someone else before you have a chance to file your papers.

It's also very important to remember that just because your name is accepted by your state filing office doesn't mean it's free and clear for you to use. As discussed in detail in Chapter 3, trademark and unfair competition laws may prevent you from using a name used by another business, including businesses that aren't included in your state's corporate, LLC, or limited partnership name databases. For instance, the name of a local general partnership wouldn't be registered in your state's corporate name database but may have been in use for years. Or the name you've chosen may have been taken by a corporation in another state, so it would not appear in your state's database. To avoid running afoul of trademark and unfair competition laws, it's wise to do a trademark search before choosing any name for your business, or for its products or services. (See Chapter 3 for a full discussion of the legal issues surrounding business names.)

Additional resources from Nolo. Nolo publishes a wide range of information on corporations, LLCs, and limited partnerships. *Nolo's Quick LLC: All You Need to Know About Limited Liability Companies* and *Form Your Own Limited Liability Company* (includes forms on disk), by Anthony Mancuso, offer guidance on creating an LLC and legal and tax information about this form of business. A software package, *LLC Maker,* and *Your Limited Liability Company: An Operating Manual,* also by Anthony Mancuso, offer detailed information on how to manage LLCs in compliance with various state and federal laws.

On the corporate side, *The Corporate Records Handbook: Meetings, Minutes & Resolutions,* by Anthony Mancuso, provides forms and instructions for running a corporation and handling corporate meetings and documentation. Nolo also publishes state-specific books for starting and running corporations in California, New York, and Texas.

For more information on limited partnerships, see *The Partnership Book: How to Write a Partnership Agreement,* by Ralph Warner and Denis Clifford.

B. Step 2: Obtain a Federal Employer Identification Number

Sole proprietors and partners don't need to explicitly "create" their business by registering with any state office; once they're engaged in business activity, their business more or less exists by default. (See Chapter 2 for more information about creating all types of businesses, including sole proprietorships and partnerships.) If you're starting a sole proprietorship or a partnership, getting a federal employer identification number (FEIN) from the Internal Revenue Service should be your first registration task, mainly because you can get one before you've registered with any other agency or filled out any other forms.

Corporations and LLCs must also apply for an FEIN, but they have to file their organizational documents with the state first. (See Step 1, above.)

1. What an FEIN Is and Who Needs One

A business's federal employer identification number (alternately called an FEIN, an EIN, or an employer ID) is roughly equivalent to a Social Security number for an individual. It's a number used by the government to identify your business, which you'll use over and over again on most of your important business documents. To mention just a few places you'll use it, you'll typically need to enter it on your business's local tax registration forms, your federal tax return, and any applications for business licenses.

Some of you are probably saying, "But I don't plan to have employees, why do I need an employer ID number?" Blame the IRS for the confusing terminology. Although it's called an "employer" ID number, FEINs are required for most businesses, even those that don't have employees. The one exception is sole proprietors with no employees, who can use their own Social Security number instead of an FEIN. Partnerships, LLCs, and corporations need FEINs whether they have employees or not.

2. Applying for an FEIN

Thanks to a mail-in and phone system, getting an FEIN is easy—and free. Simply fill out and submit IRS Form SS-4, according to the instructions just below. (This book contains two copies of Form SS-4: one in Appendix C, which you can tear out and use, and one on the CD-ROM, along with the IRS's instructions for completing the form.) If you submit the form by mail, you'll get your FEIN in about four weeks.

Better yet, by using the IRS's free Tele-TIN phone-in system, you can file by phone and get your number the same day. To do this, first fill out Form SS-4, then call the appropriate Tele-TIN number for your location (listed on the SS-4 form). You will relay your information to the IRS representative, who will then give you your FEIN over the phone. Enter the FEIN in the upper right corner of the SS-4, sign and date the form, and keep it for your records. In the past, you were asked to mail the form to the IRS within 24 hours of the phone call; this is no longer required.

A sample Form SS-4 appears below. Although most of the information you'll have to put on the form is pretty basic, the following tips will help you get the job done.

Line 1 asks for the legal name of the entity that is applying for the FEIN. Sounds simple enough, but, depending on your business, it can get a little tricky.

Sole proprietors should enter a full individual name—first, last, and middle initial. Do not enter any fictitious business name (FBN) you use or plan to use. (A fictitious business name is a name you use for your business that doesn't contain your legal name. FBNs are explained in more detail in the next section.)

A partnership should use the legal name of the partnership as it appears in the partnership agreement. For example, say Gene Cook and Beth Lynch own a partnership that they refer to as "Cook and Lynch, Partners" in their partnership agreement. This is the name they should write on Item 1. If you own a partnership but don't have a written partnership agreement, insert the name you plan to use for all official business and on all government forms—either a business name that contains each partner's last name or the trade name that you will present to the public (also known as your "fictitious business name" or your "DBA name," discussed below). (See Chapter 3 for the full spiel on the various types of business names.)

An LLC should enter the official company name as it appears in its Articles of Organization (or certificate of organization or formation).

A corporation should use its legal name as it appears in its Articles of Incorporation (or certificate of organization).

Line 2 asks for the trade name of the business. This is the same as asking for your fictitious business name or your "doing business as" (DBA) name. You can leave this line blank if you plan to do business under the same name you entered on line 1. For example, if Gene Cook and Beth Lynch plan to do business under the name Cook and Lynch, Partners, and they entered that name on line 1, they can leave line 2 blank. Similarly, if a sole proprietor named Stacey Stickler will use just her name to identify her landscape design services, she too can leave line 2 blank.

But when your company's legal name doesn't match its trade name, you should enter the trade name on line 2. For example, if Stacey Stickler decides to do business as Stickler's Landscape Design, she should enter "Stickler's Landscape Design" on line 2. A partnership that wants to do business under any name other than its legal name would do the same thing. For example, if "Cook and Lynch, Partners" want to do business under the trade name "CooLyn Enterprises," they will enter "Cook and Lynch, Partners" on line 1 and "CooLyn Enterprises" on line 2. (You'll find more on trade names and fictitious business names just below.)

While it may seem like splitting hairs, this is actually quite important. Think about it: The FEIN form introduces you and your business to the IRS and identifies you in an official way. Using the correct name will help you avoid snafus with the IRS and other government agencies. For example, if Cook and Lynch alternate between calling their business "Cook and Lynch" and "CooLyn Enterprises" on government documents, they will almost surely experience a raft of bureaucratic headaches.

Form **SS-4**

(Rev. December 2001)

Department of the Treasury
Internal Revenue Service

Application for Employer Identification Number

(For use by employers, corporations, partnerships, trusts, estates, churches, government agencies, Indian tribal entities, certain individuals, and others.)

► See separate instructions for each line.   ► Keep a copy for your records.

EIN

OMB No. 1545-0003

Type or print clearly.

1 Legal name of entity (or individual) for whom the EIN is being requested

2 Trade name of business (if different from name on line 1)

3 Executor, trustee, "care of" name

4a Mailing address (room, apt., suite no. and street, or P.O. box)

5a Street address (if different) (Do not enter a P.O. box.)

4b City, state, and ZIP code

5b City, state, and ZIP code

6 County and state where principal business is located

7a Name of principal officer, general partner, grantor, owner, or trustor

7b SSN, ITIN, or EIN

8a **Type of entity** (check only one box)

- [ ] Sole proprietor (SSN) _____
- [ ] Partnership
- [ ] Corporation (enter form number to be filed) ► _____
- [ ] Personal service corp.
- [ ] Church or church-controlled organization
- [ ] Other nonprofit organization (specify) ► _____
- [ ] Other (specify) ►

- [ ] Estate (SSN of decedent) _____
- [ ] Plan administrator (SSN) _____
- [ ] Trust (SSN of grantor) _____
- [ ] National Guard   [ ] State/local government
- [ ] Farmers' cooperative   [ ] Federal government/military
- [ ] REMIC   [ ] Indian tribal governments/enterprises
- Group Exemption Number (GEN) ► _____

8b If a corporation, name the state or foreign country (if applicable) where incorporated

State

Foreign country

9 **Reason for applying** (check only one box)

- [ ] Started new business (specify type) ► _____
- [ ] Hired employees (Check the box and see line 12.)
- [ ] Compliance with IRS withholding regulations
- [ ] Other (specify) ►

- [ ] Banking purpose (specify purpose) ► _____
- [ ] Changed type of organization (specify new type) ► _____
- [ ] Purchased going business
- [ ] Created a trust (specify type) ► _____
- [ ] Created a pension plan (specify type) ► _____

10 Date business started or acquired (month, day, year)

11 Closing month of accounting year

12 First date wages or annuities were paid or will be paid (month, day, year). **Note:** *If applicant is a withholding agent, enter date income will first be paid to nonresident alien. (month, day, year)* . . . . ►

13 Highest number of employees expected in the next 12 months. **Note:** *If the applicant does not expect to have any employees during the period, enter "-0-."* . . . . ►

Agricultural	Household	Other

14 Check **one** box that best describes the principal activity of your business.

- [ ] Construction
- [ ] Real estate
- [ ] Rental & leasing
- [ ] Manufacturing
- [ ] Transportation & warehousing
- [ ] Finance & insurance
- [ ] Health care & social assistance
- [ ] Accommodation & food service
- [ ] Other (specify)
- [ ] Wholesale–agent/broker
- [ ] Wholesale–other
- [ ] Retail

15 Indicate principal line of merchandise sold; specific construction work done; products produced; or services provided.

16a Has the applicant ever applied for an employer identification number for this or any other business? . . . . . [ ] **Yes**   [ ] **No**

Note: *If "Yes," please complete lines 16b and 16c.*

16b If you checked "Yes" on line 16a, give applicant's legal name and trade name shown on prior application if different from line 1 or 2 above.

Legal name ►   Trade name ►

16c Approximate date when, and city and state where, the application was filed. Enter previous employer identification number if known.

Approximate date when filed (mo., day, year) | City and state where filed | Previous EIN

Third Party Designee

Complete this section **only** if you want to authorize the named individual to receive the entity's EIN and answer questions about the completion of this form.

Designee's name

Designee's telephone number (include area code)
( )

Address and ZIP code

Designee's fax number (include area code)
( )

Under penalties of perjury, I declare that I have examined this application, and to the best of my knowledge and belief, it is true, correct, and complete.

Applicant's telephone number (include area code)
( )

Name and title (type or print clearly) ►

Applicant's fax number (include area code)
( )

Signature ►   Date ►

For Privacy Act and Paperwork Reduction Act Notice, see separate instructions.   Cat. No. 16055N   Form **SS-4** (Rev. 12-2001)

C. Step 3: Register Your Fictitious Business Name

As discussed in Chapter 3, any trade name that doesn't contain the legal names of the owners (for sole proprietorships or general partnerships) or that doesn't match the company's corporate, limited partnership, or LLC name on file with the state, is called a fictitious business name (FBN). Fictitious business names are sometimes called assumed names or "DBAs" for "doing business as"—as in, "Spikey Andrews, doing business as Coffee Corner," or "Alibi Corporation, doing business as Ferryville Bait and Tackle." Some states simply use the term "trade name," though this can be confusing because it doesn't indicate whether the name is the same as or different from the legal name. In this chapter and the rest of the book, the term fictitious business name will be used for any business name that doesn't contain the legal name of the business owner.

Most states require a business that uses a fictitious business name to register that name, usually with the county clerk in the county where its primary business site is located. Depending on your state, this requirement goes by different names: fictitious name certification, DBA filing, trade name registration, or something similar. FBN registrations are typically done at the county level, although, in some states, you register your FBN with the Secretary of State or other state agency. The registration process is covered in more detail below.

States like to keep track of business names for a couple of reasons: One is to prevent customer confusion between two local businesses that use the same name. (Before a business can register its fictitious business name, many states either search their business name registries or require that the business do so to make sure the name isn't already being used.) Another reason is to give customers a quick way to find out who the owner of a company is without having to hire a private investigator. This allows customers to easily contact the owners to make a complaint or to take legal action against them. Requiring owners to register their business names makes it harder for fly-by-night businesses to operate anonymously and defraud customers.

1. The Importance of Filing an FBN Statement

Do not neglect or put off registering your fictitious business name. Without proof of registration, many banks will not open an account under your business name. Also, if you don't register your name, it won't appear in any fictitious name databases in your state. This means that another business will be less likely to find out you're using it and may start using the name itself. Even though you have other legal avenues to stop another business from using a name that you used first (see Chapter 3), you don't want to create customer confusion between the two businesses and get into a name dispute with another business. If you lose a dispute over a name, at the very least you'll have to redo stationery, signs, and anything else that contains the name, such as T-shirts or maybe even your company logo.

2. Who Needs to Register

The rules for registering fictitious business names depend on which business structure you use.

Sole proprietorships. Generally speaking, a sole proprietor who includes his or her last name in the business name—such as O'Toole's Classic Cars—does not need to file an FBN statement. But it is not enough to include only initials and a nickname or part of a name. For example, a business called J.R.'s Classic Cars would likely have to file a fictitious name statement indicating that it really is John O'Toole's business.

In addition, in many states, if your business name falsely implies that more than one owner is involved, you must file a fictitious business name statement. If Jason Todd were a sole proprietor, for example, and named his business Jason Todd and Sons or Jason Todd & Associates, he would probably have to file an FBN statement, even though he included his last name in his business name. Check with your county clerk for your state's rules.

Partnerships. If a partnership includes the last names of all the partners—for example, Lawrence Anderson and Nancy Fawcett name their business "Anderson and Fawcett Metal Designs"—they don't have to file a statement. Otherwise, an FBN statement will be required. For example, if three partners, Lynch, Cook, and Briggs, did business only under the name "Lynch & Cook," they would have to file an FBN statement. Check with your county clerk for your state's specific rules.

Corporations, LLCs, and limited partnerships. A corporation, LLC, or limited partnership does not need to file an FBN statement unless it operates under a name that's different from its official name as stated in its Articles of Incorporation, Articles of Organization, or Certificate of Limited Partnership. For example, an LLC that registered with the Secretary of State under the name "Landmark Lanes, LLC" wouldn't have to file an FBN statement as long as it conducted business under that name. Any other trade name, "Landmark Bowl," for instance—or even "Landmark Lanes" without the "LLC" tacked onto the end—may be considered to be "fictitious" and would have to be registered. The same is often true for corporations: If "Inc." is included in the corporations's name in the Articles of Incorporation, but not in the company's trade name, an FBN statement usually must be filed. Check with your county clerk or Secretary of State or other state filing office to determine your state's specific rules.

3. Filing With Your County

In some states, FBN registration is accomplished through the Secretary of State or other state agency; however, in most states, you'll register your FBN at the county level. (This is generally true despite the fact that most laws governing fictitious business names are state laws.) The result is that each county in your state may have different forms and fees for registering an FBN. Your first step should be to call your county clerk's office to find out its requirements and fees. Many counties allow you to order the FBN registration form by phone; others require you to request it in writing with a self-addressed, stamped envelope. Unless you live a good distance from the nearest county clerk, it may be easiest just to go to the office and complete the form in person.

Unfortunately, most states do not provide much, if any, online information about FBN requirements, and very few states or counties offer an online filing system. (Florida is one exception.) With the rapid state of change in government websites, however, this may change in the very near future. So it's worth taking a look at your state's governmental websites to see if there are any FBN resources there. (The CD-ROM that comes with this book contains a file with links to state business-related websites. See Appendix B for information on how to use this file with your Web browser.) If you can't find any information online, you'll need to complete the process the old-fashioned way: by obtaining and filling out a paper form.

a. Searching the County (or State) Database

In many areas, you'll be instructed to search the county or state database of registered fictitious business names before submitting your statement to make sure no one else has already registered the name you want to use. Typically, you can search a county's database (often an easy-to-search computerized system) for free if you go to the office in person. Sometimes you can pay a fee for a staff person to do the search for you. If you want the clerk's office to do the search, you must usually submit the request and fee by mail.

⚠ County databases won't tell you if a name is trademarked. Oftentimes fictitious business names are registered at the county level, and you may be required to search your county database before registering your fictitious name to make sure it isn't already registered. Ironically, this requirement may well do more harm than good. The reason is that lots of people who find that no one in the county has registered a certain name are misled into believing that the name is available to use. The truth of the matter is that someone in a different county, state, or even country might own trademark rights to that name. Only owners of the tiniest of businesses can feel safe by doing merely a county-wide search of a name they want to use. If someone else has trademarked that name, you may well run into legal trouble, depending on your geographical scope and the products or services you sell. Particularly with the explosion of e-business, geographical distance is becoming irrelevant as the World Wide Web is making neighbors out of businesses on opposite sides of the globe.

To avoid being accused of unfair competition or trademark infringement, it is wise to check neighboring counties' FBN databases, look into state registries of corporate and LLC names, or even do a full international trademark search. Failing to do an appropriate search puts you at risk not only of lawsuits, but also of having to change your name down the line when you already have stationery, business signs, and invoices printed. (See Chapter 3 on trademark and business name issues for more information on choosing and researching a name that won't get you into legal trouble.)

b. Completing and Submitting an FBN Statement

If the name you've chosen is available (both at the county level and with regard to trademark issues), simply fill out the FBN statement and submit it to your county clerk (or other agency, depending on your state) along with the appropriate fees. You typically can submit the form in person or by mail.

Depending on the county, fees range from $10 to $50 for registering one business name and one business owner. Sometimes you may be charged an additional fee, around $5 to $15, to register additional business names to be used at the same business location or to register additional owners.

c. Publishing Notice of Your FBN Statement

Once you've filed your name and paid the necessary fees, you may have one more task to complete before you start doing business under that name. Many states require you to have your FBN statement published in an approved newspaper in the county where you filed it. The county clerk or state agency will provide a list of acceptable publications for posting your FBN statement, though usually any newspaper of general circulation in the county will suffice. Publishing your statement is dead simple: Just take a copy of your completed statement to your publication of choice, which will have a standard format to present the required information.

💡 Obscure publications are cheapest. As long as a newspaper is on the approved list or doesn't otherwise violate your county's rules (for instance, in some counties you can't publish an FBN statement in a free newspaper), there's nothing wrong with picking the cheapest one.

The published notice must run for a certain frequency and duration, usually once a week for a month or so. After the FBN has been published for the required period, you'll usually need to submit an affidavit (sometimes called Proof of Publication) with the county clerk or state agency to show that publication has been completed. Many newspapers that provide publication services will automatically send in the affidavit for you after your ad has completed its run. Make sure to find out whether the publication you use will do this (and double-check afterward to make sure it has actually done it). If not, you'll have to get the affidavit from the publication yourself and submit it to the county clerk or state agency within the prescribed deadline. If the affidavit isn't filed in time, you may have to start the process all over again.

Check with your county clerk for the details and requirements of publishing the FBN notice.

Save your ad receipt. For practical reasons, you may need to prove that you completed your fictitious business name filing requirements—including publication—before your ad has actually completed its publication run. Banks, for instance, want to see that you have met fictitious name rules before they allow you to open an account in that name. Fortunately, a receipt from the newspaper showing that you have paid for publication, along with a copy of the FBN statement certified by the county clerk or state agency, is generally sufficient to prove that you've met all the registration requirements, even though the ad hasn't yet run for four weeks. So be sure to get a certified copy of your FBN statement from the county clerk or state agency when you submit it, as well as a receipt from the newspaper when you pay for publishing it.

4. After You File

Your FBN registration will be good for a certain period of time, usually for five years or so, before it must be renewed. You (or someone at your business) should keep track of your expiration date, as your county clerk or state agency may not notify you when your renewal date approaches. Also, if certain facts in your statement change, such as the number of owners or your business address, you may have to renew your FBN statement. Check with your county clerk or state agency to find out which types of changes trigger a renewal requirement. If you no longer want your FBN registered, you may file a form (often called a Statement of Abandonment) to cause the registration to expire.

D. Step 4: Obtain a Local Tax Registration Certificate

Most cities require all businesses (including home businesses) to register with that city's tax collector, regardless of business type, structure, size, or name. Businesses located in rural, unincorporated areas must usually register with the county clerk rather than a city tax collector. (While this section often refers to city tax collectors and city requirements for businesses, just keep in mind that if you're operating outside of a city, the same types of requirements generally apply but are administered by county government.)

Depending on where you register, the locality may use different names for the process: tax registration, business tax application, business license application, or tax certification, for example. In this book, the terms "tax registration" and "tax registration certificate" are used—and it's best if you don't use the term "business license" when you really mean "tax registration certificate" (or whatever term is used in your locality for tax registration). True licenses, which are discussed in Section F, below, are typically administered at the state level. Certain businesses must obtain them if they engage in regulated activities, such as selling alcohol or cutting people's hair. Getting such a license often involves taking a test or otherwise proving you're qualified to do a certain activity.

Some businesses need more. Your tax registration certificate is not the same as a specialized license your business might need—such as a permit from the local health department for handling food, from the Federal Communications Commission for broadcasting over the radio waves, or from a regional air management district for emitting particles into the air. (Section F, below, discusses these specialized licenses and permits.) Whether or not you need one of these licenses or permits, you'll still need to get a tax registration certificate.

The reason you need to register with your local tax collector is that, just like the federal and state governments, your local government wants a cut of your business income. The tax registration requirement is basically your local government's way of keeping track of your business so that it will be able to collect any taxes it owes.

Cities and counties have been known to tax businesses with even more flair and creativity than the feds or the states. Localities tax businesses based on criteria such as net profit, gross income, number of employees, total payroll, number of vehicles, number of machines, and sometimes even seating capacity.

In addition, most cities categorize businesses and use different tax structures for each category. According to the structures recently in place in Charlottesville, Virginia, for instance, bakeries are charged a .2% (.002) tax on gross receipts, landscapers pay a rate of .36%, and architects and other professionals pay a rate of .58%. Other types of businesses in Charlottesville pay flat fees, such as wineries ($500 per year), coin machine operators ($150), and fortunetellers ($1,000).

In addition to being assigned a category and a tax rate, businesses may be subject to special taxes for particular activities. In Chicago, for instance, businesses that sell soft drink syrup or fountain soft drinks must pay an extra "Fountain Soft Drink" tax of 9% of the syrup price, and businesses that hold performance events must pay an extra "Amusement Tax" of 4% or 8% of the admission price, depending on the type and size of the event.

For the privilege of registering to pay local taxes, you'll usually have to pay an annual fee, which varies a lot from city to city. To register in Philadelphia, for instance, you'll need to pay a fee of $250, while Seattle charges only $90. Sometimes the annual fee depends partly on how much tax your business is expected to owe the following year, based on city (or county) tax rates. If the fee is based on estimated taxes, at least part of the registration fee may be a nonrefundable administrative fee. In that case, the other part of the fee will go toward paying your estimated taxes or will

be returned to you if your taxes turn out to be lower than expected. In Oakland, California, for instance, registering your business with the city costs $30, but you must also pay your estimated tax based on your business category and your estimated income for the next year. The estimated tax portion—but not the $30 fee—will be credited toward your tax bill for the next year.

Local rules can change without notice. Be sure to check with your local office for the most current rules and rates. The information here is relatively current, but these rules often change. The point is to give you a taste of the various ways local governments handle business taxes. As you can see, there's a lot of variation.

For your city's requirements, call your city tax collector. Look under "Tax Collector" in the city government section of your telephone book. The tax collector's office will be able to provide you with the forms necessary to register in your city, as well as any breakdown of business categories and tax tables. If you're doing business outside city limits, call your county clerk, usually listed under "County Clerk" in the county government section of the phone book.

E. Step 5: Obtain a State Seller's Permit

In most states, any business—whether it's a sole proprietorship, LLC, corporation, or any other type—must have a seller's permit if it sells any tangible goods to the public. Tangible goods are things you can touch, such as furniture or food. Businesses that sell only services are often exempt from the seller's permit requirement. In the five states that do not impose general sales taxes (Alaska, Delaware, Montana, New Hampshire, and Oregon), you may not be required to get a permit for most sales transactions. However, local governments such as cities and counties in those states may charge sales taxes (as in Alaska), and certain transactions in those states may be subject to something similar to a sales tax, though it may have a different name. If you live in one of the nontaxing states, be sure to check with the sales tax agency to find out if your specific transactions will be subject to tax and if you'll need a seller's permit. (Contact information for sales tax agencies by state is included in Appendix A.)

In states that do charge sales taxes, a seller's permit will allow your business to collect sales taxes from customers to cover any sales tax that you'll owe to the state. You'll typically pay any taxes you owe at year end, semiannually, or quarterly. Some may have to pay monthly. The general rule is that the higher your sales volume, the more often you'll owe your payment.

It's important to understand that if you plan to sell tangible goods, you'll often need a seller's permit whether or not those sales will be taxable. For instance, most states exempt certain sales from state sales tax, such as sales of food or sales to an out-of-state customer. But, in most states, you'll need a seller's permit even to conduct these types of nontaxable sales. This means you need to get a sales permit before you begin to sell tangible goods; when the sales are made, you'll distinguish the taxable ones from the nontaxable ones. When it comes time to report and pay sales taxes to the state, you'll owe tax only on the taxable sales. (See Chapter 9 for a detailed discussion of reporting and paying sales taxes.)

Keep track of your service and product sales separately. Many businesses both perform services and sell products. A metalsmith, for instance, both repairs jewelry and sells raw materials, such as precious metals and gemstones. If a business sells both labor and goods, it will need a seller's permit (assuming it's in a state that requires one). Plus, to assure proper tax reporting, that business will need to keep its labor sales separate from sales of goods, since sales of services aren't taxed in most locales. (Chapter 12 explains simple bookkeeping and how to account for taxable sales separately from tax-exempt sales.)

To obtain a seller's permit, contact the agency in your state that governs sales taxes. (Appendix A provides contact information for sales tax and seller's permit agencies by state.) The process of obtaining a seller's permit typically consists of submitting a simple application form and, sometimes, paying a fee. Some states require a deposit from businesses that have a blemished history of not paying their sales taxes on time.

F. Step 6: Obtain Specialized Licenses or Permits

Depending on the nature of your business, you might be finished with your list of bureaucratic tasks. But before you run off to rev up your cash register, cool your jets—you may be surprised to find out that even your simple little business is subject to an extra regulation or two. Some business activities are prohibited until you obtain a license or permit to engage in them, and some business locations require special approval from the local planning department. These extra requirements are especially likely to apply to your business if it has any potential for harming the environment or hurting the public, but they also apply in lots of seemingly risk-free situations.

Figuring out what additional permits or licenses you might need can be confusing, because there are literally hundreds of independent agencies from the local to the federal level that regulate various businesses. Obviously, you don't want to waste your time calling each and every one of them to find out whether your business is subject to its rules. This section will help streamline the process by first outlining the basics on what types of activities are generally regulated and by whom. This should help you figure out when your business is likely to face a special regulation. Then you'll find here a few resources that help to make sense of the crazy patchwork of local, state, and federal regulations that might apply to your business.

Regulations have different focuses. Very generally speaking, local regulations tend to focus on the location of your business and whether it poses a nuisance or a threat to public safety. State and federal regulations typically focus more on the type of work you do and your qualifications to do it.

1. Zoning and Local Permits

Local business regulations usually deal with the physical location of the business and the safety of the premises and equipment. City zoning laws regulate which activities are allowed in particular locations. For example, your zoning board might not approve your business location if it's in an area zoned exclusively for residential use, there isn't enough parking to support your business, or there are too many similar businesses nearby. Even if your business activities are acceptable for the time being, you might not be allowed to put up the sign you want or put in additional seating once your business takes off.

If your business doesn't comply with zoning laws, you'll either need to get a permit known as a conditional use permit or be granted an exception to the law, sometimes called a variance. Your city or county planning department is generally in charge of zoning laws. Contact them to find out whether your business complies with local rules and, if not, how to request a conditional use permit or a zoning variance. (Chapter 4 discusses zoning laws and picking a business location. Chapter 10 discusses zoning specifically for home businesses.)

Audrey Wackerley, owner of RetroFit, a vintage clothing store in San Francisco:

Getting the right permits turned into a total hassle for our clothing store. After we'd been in business for a year and a half, a cop walked in our store and said we needed a "second-hand" permit. We had never even heard of one! It's not like we hadn't really made an effort to get all the permits we needed. Before we opened we spent hours in all these different buildings downtown, waiting in endless lines (it's a lot like going to the DMV),

asking a million questions to find out what permits we needed to open our store. We had a business license, a seller's permit, a sign permit ... we thought we had everything we needed. But all of a sudden this cop said he'd shut us down if we didn't get the second-hand permit within five days. Five days! The permit cost $700, which was a real stretch for us right then. But what could we do? We had to scramble to get the money together and buy that stupid permit. The cop also let us know that we needed a separate jewelry permit in order to sell jewelry, but getting the second-hand permit was enough of an ordeal. We just decided to stop selling jewelry.

Assuming your business has met zoning requirements, it still might need to be approved by other city agencies, such as the fire or police departments, the building inspector, or the department of public health. To ensure compliance with local laws, such as health and fire codes, noise laws, and environmental regulations, you may need one or more permits from these agencies. When you register with your local tax collector, you may receive information on these agencies and which types of businesses need to contact them. Your county clerk might also be able to direct you to information about regulatory agencies in your area.

2. State and Federal Regulations

State regulations often focus on how you conduct your business. For instance, your state wants to make sure that your cosmetologists operating within its borders are competent and that carpenters there do safe work. Your state regulates these business activities through licensing. Businesses are more likely to need a state license or permit if they are highly specialized or if they affect the public welfare. In other words, if there's a risk that poor handling of your business activities might harm the public, chances are good that a state license is required. Common examples of state-licensed businesses are bars, auto shops, health care services, and waste management companies.

John Tilles, cofounder of Portland River Company, a river rafting outfit in Portland, Oregon:

I was impressed by Oregon's straightforward and simple process for starting a business. On the other hand, the absolute toughest and most frustrating aspect of our business is staying on top of the permit regulations in order to use state and federal land and rivers. This is a constantly changing scenario, and the politics involved are often nonsensical.

Don't assume that your business is so simple or straightforward that you don't need a special license. You'd be amazed at how many activities states regulate: to name a few, locksmiths may need a license from the Bureau of Security and Investigative Services; people who train guide dogs may need one from the State Board of Guide Dogs; and furniture makers may be subject to licensing from the Bureau of Home Furnishings. If you think some of these regulations sound far-fetched, take a look at a list of your state's regulatory agencies.

The federal government doesn't regulate small businesses as heavily as local and state offices, but you may need a federal permit or license to engage in certain activities, including:

- operating a common carrier for hire such as a trucking company (Interstate Commerce Commission)
- constructing or operating a radio or television station (Federal Communications Commission)
- manufacturing drugs or meat products (Food and Drug Administration)
- manufacturing alcohol or tobacco products, or making or selling firearms (Bureau of Alcohol, Tobacco and Firearms), and
- providing investment advice or counseling (Securities and Exchange Commission).

3. License and Permit Information Resources

Fortunately, many states have special agencies that act as clearinghouses for information on permits and issuing agencies, and several of them have very helpful websites. If you aren't sure what regulations might apply to your business, contact one or all of them to help figure out what you need to do to keep your business in full compliance. (Appendix A contains several listings of state agencies in charge of various license and permit requirements. State links to business-related websites are included on the accompanying CD-ROM. And Appendix B explains how to use these links with your Web browser.)

Keep in mind that while the Web is a potentially awesome resource for navigating the permit requirements in your area, many state and local governments are still lagging in posting this kind of practical information. Don't waste your precious time searching endlessly through a state website trying to find the information you need. If it's not readily available at the site, chances are it's either not there or is so hopelessly buried that it's not worth your time to ferret it out. In these situations, it may well be better to just get on the phone or even go to the state office in person.

☑ **Chapter 7 Checklist**

☐ File organizational documents with the Secretary of State or similar filing office (corporations, LLCs, and limited partnerships only).

☐ Obtain a federal employer identification number (FEIN).

☐ Register your fictitious business name with your county or state.

☐ Obtain a local tax registration certificate.

☐ Obtain a permit to sell retail goods and collect state sales tax.

☐ Obtain specialized vocation-related licenses or environmental permits, if necessary.

Risk Management

Chapter 2 explained the different business structures that exist and how they relate to liability issues. As discussed, creating a corporation or an LLC generally protects business owners from personal liability. If the corporation or LLC loses a lawsuit or otherwise finds itself in debt, only the business will be liable for the debt, not the owners. But in a partnership, each partner is 100% personally liable for all the business's debts and obligations. True, these debts should normally be shared among the partners, and one partner can sue the others to force them to pay up. But this not a very satisfying option if the other partners are broke or have disappeared.

Shielding owners (or employees, as discussed below) from personal liability is a totally different issue from shielding the business itself. In fact, when an individual owner or employee avoids personal liability, you can usually assume that the business will be stuck with it. The owners and employees might be happy they are not personally liable, but there's not much to cheer about when the business assets are wiped out to satisfy a judgment.

The bottom line is that a successful lawsuit against a business can be devastating, whether or not the owners are personally liable for the damages. No matter who ultimately faces liability, every business should consider where risks lurk and how to avoid them. In our litigious society, you must take liability issues seriously and take active steps to protect your business and yourself.

While the world of possible lawsuits is limited only by lawyers' imaginations, most claims arise from predictable—and often preventable—situations. If you analyze the true risks that face your business and employees, you can learn to recognize where your business is truly vulnerable and reduce the likelihood of ending up in court.

This chapter outlines the typical risks your business might face, and offers guidance on how to reduce them. It also discusses who and what may be at risk—including the owners, the staff, and the business itself. Then it offers risk management strategies and techniques to reduce your exposure to liability.

The encouraging news is that there are things you can do to protect yourself and your business. Hiring carefully, training thoroughly, having solid personnel policies in place, maintaining a safe working environment, and purchasing insurance are important risk management techniques that all businesses should use. It's crucial to do as much as you can *before* any legal issues arise.

Get advice on possible liability claims. Liability issues typically involve gray areas, so the only way to absolutely determine whether someone will be held responsible for a particular act is to find out in court—an expensive way to get an answer. Use the information in this chapter as a foundation for understanding what can go wrong, and do your best to reduce your risks, but consult an attorney if you fear possible legal trouble. And run, don't walk, to an attorney if you receive an official document such as a court order, a subpoena, or a written complaint that signals the start of a lawsuit. (See Chapter 16, Section A, for advice on finding and working with an attorney.)

A. Who Might Sue or Be Sued

Pretty much anyone you deal with in your business can sue you or the business, and vice versa. What you want to do is ward off claims by understanding your risks and taking steps to avoid problems. This section lists what could possibly go wrong for a business, divided according to which people are involved. You can read it as a checklist now, or come back later to make sure you've covered the most likely risks for your business.

The most likely kind of claim or lawsuit that could be brought by or against your business will be over a contract or agreement of some sort. That's because businesses routinely buy, rent, make, sell, or provide products or services—and all of those transactions involve contracts, whether written or oral. Most small businesses find their main problems are money-related, whether it's getting paid by reluctant customers or insurers or meeting their own financial obligations by paying their suppliers, landlord, or employees. Problems like these are called "contract" claims, because they stem from contractual agreements.

A less likely but extremely serious risk can also arise when someone in or around your business gets injured—financially or personally—by some act not related to a contract. For example, if one of your employees injures someone by being negligent, typically the business will be liable. A lot of your risk management efforts will be directed at preventing these kinds of claims—called "torts" in legalese—because they can be very costly to you and your business.

1. Co-Owners

If you are a co-owner of your business, you and the other co-owners have many obligations to each other. That's because mismanaging the business, whether on purpose or unintentionally, can damage the owners' investment and may expose all owners to liability.

Claims between and among owners can arise from one owner:

- lying—for instance, about cash flow or complaints
- self-dealing—working for personal interests instead of the business's
- stealing the business's money or taking business assets for personal use
- handing out profits incorrectly
- selling property for less than it's worth
- conspiring—for example, to defraud or push out one of the co-owners
- failing to live up to the business agreement—for instance, by not contributing the amount of time and money agreed
- mishandling company funds
- mistreating the employees
- making bad deals

- producing bad products or providing poor service
- defrauding lenders, customers, landlords, or suppliers
- failing to pay payroll and income taxes
- violating laws and regulations of various kinds: safety or securities regulations, local ordinances, employment laws, antitrust laws
- failing to properly hire, train, and supervise employees, or
- failing to observe formalities, such as recording corporate minutes or keeping personal money separate from business money.

There are many possible claims involving those who venture into business together. For example, even if you've done nothing wrong personally, a partner could sue you for your share of partnership debts, which may result in an expensive verdict or settlement. If your co-owner is your spouse and you get divorced, the business could get mired in the tussle over marital assets. Or if you and your co-owners decide to stop being in business together, you could sue each other over mismanagement, unfair competition, wrongfully expelling a partner, or other irregularities in splitting up.

2. Business Contacts

As mentioned above, business contracts are a common source of claims and problems. Lenders, suppliers, landlords, and customers could sue you—just as you could sue them—over contracts. For instance, your landlord could claim rent was in arrears or that you damaged the premises. Or you could sue your landlord for failing to make promised repairs or improvements. You could take over a lease or a contract and find that you are obligated for more than you agreed to take on. Customers could claim that your goods are shoddy and your return policy inadequate. Or you could have a supplier who gives you substandard goods.

Injuries outside of contractual agreements are the other main risk. Claims can be based on acts that were either intentionally bad or just unintentionally unfortunate. Customers could be accidentally injured on your premises or by your products. You or another partner could physically assault, harass, or make racially derogatory remarks about a supplier or customer. Your customers could claim that you were not careful enough in hiring, training, and supervising the employees—who subsequently hurt someone or something. You could have a claim if a business contact assaults your employee or steals your property. The people who hire your former employee could claim you gave a falsely positive recommendation. (Employees' claims against owners are a distinct category, discussed below in Section 3c.)

3. Employees

Many businesses simply can't operate without employees to help. But while these extra minds and bodies may be essential to the business, they can also be the targets and sources of liabilities and lawsuits.

a.   Owner's Claims Against Employees

A business owner may sometimes be compelled to sue an employee. Theft and property damages are common impetuses—although it may not be cost-effective to take a pilfering employee to court for small reimbursements or money owed for small repairs.

In almost every case, someone who is injured by your employee will choose to sue you—not the employee. An injured person nearly always looks for a way to sue the employer, who usually has assets, including insurance. An employer who has to pay an injured person for harm caused by an employee could theoretically sue the employee for reimbursement, but it's not worth the trouble if the employee has no money.

A rare but important problem is that employees sometimes steal customer lists or a secret process or invention, then go into business in competition with their former bosses. An employee with a head full of business information and years of experience in the field can be a formidable competitor, even without stealing trade secrets or a customer list.

For more information on restricting business information. State laws vary considerably on how much and how long you can effectively restrict a former employee or associate from going into competition with you. For guidance, see, *How to Create a Noncompete Agreement,* by Shannon Miehe, and *Nondisclosure Agreements: Protect Your Trade Secrets & More,* by Richard Stim and Stephen Fishman (both published by Nolo).

Risks Facing Employees

Employees may have to pay an injured person for damages for injuries they cause at work by:

- failing to act reasonably and carefully—for example, working without enough sleep when they need to stay alert
- acting with reckless disregard for the safety or interests of others—for example, removing safety equipment from a machine or ignoring warnings, or
- hurting someone deliberately or breaking the law.

If the person injured is a coworker, the legal relief is usually limited to workers' compensation benefits.

---

b.   Owner's Responsibility for Claims Against Employees

A business owner's responsibility for harm done by an employee is an area of potentially very serious liability. There are two different ways an employer may be held responsible for the harmful acts of an employee: when the employer is at fault in some way, and when the employer isn't at fault at all. This is surprising, but unfortunately true.

In general, an employer is liable for everything an employee does "within the course and scope of employment," because the employee acts as the employer's agent. This means that for legal purposes, it is as if the employer directed an employee's every move, simply by authorizing the employee to act. For instance, the U.S. Supreme Court recently held that a real estate corporation was "vicariously liable" for its salesman's illegal discrimination when he refused to accept a biracial couple's offer to buy a house. (*Meyer v. Holley*, 537 U.S. 280 (2003).) The ruling expressly held that the corporation's sole owner was not personally liable. This effectively protected the corporation owner's other assets by limiting liability to the corporation itself—exactly why some business owners choose to incorporate.

An employer obviously should be held responsible when the employer tells the employee to do something and the employer knows that act will probably cause harm. An employer who knows or should know that the employee is harming someone or something will also be held culpable.

In addition, an employer is often legally responsible for an employee's acts—even when the employer did not direct the employee to do the act that caused the trouble and didn't know that the employee was doing it—if the employer *should have* done something to prevent the situation from arising. For example, an employer may be liable for carelessness in hiring, training, or supervising an employee who causes some harm on the job. This can be true even when the harm happens after work hours or away from the work premises, as long as there is some connection to the job.

For more in-depth information on employers' potential liabilities. See *The Employer's Legal Handbook*, by Fred S. Steingold, and *Everyday Employment Law: The Basics*, by Lisa Guerin and Amy DelPo (both published by Nolo).

Liability for Independent Contractors

An independent contractor is someone who works for you but is not a regular employee. (For a discussion of the differences between an independent contractor and an employee, see Chapter 15, Section A.)

Employer liability for an independent contractor's acts is a complex area. Because a typical independent contractor works offsite, using his or her own equipment, without direct supervision, a business owner usually has little control over how the work is done. Nonetheless, the employer may still be liable to anyone who is hurt by the finished product that the independent contractor produces—for instance, if the employer uses the product at the business site or sells it to the public.

Fortunately, independent contractors often have insurance, so an employer who is sued can in turn sue the independent contractor for mistakes. For more information, see *Hiring Independent Contractors: The Employer's Legal Guide*, by Stephen Fishman, and *The Employer's Legal Handbook*, by Fred S. Steingold (both published by Nolo).

c. Claims by Employees Against Owners

Employment-related claims may pose a major liability risk to businesses with employees. Lawsuits alleging wrongful termination, sexual harassment, or other types of illegal discrimination are a serious risk to all businesses—and possibly to individual owners, managers, and employees. Here's an extremely brief and simplified outline of the types of workplace-related suits commonly faced by businesses.

For more information on employee lawsuits.
See *The Employer's Legal Handbook,* by Fred S. Steingold; *Dealing With Problem Employees: A Legal Guide,* by Amy DelPo and Lisa Guerin; *Everyday Employment Law: The Basics,* by Lisa Guerin and Amy DelPo; and *Federal Employment Laws: A Desk Reference,* by Lisa Guerin and Amy DelPo (all published by Nolo). You can also get lots of free information online from Nolo's website at www.nolo.com under the heading Business & Human Resources.

1. Wrongful termination

In every state but Montana, every employee without a written employment contract has a job only as long as both the employer and the employee agree to continue the employment. An employee can quit at any time, for any reason or no reason, and the employer can fire the employee any time, for any or no reason. This is a legal doctrine called "employment at will."

There are major qualifications to that general rule, however, that may open an employer to a lawsuit for firing a worker. For instance, an employer can't fire someone for an illegal reason, such as wrongful discrimination (discussed below), in retaliation for union organizing, or whistle-blowing—reporting the employer's wrongdoing to a government agency. In these cases, the employees could sue their former employers for wrongful termination.

And employees who have written contracts setting out conditions of termination—an increasingly rare breed—can sue a business on a claim that the company did not have "good cause" to terminate the employment. This is a "breach of contract" claim. Most businesses avoid these claims by making it clear in writing that all their employees are at-will.

For more on potential liability for firing workers. See *Everyday Employment Law: The Basics,* by Lisa Guerin and Amy DelPo (Nolo).

2. Defamation

A business that gives out false and damaging information about a former employee may be sued for harming that individual's reputation—also called defamation.

Defamation may rear its head to business owners and managers who are asked to give references for former employees. In most states, there is a legal defense called a "privilege" that protects people who give job references in good faith or when negative information is true. However, if sued for defaming a former employee, it would still cost time and money to prove that defense in court and win the case.

Another problem is that, while you may believe something to be true, it is always possible to argue about the truth of subjective evaluations and personal experiences. To combat this, some managers refuse to comment at all about any former employee, except to confirm that the employee worked for the business and when. While this may be a wise policy for problem former employees, it also limits the opportunity to pass along good information about good workers. It's best to use discretion.

Another time for business owners and managers to beware of the possibility of defaming a worker is during the firing process, when emotions often run high. It's always wise to keep termination discussions brief—and tied to specifics about an individual's work performance.

3. Sexual harassment

Sexual harassment is any unwelcome sexual conduct on the job that creates an intimidating, hostile, or offensive work environment—and by now you're surely aware that it can expose a business to liability. Some courts categorize harassing behavior as either "quid pro quo" or "hostile environment." In quid pro quo harassment—literally, "do this for that"—a worker is confronted with demands for sexual favors to keep a job or get a promotion. Hostile environment harassment is found when sexual jokes, pictures, innuendoes, or comments are allowed to persist in the workplace.

A business can help avoid these types of claims by putting a strong sexual harassment policy in place and strictly enforcing it—along with offering periodic training for all employees on how to recognize and report sexual harassment on the job.

For in-depth information on liability for sexual harassment. See *Sexual Harassment on the Job: What It Is & How to Stop It,* by William Petrocelli and Barbara Kate Repa (Nolo).

4. Illegal discrimination

Federal law prohibits discrimination in employment based on race, skin color, gender, religious beliefs, national origin, disability, or age. And state and local ordinances sometimes protect additional characteristics, such as marital status, obesity, or sexual orientation. That makes it illegal to use any of these factors in decisions about hiring, promoting, making job assignments, firing, or paying workers. It is even a bad idea to ask questions about those parts of an applicant's background before the business gives the offer to hire. Most businesses use clear job descriptions, review standards, and termination guidelines to avoid claims of discrimination. And, of course, epithets or hostility on the job based on these protected characteristics should not be tolerated.

But discrimination law can get more complicated, making it necessary to pay attention to reality rather than blindly enforce workplace policies. An apparently neutral job requirement may disproportionately harm members of a protected group. For instance, in several states, black male employees have successfully challenged grooming codes requiring all workers to be clean-shaven, based on medical evidence that black men are disproportionately likely to suffer from a skin disorder giving them painful ingrown hairs after shaving.

A growing number of discrimination complaints these days are filed by employees who have disabilities. A federal law, the Americans With Disabilities Act, requires an employer to make "reasonable accommodations" for an employee who has a disability but is otherwise able to do the job—as long as the employee requests an accommodation and the business can provide it without suffering hardship. The accommodation may be buying a special chair, computer, or other equipment, or installing a safety bar in the restroom. It may be allowing the employee to reduce work hours to undergo chemotherapy, or reassigning an employee to a job that requires less lifting or standing.

How far the employer must go to accommodate the employee varies on the facts of each situation. The employer need not always provide the most expensive accommodation or the one the employee requests first or most stridently. At a minimum, the employer and the employee should discuss and negotiate what accommodations are possible and reasonable.

The Americans With Disabilities Act also requires many businesses and buildings to be made accessible to people with disabilities. Not complying with that law is another form of illegal discrimination.

Another growing area of discrimination claims arises from bringing religion into the workplace. Employees may complain that they are being harassed by evangelical coworkers of a different religion or upset by required prayers at business meetings. But if the business forbids all religious practice, employees may claim that they have a right to practice their religion at work, including praying and proselytizing. Employers often handle this by restricting religious and personal postings to a designated bulletin board and prayer groups to nonwork times. However, a business should generally accommodate employees' religious practices, including religious garb and religious holidays.

For more on illegal discrimination in the workplace. See *Federal Employment Laws: A Desk Reference,* by Lisa Guerin and Amy DelPo (Nolo).

5. Privacy

The flip side of bringing an employee's personal beliefs into the workplace is that many employees do not want an employer to know about their lives outside the office. Be sure to check the laws in your state before you start monitoring employees' off-duty pursuits or drug use. A manager who inquires about whether an employee went to church on Sunday may be both invading privacy and appearing to discriminate based on religious beliefs.

In some states, a business may legitimately require a drug test prior to offering a job. The employer may also require drug testing on the job if there are specific and significant reasons why drug testing is necessary, such as when employees handle dangerous machinery or drive on the job. However, many potential legal hazards can be addressed simply by having a rule that forbids being "under the influence" of any substance at work. An employee can be held responsible for truly dangerous or inappropriate behavior without requiring an invasive or humiliating test. Keep in mind that some prescription and over-the-counter drugs also may temporarily affect an employee's mood or concentration.

For more on drug testing and privacy issues in the workplace. See *Everyday Employment Law: The Basics,* by Lisa Guerin and Amy DelPo (Nolo).

6. Personal injuries

An employee who is injured on the job cannot usually sue the employer or another employee for damages, because state workers' compensation laws provide insurance benefits to cover those injuries. State or private disability insurance may also help compensate an injured employee, although only a handful of states have disability insurance programs.

For more information on workers' compensation laws and disability insurance. See *The Employer's Legal Handbook,* by Fred S. Steingold (Nolo).

4. Outsiders

People you never expect to come into contact with your product or service could be injured by it. In some states, even trespassers who get injured on your property can sue you. And you or your employee might get into an auto accident in a company car, or on company business, and sue or be sued. You might also commit a crime that, as a side effect, harms someone.

B. Risk Management Strategies

"Risk management" refers to actively addressing, managing, and reducing risks for any business. It is a rapidly growing field, partly because of the widespread and realistic fear of lawsuits. Your first goal is not to win a lawsuit, but to avoid a claim altogether. Your second goal is to resolve any claim as quickly and cheaply as appropriate, without a lawsuit. Only as a last resort should you venture to court, because that is usually very expensive and the outcome is always a gamble.

Insurance is part of a risk management program, but beware that it does not in itself constitute risk management. Sometimes the protection of insurance is adequate, but in some cases insurance may be either too expensive or simply unavailable for particular activities. (See Section C, below, for more specifics on insurance.)

Here's one example of risk management: Many commercial and industrial sites have residual contamination from solvents, metals, and chemicals. If you buy the property, you may legally have to pay for environmental cleanup, even though the mess wasn't your fault. So, before you purchase, you should consider some ways to manage your risk.

Here are some possibilities.

- You could evaluate the likelihood and extent of contamination with scientific sampling by an engineering firm that also provides an estimate of the probable cost of cleanup. Then you would weigh whether the purchase is worth the additional costs.

- You could try to get protection through contracts—for instance, you could try to purchase insurance directly, or to negotiate a reimbursement agreement or an agreement to purchase environmental insurance from the seller.

- You could ask the relevant government agencies for a "comfort letter," in which they promise—or at least come close to promising—that their lawyers will not go after innocent landowners. Your bank may require this letter as a condition of a loan.

- You could look into a federal "brownfields" program, which gives you certain immunities from future surprise liability if you clean up urban industrial land.

As you can see, many options are available to manage that one potentially expensive risk.

1. Find Out What Can Go Wrong

A good place to start your risk management program is to outline what you are trying to protect. Most businesses will have a similar list: its people, its physical and financial assets, and its reputation. Keeping these items in mind, you can move ahead to anticipating potential threats to them.

In addition to general risks, find out what can go wrong in your field. Talking with an insurance agent who is familiar with your type of business is one of the best ways to assess the possible risks

you face. Talking with people who own or work in similar businesses is also useful, especially outside your local area; if they don't compete with you, it's more likely you can trust what they tell you. Reading trade magazines and the newspapers will keep you abreast of the kinds of lawsuits being brought. And, finally, ask your employees what risks they see and what problems are waiting to happen. They may be one of your best sources for ideas to prevent problems.

Liability Lurks All Around You

There is a sea of laws and regulations controlling safety, land use, business, employment, and other matters that business owners must abide by—and ignorance of them is no excuse. You never know when you will be hauled up short for parking too many cars on the street, having an unsafe workplace, or causing an environmental disaster. You should have a pretty good idea, though, of the kinds of laws that apply to you, especially if you are in a heavily regulated industry such as manufacturing, food preparation, or professional services. There can be harsh penalties (including prison time) if, for example, you fail to report a workplace death to the appropriate agency.

Finally, it should be no surprise that you can also get in trouble by breaking various criminal laws. Businesses traditionally have special problems with failing to pay taxes; with property crimes such as theft, fraud, and arson; and with antitrust laws that prohibit forming monopolies.

---

2. Focus on Prevention

Once you've identified the main ways that your business is vulnerable, you should brainstorm ways to protect against these risks.

a.   Setting a Solid Foundation

Most obviously, you should choose your partners, lenders, landlords, business sites, vendors, agents, and employees carefully. In particular, investigate in depth any deal that seems too good to be true—including the sales pitches of people who encourage you to set up in a franchise or buy expensive equipment.

Next, if you will be a joint owner of the business, get a clear understanding with your co-owners about all aspects of your business: what you want to accomplish, what you expect from one another, and how or when you might split up or buy out. Agreements known as buy-sell agreements outline how the business will handle transfers of ownership. (Buy-sell agreements are discussed in Chapter 14.) Money is usually the first big issue; control is next. You would be wise to have your business formation agreement in writing, whether it's a simple one-page partnership agreement or a detailed Operating Agreement for an LLC. If possible, co-owners should agree to mediate disputes. Mediation is generally quicker, simpler, and cheaper than a lawsuit, which is why the business community has adopted it enthusiastically.

It goes without saying that you should operate your business on the up-and-up. That includes:

- filing all the required papers and getting the right permits
- telling the truth on all documents and to everyone with whom you deal
- keeping track of company funds, inventory, and important documents
- paying your debts
- delivering what you promise
- observing business formalities, such as keeping your personal money separate from business accounts
- maintaining safety standards, and
- complying with all applicable laws, especially by paying your income and payroll taxes quarterly.

Owners must make sure their businesses comply with bureaucratic requirements. Applying for permits and licenses, filing reports, paying taxes, and so on are necessary evils for all businesses, and failing to do so may, in some cases, expose the owners to personal liability. (The preliminary bureaucratic hurdles are covered in detail in Chapter 7.) Even if a manager or another employee is in charge of filling out and filing the paperwork, ultimately it's your responsibility as an owner to make sure your business is in compliance. Check in regularly to make sure that paperwork is getting done.

Risk management can affect your decisions about what your business actually does. You may need to change or eliminate certain activities that are uninsurable or too risky. What is too risky may depend on the law and the availability of insurance in your state—especially for construction, manufacturing, and professional services.

b.   Covering Employee Issues

Employees make businesses vulnerable. Every business owner who hires employees should be very concerned about workplace-related liability issues and take steps to decrease the risks from possible claims and lawsuits. Lay the groundwork to hire carefully, train thoroughly, supervise adequately, have solid personnel policies in place, and maintain a safe working environment.

If you are unsure what your employment policies should be and what laws you must follow, check the Small Business Compliance section of the U.S. Department of Labor website (www.dol .gov) and your own state's department of labor. (To contact your state's labor agency, see Appendix A under "State Unemployment Compensation Agencies.") You can also consult a personnel specialist or HR manager, or review other employers' personnel manuals to see what's covered. Websites such as The Human Resources Learning Center (www.human-resources.org) and Nolo (www.nolo.com) also provide good free information.

For in-depth information on employment matters. See *The Employer's Legal Handbook,* by Fred S. Steingold; *Dealing With Problem Employees: A Legal Guide,* by Amy DelPo and Lisa Guerin; *Everyday Employment Law: The Basics,* by Lisa Guerin and Amy DelPo; *Create Your Own Employee Handbook: A Legal and Practical Guide,* by Lisa Guerin and Amy DelPo; and *Federal Employment Laws: A Desk Reference,* by Lisa Guerin and Amy DelPo (all published by Nolo).

With many workplace issues, the most effective risk management technique is to implement effective policies and training programs. For instance, straightforward hiring and firing policies, including a written policy that employment is "at will," help protect you against claims of discrimination and wrongful termination. A solid orientation and annual training program for employees on sexual harassment and discrimination issues will significantly reduce your liability exposure in those areas. Every business with employees should have written, posted policies to clarify what behavior is expected and what will not be tolerated.

Similarly, workplace safety issues can be addressed through training programs and posted materials. You can ask consultants who know your type of business to evaluate your workplace for compliance with the Occupational Safety and Health Administration (OSHA)—the agency that establishes and oversees workplace safety standards. Workplace safety will be an ongoing consideration and expense.

Beyond establishing and communicating personnel and other policies, your business needs to have enforcement mechanisms in place. The toughest written sexual harassment or safety policy won't protect a business from a major lawsuit if there's no one to complain to who has power to change the situation, or if complaints go uninvestigated and policies unenforced.

An "open door" policy and a safe channel to launch complaints are very helpful. Employees who understand that their employer is taking care of their concerns are less likely to become frustrated and sue.

In many states, you can ask the employee to agree to refer serious issues to a mediator and then, if they can't be resolved within a reasonable time, to an arbitrator. A mediator is someone who helps people come to an agreement, while an arbitrator makes a binding decision. Some states automatically refer civil lawsuits to a mediator to see if the parties can settle before a judge will hear the case. Many employers have such an agreement in their personnel manuals, which every new employee reads and signs.

It helps morale if the employer pays the costs of mediation and arbitration. After all, the employee probably has very little spare money, and a one-day mediation can commonly cost anywhere from $500 to $3,000. Some community mediation groups will take on small business claims for free or a nominal cost.

A lawsuit may still be possible. Agreements between employers and employees that make arbitration the employee's exclusive remedy are not always binding. Judges do not like to see employees give up their rights to complain to government agencies or to bring lawsuits, especially if the employee has to agree to arbitrate future disputes as a nonnegotiable condition of employment, such as in a written employment contract. The law in this area is changing rapidly, so you should find out what is legal in your own state. For a good short discussion of mandatory arbitration, see *The Employer's Legal Handbook,* by Fred S. Steingold (Nolo).

3. Deal With Problems

When a problem does arise, stay as calm as possible while you get as much information as you need to decide what to do. You won't do yourself or your business any good with an unconsidered response.

If a problem comes up in an area that is addressed in a written contract, a calm meeting or phone call is a good idea, followed up by a letter summarizing the meeting or conversation. Any meeting with a problem employee should be witnessed by at least one person who is neutral. If you are out of your depth, contact an expert such as an accountant, a lawyer, a doctor, an employment law specialist, or a mediator. Keep employment matters confidential.

For in-depth information on many business problems. See *Legal Guide for Starting & Running a Small Business* and *The Employer's Legal Handbook*, by Fred S. Steingold; *Dealing With Problem Employees: A Legal Guide*, by Amy DelPo and Lisa Guerin; and *Tax Savvy for Small Business*, by Frederick W. Daily (all published by Nolo). There are also numerous articles on lawsuits and personal injuries at Nolo's website at www.nolo.com.

Finally, realize that you might end up paying something to settle a claim or to defend yourself, whether or not you feel responsible for what went wrong. As discussed in Chapter 2, owners of sole proprietorships and partnerships are personally liable for all business debts, including damages stemming from a lawsuit against the business. It doesn't matter much whether these owners are personally named or found liable in a lawsuit, or whether only the business itself is—either way, they'll be personally responsible for paying the damages. This fundamental rule regarding sole proprietorships and partnerships is a major reason why many business owners choose to create an LLC or corporation.

If your small business is an LLC or a corporation (or if you are a limited partner in the business), then you, and owners like you, will ordinarily not be personally responsible for any damage awards against the business. Only business assets can be used to satisfy those debts. Of course, that could wipe out your business.

Personal guarantees may bind you. As a practical matter, most suppliers and banks require a personal guarantee from small business owners on contracts and loans. This means that there will be personal, individual liability on claims arising from those contracts. Similarly, business owners will personally sign the document that creates their businesses, so the co-owners can sue one another personally on claims that arise out of starting, running, or winding up the business.

All business owners—even owners of corporations and LLCs—may face personal liability in certain situations. Those who recklessly or intentionally cause harm may be found personally liable for injuries caused by their actions. The same is true for business owners who don't carefully investigate a deal before making a business decision.

Paying for What Goes Wrong

If you have been prudent, and if the business is reasonably successful, there will be some extra money in the bank for emergencies. There may be business assets, such as machinery or a building or inventory, that you can sell or pledge to raise money—subject, of course, to agreement by your co-owners. You may also have some insurance that applies. An insurance company has to pay for an attorney to defend you against a claim your policy covers. It will likely also pay some, maybe most, of any eventual settlement or judgment against you if the claim is covered by your policy. (Insurance is discussed in more detail below.)

C. Insurance and Warranties

Insurance coverage is a powerful tool in risk management. However, there's no requirement that you obtain property or liability insurance for your business, unless:

- your state requires liability insurance for a company vehicle
- state and federal law requires it because you have employees, or

• your lender requires it as a condition for getting a loan.

But just because you don't have to get insurance doesn't mean you shouldn't. Even if you form a corporation or an LLC, which shields your personal assets from business liabilities (see Chapter 2), it won't protect you from losing your business if disaster strikes. Careful as you may be, fate sometimes deals an unforeseen blow. If you face unexpected trouble, you'll be thankful you've taken steps to protect yourself.

Employers are subject to special insurance requirements. Employers must typically pay for workers' compensation insurance and unemployment insurance. A handful of states also require employers to pay into a state disability insurance fund. All of these insurance programs are specifically set up for employers and are largely regulated by state agencies. (See Chapter 15 for some of the special rules governing employers' and employees' contributions to these insurance programs.)

There is an art to insuring your business: You want to get the maximum protection from insurance without blowing your whole bankroll on policies for every conceivable risk. Once you start to look, you'll find every imaginable type of insurance policy out there, although your business will probably need only a few of them at most. The two most common and generally useful types of policies are property insurance and liability insurance. This section will explain the basics of these and introduce you to many other kinds of policies that cover specific risks involved in your business. It will also shine some light on the process of shopping for and buying the policies you need.

Caring for your policy. Treat your insurance policy just as the precious, and possibly irreplaceable, document that it is. Store it carefully. Keep an old policy even after you change insurance providers. A claim could come up that arises from a long-ago event, and that document may be your only way to track down an insurer that you had in the past. Believe it or not, if the insurance company or its successor is still in business and you have a copy of the old policy to prove it covered that event, the insurance company should provide the protection you paid for at the time.

1. Property Insurance

This chapter concentrates mostly on liability issues, but other types of losses can also be devastating to a business. Property insurance can cover your business for damages or loss to your business property due to theft, fire, or other causes. There is a good deal of variation among policies on what property and what risks are covered and what the coverage is. Be sure you're absolutely clear on these terms when you choose a policy.

You'll want to make sure that your property insurance covers the premises themselves as well as the business's assets that are kept there, including:

• fixtures to the property, such as lighting systems or carpeting
• equipment and machinery
• office furniture
• computers, telephones, and other office machines, and
• inventory and supplies.

Most basic property insurance policies will cover these items.

If you rent your business space. Your lease may require you to get a specific amount or type of property coverage. Be sure to check your lease for any insurance requirements before you purchase a policy.

If you purchased your business property. You almost certainly paid for title insurance, which protects you from challenges to your ownership of the property. You may also want to purchase a life insurance policy that is dedicated to paying the mortgage if anything happens to you. You usually get the best deal if you buy this on your own, not from your mortgage lender or broker.

You'll need to understand not only which property is covered by your policy but what types of losses will be covered. Read it carefully to determine what causes of damage are insurable. Most general business property insurance policies will provide *basic, broad,* or *special* coverage—with special offering the broadest coverage and basic the narrowest.

A basic form policy will normally cover fire, explosions, storms, smoke, riots, vandalism, and sprinkler leaks. A broad form policy typically covers damage from broken windows and other structural glass, falling objects, and water damage. With both basic and broad form policies, certain risks may be listed as excluded—that is, not covered. Note that theft isn't typically covered under either a basic or broad form policy, a fact that surprises many business owners. (See Section 3e, below.)

Special form coverage offers the widest range of protection, as it typically covers all risks—including theft—except for those risks that are specifically excluded. While premiums for special form policies are more expensive, it may be worth the added expense if your business faces unusual risks—or simply to make sure you're covered against theft.

A basic policy may not cover the other property that you have at your business premises—for instance, if you rent a laptop or other equipment, or if customers leave their goods with you as happens at a jeweler, dry cleaner, or repair shop. If you expect to regularly have property that belongs to others at your business, get a policy that covers it.

If the policy you are considering excludes one or more items that you want covered, find out whether it can be included and at what cost. You may have to purchase what's commonly called a "rider" or an "endorsement" to add special coverage to the policy. For example, accounting records, cash, and deeds are often excluded from standard property insurance policies but can usually be covered with some extra paperwork—and an additional premium.

You may find other ways to bring the property you want covered under the scope of the policy. For example, if you want the policy to cover your personal stereo that you keep at the office, but the policy only covers business property, one option is to transfer title of the stereo to the business.

Be sure that you clearly understand the dollar limits on your policy and any deductibles or co-payments you'll have to make. Also, make sure the policy covers the replacement cost of the property, not merely its depreciated value. Computer equipment, for example, loses value incredibly fast. If you lose your two-year-old computer to theft, you'd definitely want your insurance to pay for a new computer rather than the value of the stolen one, which might be barely enough to cover the shipping costs of a new machine.

⚠️ **Possible policy adjustments for home-based businesses.** Owners of home-based businesses should figure out whether their homeowner's or renter's policies forbid business use of the home or exclude coverage of business-related claims. Make sure that your policy won't be limited or voided entirely by running a business out of your home. It's better to come clean with your insurance company about your home business and maybe spend some extra premium dollars than to find out after a catastrophe that you had no insurance after all. (See Chapter 10, Section C, for more on insurance and home businesses.)

2. Liability Insurance

Find out what an available "commercial general liability" (CGL) insurance policy will cover. Ask, for instance, whether it covers negligence—that is, carelessness or recklessness. Most CGL policies do not cover certain employment law claims such as harassment, discrimination, and wrongful termination. And all insurance companies will refuse to insure you against bad business decisions, criminal acts, or intentional acts of harm.

a. Personal Injury Liability Insurance

Say, for instance, that someone—a customer or supplier—puts a foot through a floorboard weakened by dry rot, trips on an electric cord, or is hit by a shelving unit that falls over. One accident like that could result in a verdict against your business for tens of thousands or even millions of dollars, even if you were only marginally at fault. For this reason, liability insurance is probably a wise investment for any business that has even minimal contact with the public.

Liability coverage insures you against the notorious slip-and-fall situation, when someone gets injured on your premises and sues you for the ranch. A general liability policy (versus a product liability or vehicle liability policy, discussed below) will cover damages that your business is ordered to pay to an individual such as a customer, supplier, or business associate who was injured on your property.

b. Product Liability Insurance

A related, though technically different, type of insurance is product liability insurance, which protects you from lawsuits by customers claiming to be hurt by a product you made, sold, or provided. If your business has a product that has a risk of harming anyone, no matter how far-fetched, you might consider this type of insurance. Plaintiffs have won product liability lawsuits even when they were ignoring warnings or misusing the product. An insurance premium will be less expensive than a big award to a tragically injured plaintiff.

c. Auto Insurance

Auto liability coverage will not be provided by a general business liability policy, but it is legally required in most states. Even if it's not required in your state, it's foolish not to protect yourself against this potentially devastating risk. Insurance coverage for employees' personal cars that are used for business is known as "nonowned auto" liability insurance. This protects your business if an employee hurts someone or damages property while driving his or her car on the job. If your em-

ployees will use their own cars for business activities, it's important that you get this type of coverage even if your state doesn't require it. Many nonowned auto liability insurance policies do not protect employees themselves, just the business; employees usually need to get their own coverage.

In addition, some states require drivers to be covered by other types of auto insurance, including personal injury protection (PIP) coverage and uninsured/underinsured motorist (UM/UIM) coverage. If your state mandates certain types of coverage, it will generally also require that you purchase a minimum level of the insurance. Check with your state's department of motor vehicles to find out insurance requirements for drivers in your state.

3. Specialized Insurance

Property and liability insurance are the two most important types of coverage for small businesses, but there are many other kinds of policies. Some of the more common ones are listed below. Keep in mind that a broad property or liability policy might already cover one or more risks listed here. For instance, if you have special form property insurance (discussed above), you'll probably be insured against theft.

a. Employment Practices Liability Insurance

This is a relatively new kind of insurance. It can protect you against a number of employee claims including harassment, discrimination, and wrongful termination. It can be a very useful supplement to commercial general liability insurance.

b. Business Interruption Insurance

This type of insurance will cover you if your business is forced to close for a period of time for a reason covered under the policy, such as damage from a fire or earthquake. In that case, your policy will pay approximately what you would have earned if you had been open as normal.

c. "Key Man" Insurance

This is a life insurance policy that the business owns, pays for, and collects on. It protects the business when a crucial person dies unexpectedly and the business grinds to a halt. The "key" person whose life is insured can be the founder, the owner, or an employee—the person who knows everything and holds things together, especially in a small business. This insurance gives the business some extra cash that buys time to decide what to do: whether to hire a replacement, sell the business as a going concern, or wind down gracefully. It is similar in effect to business interruption insurance.

d. Malpractice Insurance

Often expensive, this type of insurance protects you from lawsuits arising from professional mistakes. Doctors, lawyers, real estate agents, accountants, and a number of other professionals typically need malpractice insurance. It is also known as "errors and omissions" (E & O) insurance.

e. Theft Insurance

Since many basic policies do not cover losses due to theft, you may want to purchase specific insurance to cover you in case office equipment is stolen. Be sure to find out whether the policy covers employee theft as well as ordinary burglary and robbery. If not, you can usually purchase that type of coverage separately.

f. Special Coverage

Other types of insurance include credit insurance for accounts receivable, insurance for intellectual property such as trade secrets, or patents, and disability insurance for owners of the business. (This is not the same as state-mandated disability insurance for employees, discussed in Chapter 15.) Some businesses need insurance for issues that arise out of advertising, while others might need to guard against a big bill for environmental cleanup of purchased real estate. If you are an importer and travel frequently to dangerous foreign locations, you might want kidnap and ransom insurance. Talk with an insurance agent or broker about whether your specific business activities might warrant one or more of these special types of coverage.

Many corporations have special liability insurance called "directors' and officers'" (D & O) insurance, because there are occasions when directors and officers are sued individually for making employment and other decisions. This comes up, for example, in sexual harassment cases. An insurance agent can tell you when a small corporation needs this type of coverage.

4. Investigating and Purchasing a Policy

You have to do your homework to make an intelligent and cost-effective insurance purchase. You must understand both the large and fine print so you can compare policies and purchase the best one for your business. For example, when comparison shopping among different insurance companies, it's useless to compare two policies unless they cover the same types of property, the same risks, and the same payouts and deductibles. You can't make an informed decision until you understand all these details.

Insurance brokers who gather information from different insurance companies can help you decipher policies and figure out your best deal. Make sure any broker you consult understands all the nooks and crannies of your specific business activities and the risks that may be involved. Try to find one who specializes in policies for your type of business. You may be surprised to learn that specially tailored policies already exist that cover your particular needs. For instance, a "producer's package policy" for filmmakers covers several risks unique to the film business, such as the costs of production—often in the tens or hundreds of thousands of dollars—in case your negatives are destroyed. An insurance broker who knows your type of business will be able to direct you to these specialized policies, while a run-of-the-mill broker may not. Check trade magazines for the ads of specialized brokers, and ask other business owners who they use and what they buy.

You'll probably encounter insurance companies that offer package deals that are cheaper than buying several individual policies separately. As long as all your needs are met—and not exceeded—these deals can be a good way to go. As always, be sure you understand the extent of coverage in each area rather than relying on any general promises that the package covers "all your business needs."

Finding help on the Internet. A couple of websites that may be helpful are the Business Insurance Oracle Home Page at www .insuranceoracle.com and the Insurance Information Institute at www.iii.org.

5. Manufacturer's and Extended Warranties

While insurance can protect you when property is damaged or stolen, product warranties can protect you in case equipment malfunctions for various reasons. Don't overlook the value of warranties when considering ways to reduce risks and potential losses related to your equipment.

Most products come with a standard manufacturer's warranty against defects for a certain period of time. Warranties generally range from 90 days to one year of coverage. It's not uncommon for the warranty to cover parts and labor for time periods—for example, parts might be covered for one year, and labor for 90 days.

In addition, you can purchase extended warranties for most equipment that offer coverage for longer periods, generally from two to five years. While some manufacturers offer extended warranties to supplement the standard manufacturer's warranty, many extended warranties are sold by companies other than the manufacturer. These companies make big profit margins on extended warranties, leading many consumer advocates, including *Consumer Reports* magazine, to advise people generally against purchasing an extended warranty. However, a *Consumer Reports* article from September 2005 advises that extended warranties might be a good safety net for products such as laptops and plasma TVs due to their high cost and relatively high repair rates.

The truth is there may be some situations in which purchasing an extended warranty makes sense for your business. Generally speaking, the more expensive and important a piece of equipment is to your business, the more an extended warranty might be a smart idea. For example, if your business cannot live without a certain piece of equipment such as a computer, and would be financially hard-pressed to replace it if it went south, an extended warranty might be a godsend—but always account for the repair time during which you won't be able to use the equipment.

When considering whether to buy an extended warranty, be sure to consider the following factors.

Be clear about when the extended warranty coverage begins and how long it lasts. In particular, don't pay for extended coverage that overlaps with the original manufacturer's warranty. If coverage begins as of the date of purchase of the extended warranty, as opposed to the date of purchase of the equipment, then wait until the original warranty is about to expire before purchasing the extended warranty. Most warranty companies allow this—but be aware that you will usually not be able to purchase an extended warranty if the original warranty has expired. Find out in advance what deadlines apply to the extended warranty purchase.

Make sure you trust the warranty company. Particularly if the warranty is being sold by a third-party warranty company, evaluate the reputation and reliability of that company. If the extended warranty is being sold through a major national retailer, chances are that it is not a fly-by-night scam—though it still may not be worthwhile. But be aware that scam warranty companies do exist.

Evaluate the value of the extended coverage. Weigh the cost of the extended warranty and what it will cover, against the cost of the equipment and the likelihood it will need repair. Just as with insurance, warranties generally exclude certain types of damage from coverage. The more limitations on coverage, the lower the value of the warranty.

When you do have warranty protection, whether from an original manufacturer's warranty or an extended warranty, it's crucial to keep track of important warranty details—especially the expiration dates, so that you can purchase extended coverage if you so choose. As mentioned above, you will usually not be allowed to purchase an extended warranty if the original or previous extended warranty has expired—so be careful not to let those important dates slip by if you intend to purchase extended coverage.

On the CD-ROM that comes with this book, you'll find a worksheet to help you track your warranty information. The file name of the worksheet is warrantytrack_worksheet.xls. The file is meant to be used with a spreadsheet program such as Microsoft Excel, but it may also be opened in Microsoft Word. Note that sorting and other features will be affected if you do not use Excel or another spreadsheet program.

Simply enter all relevant information into the worksheet about warranty coverage for every piece of business equipment you buy. If you don't have information for every column, it's okay, but be sure to include the Warranty Expiration Date. Keep the list sorted by "Warranty Expiration Date" (Column C) in ascending order, so that the warranties about to expire will be at the top of the list. Make it a habit to enter this information as soon as you purchase any equipment, and to review and update the worksheet periodically so that you don't miss any expiration dates and the chance to purchase extended coverage.

☑ Chapter 8 Checklist

☐ Have active risk management strategies. Start by evaluating your risks and identifying specific ways to reduce them.

☐ If your business has employees, establish personnel policies including hiring and firing guidelines, policies prohibiting sexual harassment and discrimination, and effective enforcement mechanisms.

☐ Research and purchase appropriate insurance for your business. Contact an insurance agent or broker familiar with your business to answer your questions and to price out various policies.

☐ Get a property insurance policy that covers against all the types of losses that your business may face, such as theft, fire, and water damage.

☐ Get a liability insurance policy if your business will have any contact with the general public, or if you determine there's a significant risk that someone could sue your business for injuries or other damage.

☐ Get auto liability coverage for any vehicles used for business, including the personal cars of employees that are used for business.

☐ Consider other, specialized insurance coverage.

CHAPTER 9

Paying Your Taxes

It's no fun for any profitable business to share its hard-won earnings with the government. But, like it or not, as soon as your business is in the black, everyone—from your city and county to your state and, of course, the IRS—will demand a piece of the action. Although it's not necessary to become a tax expert before going into business, you do need to know what taxes you'll have to pay and how to pay them. Understanding your tax liability will help you be better able to:

- plan your finances, including whether you'll have enough cash to stay in business
- avoid tax-reporting and deposit errors, which can result in hefty—sometimes even business-threatening—penalties, and
- make good business decisions that will reduce your tax burden.

Even if your business won't make a fast profit, you may owe taxes. Lots of new businesspeople believe that if there is no profit, there is no tax. Sadly, this is not the case. Local taxes on gross receipts and taxes on sales of retail goods (sales taxes) are but two examples of taxes that may need to be paid regardless of whether a business is turning a profit. So, even if your business may not be profitable for a year or two, you need to prepare for the possibility of owing some taxes.

This chapter gives you simple, straightforward information on the taxes that owners of sole proprietorships, partnerships, and LLCs will face. It provides basic instructions for filing returns and paying taxes correctly and on time. After covering the basics, it offers three sections that discuss the specific tax rules that apply to each business type—there's a separate section for sole proprietorships, partnerships, and LLCs. Simply read the section that's appropriate for your business form and skip the others. The last three sections cover paying estimated taxes, local taxes, and sales taxes—all of which apply more or less evenly to all business types. If your business has employees, refer to Chapter 15, "Building Your Business and Hiring Workers," for information on the special taxes employers face.

Help with corporate taxation. This chapter offers only some broad outlines of corporate taxation. The full maze of corporate tax rules is far too complicated to cover in detail here. If you're thinking about incorporating, keep in mind that doing so will subject you to more complicated (and occasionally unpleasant) tax rules. There is an overview of the potential tax advantages and disadvantages of the corporation in Chapter 2, Section D. If you need more detailed information, take a look at *Tax Savvy for Small Business*, by Frederick W. Daily, or *Incorporate Your Business: A 50-State Legal Guide to Forming a Corporation*, by Anthony Mancuso (both published by Nolo).

Get professional help to deal with your taxes. Tax rules and filing procedures can be quite complex, even for a relatively simple business. This chapter is meant to give you the big picture. Especially if your business is large, is incorporated, or has a number of employees, you will likely need to do additional reading and possibly hire an experienced accountant or even a tax lawyer. Chapter 16 discusses other resources and publications for small business owners, as well as how to work with experts.

A. Tax Basics

One of the first things you should understand is that there's little rhyme or reason to the world of taxes. Don't drive yourself nuts by trying to figure out the logic of a system that has virtually none. The bottom line is that the federal, state, and local governments tend to tax everything that they legally can. And this includes virtually every aspect of a business that can be quantified. For example, depending on the type of business and its location, a business might have to pay taxes based on its gross income, net profit, or gross retail sales; how many employees it has; how much employees are paid; how much property it owns or leases; its

Talking About Income—Key Terms Defined

A lot of different jargon is used to describe the money that comes into and flows out of your business. These financial terms are discussed in more detail elsewhere in the book where we discuss financial projections and accounting. (See Chapters 5 and 12.) But since these concepts are also important in understanding your taxes, here are some brief definitions.

- **Gross vs. net.** It's crucial to understand this distinction. "Gross" generally refers to total revenue, before deducting expenses such as salaries, rent, product costs, or office supplies. "Net" means what's left over after subtracting costs and expenses. (As you can see, a "gross" figure will be higher than a "net" figure, since deductions come out of the "gross" and result in the "net.") Thus "gross income" (sometimes called "gross receipts" or "gross sales") refers to the total money your business brings in, before you've begun to cover any of your costs. "Net profit" refers to your income after deducting costs and expenses. In some contexts, "net" may refer to your after-tax profit. In other words, it may reflect not only your costs and expenses, but also any taxes you owe on your income. Be aware that the terms "gross" and "net" are often bandied about loosely. It's important to understand which deductions are included when using these terms.

- **Fixed vs. variable expenses.** Fixed expenses are the ones that will be more or less the same regardless of how well your business is doing. They include rent, utility bills, insurance premiums, and loan payments. Variable expenses are the costs of the products or services themselves and anything that goes along with your product, including packaging or shipping. Variable expenses increase or decrease depending on how much business you're doing.

- **Gross profit.** Gross profit refers to how much money you make on each sale above the cost of the item itself (its variable cost). Unlike the term "gross income," which refers to all the money your business brings in before expenses are accounted for, the term "gross profit" does take into account the cost of the product or service you're selling. For example, if a widget costs you $3 and you sell it for $5, your gross profit is $2. The terms "profit margin" or "gross margin" are sometimes used to mean the same thing. The key thing to remember about gross profit is that fixed expenses such as rent or utility bills are not deducted—only the cost of the product or service itself.

- **Net profit.** This is what's left over after subtracting fixed expenses from gross profit. Put another way, net profit means the amount of money you have left over after subtracting all expenses—fixed and variable—from your gross income. Sometimes the term "net income" is used to mean the same thing as net profit.

- **Current vs. capital expenses.** Current expenses include ordinary, day-to-day business expenses such as office supplies or salaries. For tax purposes, you can deduct them from your business income in the year that you pay for them. Capital expenses, on the other hand, include payments for business assets (also called "capital," "fixed," or "depreciable" assets) that have a useful life of one year or more, such as computers or office furniture. Capital expenses generally can't be fully deducted in the year they are incurred but must be deducted over a number of years—a process known as depreciation, capitalization, or amortization.

seating capacity; or how many vehicles the business owns—and the list goes on and on.

To complicate matters further, the many different taxes are administered by different government agencies, each with its own rules, forms, and filing procedures. It's little wonder that the mere mention of taxes often induces anxiety and sometimes even panic in otherwise well-adjusted businesspeople.

1. The Agencies Behind the Taxes

The first step in understanding small business taxes is to recognize who levies which taxes. Here's a quick breakdown.

- **Federal taxes.** The United States Internal Revenue Service, the top dog of tax agencies, collects the following taxes from small businesses and their owners: taxes on individual or corporate income, self-employment taxes (which go to the Social Security and Medicare systems), and payroll taxes. (See Chapter 15, Section B, for information on payroll taxes.)
- **State taxes.** While not all states are the same, states typically collect the following taxes from businesses: taxes on business income, sales taxes on sales of retail goods (after the business has collected the sales tax from its customers), and payroll taxes. (See Chapter 15, Section B, for information on payroll taxes.) States also often collect special taxes (called "excise taxes") on certain types of business activities such as distributing alcohol, cigarettes, or gasoline. In addition, some states collect taxes on corporations, LLCs, and limited partnerships.
- **County and city taxes.** Cities, counties, or sometimes both typically impose taxes on businesses based on several factors. Most cities assign businesses to categories (for example, retail businesses, wholesalers, and services) and then tax each category based on certain criteria, such as gross receipts, gross payroll, or number of employees. In addition, counties often assess and collect

property taxes on real and personal property owned by businesses within the county. Cities and counties also may impose a sales tax. This tax may be collected by the state along with the state sales tax.

Forms and Schedules and Returns, Oh My!

This chapter makes many mentions of tax forms, tax schedules, and tax returns. Basically, these are simply different names for the papers you have to fill out and submit to your federal, state, and local tax agencies.

Technically, a "tax form" is the principal document that businesses and their owners must use to report all the basic information about the business's or individual's income. For instance, every individual who earns income must fill out Form 1040, *Individual Income Tax Return,* and all partnerships and LLCs must file Form 1065, *Partnership Return of Income.*

A "schedule" is an additional sheet of information the IRS requires businesses and business owners to attach to their tax forms. For instance, sole proprietors must submit Schedule C with their Form 1040 to report their income from their business, and partners and LLC owners usually need to report their business income on Schedule E. Partnerships and LLCs also must include various schedules with their Form 1065s.

Finally, a "tax return" is simply a general term for the whole package you send off to the IRS: your tax form, any schedules, and any attached documents.

A tax by any other name is … a fee. In addition to the taxes listed above, your business may have to pay additional fees for business licenses or tax registration. For instance, many cities and counties require all businesses in the area to register with the local tax collector and pay a registration fee. And, if your business requires a special license such as a permit to handle food or a cosmetology license, you'll usually have to pay for it. While these fees arguably could be called taxes, this chapter does not deal with them as such. The various registration, permit, and license requirements—including their associated fees—are covered in Chapter 7, "Federal, State, and Local Start-Up Requirements."

2.   Understanding Deductions

Increasing profits while keeping taxes as low as possible is the name of the game in any business. The main way to do this is by claiming business deductions. When you deduct an expense, you subtract it from your taxable income—which means you'll have less income to report and pay taxes on. Of course, you can't deduct just any old expense you want. To stay out of trouble with the IRS, your state tax agency, and your local tax collector, you need to understand which deductions are allowed and which are not.

a.   What Expenses Are Deductible?

Allowable deductions are outlined in great length (to put it mildly) in the Internal Revenue Code— although the basic guidelines are summarized here below. You'll need to follow these rules when filling out your federal tax return, which you use to report your business income and deductions. When you file your state income tax return, you'll generally fill out a form that uses the information from your federal return, with a few adjustments to reflect your state's rules on deducting business expenses. As far as local taxes go, they may simply be based on gross income (also called "gross receipts") without taking any deductions into account. Your main concern should be the federal rules.

The Internal Revenue Code (IRC) states that any "ordinary and necessary" business expenses can be subtracted from your business income for federal tax purposes. (IRC § 162.) Figuring out whether most expenses qualify is a no-brainer. Product costs, office rent, equipment and machinery, office supplies, your business computer system, business insurance, salaries, payroll taxes, and office utility bills are just a few examples of costs that easily count as deductible expenses. As long as an expenditure is in fact made for business—not personal—purposes, the general rule is that you can deduct it from your business's gross income.

It gets a little more complicated when expenditures aren't clearly made for business reasons. The IRS has special rules for expenses that border on the personal, such as travel, entertainment, and vehicle expenses. These costs are deductible, but only according to special IRS rules.

Resources for the details on expenses. The rules on allowable travel and entertainment expenses are fully explained in *Tax Savvy for Small Business*, by Frederick W. Daily (Nolo), and in the IRS's Publication 535, *Business Expenses*, available online at www.irs.gov/formspubs/index.htm.

b.   How Are Expenses Deducted?

In addition to figuring out whether an expense is deductible, you need to understand how particular expenses may be deducted. First, you need to know that there's a major distinction between current and capital expenses. Current expenses can best be described as your everyday costs of doing business, such as rent, supplies, utility bills, and the like. These expenses are fully deductible in the year they occur. Capital expenses, on the other hand, are not fully deductible in the year you incur them. You incur a capital expense when you purchase an item with a useful life of at least one year—called a "business asset." Business assets include items such as vehicles, furniture, heavy equipment (like a forklift or printing press), and real estate.

Rather than fully deducting a capital expense in the year it was made, you must spread out the deduction over a number of years. (A major exception to this, the 179 deduction, is discussed below.) This process is variously called "depreciation," "amortization," or "capitalization." Different types of assets have different depreciation rules, and the number of years over which the cost of an item must be depreciated varies. Depreciation rules are explained in IRS Publication 534, *Depreciation*, available online at www.irs.gov/formspubs/ index.html, as well as in other IRS publications that cover specific types of assets.

The Section 179 Deduction

The IRS allows every business to treat a certain amount of capital expenditures as current expenses and fully deduct them in the year they were made. This major exception is known as a "179 deduction," because it's established in Internal Revenue Code § 179. In 2003, the limit was dramatically increased from $25,000 to $100,000—allowing businesses to write off up to $100,000 in expenditures that would normally qualify as capital expenses. This limit applied to tax years 2004 and 2005. Unless Congress votes to extend the higher limit, it will go back to $25,000 for the tax years 2006 and beyond.

Whether and to what extent you should take advantage of a 179 deduction depends on your circumstances. Generally, you should take a 179 deduction only when your taxable income is high enough that you'll get a decent tax benefit right away. Businesses with low incomes might want to depreciate assets instead (take their deductions slowly) so that they'll have more deductions available in future years when their income might be higher.

Start-up expenses must be depreciated over time—you can't deduct their full cost in the year you incur them. For lots of businesses, this rule doesn't matter because their profits in the first year of operation are small—or, as is often the case, nonexistent—so a big tax deduction wouldn't result in a lot of savings, anyway.

Learn more about tax deductions. This introduction to tax deductions only begins to scratch the surface of a huge and complex body of information. *Tax Savvy for Small Business*, by Frederick W. Daily (Nolo), does an excellent job of leading you through the maze.

Consider working with a tax expert. Especially as your business grows and its finances become more complicated, you may well want to hire a tax adviser to help you use the tax rules to your best advantage. (See Chapter 16, Section B, on hiring and working with tax professionals.)

Where to Get Tax Forms and Schedules

Although this book does provide several tax forms in Appendix C and on the CD-ROM (a list is included at the beginning of Appendix C), many federal and state tax forms have been left out because they change from year to year and are readily available from other sources. Besides the flood of tax forms that are available at libraries as April 15 comes near, you can always obtain the most current forms, schedules, and publications by ordering them over the phone or downloading them off the Web.

- Order federal tax forms and other publications from the IRS by calling 800-829-3676. Or download them from the Web at www.irs.gov/formspubs/index.html.

- For state tax forms, contact your state tax agency. You'll find contact information in Appendix A for tax agencies in each state. Also, most states have tax forms and information available online. On the CD-ROM that comes with this book, there is a list of links to business- and tax-related websites for each state. You can use this file with your Web browser to link directly to these sites. (See Appendix B for instructions on how to use this list with your browser.)

- Local tax forms and instructions are often automatically sent to businesses once they've registered with their city or county. Otherwise, contact the agency in charge of business taxes in your city or county (depending on where your business is located) for more information on how to obtain local tax forms. To find your local tax agency, look in the city and county government sections of your telephone book under "Tax Collector," "Business Tax Division," or "City Clerk."

3. Hobby Businesses

For many small business owners, their "business" is more a labor of love than a reliable source of income. This is most often the case when an owner has other means of financial support—such as a regular job or a spouse who brings home wages or other income—that allows a micro-business to continue even though it makes little or no money. These types of tiny businesses are usually operated from the home (renting an office would be too expensive) and are often based on activities near and dear to the owner, which has earned them the nickname "hobby businesses."

There is no one type of hobby business. Examples might include a basement jewelry studio, a jazz band for hire, or an antique-refinishing business. The owners would probably keep on making jewelry, playing jazz, or restoring antiques even if they never made a penny, but are trying to turn their hobbies into profitable businesses.

Often, profits fail to materialize. For most regular businesses, spending more than a year or so of losing money is a cue to close up shop. But if you love what you're doing, it might make sense for you to stick with your losing business rather than fold it up. This is true because if you have another source of income (as many owners of hobby businesses do), the losses from your hobby business can be used to offset that income. Deducting business losses—including everyday expenses and depreciation on assets such as computer equipment—not only lowers the amount of income on which taxes are calculated, but also may drop you into a lower tax bracket. This is what is commonly referred to as a tax shelter: an unprofitable business whose losses offset the owner's taxable income from other sources.

Of course, most entrepreneurs would much rather earn a healthy profit than lose money. And the savings made possible by a tax shelter do not always justify continuing a marginal or losing business. But they definitely can make a difference in deciding whether it's worth it to keep your unprofitable—but enjoyable—business going.

> **EXAMPLE:** Kay and Reza are married and file joint tax returns. Reza earns a salary as a chef in a local restaurant, and Kay is a magazine editor. Kay has a passion for plants and decides to try to make a business of selling some of the hundreds of plants she grows and propagates in her backyard greenhouse. After she's spent thousands of dollars on exotic plants and better lighting equipment, the greenhouse heater goes on the fritz and over 300 of Kay's expensive, exotic plants die. Her expenses for the year total nearly $10,000, and she has not yet sold any plants. The silver lining for Kay and Reza comes at tax time, when they deduct the $10,000 loss from their joint taxable income of $105,000. This not only reduces their taxable income, but—depending on their income level and any other deductions they take—might drop them into a lower tax bracket as well.

On the down side, if you consistently use your unprofitable business as a tax shelter, deducting your losses from your other income year after year, you'll probably attract the attention of the IRS. An issue that often arises with hobby businesses is whether the venture is really a business at all. To deduct expenses from your taxable income, those expenses must have been incurred by a legitimate profit-motivated business—not merely a personal hobby. As you might expect, not every hobby counts as a business. If you claim a loss from your hobby business and you're audited, you'll have to prove to the IRS that your hobby is in fact a legitimate business.

a.   Proving Your Hobby Is a Business

Before you start claiming deductions for the costs of your favorite art projects or toy car collections, make sure your venture will pass IRS scrutiny and qualify as a real business. Thankfully, the IRS's definition is fairly broad. Basically, any activity that you undertake to make a profit counts as a business. In other words, you need only prove to the IRS that you're trying—not necessarily succeeding—to make a profit with your venture. The IRS uses a few different criteria to decide whether your business truly has a profit motive.

The main test for profit motive is called the "3-of-5" test. If your business makes a profit in three out of five consecutive years, it is legally presumed to have a profit motive.

While the IRS gives a lot of weight to the 3-of-5 test, it is not conclusive. In other words, if you flunk the 3-of-5 test, you still may be able to prove that your business is motivated by profit. You can use virtually any kind of evidence to prove this. Business cards, a well-maintained set of books, a separate business bank account, current business licenses and permits, and proof of advertising will all help to persuade an IRS auditor that your activity really is a business.

b.   Watch Out for Local Tax Rules

When planning out your hobby business, don't forget that local requirements and taxes will increase your costs of doing business, both in time and money. Lots of small business owners are surprised to find out that state and local tax regulations for small businesses can be more of a bear than IRS rules. For example, if you sell tangible products, you may be subject to state sales taxes. Plus, many cities impose taxes or fees on small businesses and require them to go through some sort of registration process, and counties often have similar requirements for businesses in rural areas. Generally speaking, these rules apply to any money-making activity within the locality—even if the hobby business doesn't intend to claim any federal or state tax deductions. (Local taxes and fees are discussed later in this chapter, in Section F, as well as in Chapter 7, Section D.)

In practice, many tiny hobby businesses—so tiny that the word "business" even seems excessive—might be able to get away unnoticed, assuming you don't deduct business losses on your tax return. Even so, you should be aware that, depending on your local rules, you may be penalized if you're caught doing business without the permits or licenses required by your state or local government. These penalties may include fines and back taxes.

John Tilles, cofounder of Portland River Company, a river rafting outfit in Portland, Oregon:

The real can of worms for us was in dealing with taxes. As a new and undercapitalized business, a professional accountant was out of the question. This left me to figure it out as I went, which was pretty straightforward in the early days, but, as the years went on and things became more complicated, I finally had to use a professional C.P.A.

B. Income Taxes for Sole Proprietors

As mentioned throughout this book, a sole proprietorship is one and the same as its owner (the sole proprietor) for most legal and tax purposes. It follows that the sole proprietor must report and pay federal and state income taxes on all business profits, including any profits the sole proprietor leaves in the business for expansion. In other words, the business itself does not file tax returns or pay income taxes.

1. Federal Income Taxes

You're probably already familiar with the process of filing IRS Form 1040, based on income you earned at a job. Good—this means much of the process of filing federal income taxes as a sole proprietor will already be familiar to you. That's because income from your business will be treated as personal income, which you report on Form 1040 much as you report wages or returns on investments. But there are two additional steps you'll have to take: You'll have to use a separate sheet (called Schedule C) to report your business profit, and you'll also have to pay self-employment taxes based on your income, reported on Schedule SE.

a. Income Tax

You report business profits or losses on Schedule C (*Profit or Loss From Business*), which is submitted once a year with your 1040 return, usually by April 15. (See "Defining Your Business Year" in Section E2, below, for information on using a business year other than the calendar year for tax-reporting purposes.) A sole proprietor who owns more than one business must file a separate Schedule C for each business. (See "Where to Get Tax Forms and Schedules" in Section A2, above, for information on obtaining the most current forms.)

You're not required to file Schedule C if your sole proprietorship doesn't make at least $400 profit in the business year, though it's a good idea to file one anyway. If your business loses money in any year, filing Schedule C allows the loss to be deducted from any other income you make for that year, reducing your total taxable income. Or, you can carry over the loss into a future profitable year to offset those profits and thereby reduce your taxes. Another reason to report losses or profits under $400 on Schedule C is that doing so triggers the beginning of the time window during which the IRS can audit you. Otherwise, the IRS can audit you anytime, virtually forever.

Simplified Tax Schedule for Super-Small Sole Proprietorships

Extra-small sole proprietorships may be able to use a simplified schedule to report their income, Schedule C-EZ. (This schedule may only be used by sole proprietors.) To use this simplified form, which works just like Schedule C, you must have:

- less than $2,500 in business expenses
- no inventory during the year
- no employees during the year
- used the cash method of accounting; see Chapter 12, Section B, for an explanation of the difference between the cash and accrual methods of accounting
- owned and operated only one sole proprietorship during the year
- no expenses deducted for business use of your home, and
- not reported a net business loss.

If you depreciate assets or have unallowed passive activity losses from previous years, you may not be able to use this schedule. See the IRS instructions for details on who may use Schedule C-EZ.

Though Schedule C-EZ is easier to fill out than Schedule C, you won't save enough time or trouble to warrant trying to squeeze a too-large business into it. Don't, for example, neglect to claim more than $2,500 in business expenses or to claim depreciation expenses just so you qualify to use the schedule. The marginal convenience of the simplified schedule just isn't worth it.

There's an important procedural difference between reporting and paying taxes on income from a job and income from a sole proprietorship: Regular employees are subject to tax withholding by their employers, but sole proprietors usually have to estimate their taxes for the year and pay them in quarterly installments. The IRS is a stickler when it comes to making these quarterly payments and won't hesitate to fine you for doing it incorrectly or late, and especially for not doing it at all. Even if you pay your taxes in full by April 15 (or whenever your business year ends), failure to make quarterly payments means you'll be charged a penalty (typically about 9%). (See Section E, below, for details on who needs to make estimated quarterly tax payments and how to do it.)

b. Self-Employment Taxes

Sole proprietors must also make contributions to the Social Security and Medicare systems, called "self-employment taxes." Regular employees contribute to these two programs through deductions from their paychecks. Sole proprietors must make their contributions when paying their other income taxes. And they have to pay more than employees do—employees only have to pay half as much into these programs, because their contributions are matched by their employers. Sole proprietors must pay the entire amount themselves.

For tax year 2005, self-employment taxes include:

- Social Security tax of 12.4% on profits up to $90,000, and
- Medicare tax of 2.9% on all profits.

In other words, profits of $90,000 and less will be taxed at 15.3% (Social Security and Medicare combined), and profits above that will be taxed at 2.9% (Medicare only). In comparison, regular employees only pay a 7.65% tax on wages of $90,000 or less, and a 1.45% tax on wages above that.

Fortunately, there is a small silver lining to this dark tax cloud: Half of the total self-employment tax you'll pay can be deducted from your taxable income at year end. And if your sole proprietorship makes less than $400 profit in the business year, you don't have to pay self-employment taxes.

Reporting and Paying Are Not the Same

As you read about the often-complex rules of taxes, keep in mind that having to report income is not the same as owing tax on that income. Sometimes, a tax agency like the IRS or your state tax office requires you to submit a tax return even if you don't owe any taxes. Generally, a "filing" or "reporting" requirement means simply that you need to provide income and expense information, which may or may not add up to an actual tax obligation.

Self-employment taxes are reported on Schedule SE, which, like Schedule C (*Profit or Loss From a Business*), is submitted yearly with your 1040 income tax return. (See "Where to Get Tax Forms and Schedules" in Section A2, above, for information on obtaining the latest forms.) Once you determine the amount of self-employment taxes you owe on Schedule SE, you enter the result on your 1040 form in the "Other Taxes" section and add it to your personal income tax obligation. Remember, however, that most sole proprietors must estimate their total taxes for the year and pay them in quarterly installments. (See Section E, below, for details on estimated tax payments, which most business owners must pay.)

2. State Income Taxes

You must report and pay state income taxes in much the same way as federal income tax. Any profit generated by a sole proprietorship is generally treated as personal income of the sole proprietor and reported on an individual state tax return. In most states the sole proprietor will need to attach a separate schedule, similar to the federal Schedule C, to report business income. Unlike the federal rule, some states require this schedule to be filed even if a business loses money or makes less than $400 profit. In these states you won't owe any taxes unless you've made a profit, but you must file the form in any case.

Like federal taxes, many states require businesses to estimate and pay their income taxes in quarterly installments. (Estimating your taxes and making quarterly payments is covered in Section E, below.)

Tax rules vary considerably from state to state, so it's important that you check with your state tax agency for its requirements. (Appendix A includes contact information for state tax agencies, and the CD-ROM that comes with this book contains a list of links to state tax websites. See Appendix B for information on how to use this file with your Web browser.)

C. Income Taxes for Partnerships

Although a partnership itself does not pay taxes (its owners do), it does need to submit an annual informational return to the IRS and usually the state to report its income. As is true for sole proprietorships, taxes are paid only by the partners (business owners), not the business itself, and the partners have to pay taxes on all business profits, whether or not they take any money out of the business. This section explains what partnerships need to do to comply with the IRS and state rules.

1. Federal Income Taxes

Partnerships are called "pass-through tax entities," which means that profits pass right through the business to the owners, who report them on their individual income tax returns. The partnership itself is not taxed, though it must report its income and losses each year. (Although few do, a partnership can also elect to be taxed as a corporation, by submitting Form 8832 and electing corporate tax status.) Besides income taxes, partners must also file and pay self-employment taxes.

a. Income Tax

Even though the partnership itself does not pay taxes on profits, it must report profits and losses on an informational return, Form 1065, *U.S. Partnership Return of Income.* No tax is due with this return, which is generally due by April 15. (See "Defining Your Business Year" in Section E2, below, for information on using a business year other than the calendar year.)

Along with Form 1065, the partnership must also submit a Schedule K-1, *Partner's Share of Income, Credit, and Deductions,* for each partner, reporting each partner's share of profits or losses. The K-1 schedule is used to inform the IRS of the partners' chosen profit division. Often, partners own equal shares of the business, which normally means they will choose to share profits and pay taxes equally—such as four partners each getting ¼ of a business's profits and paying ¼ of its taxes. But if they so choose, partners can divide profits and losses unequally. (See Chapter 2, Section B, for more on partnerships.) A copy of the completed K-1 must also be given to each partner on or before the date that the partnership return is due to the IRS. (Section A2, above, includes information on obtaining current tax forms.)

As mentioned, profits earned by a partnership are taxed as personal income of the individual partners. Each partner reports an allocated share of business income or losses on an individual federal income tax return (Form 1040) using Schedule E, *Supplemental Income and Loss.* Schedule E repeats the income information reported on Schedule K-1 (which each partner should have received from the partnership). Since the partnership already filed Schedule K-1 with the IRS, partners do not need to submit this schedule with their individual tax returns.

Partners who earn income from a profitable partnership often must estimate their taxes and pay the total in quarterly installments. (Section E, below, covers estimated tax payments, an important aspect of taxes for all small businesses.)

When partners don't share and share alike. Remember that each partner is taxed on his or her allocated share of the partnership profits, not on the amount actually distributed. However, it is possible in some circumstances for partners to legally divide items on a less-than-even basis. For instance, they could agree that one partner may deduct, on his or her personal tax return, all the interest paid on a partnership-property mortgage. But a partner's share of partnership losses that can be deducted is limited to the partner's basis (investment) in the partnership. You should see a tax attorney if you want to get into this kind of tax planning.

b. Self-Employment Taxes

Partners and other self-employed individuals who earn more than $400 profit during the business year must contribute to Social Security and Medicare through federal self-employment taxes (FICA). In 2005, self-employment taxes include:

- Social Security tax of 12.4% on profits up to $90,000, and
- Medicare tax of 2.9% on all profits.

Put another way, profits of $90,000 and less will be taxed at 15.3% (Social Security and Medicare combined), and profits above that will be taxed at 2.9% (Medicare only).

On a brighter note, you can deduct half of the total self-employment tax you'll pay from your taxable income at year-end. And if your partnership makes less than $400 in profit, no self-employment taxes need be filed or paid. (See "Reporting and Paying Are Not the Same" in Section B1, above, if you're confused about the difference between filing taxes and paying them.)

Self-employment taxes are reported on Schedule SE, which, like Schedule E (*Supplemental Income and Loss*), is submitted yearly with a partner's 1040 return. Once you determine your self-employment tax with Schedule SE, enter the result on your 1040 form in the "Other Taxes" section, which you must add to your personal income tax obligation. But don't forget about estimating and paying taxes quarterly—most partners of profitable businesses must do so, or face the IRS's penalties. (See Section E, below, on how to estimate and pay your taxes.) A husband and wife who operate a business as partners must each report their share of the business profits as net earnings on separate Schedule SEs, even if they file a joint 1040 return.

2. State Income Taxes

Like the federal government, most states require partnerships to file informational returns reporting business income and losses. Fortunately, many of these state forms are almost identical to the federal Form 1065. Partnerships may also be required to file a schedule analogous to the federal Schedule K-1 for each partner, indicating the partner's share of the business profit or loss. The partnership must give each partner a copy. Typically, the state schedules are similar to the federal version but account for differences between state and federal tax laws. Generally, no tax is due with the partnership return or schedules.

Any partnership profit is taxed as personal income of the partners, who report their shares on their individual state income tax return. Partnership income is usually recorded on a schedule similar to the federal Schedule E and included with the state tax form. Keep in mind that some states require partners to file this schedule even if the partnership loses money and no taxes are due.

Finally, like federal taxes, state income taxes must often be paid in quarterly installments. (Estimating your taxes and making quarterly payments are covered in Section E, below.)

D. Income Taxes for LLCs

The limited liability company or LLC (explained in greater detail in Chapter 2, Section C), is a relatively new business ownership structure. LLCs combine several key attributes that distinguish the traditional partnership and corporation, allowing LLC owners (usually called "members") to enjoy the protection from personal liability that a corporation offers yet avoid the complicated and often expensive corporate tax system. LLC profits are taxed to the owners as individuals (like a sole proprietor or owners of a partnership). Although LLC members (owners) can instead choose to be taxed like a corporation, this choice is somewhat unusual. (But see Chapter 2, Section C, for reasons why some LLCs may want to be taxed like a corporation.) In this section, assume your LLC will stick with pass-through tax status.

1. Federal Income Taxes

Like owners of partnerships, most LLC owners will report business profits on their individual federal income tax returns. Although this means the LLC itself is not taxed, it must still report its income and losses to the IRS each year if it has two or more members. In addition to regular income taxes, members may be obligated to pay self-employment taxes, which are also based on business income.

a. Income Tax

LLCs with only one member are treated as sole proprietorships for tax purposes, so that business profits and losses are reported on Schedule C, to be submitted with the member's regular individual income tax return. If the LLC has two or more members, it must file an annual informational return with the IRS, similar to the requirement faced by partnerships. Since the IRS hasn't yet come up with tax forms specifically for LLCs, LLC profits and losses are reported on Form 1065, *U.S. Partnership Return of Income.* No tax is paid with this return, which is generally due by April 15. (See "Defining Your Business Year" in Section E2, below, for information on using a business year other than the calendar year.)

Along with Form 1065, an LLC must also submit a Schedule K-1 (again, the same schedule used by partnerships) to the IRS for each member, reporting each member's share of profits or losses. The K-1 schedule is used to inform the IRS of the members' chosen profit division. A copy of the completed K-1 must also be given to each member on or before the date that the LLC return is due to the IRS.

Often, members own equal shares of the business, which normally means they will choose to share profits and pay taxes equally—such as four members each getting ¼ of a business's profits and paying ¼ of its taxes. But if they so choose, LLC members can divide profits and losses unequally. (See Chapter 2, Section C, for more on LLCs and profit allocations.)

Profits earned by an LLC are taxed as personal income of the individual members. Members use the information from Schedule K-1 to report business income or losses on their individual federal income tax returns (Form 1040) using Schedule E (*Supplemental Income and Loss*). Since the LLC already filed Schedule K-1s with the IRS, members do not need to submit this form with their returns. (See "Where to Get Tax Forms and Schedules" in Section A2, above, for information on obtaining the latest forms.)

Like sole proprietors and partners, LLC members will have to estimate their taxes for the year and pay them in quarterly installments. (Read Section E, below, for information on estimated tax payments.)

b.   Self-Employment Taxes

The current rule is that LLC members who are actively involved in the business must pay self-employment taxes, which include payments into the Social Security and Medicare systems (FICA). An LLC member who is nonactive and merely invests in the company may be exempt from the self-employment tax obligation.

The rules on self-employment taxes for LLCs are far from settled. Due to the somewhat contradictory nature of LLCs—partnership-like in some respects, corporate in others—it's not clear to what extent LLC owners are subject to self-employment tax. If the issue affects you, it may be wise to do some research or consult a business attorney to find out the latest word on how these taxes apply to LLC members. (Chapter 16 gives information on legal resources beyond this book.)

For tax year 2005, self-employment taxes include:
- Social Security tax of 12.4% on profits up to $90,000, and
- Medicare tax of 2.9% on all profits.

This translates into a 15.3% tax on profits up to $90,000 (Social Security and Medicare combined), and a 2.9% tax on profits above that amount (Medicare only). In comparison, regular employees pay only a 7.65% tax on wages of $90,000 or less, and a 1.45% tax on wages above that.

Fortunately, if self-employment taxes are due, you can deduct half of the total self-employment taxes you pay from your taxable income at year-end. And if your LLC made less than $400 profit in the business year or lost money, you're totally exempt from having to pay self-employment taxes. (See "Reporting and Paying Are Not the Same" in Section B1, above, on the distinction between filing taxes and paying them.)

Self-employment taxes are reported on Schedule SE, which, like Schedule E (*Supplemental Income and Loss*), is submitted yearly with an LLC member's 1040 return. Once you determine the self-employment taxes you owe on Schedule SE, the result is entered on your 1040 form in the "Other Taxes" section, which is added to your individual income tax obligation. If the LLC member is required to pay advance quarterly tax installments, however, any self-employment taxes will be included in those payments. (See Section E, below, for information on estimating taxes and paying them quarterly.)

2. State Taxes

While the federal government treats LLCs with pass-through tax status almost exactly like partnerships, the tax treatment LLCs receive in their states of formation may vary somewhat. Most states follow the IRS's lead and treat LLCs as pass-through entities unless the members have elected corporate tax treatment for the LLC. However, some states also impose special taxes on LLCs themselves, despite treating them as pass-through tax entities in most other respects.

First, most states collect income tax from LLC members on their share of business profits. Essentially, most states simply follow the IRS classification scheme for LLCs, which translates into treatment as either a partnership or a sole proprietorship. An LLC with a single owner is usually treated as a sole proprietorship, and business profits will be taxed on the sole member's individual state income tax return. LLCs with two or more owners will typically be treated as partnerships and must file the same tax returns as owners of partnerships in that state.

Unlike the IRS, which imposes no taxes on LLCs themselves, several states levy taxes on LLCs in addition to taxing LLC members on their share of LLC income. These taxes are alternately called "franchise taxes," "annual fees," "surcharge taxes," or other similar names. Depending on the state, these additional costs can range from $10 to thousands of dollars, so be sure to understand your state's rules well in advance of tax time. (Appendix A includes contact information for state tax agencies, which can tell you how your state treats LLCs taxwise. You'll also find information there on where to get the latest forms for your state.)

Like federal taxes, state income taxes for members must often be paid in quarterly installments. (Estimating your taxes and making quarterly payments is covered in Section E, just below.)

E. Estimating and Paying Your Taxes Quarterly

Anyone who earns income from a business must generally pay income taxes in quarterly installments over the course of the business year. Some businesspeople who expect to owe little or no income tax are exempt from these estimated payment requirements. (See Section 1, below.) At year end, if you've paid more than what you owe, you'll get a refund. On the other hand, if you didn't pay enough in your quarterly installments, you will owe more.

While it might not seem so at first, this system isn't all that different from the way taxes on employment wages are handled. From each paycheck, the federal (and often state) government requires an employer to withhold income taxes from each employee's wages based on the employee's expected annual salary or hourly pay. At year end, the employee calculates and reports a personal tax obligation based on how much money was actually earned during the year. Depending on the dollar amount of the tax obligation, the employee will either owe more money (if the employer didn't withhold enough) or be due a refund (if the employer withheld too much).

The IRS and state tax agencies collect withholdings or advance payment of estimated taxes for a simple, practical reason: They know that a sudden multithousand-dollar bill on April 15 can be difficult for anyone. Spreading out payments by wage withholding or estimated payments is the tax agencies' way of making your life a little easier—and making sure they get their money.

Unfortunately, it's much easier for an employer to figure out an employee's estimated tax burden based on individual yearly salary or hourly wage than it is for a small business owner to estimate taxes based on future income from a new and unproven business. If you're wondering how you can estimate taxes on business income that hasn't come in yet, you're not alone. Projecting future income in order to estimate your tax obligation can be a dicey task, especially for brand-new business owners whose income hasn't yet evened out into any predictable rhythm. To make matters worse, you'll be socked with a penalty if your estimates are off and you don't pay enough each quarter.

But here's the good news: You don't need to start making estimated tax payments until you earn enough income to subject you to a threshold quarterly payment requirement. This should give you enough time to get a pretty good feel for how much and how quickly money—and, by extension, taxable profits—are coming into your business. And even if you do underestimate your taxes and face a penalty of a few hundred dollars, you can at least take heart that you owe extra only because your business has become profitable sooner than you anticipated.

In addition to the IRS, many state tax agencies also require profitable businesses to make estimated tax payments. For the most part, these states' rules are similar to the federal one, but they use slightly different formulas. The rest of this section will address just the federal requirement; check with your state tax agency to find out its formula for estimating taxes. (Contact information for each state's tax agency is included in Appendix A.)

1. Who Must Pay Estimated Taxes?

In a nutshell, business owners have to pay federal estimated taxes if they expect to owe at least $1,000 in federal taxes for any particular year (including income taxes and self-employment taxes). Generally, this means you'll have to make estimated payments if your adjusted gross income (taxable net profits minus tax exemptions, deductions, and credits) will be between $3,000 and $6,000, depending on your tax bracket. The point here is, if your business is at all profitable, count on estimating and paying your taxes quarterly. On the other hand, if you're operating at a net business loss or making next to nothing, you may not have to make estimated payments.

EXAMPLE: On December 31, as part of a New Year's resolution, Jason quits his job as computer salesman and opens a river rafting outfit called the Rapids Transit Company. For the first few months of the next year, every dollar he takes in pays for equipment, insurance, and marketing. At the rate he's going, he doesn't know if he'll make a profit at all that year, so he doesn't worry about estimated taxes. However, starting in June with the heavy tourist season, he starts clearing about $1,300 per month, after all deductions. He thinks he may have at least four more months like that before winter slows business down. If so, his annual profit will be about $6,500 ($1,300 x five months). Depending on his tax status, he'll probably owe between $1,000 and $2,000 in taxes at the end of the year. He realizes he'd better start making estimated quarterly payments to be safe, or risk a penalty.

Your Day Job May Help You Avoid Estimated Taxes

If, in addition to the business you own, you work at a job on which taxes are withheld from your income, you might not have to pay estimated taxes if your income from your business is not a significant part of your total income. This is because the taxes withheld from your job may cover you for any estimated taxes owed on your business income. In other words, the IRS wants to make sure that a certain portion of the total taxes you'll owe are paid in installments over the year, but it doesn't care whether those taxes are withheld from your paycheck or paid as estimated taxes. It's possible that the taxes withheld from your paycheck will be enough to meet your entire tax obligation. On the other hand, if your business is bringing in significant income, chances are that your wage withholding won't cover your tax bill.

Now for the nitty-gritty. The IRS has a relatively straightforward formula (okay, that may be stretching this just a bit) for determining whether you need to estimate and pay your taxes in installments. For the year 2005, for example, you'll have to pay estimated taxes if:

- you expect to owe at least $1,000 in federal taxes (including income taxes and self-employment taxes) for the current year, after subtracting any withheld taxes, and
- you expect your withheld taxes and credits to be less than the smaller of:
  - 100% of your total tax owed for the previous year, or
  - 90% of your total tax obligation for the current year.

This formula sounds complicated, but it's not. First, it requires you to make estimated payments only if you expect to owe at least $1,000 to the IRS at year end, above and beyond any taxes withheld from wages. This translates to about $3,000 to $6,000 in adjusted gross income from your business, depending on your tax bracket. So if your business is barely breaking even, you probably won't have to make estimated payments.

Second, if you do expect to make at least that amount from your business, you may not have to pay estimated taxes on your business income if enough taxes are withheld from a paycheck (assuming you receive one). If the taxes that are withheld from your paycheck in 2005 will add up to more than 90% of what you'll owe in taxes for the year, you won't have to make estimated payments. Or, if that's not true, there's one more way you can escape paying estimated tax payments: If the taxes withheld in 2005 will add up to at least what your entire tax bill was in 2004, you're free of the estimated tax requirement.

> **EXAMPLE:** Nels works as a manager of an auto parts store, which pays him a salary and deducts federal and state taxes from each paycheck. He starts a sole proprietorship called Falcon's Auto Tow. In the first few months of his auto-towing business, Nels operates at a loss. Since his only taxable income during those months is from his paychecks, on which taxes are withheld, he doesn't have to worry about estimated payments. In the fifth month he starts to turn a profit, at which point Nels starts to pay attention to whether he must pay estimated taxes. If he thinks his wage withholding will account for at least 90% of his total tax bill at the end of the year, he doesn't need to file and pay estimated taxes. In other words, if he thinks that taxes on his small business income will account for less than 10% of his total tax bill, he'll just file his taxes at year end like most people whose entire income is all subject to wage withholding.

If you're not sure whether you have to pay federal estimated taxes, help is available. IRS Form 1040-ES contains a worksheet to use to calculate your estimated taxes, and Publication 505, *Tax Withholding and Estimated Tax*, explains in detail whether you have to pay estimated taxes. You can obtain these by calling 800-829-3676, or at www.irs.gov/formspubs/index.html. Another option is to use an online calculator to figure your estimated taxes. The TuboTax website at www.turbotax.com offers free tax calculators; look in the "Tips & Resources" section. Or, you may be able to do the calculation quickly and easily with your accounting software.

2. When to Make Estimated Tax Payments

As just discussed, you become subject to the federal estimated tax payment requirement when you expect to earn enough profit during a business year to trigger the payment requirement. Once you expect to earn that much income, you need to do your best to estimate your income for the year and pay a quarterly installment based on the taxes due. (See Section 3, below, for more.) Each quarterly payment must be filed a half-month after the end of the quarter. For federal estimated taxes, the quarterly due dates are as follows:

Income made during:	Tax installment due:
Jan. 1 through Mar. 31	April 15
Apr. 1 through May 31	June 15
June 1 through Aug. 31	September 15
Sept. 1 through Dec. 31	January 15 of the next year

If your business uses a fiscal rather than a calendar year, your payments will be due on the 15th day of the 4th, 6th, and 9th months of your fiscal year and the 1st month of the following fiscal year.

Defining Your Business Year

Except for C corporations, a business must use the calendar year as its business year unless it gets permission from the IRS to choose a different starting and ending point. A bit of tax jargon is important here. Any one-year period other than the calendar year (ending on December 31) that a business uses for tax purposes is called a "fiscal year," a "tax year," or an "accounting period." The IRS allows sole proprietorships, partnerships, LLCs, and S corporations to use a fiscal year only if there is a valid business reason for it, such as significant seasonal fluctuations in business. Fiscal years must begin on the first day of a month and end on the last day of the previous month one year later. An unincorporated business that wants to use a fiscal year must submit Form 8716, *Election To Have a Tax Year Other Than a Required Tax Year,* to the IRS and have it approved. (This form is included in Appendix C and on the CD-ROM that accompanies this book.)

---

3. Calculating and Paying Your Estimated Taxes

There are three ways to estimate your taxes properly. You can:

- base them on how much tax you owed last year
- estimate your current year's income and deductions, then calculate the taxes you'd owe for those figures, or
- calculate your tax liability after each quarter (called the "annualized income installment method"), prorating your deductions and personal exemptions. You must file Form 2210 if you use this method.

With the exception of the first method, you'll need help making these calculations. Instructions and worksheets that can help you calculate your estimated tax payments are included with the federal Form 1040-ES (the form you'll send to the IRS). This form also includes vouchers to submit with each periodic payment. Both Appendix B and the CD-ROM that accompanies this book offer information on getting the latest forms. For more information on federal estimated tax payments, refer to IRS Publication 505, *Tax Withholding and Estimated Tax,* available online at www.irs.gov/formspubs/index.html.

Don't overlook your self-employment taxes. Self-employment taxes (see Section B1b, C1b, or D1b, above), like income taxes, are subject to the estimated tax payment requirement. Be sure to include them when figuring your estimated tax burden for the year.

F. City and County Taxes

Unlike the federal or state governments, many cities and counties impose taxes directly on your business, even if your business is a pass-through entity such as a sole proprietorship, partnership, or limited liability company. Of course, you, as the owner of the business, are personally liable for these financial obligations, but the difference is that your business itself—not merely the profits that flow through to you and any other owners— incurs taxes by local governments. Often, these taxes can be more of a burden than federal or state ones, because many of them are based on your business income before you deduct business costs and expenses. Some areas, for instance, impose a gross receipts tax, which calculates the tax based simply on how much total income your business brings in, without regard for your expenses.

Local taxes vary a lot from one area to the next, but your business can always expect to face some sort of "business taxes" from your city or county, which may include property taxes.

1. Business Taxes

The vague term "business taxes" simply refers to the tax your local government imposes on all businesses within the city or county limits. Businesses in rural areas will probably only deal with their county tax authority. Whether the tax is imposed by a city or a county tax authority, the information about business taxes provided in this section generally applies.

Unlike the IRS and most state tax agencies, which simply collect taxes after they're incurred, most local tax collectors require you to go through a tax registration process before you start your business. (Information on how the registration process generally works is provided in Chapter 7, Section D.) Once you've registered, you'll obtain what's commonly called a "tax registration certificate" (or, sometimes, a "business license"). Registration gives notice to your local tax authorities that your business exists and allows them to tax it, based on whatever method your locality has adopted for your type of business.

In many cities and counties, you actually start paying your local taxes when you purchase your business license or registration certificate. Often, a

locality will base its registration fee on your expected local tax for the year. In some localities, your registration fee is like a prepaid tax that can be applied toward your total year-end tax. In other places, the registration cost is purely an administrative fee and cannot be applied to your tax bill. And in still other areas, part of the registration cost is a prepaid tax that can be credited toward your tax bill, and part is an administrative fee.

The taxing schemes used in various cities and counties are usually based on certain attributes of your business. Most localities divide businesses into a number of different categories or types, such as retail sales, wholesale sales, hotels/apartments, and service businesses. Each category uses a certain criterion to calculate taxes, usually called a "tax base." The most common tax base, for example, is "gross receipts" (total income, before expenses). Each category has a certain tax rate for each tax base.

For example, in San Francisco, retail sales businesses (category 08) must pay $1.50 per $1,000 of gross receipts (the tax base). Contractors (category 02) in San Francisco also have gross receipts as their tax base, but they must pay $3 per $1,000. Other criteria used as tax bases include total payroll, number of employees, or number of company vehicles. Other tax bases exist as well. Certain professionals, such as accountants, attorneys, and podiatrists, pay taxes based on the number of years they have been licensed in the state. The moral of the story here is that local tax systems have just about as many ways of taxing your business as there are types of businesses.

Since rules vary widely from city to city and county to county, you'll need to check with your local tax agency to find out how it will tax your business. When searching for the appropriate tax agency, look in the government section of your telephone book under City Government (or County Government if you live in an unincorporated area) for names such as "Tax Collector," "Business Licenses and Permits," or "Business Tax Division." And, since local taxation of businesses is usually closely tied to start-up registration requirements, most businesses will automatically receive tax-filing information either when they register or soon after by mail. (For more information on start-up registration requirements, see Chapter 7.)

2. Property Taxes

Many localities impose taxes on certain kinds of business property, such as real estate, business equipment, furniture, and vehicles. Property tax reporting procedures vary considerably from area to area, but a common requirement is for businesses to provide their local tax authority with an itemized list of business property subject to tax. Check in your area to determine whether any property taxes apply to your business and how to go about paying them.

G. Sales Taxes

In many states, retail sales are subject to state, county, and local district sales taxes. They are often just referred to as state sales taxes, since they're often filed and paid to one state sales tax agency with just one return. In states that use this system, it's up to the state sales tax agency to distribute the collected taxes to the counties and districts across the state.

⚠️ **Sales tax rules are closely related to seller's permit requirements.** Recall from Chapter 7, Section E, that most businesses that engage in retail sales must apply for a seller's permit. This can be true even if the business ultimately makes no taxable sales—for instance, if all sales fall into a tax-exempt category, like groceries. (See Chapter 7, Section E, for help in figuring out whether your business needs a seller's permit.)

1. Taxable vs. Nontaxable Sales

In most states that impose sales taxes, the general rule for whether a transaction is taxable is that the sale must:

- involve the sale of a tangible item, and
- be made to the final user of the item.

Tangible items are things you can touch, such as books, toys, or furniture. Nontangible items might include services, downloadable books, software, or intellectual property such as patents or copyrights.

A final user is a consumer—either an individual or a business—rather than a reseller (a wholesaler or distributor). Sales that are made directly to end users (consumers), rather than resellers, are retail sales (taxable). Sales to resellers are wholesale sales (nontaxable). This means that if you operate as a wholesaler and sell tangible goods to resellers who will in turn sell them to consumers, your sales are likely exempt from sales tax. (See Section 4, below, for rules on sales to resellers.)

Keep in mind, however, that this rule is by no means uniform from state to state. For instance, while some states may consider sales of software to be taxable sales of tangible items, others will not. A common source of confusion is the fact that states often have unique (to put it delicately) definitions of the terms "tangible item," "final user," or whatever other terms apply within the state. For example, in the late 1990s, more than a few graphic artists in California were surprised to learn that the state did not consider their transactions to be services (which are not taxable in California), but instead to be taxable sales of tangible items, merely because the artists' work was given to the client on a physical piece of paper. The sales tax regulations were amended in 2002, resulting in more fair treatment of graphic artists' work. The point here is not to rely on common definitions, but to find out specifically how your state tax agency interprets sales tax terminology.

Besides the fact that many states use broad definitions in deciding what is taxable, a few states diverge from the general rule described above. Unlike the majority of states, Hawaii, New Mexico, and South Dakota impose sales taxes on all services. Still other states charge sales taxes on certain services, and others tax services when they're performed along with a taxable sale of a tangible item, such as charges for delivering a taxable item. Again, the state rules regarding these sales tax situations are complex and fraught with exceptions, so it's crucial that you check with your state agency to find out the details that apply to your business. (Appendix A contains contact information for state sales tax agencies, including Web addresses and phone numbers.)

Sales Tax Exemptions

Part of the reason that the rules on sales taxes can be so convoluted is that the "rules" are clouded by swarms of exceptions and exemptions. Here are several examples of common exemptions from sales tax:

- most groceries (but not restaurant or take-out food)
- sales to out-of-state customers
- sales to the U.S. government, and
- some sales related to the entertainment industry.

Rules vary from state to state, so be sure to check with your state sales tax agency about which sales are exempt from sales tax. For general information, see The Sales Tax Clearinghouse, http://thestc.com.

You may need a permit to sell tangible goods. As we mentioned earlier, businesses that sell tangible goods must typically obtain a seller's permit from the state before sales begin, even if the sales aren't taxable (such as wholesale sales, discussed below). Selling tangible goods without a seller's permit is a misdemeanor crime in some states, but, typically, the state sales tax agency will give you the opportunity to comply by getting a permit before it files any criminal charges. But keep in mind that if you made any sales that were taxable before you got your seller's permit, you may be required not only to get a permit, but to pay all back taxes that are due.

2. The Nexus Requirement

Not all sales of tangible goods to end users are subject to sales tax. Such a sale is taxable only if it is made to a customer who is a resident of the state in which you're doing business. In other words, sales to out-of-state customers (such as by mail order) are not subject to sales tax.

The general rule—established by the U.S. Supreme Court in *Quill v. North Dakota,* 504 U.S. 298 (1992)—is that your business must collect sales taxes only on sales conducted within states in which your business is physically located. In legal terms, this is known as having a "nexus," which essentially means a physical presence. For instance, if your business has a store in California and warehouses in Texas and Illinois, then your business would have a nexus in all those states and would need to collect sales taxes from customers there. On the other hand, orders shipped to customers in Wisconsin, where your business has no physical presence, would not be taxed. This explains why mail order forms often contain language such as "California residents add 8.5% sales tax." When you see such language, you know that the business is located in California and must collect sales tax from customers in the state, but not from residents of other states.

Your business is likely to be deemed to have a nexus in a state if:

- you operate a retail store in the state
- your company's salespeople conduct business within the state, or
- you own or lease a warehouse or office in the state, even if it's not open to the public.

Generally, simply shipping a product or a catalogue to a customer in a certain state isn't enough to establish a nexus in that state (assuming that you use a third-party shipper such as UPS or the U.S. Postal Service).

Once a nexus exists in a given state, your business will be subject to all of that state's sales tax laws, including any seller's permit and sales tax collecting and reporting requirements. For this reason, many businesses limit their physical presence to one or two states and conduct nationwide business by mail order or e-commerce. This approach is sound in theory, but the explosion of e-commerce has created a number of wrinkles you should know about. (These are discussed in the next section.)

3. Sales Taxes Online

While the Web can help you leap geographical boundaries and bring the world into your living room, it also makes a quagmire out of state and local laws that are supposed to apply only to specific areas on the map. Sales tax laws have had a particularly hard time adapting to the world of e-commerce. As more and more companies have started selling products online, there's been increasing confusion over which of these sales are subject to sales tax and which state's rules apply. Online businesses charge sales tax in a seemingly random manner, causing many lawmakers and businesspeople to call for the reform of sales tax laws. In particular, brick-and-mortar businesses are bitter that many online businesses "unfairly" escape paying sales taxes, giving them a competitive advantage over the real-world stores. Before going into any details, simply keep in mind that

online sales tax rules are still emerging and highly controversial. Expect a good deal of development and change over the next few years.

Currently, the rules that apply to businesses that sell products online are no different from those applying to non-Web retailers. Businesses that sell products over the Web are subject to the sales tax laws in the states in which the business has a physical presence. Even for online businesses, only a traditional physical presence counts with regard to sales taxes; the fact that customers can access your website from a particular state currently isn't enough to create a nexus in that state. Online retailers don't need to pay sales taxes on transactions in every state where the website appears (which, of course, is everywhere). E-tailers need only to pay sales taxes on sales in states in which the business has an office, salespeople, or other type of physical presence. Of course, if the business has a nexus in a state that doesn't charge sales taxes, then transactions there are tax-free.

EXAMPLE: Killer Computers sells computers and related accessories from its website, killercomputers.com. Killer Computers has a main office and a phone bank in Nebraska and warehouses in New Hampshire, Oregon, and Texas. Because of its physical presence in these four states, Killer Computers will need to comply with those states' sales tax laws. This means that when killercomputers.com sells computers to customers in Nebraska, New Hampshire, Oregon, and Texas, the sales tax laws of those states will apply to those transactions. Since Oregon and New Hampshire don't charge sales taxes, Killer Computers doesn't have to worry about paying sales taxes when it sells computers to customers in those two states. Nebraska and Texas, on the other hand, do charge sales taxes on retail sales, so when killercomputers.com sells to Nebraska or Texas residents, those sales will be subject to sales taxes.

If you think that the rules for online retailers sound pretty much like the rules for other businesses, you're right. Things get a little kooky, however, when it comes to certain large e-tailers. Major chains such as Barnes & Noble and Wal-Mart have found a way to sell their goods online free of sales tax, even to customers who live in states teeming with Barnes & Noble and Wal-Mart retail stores. They get away with paying no sales tax on their online sales, even in states where they have a physical presence by doing what big corporations do best: being crafty. The website called barnesandnoble.com is a different legal entity from the Barnes & Noble company, so the fact that Barnes & Noble has a physical presence in virtually every state doesn't matter. The barnesandnoble.com website only needs to charge sales taxes on sales to residents in states in which the website is headquartered or has some other physical presence. And its website has a nexus only in states that don't charge sales tax (Alaska, Delaware, Montana, New Hampshire, and Oregon).

It's tough to say what the future holds. The questionable practice of creating legally separate, tax-free websites is under attack, and the e-business boom in general is being blamed for billions of dollars of lost sales tax revenues each year. State revenue departments as well as brick-and-mortar companies are lobbying heavily for sales tax reform to make the system more fair for everyone.

It may be a while before any significant reform takes place. There is a flurry of legislative activity on the issue, much of it focused on streamlining the state sales tax systems so that sellers who operate in more than one state can reasonably comply with more than one state's rules and regulations. Under an initiative known as the Streamlined Sales and Use Tax Agreement (SSUTA), states are working together to simplify their sales tax systems with the ultimate goal of compelling out-of-state sellers to comply with their sales tax laws. The states' plan is to meet certain measures of streamlining—for instance, with coordinated automatic tax collection systems—then to appeal to the U.S. Congress for expanded powers to collect sales taxes from out-of-state sellers. Approximately half the states have now passed SSUTA legislation and are working through the details of streamlining their complex sales tax codes. The sheer immensity of the task makes progress slow going, however, so it's hard to say what the long-term future holds. One source of updated information is available at the website of Vertex, Inc., a company specializing in tax software. Go to www.vertexinc.com and look for SSUTA updates.

Staying up to date on e-taxes. For information on the ever-changing world of e-commerce taxes, check out the Vertex Tax Cybrary at www .vertexinc.com/taxcybrary.

4. Sales to Final Users vs. Sales to Resellers

As mentioned above, states generally tax only sales to the final user. The idea behind this rule is to make sure that items are taxed only once. Rather than taxing the sale of a lamp, for instance, each time it is sold—from its manufacturer, to the wholesaler, to the final customer—it is taxed only when it is sold to the final consumer. (Some transactions that are exempt from sales tax, however, may be subject to a nearly identical tax, a "use tax." See Section 6, below.)

How can you be sure that a customer is a final user? Customers who intend to resell your product should present you with a "resale certificate," which states that the product is being purchased for resale. Depending on your state's law, the certificate must usually contain certain information, including:

- the purchaser's name and address
- the number of the purchaser's seller's permit
- a description of the property to be purchased
- a statement that the property is being used for resale, in terms such as "will be resold" or "for resale" (language such as "nontaxable" or "exempt" is not enough)
- the date of the sale, and

- the signature of the purchaser or an authorized agent.

If you are not presented with such a certificate, you should assume the customer is the final user and treat the sale as taxable. If you sell to the same customer repeatedly, you'll usually need to collect only one resale certificate, which you should keep on file at your office. From then on, whenever you sell items to that company, you shouldn't have to collect another resale certificate.

5. Using Resale Certificates

Just as your customers can escape paying you sales taxes by presenting a resale certificate, you can use one to purchase goods and supplies free of sales tax, as long as the goods and supplies are for legitimate resale. This applies whether you'll resell purchased goods as is, or whether you'll incorporate purchased supplies into your products. (But see the discussion of "use tax" in Section 6, below.) If you buy regularly from the same supplier, you should only have to present your resale certificate once.

This exception doesn't apply to goods and supplies that you don't plan to resell or use in manufacturing products. You must pay sales taxes on all items that you'll use in your business and not pass on to a customer. In other words, when you are actually the final user, you have to pay sales tax like anyone else. This includes sales tax on goods and supplies you use to perform services or operate your business. For example, a hairdresser must pay sales tax on the shampoo used to wash hair. Similarly, if you purchase a computer to keep track of your sales, you should pay the sales tax on that purchase. When purchasing a combination of goods, only some of which you intend to resell, you should clearly indicate which items are for resale and pay sales taxes on the rest.

6. Use Taxes

While it's true that some sales of tangible goods are exempt from sales tax, many of these transactions are actually subject to a use tax. In keeping with its name, a use tax is due when you use a tangible good on which you didn't pay sales tax.

Use taxes commonly apply to purchases of tangible goods from outside your state. For instance, if you order 20 computers, 20 chairs, and 20 desks for your office from an out-of-state mail order catalogue, you probably didn't pay sales taxes on those items, because most states don't require businesses to collect sales tax from out-of-state purchasers. But under use tax laws in many states, your state can collect use taxes from you, the buyer, to make up for the revenue it would have gotten if you had bought the equipment within the state.

Other transactions subject to use tax include purchases of items you originally intended to resell (and bought tax-free because you used your resale certificate) but used for another purpose. Also, items that you buy to incorporate into a new product to sell, as well as items you lease, are subject to the use tax (assuming you bought them free from sales tax with a resale certificate). Inventory that you store for future resale is not subject to use tax.

To pay use taxes, you typically fill out a use tax return, which is often the same as or related to the one that your business will use for paying sales taxes to the state. Essentially, you'll enter information on the form about the purchases you made that are subject to use tax, and follow the form's instructions for calculating your tax. There's not much more to it than sending it off to the state sales tax office, along with a check (assuming you owe money).

There's a high blow-off factor when it comes to use taxes. Use taxes have largely been ignored by individuals and businesses, and the inherent difficulty of enforcing this tax allows virtually everyone to get away with it. However, some states that have traditionally been lax in enforcing and collecting use taxes are now stepping up their efforts to collect them. Particularly in today's environment of thriving e-commerce and state budget deficits, sales taxes on out-of-state purchases is becoming a burning issue. Keep an eye out for developments in this area, and don't get caught with your use taxes down.

Who Actually Owes Sales Taxes?

Despite the fact that most consumers pay sales taxes on a daily basis, there's a lot of misunderstanding out there over who really owes sales taxes—purchasers or sellers. Here's the deal: In most states, consumers are technically responsible for paying sales taxes. In these states, the retailer is essentially merely a collector for the sales tax owed by the consumer. In some states, however, the actual responsibility for sales taxes falls on the retailer. This sort of tax is sometimes called a "privilege tax," since businesses are taxed for the privilege of conducting retail sales.

Keep in mind that these are often technical distinctions without a whole lot of practical effect. For example, if consumers are legally responsible for paying sales taxes in a certain state, that doesn't mean that businesses can escape paying state sales taxes. Usually, all it means is that the business must state the selling price and the sales tax separately on receipts and invoices. That way, consumers see that they are in fact being charged sales tax.

---

7. Keeping Track of Your Sales

When you obtain a seller's permit in most states, you obligate yourself to file a sales (and use) tax return. This means that you'll need to keep careful records of both your sales and purchases. Most state sales tax agencies require that you keep:

- books or computer files recording your sales and purchases
- bills, receipts, invoices, contracts, or other documents (called "documents of original entry") that support your books, and
- schedules and working papers used in preparing your tax returns.

In addition, if you conduct business in more than one county, city, or other local tax district, you may need to keep separate records of sales made in each area.

Finally, your records should show all sales your business makes, even sales that aren't taxable.

8. Calculating, Paying, and Filing Sales Taxes

Sales taxes in many states are actually a combination of state, county, and city sales taxes. For example, an 8% sales tax may actually break down into a 5% state tax, a 2% county tax, and a 1% city tax. The sales taxes that apply to your business will often depend on where your taxable sales are being conducted. If you conduct taxable sales in more than one tax district, you may end up paying several different rates. Conveniently, many states allow businesses to file just one state tax return that includes all taxes for all applicable districts. The return will usually ask you to identify where

your sales were made so that the state can allocate the fair share of taxes to each tax district.

Businesses that have been issued a seller's permit will often receive their state sales tax return package automatically, along with an account number, due date, and filing instructions. Depending on your sales volume, you'll need to submit your sales tax return yearly, quarterly, or monthly. Contact your state agency for details.

Filling out the sales tax return is generally fairly straightforward and will vary only slightly in format depending on the form used by your state. Basically, you'll enter sales information for each tax district in your state where you conducted taxable sales and identify the tax rates that apply to each of these sales. The return will typically walk you though the calculations and will tell you whether and how much sales tax you owe. In most states, you can get telephone assistance if you're having trouble filling out your return. Consult your state sales tax agency (contact information is included in Appendix A) for detailed instructions on filing your sales tax return.

Sellers' may be required to file sales tax returns. If you applied for and received a seller's permit because you anticipated selling goods, you may need to submit your sales tax return even if you never made a sale. If you didn't make any taxable sales, you shouldn't owe any

taxes, but you may still need to submit the form. If you don't, you may risk losing your seller's permit, which could mean you couldn't legally make any sales at all. Check with your state agency (listed in Appendix A) for its requirements.

Chapter 9 Checklist

☐ Become familiar with the general scheme of taxes faced by small businesses.

☐ Remember that you may have to pay estimated taxes in quarterly installments. Other taxes may also have to be paid more often than once a year, such as your state sales taxes. Make a calendar of important tax dates so you don't miss them and incur penalties.

☐ Keep careful track of your expenses so that you may deduct them.

☐ Consult a tax professional at least once a year to help you organize your books and keep your taxes to a minimum.

☐ File and pay your annual taxes each year, and other taxes as they become due.

Laws, Taxes, and Other Issues for Home Businesses

It's not an exaggeration to say that the explosion of home-based businesses has radically reshaped the small business landscape. By most accounts, the number of home-based businesses in the United States exceeds 30 million and is growing strong. Along with the boom in home businesses, whole new industries have emerged, such as major office supply chains; home office networking equipment dealers; home business consultants; and a host of magazines, websites, and other media dedicated to home business issues. No question about it, home businesses—and the industries that have grown around them—are here to stay.

While growing phenomenally, the home business sector has achieved a new level of respect. Entrepreneurs of all stripes and funding levels have discovered that setting up shop in a home can be a cost-efficient, flexible way to get a business venture off the ground. While many businesses eventually move into company digs, an increasing number are staying put at their founders' homes. "Home business" no longer means Tupperware parties or shady multilevel marketing schemes. Even the most professional, reputable, and aggressively growth-minded companies are joining the ranks of home-based businesses.

It's no secret why the idea of starting a business from home is so attractive to so many. The convenience of working at home is a major draw, especially to parents who want to cut commute times and increase time with the family. Not having to pay rent for an external office helps the bottom line of any business—especially important in the start-up days. And thanks to fast, affordable Internet connections and wireless networks, it's never been easier to exchange documents, do research, send emails, teleconference, and otherwise be connected to the world from home.

In addition to communications and networking, a number of other technologies have advanced by leaps and bounds to help home businesses get firmly established. Prosumer—a hybrid of professional and consumer—imaging products such as digital cameras, scanners and printers, and easy-to-use Web development software allow home businesses to create professional-looking brochures, websites, and other marketing materials. With all this new technology, a home business can develop a much more professional image than was possible a decade ago.

Before you hang out your shingle, however, it's important to realize that a home business isn't immune from a number of the requirements that affect businesses in general. Similar to a business operated from a commercial office space, a business run from home must comply with zoning requirements in your area. And there are several special tax rules for home businesses, as well as insurance issues, that you should understand. All of this is discussed in this chapter.

Is a Home-Based Business Right for You?

While many types of businesses lend themselves to being run out of a residence, others don't. Make sure you've considered whether using your home as your office is a good idea. Ask yourself the following questions:

- How will you deal with customers and suppliers? Will they be able to easily park and pick up or unload material if necessary?
- Will customers take you and your company seriously if you work out of your house?
- Will your business require a lot of space for performing services or storing supplies?
- Can you work productively in your home, considering potential distractions such as kids, the couch, the refrigerator, and the TV?
- If you rent, will your landlord give your business the okay?

Businesses that require nothing but a small office and don't generate much traffic coming and going—such as graphic design, accounting, and Web development—and those in which most of the dirty work is routinely done offsite—such as construction and plumbing—are particularly well suited for home businesses.

A. Zoning Restrictions

As with leased office spaces, you need to make sure that the business activities you plan to carry on in your home are within the letter of your local zoning laws. You may also have to apply for a special "home occupation permit" before you begin. (Zoning laws typically refer to home businesses as "home occupations.")

Since your home is most likely in an area zoned for residential use only (some loft-type or urban apartments might be zoned for mixed use), the types of businesses your neighborhood ordinances allow to operate will likely be pretty limited. A few areas actually forbid home businesses altogether. But most cities and counties allow home businesses that have little likelihood of causing noise or pollution, creating traffic, or otherwise disturbing the neighbors. Writers, artists, attorneys, accountants, architects, insurance brokers, and piano teachers are examples of businesspeople commonly allowed to work from home. Typically not allowed are retailers, automotive repair shops, cafés and bars, animal hospitals and breeders, or any type of adult-oriented businesses.

Watch out for private land use restrictions. If you live in a condo, co-op, planned subdivision, or rental property, you are likely subject to private land use restrictions in addition to your local laws. Condo regulations, for instance, often contain language restricting or sometimes even prohibiting business use of the premises. Or your apartment lease might prohibit business on the property. Check the documents governing your property to see if you are bound by any such rules.

1. Check With the Planning Department

To find out how your city or county deals with home businesses, call the planning department or visit its website if it has one. Ask or look for any information available on home occupations. Some areas have websites or pamphlets with information explaining home business restrictions and how to obtain any necessary permits. In other places, all that's available might be a grainy photocopy of the municipal code, which you'll have to decipher yourself. If there's no approval or permit process for home businesses in your area, it's generally up to you to comply with the local zoning codes. And those codes are subject to change; be sure to check with the local zoning offices for updates.

The most foolproof way to avoid trouble with zoning officials is to do your best to keep down your business's impact on the neighborhood. As long as you're not in flagrant violation of the zoning laws regarding home businesses and your neighbors are happy, you'll probably be fine.

Let your neighbors in on your business plans. Getting to know your neighbors can be a huge help in avoiding problems with zoning officials. For instance, if your business requires people to come and go from your house or packages to be delivered daily, your neighbors might jump to the nutty conclusion that you're a drug dealer and report you to the city. Even though you can show your drug of choice is vitamin C, the city might unearth technical zoning violations that never would have otherwise turned up. As preventive measures, communicating with your neighbors and dealing with their concerns about issues such as parking and noise will greatly reduce the likelihood that the zoning police will come knocking on your door.

2. Understand Common Restrictions

Assuming that your local zoning laws do allow your type of home business, they are likely to impose some restrictions, such as allowing only residents of your home to be employees, restricting the number of customers that may come to your house, limiting the percentage of your home's floor space that can be used for business, or prohibiting signs outside of your house that advertise the business. In Milwaukee, Wisconsin, for example, home businesses cannot employ anyone who doesn't live at the residence, and the business may not use more than 20% of the usable floor area of the home, including the basement. In Austin, Texas, it is illegal for any equipment or materials associated with the home business to be visible from the street. And in Sacramento, California, home businesses are not allowed to use any trucks larger than one-half ton—which rules out many full-size pickup trucks.

In addition to these general limitations, cities often impose restrictions on specific types of home businesses. For instance, while a city might forbid any type of home business from having a neon sign, it might also have a special rule for landscapers that prohibits landscaping supplies from being kept at the home office. Be sure to find out from zoning officials or the local city hall whether there are special rules for your type of business.

3. Comply With Local Requirements

If you find out that your city does allow your type of home business in your area, you may have no further need to contact the zoning office. Many cities do not require any special permits, as long as a home business complies with all of the rules and restrictions contained in its planning code (as discussed above). Some cities, however, require all home business owners to get a "home occupation permit." Obtaining such a permit is usually a simple matter of filling out a form provided by the planning department and paying whatever fee may be required. If your business meets the restrictions your city imposes, your permit will be issued.

If you don't meet all of your city's rules for having a home occupation, or your area isn't zoned for your type of home business, you may be out of luck and simply not allowed to run your business from home. In some locales, however, a home business that meets most but not all of the city's restrictions may be allowed to operate, but only after obtaining a home occupation permit. In San Diego, for instance, no permit is required for home businesses that meet all of the city's criteria: no business signs, no nonresident employees on the premises, and so on. If the home business deviates from the criteria, the city may allow the business to proceed, but only with a permit. Acceptable deviations in San Diego include having one nonresident employee, having one client who visits your home office by appointment, and using more than one vehicle for business.

Keep in mind that the zoning agency is probably not the only land use regulatory agency in your area. While your activity might be okay with zoning officials, operating out of your home may not pass other departments' requirements. For example, if you're starting a catering business, chances are your county health department won't let you work out of your home kitchen. You may be allowed to convert your garage or another separate structure into a professional kitchen—but, of course, that is likely to necessitate securing building permits and passing county health inspections, in addition to zoning compliance or permission. (See Chapter 7 for more on permits for your specific business.)

B. The Home Business Tax Deduction

If your office is located in your home, you may be able to claim a portion of your home expenses—such as rent or depreciation, property taxes, utilities, and insurance—as a special deduction when reporting federal taxes. The IRS's general rule is that if your business qualifies (discussed below), you can deduct a pro rata share of home business expenses. "Pro rata" simply means a share that's proportional to the percentage of home space that you use for your business.

This section explains which businesses may qualify for the home business tax deduction, how the deduction is calculated, and other tax issues that apply. (For information on how businesses in general are taxed, see Chapter 9, "Paying Your Taxes.")

Many expenses are automatically fully deductible. Many taxpayers mistakenly believe that they need to qualify for the home business deduction before they can claim any expenses associated with a home-based business. But, in fact, you can deduct business expenses necessary for your business whether they're incurred in your home or anywhere else, even if you don't qualify for the home business deduction. For instance, you can always deduct the portion of your home long-distance phone bill that you spend on business-related calls. Other deductible business expenses might include office supplies, furniture, and equipment that you use in your home office, and the cost of bringing a second telephone line into your home for business use. As used in this chapter, "home business expenses" will refer to expenses that can only be claimed with the home business deduction.

1. IRS Requirements

Before tackling the nitty-gritty requirements, look at a couple basics. First, the IRS definition of "home" is pretty broad, generally including any type of dwelling in which you can cook and sleep. This includes houses, condos, apartment units, mobile homes, boats, and wherever else you reside. Both renters and owners are eligible for taking the home tax deduction.

Moving on to the meat of the criteria, the IRS has two requirements for any business owner who wants to deduct expenses for using part of a home as a business:

1. You must regularly use part of your home exclusively for a trade or business (see Subsection a, below).
2. You must be able to show that you:
   - use your home as your principal place of business (see Subsection b, below), or
   - meet patients, clients, or customers at home (see Subsection c, below), or
   - use a separate structure on your property exclusively for business purposes (see Subsection d, below).

Each of these criteria is examined a bit more closely below.

a. Exclusive and Regular Use for Business

The IRS will allow you to deduct home business expenses only for space in your home that is 100% dedicated to business use. For example, a graphic designer who sometimes sits at the kitchen table to do illustrations can't claim business deductions for using the kitchen—assuming the kitchen is also sometimes used for nonbusiness purposes such as cooking and eating. A spare room, however, that's set up as an office space and used only for business would probably meet the exclusive use test. But if the room contains a bed for the occasional overnight guest or doubles as storage space for clothing, then, technically, it wouldn't qualify.

The regular use test is generally pretty easy to pass. As long as you use your home business space for business on a frequent, continuing basis, rather than for a once-in-a-while garage sale or other sporadic business activity, you'll probably make the cut.

> **EXAMPLE:** Stacey runs a hat-making business. She makes the hats in an extra room of her house in which she has a sewing machine and all her supplies, as well as a computer and a file cabinet containing her sales and other financial information. Since the only use of that room is for the hat-making business, it will meet the IRS's criteria of exclusive use. And since Stacey has made and sold hats for a couple of years, with consistent monthly sales, she'll have no trouble proving that she uses the space regularly for business.

> **EXAMPLE:** Parisha has a full-time job at a plant nursery, but also does occasional freelance photography work. She has a darkroom in her basement that she uses to develop photos for her assignments. Her darkroom is dedicated to

her photography business, but she spends most of her time working at the plant nursery and has only done one photo shoot in the last six months. Parisha would be ill-advised to claim her darkroom expenses as a home business deduction, since she doesn't regularly use it for business.

There are two exceptions to the exclusive use rule: If your business use is either storing inventory or product samples, or running a qualified day care center, you don't have to meet the exclusive use test. In these two cases, the parts of the home you use for business—say, a closet for inventory storage or a living room for the day care center— may also be used for personal activities, and you will still qualify for the home business tax deduction. (See IRS Publication 587, *Business Use of Your Home,* for details. It's available online at www.irs.gov/formspubs/index.html.)

Exceptions to the Home Storage Exception

In its inimitable fashion, the IRS has created two exceptions to the home storage exception. First, you won't qualify for the deduction if you have an office or other business location outside your home. Second, you must store the products in a specific, identifiable space such as your garage, a closet, or extra room—not just stacked against the wall of your garage or in the corner of your basement. It's okay to use the storage space for other purposes as well, as long as you regularly use it for storing inventory or samples.

EXAMPLE: Mariana teaches ballet lessons to children at a studio in her home. She also sells instructional dance videos and regularly stores the inventory of VHS tapes in a large closet in her basement. Since Mariana has no other business location away from her home, she can claim a home business deduction for the basement closet. This is true even though she also stores other things in that closet such as skis and boxes of books. However, if Mariana ever opens a studio outside her home, she will not be able to deduct the expenses of the storage space.

b. Principal Place of Business

In addition to fulfilling the exclusive and regular use requirements, your home business space must also be the main place where you do business— with two exceptions as explained below in Subsections c and d. Thankfully, since 1999, the principal place of business rule has been fairly easy to satisfy. Before 1999, business owners often had to use an imprecise formula to balance how "primary" their places of business were. Now, however, the rule is simple. Your home office will qualify as the principal place of business if you:

- use the office to conduct administrative or management activities, and
- do not have an office or other business location outside your home set up to conduct these activities.

This rule is just as straightforward as it sounds. As long as you use your home office to keep track of your business files, do your bookkeeping and accounting, maintain your client databases, or conduct whatever other type of administration is required, and you don't have a space away from home set up for these activities, your home office will be considered your principal place of business.

c. Meeting Clients or Customers

If your home office doesn't qualify as your principal place of business under the test described above, you can still qualify for the home business deduction if you regularly and exclusively use your space to meet with clients or customers. As long as you regularly use the home space to meet clients—say, once or twice a week—and don't use the space for nonbusiness purposes, you can claim the deduction for the space even if you have an office away from home.

d. Home Business in a Separate Structure

Finally, another way to qualify for the home business deduction is to use an external structure on your property—a detached garage, shed, or in-law unit, for example—regularly and exclusively for your business. Again, this rule applies even if you have another business space such as a storefront or office, and regardless of whether you meet clients or customers there. If the space is used regularly and exclusively for business and is not physically connected to your house, you can deduct expenses for it.

⚠️ **Tax concerns for separate structures.** If you use a separate structure on your property for your home business, beware of possible tax repercussions when you sell your home. When a separate structure is used, the business portion of the home will be subject to capital gains tax when sold. (Be sure to read Section B3, below.)

Tips on Establishing Home Business Use

Home business owners should make an effort to clearly establish their home offices as places of business. Here are some ways you can accomplish this.

- Take pictures of your home office that show its business character.
- Draw a diagram showing the floor plan of the house with the home office clearly defined. Include room dimensions if possible.
- Keep a log of the times you work in the office.
- Keep a record of all client meetings at your office—including whom you met, when, and the subject of the meeting. Recording client visits to your home office is especially important if you also have an outside office.
- Have your business mail sent to your home.
- Get a separate phone line for the business.

---

2. Figuring Deductible Home Business Expenses

Once you've determined that you do in fact qualify for the home business tax deduction, you'll need to figure out exactly how much you can deduct. Obviously, you can't deduct all of your housing costs—only the expenses attributable to business purposes qualify.

At the outset, you'll need to determine a "business percentage" for your home—simply, the percentage of your home that is used for business. Then you'll need to look at your home expenses and figure out to what extent they may be deducted.

a. Calculating Business Percentage

You can calculate the percentage of your home used for business in one of two ways: the "square footage" method or the "number of rooms" method. Either approach is acceptable to the IRS.

The square footage method simply divides the square footage of the business space by the square footage of the whole house. For instance, if you use 250 square feet for business, and your entire house takes up 1,000 square feet, then your business space uses 25% (250 ÷ 1,000) of your home.

The number-of-rooms method is just as simple: If your house has five similarly sized rooms, and you use one of them for business, then the business uses 20% (1 ÷ 5) of your home.

b.   Categorizing and Deducting Expenses

Once you have calculated a space percentage for your business, use it to calculate the portion of your home expenses that is deductible to the business. Home expenses fall into one of three categories, with different deductibility rules for each.

Unrelated expenses. Expenses that are unrelated to your business space are not deductible at all. For example, you can't deduct the cost of repainting your bedroom or replacing your dining room window.

Direct expenses. You can fully deduct expenses that directly affect your business space, such as the cost of installing new carpeting, replacing a broken window, or repairing the heating vent in your office space. Note that direct expenses for a day care center may not be fully deductible. (For more information, see IRS Publication 587, *Business Use of Your Home,* available online at www.irs.gov/formspubs.index.html.)

Indirect expenses. Expenses that affect the whole house—called indirect expenses—are deductible, but only partially so, based on the percentage of your home that is used for business. For instance, you can deduct a percentage of the cost of plumbing services, root repairs, mortgage interest, real estate taxes, and utility bills.

To calculate the portion of indirect expenses attributable to your business, you generally multiply the indirect expense by your business percentage. Rent, for example, is an easy expense to prorate. If your business uses 25% of your home, and your rent is $800 per month, then $200 per month is a deductible home business expense (25% x $800). The same simple approach generally works for calculating the deductible business portion of many other indirect expenses such as homeowner's insurance, mortgage interest, home utilities, and repairs.

Repairs are generally deductible; permanent improvements are not. The IRS won't let you deduct the cost of major projects it considers "permanent improvements"—those that increase the value of property, add to its life, or give it a new or different use. The cost of repairs, on the other hand, may be deducted—either fully if a direct expense or partially if an indirect expense. The IRS defines "repairs" as those that "keep your home in good working order over its useful life." (For more details on the IRS's distinction between repairs and permanent improvements, see IRS Publication 587, *Business Use of Your Home,* available online at www.irs.gov/formspubs.index.html.)

For more on the home office deduction. For more detailed information on tax deductions for home businesses, read *Tax Savvy for Small Business,* by Frederick W. Daily (Nolo).

c.   Calculating a Depreciation Deduction

If you own your home and you qualify for the home business tax deduction, an indirect expense that you may deduct is the depreciation of your home. Depreciation of your home is an allowance for the wear and tear inflicted upon it. And the home business depreciation deduction is simply a deduction for the business portion of this. Calculating this deduction is slightly more involved than the indirect expense deductions mentioned above. This section offers an overview below of how to calculate the depreciation deduction; detailed instructions are included in IRS Publication 587, *Business Use of Your Home,* available online at www.irs.gov/formspubs.index.html.

Keep in mind that depreciation is calculated for the building only—not the land. Property tax assessments usually show the breakdown of home value versus land value.

In a nutshell, calculating the depreciation deduction works like this.

- To start, figure out the adjusted basis of your home (don't include land value) at the time you started using it for business. The adjusted basis of your home is generally its cost, plus the cost of any permanent improvements, minus any casualty losses (sudden losses from accidents such as a fire or damages from a falling tree) or depreciation deducted in earlier tax years. (The IRS explains adjusted basis in its Publication 551, *Basis of Assets*, available online at www.irs.gov/formspubs.index.html.)

- Next, figure out the fair market value of the home (again, not the land) at the time you started using the home office. The IRS defines fair market value as follows: "The price at which the property would change hands between a buyer and a seller, neither having to buy or sell, and both having reasonable knowledge of all necessary facts." Information such as appraisals or the selling price of similar homes in your area when you started using yours for business will help you determine its fair market value.

- The next step is to calculate the portion of the cost of your home that can be depreciated. This amount is called the "depreciable basis." Calculate the depreciable basis by multiplying the percentage of your home used for business by the smaller of:
    —the adjusted basis of your home (excluding land) on the date you began using it for business, or
    —the fair market value of your home (excluding land) when you began using it for business.

The result of this calculation—the depreciable basis—is the portion of the home's value attributable to the business.

- Last, calculate the actual deduction that your home business will be able to claim. To oversimplify, this deduction is calculated by multiplying your depreciable basis by a certain percentage, set by the IRS. The percentage and specific depreciation method to use will depend on when you started your home business.

There are many more details involved than this book can cover, so you would be wise to consult the IRS publications mentioned before tackling the depreciation deduction on your own. Or consider handing the job over to an experienced business accountant. (See Chapter 16, Section B, for more on this.)

3. Tax Issues When You Sell Your Home

Homeowners with home businesses face a couple tax issues if they end up selling their homes: capital gains taxes and depreciation recapture. These concepts are widely misunderstood, with the result that many home business owners don't claim their rightful share of deductions for fear of the tax implications. Don't make this mistake. Not only are the rules relatively easy to understand, they're quite favorable to home business owners.

a. No Tax on Proportional Gain

Before 2002, a home business owner who sold a home at a profit had to pay capital gains tax on the portion of the home used by the business. This was a widely cursed exception to the general IRS rule that exempted home sellers from capital gains taxes on gains up to $250,000 ($500,000 for married couples), as long as they owned and lived in the home for at least two of the last five years. For home business owners, even if the profit from the home sale was within the exempt limits, capital gains taxes would be due on the portion allocated to the home business. One way around this was to stop claiming home business deductions—which is exactly what many home business owners did, kissing goodbye to hundreds or thousands of dollars in potential tax savings.

Mercifully, in December 2002, the IRS reversed itself with a new regulation. Now, when you sell your home at a gain, you do not need to allocate a portion of that gain to your home business. You can go ahead and claim all the home business tax deductions you're entitled to, without worrying that you'll be stuck with capital gains taxes for your home business portion. You'll only have to pay capital gains taxes if you exceeded the limits of $250,000 gain ($500,000 for married couples), which would apply whether or not you had a home business.

An important exception to the IRS's 2002 rule is that home businesses located in a separate structure will continue to be subject to capital gains taxes. So if you run your business from a separate, freestanding garage or shed, for example, you'll be stuck paying the gains taxes when you sell your home. To avoid this, stop claiming the home business tax deduction two years before you sell your home.

b. Recaptured Depreciation Tax

The IRS's 2002 rule change does *not* change what's known as "depreciation recapture," however. As in the past, home business owners who sell their homes must still pay taxes on the depreciation deductions they've taken over the years. In other words, if you claim depreciation deductions for a home business, the total of those deductions will be taxed—"recaptured," if you will—when you sell your house.

> **EXAMPLE:** Patrice, a yoga instructor, sells her house at a gain of $200,000. Her home studio takes up 10% of her home. Under current IRS rules, she will not be subject to capital gains

taxes for the 10% of her home used for business activities. However, Patrice must pay depreciation recapture tax on the total depreciation deductions she's taken in the five years of operating her home teaching studio.

This rule isn't really so bad when you consider the depreciation recapture rate is only 25%. Most business owners pay much more than this on income—self-employment tax at a rate of 15.3%, plus their federal personal tax rate of 15%, 28%, or higher, plus state tax rates—so that depreciation deductions can easily offer savings of 40% or more each year. The bottom line is that it's worth it to take the depreciation deductions, since you'll almost certainly save more in cumulative savings over the years than you'll end up paying when you sell your home.

C. Risks and Insurance

Just because you run a business from your home, don't make the mistake of taking risk management and insurance issues lightly. Home businesses are often just as vulnerable to theft, fire, personal liability claims, and other risks as businesses based in storefronts or office buildings—sometimes even more vulnerable. It can be a real catastrophe if your computer system is stolen or destroyed, or if a client trips and falls over your garden hose on the way up your front walk.

If you assume that your homeowner's policy will protect you against these risks, you may well find out the hard way that you're horribly wrong. Potentially even more important, home business owners need to make sure that none of their business pursuits jeopardize their regular homeowner's policy for nonbusiness-related claims.

This section discusses the insurance and risk management issues particular to home businesses. (Chapter 8 offers a full discussion of these topics as they apply to all businesses. Be sure to read that chapter in addition to the material below.)

Start by evaluating your risks. All risk management and insurance decisions must begin with a realistic assessment of what risks your business faces. Only after you do this assessment will you be able to decide how to reduce your risks with insurance or other strategies. While some basic insurance protection for your business assets is never a bad idea, some home business owners may sensibly conclude that insurance is not necessary. (See Chapter 8.) Much of the discussion in this chapter presumes that you've decided some insurance is necessary.

1. Limitations of Homeowner's Policies

A common mistake among owners of home-based businesses is to assume that business losses will be covered by their homeowner's or renter's policies. This is a very dangerous assumption. While many insurance companies will extend homeowner's coverage to a home business, they'll often require an endorsement—sometimes called a "floater" or "rider"—to a policy that specifically authorizes the coverage. You'll generally have to pay an extra premium for such an endorsement. Without one, the insurance company may deny claims related to a home business.

Honesty is the best insurance policy. You might wonder how an insurance company would find out that you are quietly operating a home business. Apart from the fact that trying to deceive your insurance company is just a foolish idea, the insurance company's suspicion can easily be aroused by claims involving major business assets such as high-end computer systems, machine equipment, or inventories that seem unsuited for home use. All it could take is a few questions or a visit from an insurance adjuster to blow your cover. When it comes to communicating with your insurer, the best advice is not to mess with the truth.

In addition to requiring home businesses to jump through extra hoops, some insurance companies exact harsh consequences if you run a business from home without informing them first. In some cases, an insurance company may terminate your coverage altogether—even for nonbusiness claims—if it discovers that you've been running a business from your home without its authorization. This is a sobering possibility.

And even when homeowner's policies do cover home businesses—either with or without an endorsement—the coverage may be only for property loss, not for other claims such as liability or business interruption. If a client is injured on your slippery floor, your business may have to pay for any damages awarded in a personal injury lawsuit, without any coverage from the homeowner's policy. And if your business records are destroyed in a fire, it's highly unlikely that your homeowner's policy would cover your inability to collect accounts receivable or your lost income from business down time.

The bottom line is that no home business owner should make the mistake of finding out what is or isn't covered the hard way. If you have homeowner's or renter's insurance, contact the providing company and find out specifically how it deals with home businesses and what kinds of claims are covered. If you're like many home business owners, you'll likely find that your coverage isn't quite what you hoped it might be. Your next step will be to fill in those gaps, either by getting an endorsement to your existing homeowner's policy or purchasing separate coverage.

2. Finding and Purchasing Coverage

An increasing number of insurance companies are willing to insure home businesses, no doubt due to the massive growth of this market. And despite what you might fear, costs are generally not prohibitive. An endorsement for a home business is typically no more than $1,000 a year—and sometimes much less. Another option is a "home business-type" policy that's becoming more common. These are distinct from homeowner's policies but aren't quite as robust as full commercial policies, and as a result are generally a good value. Larger businesses with significant assets or risks may need to look at full commercial policies, which may be somewhat more expensive.

If you have a homeowner's or renter's policy, start your search by contacting your current insurance provider. If an endorsement is required, the process is generally a simple matter of paying an extra premium and having documents drafted reflecting the home business coverage. Of course, you'll need to check that the coverage limits are sufficient to cover the value of your business equipment. Also find out whether liability or loss-of-income claims are covered. If not, and if these risks are a concern, you may need to purchase additional coverage.

If your current insurer doesn't offer the coverage you need, one possibility is to find a policy with a different company that meets your requirements. Another option, whether or not you have existing home coverage, is to look for a separate business policy. Business policies can get complicated and expensive, so it's a good idea to use a broker who can present you with options from a range of companies. (See Chapter 8 for general tips for buying insurance.)

Home business owners sometimes can get good deals through trade associations or other organizations that offer coverage options for their members. Organizations tend to get favorable group rates from insurance companies, so these resources are definitely worth a look.

Chapter 10 Checklist

☐ Evaluate whether your business activities can be run well from your home.

☐ Fine out whether any city or county restrictions apply to running a business at home—commonly called home occupation regulations—and obtain any necessary permits.

☐ To satisfy IRS requirements for the home business tax deduction, use your home business space exclusively for business and not for any personal uses. Review other IRS rules such as the "principal place of business" rule to make sure your home business qualifies for the tax deduction.

☐ Take photos of your home business space to establish its business use.

☐ Do not rely on homeowner's insurance to protect you against losses related to your home business. Even more important, make sure your homeowner's policy is not voided entirely—even for personal claims—by running a business from home.

■

Entering Into Contracts and Agreements

As a business owner, you'll often have to enter into contracts (legal agreements) with other businesses and people: suppliers, customers, creditors, and landlords, for example. While a few of these transactions will be simple enough to complete with a handshake, most will be sufficiently complicated, long-term, or financially important to require a written contract.

Thankfully—and contrary to what many people believe—a contract is often a fairly simple legal document. It sets out mutual promises to do specific acts: "A promises to pay B $1,000 if B delivers 50,000 twist-ties to A's warehouse on or before March 1, 20xx." A written contract will usually include the main terms of the agreement: the price of goods, important dates, and the time and place of delivery. For most contractual agreements, standard forms are readily available. Except in the relatively few instances in which lots of money or new legal issues are involved, you probably won't need a lawyer to complete your contract.

Simple as some types of contracts may be, you must remember that they are legally enforceable. If you fail to keep your end of the bargain, you can be sued and forced to pay damages to the other side or, in some circumstances, to do the things you promised in the contract.

This chapter explains some contract basics, including what makes a contract enforceable and which contracts are legally required to be in writing.

A. Contract Basics

Although lots of contracts are filled with mind-bending legal gibberish, there's no reason why this has to be true. For most contracts, legalese is not essential or even helpful. On the contrary, the agreements you'll want to put into a written contract are best expressed in simple, everyday English.

Don't be afraid to redraft contract language. When reading a contract that has been presented to you, your first task is to make sure you understand all of its terms. It is just plain foolish to sign a contract if you're unclear on the meaning of any of its language. If a clause is poorly written, hard to understand, or doesn't accomplish your key goals, rewrite it to be clear. By refusing to sign at the "X" unless your goals are clearly met, you'll be less likely to find yourself in a breach-of-contract lawsuit later on. A breach of contract occurs when one party fails to live up to the terms or promises in the contract. (For more on changing contract language, see Section D, below.)

1. Elements of a Valid Contract

A contract will be valid if all of the following are true:

- All parties are in agreement (after an offer has been made by one party and accepted by the other).
- Something of value has been exchanged, such as cash, services, or goods, for something else of value (or there is a promise to exchange an item for something else of value).
- In a few situations, such as the sale of real estate, the agreement must be in writing. (See Section 2, below.) Of course, because oral contracts can be difficult or impossible to prove, it is wise to write out most agreements.

Each of these elements is described below in more detail.

a. Agreement Between Parties

Although it may seem like stating the obvious, an essential element of a valid contract is that all parties really do agree on all major issues. In real life there are plenty of situations that blur the line between a full agreement and a preliminary discussion about the possibility of making an agreement. To help clarify these borderline cases, legal rules have developed to define when an agreement exists.

The most basic rule of contract law is the "offer and acceptance" rule: A legal contract exists when one party makes an offer and the other party accepts it. For most types of contracts, this can be done either orally or in writing. (For a few, discussed in Section 2, below, the offer and acceptance must be made in writing.)

Let's say, for instance, you're shopping around for a print shop to produce brochures for your business. One printer confirms, either orally or in writing, that he'll print 5,000 two-color flyers for $200. This constitutes his offer. If you tell him to go ahead with the job, you've accepted his offer. In the eyes of the law, when you tell the printer to go ahead, you create a contract, which means you're liable for your side of the bargain—in this case, payment of $200. But if you tell the printer you're not sure and want to continue shopping around (or don't even respond, for that matter), you clearly haven't accepted his offer, and no agreement has been reached. Or, if you say his offer sounds great, except that you want three colors instead of two, no contract has been made, since you have not accepted all of the important terms of the offer—you've changed one. (Depending on your wording, you may have made a "counteroffer," which is discussed below.)

Advertisements as Offers

Generally speaking, an advertisement to the public does not count as an offer in the legal sense. In other words, if you advertised your catering services in your local weekly newspaper, and included a price quote of $300 for your standard menu serving 20 people, you would not be legally bound to live up to that service if someone called you and said, "I accept!" If, for instance, you were too busy with other catering jobs and unable to do the job for the eager caller, you could decline. Since your ad wasn't, legally speaking, an offer, the caller couldn't claim a legal acceptance of it to create a binding contract.

Despite this, however, you do need to watch what you say in your advertisements. Some states require retailers to stock enough of an advertised item to meet reasonably expected demand, or else your ad must state that stock is limited.

Of course, false or misleading advertising is always a bad idea. Federal laws regulating trade and state consumer protection laws prohibit deceptive advertising, even if no one was actually misled. And check your ad's facts; false advertising is illegal, even if you believed the ad to be truthful when you ran it.

In real, day-to-day business, the seemingly simple steps of offer and acceptance can become quite convoluted. For instance, sometimes when you make an offer, it isn't quickly and unequivocally accepted; the other party may want to think about it for a while or try to get a better deal. And before your offer is accepted by anyone, you might change your mind and want to withdraw or amend it. Delaying acceptance of an offer, revoking an offer, and making a counteroffer are common situations in business transactions that often lead to confusion and conflict. To cut down on the potential for disputes, make sure you understand the following issues and rules.

- **How long an offer stays open.** Unless an offer includes a stated expiration date, it remains open for a "reasonable" period of time. What's "reasonable," of course, is open to interpretation and will depend on the type of business and the particular situation. Because the law in this area is so vague, if you want to accept someone else's offer, the best approach is to do it as soon as possible, while there's little doubt that the offer is still open. Keep in mind that until you accept, the person or company who made the offer—called the offeror—may revoke it.

  If you are the offeror, it's best to be very clear about how long your offer will remain open. The best way to do this is to include an expiration date in the offer. But to leave yourself room to revoke the offer, avoid wording such as, "This offer will remain open until December 31, 20xx." Instead, use language such as, "This offer will expire on December 31, 20xx"

Include an expiration date clause. In many types of businesses, from replacing roofs to redesigning websites, it is common to bid (in other words, to make an offer to create a contract) on lots more jobs than you really need or want. But sometimes this strategy can backfire. With lots of offers floating around, there is always the possibility that too many will be accepted, which could raise the embarrassing possibility that you might not be able to deliver on all the work. One easy way to eliminate this problem is to print right on your bid or offer form that all offers are good for only ten days (or some other relatively short period) unless extended in writing.

- **Revoking an offer.** Whoever makes an offer can revoke it as long as it hasn't yet been accepted. This means if you make an offer and the other party wants some time to think it through, you can revoke your original offer. If your offer is accepted while it is still open, however, you'll have a binding agreement. In other words, revocation must happen before acceptance.

- **Options.** Sometimes the offeror promises that an offer will remain open for a stated period of time—and that it cannot and will not be revoked during that time. This type of agreement is called an option, and options don't usually come for free. Say someone offers to sell you a forklift for $10,000, and you want to think the offer over, without having to worry that the seller will revoke the offer or sell to someone else. You and the seller could agree that the offer will stay open for a certain period of time, say, 30 days. Often, however, the offeror will ask you to pay for this 30-day option—which is understandable, since, during the 30-day option period, he or she can't sell to anyone else. But payment or no payment, when an option agreement exists, the offeror cannot revoke the offer until the time period ends.

- **Counteroffers.** Often when an offer is made, the other party's response will not be to accept the terms of the offer right off, but to start bargaining. Of course, haggling over price is the most common type of negotiating that occurs in business situations. When one party responds to an offer by proposing something different, this proposal is called a "counteroffer." When a counteroffer is made, the legal responsibility to accept or decline the offer or make another counteroffer shifts to the original offeror. For instance, if your printer (here, the original offeror) offers to print 5,000 brochures for you for $300, and you respond by saying you'll pay $250 for the job, you have not accepted his offer (no contract has been formed), but instead have made a counteroffer. It is then up to your printer to accept, decline, or make another counteroffer. If your printer agrees to do the job exactly as you have specified for $250, he's accepted your counteroffer and a legal contract has been formed.

b. Exchange of Things of Value

Even if both parties agree to the terms, a contract isn't valid unless the parties exchange something of value in anticipation of the completion of the contract. The "thing of value" being exchanged—called "consideration" in legal terms—is most often a promise to do something in the future, such as a promise to perform a certain job or a promise to pay a fee for that job. Returning to the example of the print job, once you and the printer agree on terms, there is an exchange of things of value (consideration): The printer has promised to print the 5,000 brochures, and you have promised to pay $250 for them.

This requirement helps differentiate a contract from generous statements and one-sided promises that are not enforceable by law. If your friend Leili offers you a favor, for instance, such as to help you move a pile of rocks without asking anything in return, that arrangement wouldn't count as a contract, because you didn't give or promise anything of value. If Leili never followed through with the favor, you would not be able to force her to keep that promise. However, if, in exchange for helping you move rocks on Saturday, you promise to help Leili weed a vegetable garden on Sunday, the two of you have a contract.

Although the exchange-of-value requirement is met in most business transactions by an exchange of promises ("I'll promise to pay money if you promise to paint my building next month"), actually doing the work or paying the money can also satisfy the rule. If, for instance, you leave your printer a voice mail message that you'll pay an extra $100 if your brochures are cut and stapled when you pick them up, the printer doesn't have

to respond; he can create a binding contract by actually doing the cutting and stapling. And, once he does so, you can't weasel out of the deal by claiming you changed your mind.

2. Oral vs. Written Contracts

Before you learn more about which contracts have to be in writing to be legally enforceable, here's some advice: Put all of your contracts in writing. For compelling practical reasons, all contracts of more than a trivial nature should be written out and signed by both parties. Here is why.

- Writing down terms tends to make both parties review them more carefully, eliminating misunderstandings and incorrect assumptions right from the start.
- An oral agreement—no matter how honestly made—is hard to remember accurately.
- Oral agreements are subject to willful misinterpretation by a not-so-innocent party who wants to get out of the deal.
- Oral contracts are sometimes difficult, and often impossible, to prove, making them hard to enforce in court.

EXAMPLE: Kay opens a plant shop called The Green Scene. Because she needs specialized grow-lights for her extensive line of tropical plants, she checks with several contractors who install lighting systems. One company, Got a Light, says it will install a system for $3,000, which would include the cost of the lights themselves and installation charges. That quote is the lowest among the companies Kay has checked, so she tells Got a Light she'll accept the offer, but only with a written contract.

When Got a Light sends Kay a contract, she notices that it doesn't address rewiring her shop. She calls Got a Light and talks with Dan, who tells her that she needs to have an electrician add several new circuits and provide six specialized outlets before Got a Light can install the lighting system. Based on this discovery, Kay and Dan discuss exactly what needs to be done before Got a Light's work begins and include this new agreement in an additional contract clause. Dan recommends an electrician, whom Kay hires to do the rewiring. She also manages to negotiate a lower price with Got a Light, based on the fact that the rewiring will be done according to Got a Light's specifications, making the installation much easier.

The best advice is to get every contract in writing. Now here's what the law says: All states have laws that require certain contracts to be in writing. These laws often go by the name "Statute of Frauds" and are quite similar from state to state. They typically require the following types of contracts to be in writing.

- An agreement that by its terms can't be completed in a year or less. For example, a contract for a bakery to provide fresh bread to a restaurant for two years must be in writing. On the other hand, if the contract might take longer than a year to complete but could be completed within a year, it doesn't need to be in writing. For example, a contract for a gardener to landscape five big properties would not need to be written, because it is quite possible that the gardener would finish the work within one year. Similarly, a contract for a bakery to bake bread for a restaurant with no time period stated would not need to be in writing.
- A lease for a term (or time period) longer than one year, or an agreement authorizing an agent to execute such a lease on your behalf.
- Any sale of real estate (or of an interest in real estate), or an agreement authorizing an agent to purchase or sell it on your behalf.
- An agreement that by its terms will not be completed during the lifetime of one of the parties. This includes a promise to leave someone your business when you die.

- A promise to pay someone else's debt, such as a business partner's promise to pay your car payments or an agreement that the person who prints your brochure will also pay the cost of photographic work done at another shop.

In addition to the Statute of Frauds laws, each state has a special body of law on commercial issues called the Uniform Commercial Code (UCC). (While Louisiana has not fully adopted the UCC, it has implemented some of its more important provisions.) Under the UCC, a sale of goods for $500 or more requires at least a brief written note or memo indicating the agreement between the buyer and the seller. The note can be much less detailed than a normal contract; it needs only to show an agreement between the parties and the quantity of goods being sold. Other terms that are typically covered in contracts, such as the price of goods or the time and place of delivery, aren't required. This written memo usually has to be signed, although if one party doesn't object to the memo within ten days of receiving it, then his or her signature isn't required.

Special State Requirements for Contracts

Various state laws impose additional requirements for contracts involving particular businesses or certain kinds of transactions. In California, for instance, contracts for weight-loss services and dating services must be in writing. Plus, the law requires some contracts to include special language. For example, California dating service contracts must include the following language in at least 10-point boldface type:

> **"You, the buyer, may cancel this agreement, without any penalty or obligation, at any time prior to midnight of the original contract seller's third business day following the date of this contract, excluding Sundays and holidays. To cancel this agreement, mail or deliver a signed and dated notice, or send a telegram which states that you, the buyer, are canceling this agreement, or words of similar effect." (Cal. Civ. Code § 1694.2.)**

Unfortunately, there's no centralized place where a business owner can learn if any special contract laws apply to a particular type of business. Talking with people in your line of business is one option. Another is to do research in a library or online.

If doing legal research to find any required contract language is too time-consuming or overwhelming for you, a good alternative is to use the limited help of a lawyer who's generally familiar with small business issues and, if possible, already works with businesses in your field (other plant nurseries, website designers, or restaurants, for example). Many small business lawyers are now more flexible in offering just as much or as little help as clients need, and offer coaching services to those who want to handle their simple legal affairs themselves. Using a legal coach is especially useful for small business owners, who often need answers to simple legal questions rather than full-blown attorney services. Chapter 16, Section A, discusses working with lawyers and finding one who's willing to coach you through simple legal matters.

Now that you have an idea of which contracts must by law be in writing, it bears mentioning again that, in practice, written contracts are almost always preferable over oral ones—whether legally required or not.

B. Using Standard Contracts

By now you should understand that your contracts should be written, but you may still have no idea about how to write the ones you'll need. Luckily for you and most other businesspeople, virtually every type of business transaction is covered by a readily available standard contract. Service contracts, rental agreements, independent contractor agreements, contracts for sales of goods, and licensing agreements are just a few examples of blank-form contracts you should easily be able to find.

Anyone who has ever picked up a fill-in-the-blanks lease or promissory note from an office supply store, torn a form out of a self-help law book, or downloaded one from a website is familiar with how this works. Blank rental agreements, for example, are widely available at office supply stores, through landlords' associations, at most public libraries, and from many other sources. Once you find the blank-form contract you need, you simply fill it in and, if necessary, modify it before signing.

If you can't easily find a blank-form contract that meets your needs, try the sources described here.

- Trade associations are excellent resources for fill-in-the-blanks contracts.
- Your competitors might be less than willing to share their contracts with you, but similar businesses in faraway locations (which you won't be competing with) might be willing to show you theirs.
- The Web has oceans of information for small businesses, including sample contracts. Try searching for terms particular to your type of business to find specific contracts you need.
- Nolo books offer many different blank-form agreements. For general business contracts, a great resource is *Legal Forms for Starting & Running a Small Business,* by Fred S. Steingold.

Once you've found a contract that generally fits your needs, you can amend it for your particular situation. It's entirely appropriate and often necessary to change clauses of a fill-in-the-blanks contract to suit your needs. Of course, it's crucial that you understand what you're doing. Don't just strike a clause because you don't understand what it means or add a clause without fully knowing the consequences of including it. To help you educate yourself about typical contract language, the next section explains which clauses commonly appear in contracts and what they mean.

C. How to Draft a Contract

If you can't find a form agreement, or if you find one that needs a load of revisions, you may need to write a clause or two—or possibly even the whole contract—from scratch. Don't be intimidated. Either way, your goal is simple: to state clearly what each party is agreeing to do and the specifics of how they'll do it (usually called the terms of the contract). Put another way, your written contract should be the most accurate reflection possible of the understanding you have with the other party.

Good Ideas to Keep Your Contracts Crystal Clear

- Avoid the use of "he," "she," "they," or other pronouns in your contracts as they can easily lead to confusion over what parties you're talking about. Use either the actual names of the parties or their roles, such as Landlord and Tenant. It might seem repetitive or clumsy to write this way, but your goal is to be clear—not to write beautiful prose.
- Stay away from legalistic words such as wherefore, herewith, or hereinafter. Far from making your contract sound more impressive, this type of language is simply unnecessary and outdated. Stick to modern, clear English. And don't include legal expressions you think you may have heard elsewhere. Legal-sounding jargon will not make your contract more binding—and if you get it wrong, you may be bound to terms you didn't want, or your contract may be void.
- Make at least a couple drafts of your contract. After the first draft, let it rest a day or so, and then reread it. Does it leave any questions in your mind? If it does, you need to fill in the gaps with more information.

This section explains the important things to include in most contracts and alerts you to the situations that might require more specialized provisions. The information provided here will help you in editing or drafting amendments to a standard contract, or in drafting a contract from scratch, if necessary. You'll also find examples of how to state certain terms—although, as mentioned above, clear English is really all that's usually necessary.

Don't get too specific. Although a good contract covers all the important aspects of a deal, there is no need to be too anal when it comes to specifying every tiny detail. For instance, if you hire a cleaning service to scrub your floors, you probably don't need to specify what type of brushes it will use. Better to put your energy into picking the right person or company to do the job and to leave some of the specifics of the actual work up to those who will do it. In deciding how much detail is enough, you'll simply have to judge for yourself which nit-picky details are so important that they should be covered in your contract, and which ones you can safely ignore. For example, if you need fresh salmon for a party at 6 p.m., the time of delivery and quality of the fish are extremely important points, but the exact weight of each fish or the method of delivery may be a lot less so.

1. What to Include in a Basic Contract

So you've reached an agreement with another party and are ready to put it into writing. Before you start editing a form contract or writing one on your own, step back a moment to consider that the goals of all contracts are to:

- clearly outline what each party is agreeing to do (including timelines and payment arrangements)
- anticipate areas of confusion or points of potential conflict, and
- provide for recourse (a remedy) in case the agreement is not followed through to completion.

Also remember that the more you have at stake, the more carefully you'll have to approach the task of putting together your contract. For example, if you're entering into a contract to buy a truckload of bicycle tires for $1,000, you won't need your agreement to be outlined nearly as meticulously as you would in a contract for the construction of a building.

For complex agreements, you may need an attorney. Complex contracts—especially those in areas unfamiliar to you—are often best handled with the help of a lawyer. Certainly, if a transaction is so huge or elaborate that it makes your head spin, you shouldn't go it alone. First, decide how much help you need. Rather than having an attorney draft your contract from start to finish, you could simply have him or her look over a contract that you or the other party has written. Ideally, you should hire a lawyer with some experience with small business, preferably your type of business. Even better would be an attorney who knows the ins and outs of your business based on a long-term working relationship. (See Chapter 16, Section A, on getting legal assistance.)

Let's look at the information most contracts include to fulfill these three goals, and how to present it. Except where noted, you don't need to use any special language.

- **Title.** Generally, a contract will have a simple, to-the-point title such as "Contract for Printing Services" or "Agreement for Sale of Ball Bearings."
- **The names and addresses of all the parties.** It should be clear what role each party has in the contract, such as seller or buyer; landlord or tenant; client or service provider.

    EXAMPLE: Christopher Johnson ("Client") desires to enter into a contract with Virgil's Printing ("Printer") for printing services for Client's newspaper.

    The addresses of the parties generally appear at the end of a contract in the section with the signatures.

- **A brief description of the background of the agreement (called "recitals").** While not always included, this type of information is often necessary to frame the contents of the agreement. Typically, this section includes a brief description of what kinds of businesses the parties run and the nature of the transaction covered in the contract.

EXAMPLE: Client prints and distributes a free, weekly, 24-page newspaper called *El Norte* with a circulation of 40,000. Printer operates a full-service print shop with three printing presses. The subject of this contract is an agreement that Printer shall print Client's newspaper each week in exchange for payment.

- **A full description of what each party is promising to do as part of the agreement.** This section, sometimes called the "specifications" or just "specs," describes the terms of the deal. If a product is being sold, describe the product and delivery terms. If a service is being performed, describe the job and then state when it will be completed, including any intermediate deadlines that must be met before the final completion date. If strict compliance with deadlines is necessary, throw in the phrase, "Time is of the essence." This is a standard phrase used in contracts. It simply means that deadlines will be enforced strictly.

  If specifications are complicated (for example, intricate performance details for a software contract), they should normally be set out in attachments to the contract, which may include scale drawings, formulas, or other detailed information about the transaction.

  EXAMPLE: Client promises to deliver materials ("boards") for printing to Printer's shop no later than 10:00 a.m. each Wednesday morning. Printer promises to print, fold, and bundle 40,000 copies of Client's newspaper and have them ready for Client to pick up from Printer's shop by 8:00 p.m. that same Wednesday. Time is of the essence regarding this contract. If, however, Client fails to deliver boards to Printer by 10:00 a.m. Wednesday morning, Printer may take extra time to complete the job. The amount of extra time will depend on how late Client is in delivering the boards and on Printer's schedule of other jobs, but in no case shall be longer than 24 hours after delivery of the boards.

- **The price of the product or service.** This section states how much one party will pay for the other party's goods or services. If the price may vary (say, based on the time or quality of performance) or if it will be established later, a description of how it will be calculated should be included.

  EXAMPLE: Client will pay Printer $1,000 for every 10,000 24-page newspapers printed, up to 50,000 newspapers. The price will be renegotiated if Client orders more than 50,000 newspapers, or if the number of pages per newspaper changes.

- **Payment arrangements.** This section should explain when payment is due, whether it will be paid all at once or in installments, and whether interest will be charged if payments are late. Also include any other special requirements, such as whether payment must be by certified or cashier's check. Otherwise, a garden-variety check will normally suffice. Again, if strict compliance with payment deadlines is necessary, use the phrase "Time is of the essence."

  EXAMPLE: Client will pay Printer the full amount of each week's printing cost within three days of picking up the completed newspapers.

- **A statement of any warranties made by either party regarding the product or service being provided.** A warranty is essentially a guarantee made by one party to another that a product or service will meet certain standards. If either party gives a warranty, the contract should state what will happen if the guarantee isn't satisfied—for instance, if certain standards aren't met, the party who got the raw end of the deal will be given a refund or may give the other party another chance to do the job right at no additional cost.

Automatic Warranties

Under the Uniform Commercial Code, which is adopted in some form in all 50 states, all sales of products are automatically covered by some warranties whether or not the seller promised anything to the buyer. These warranties are called "implied warranties" and include two guarantees: that the product is fit for its ordinary use and that it is fit for any special purpose for which the seller knows the buyer wants to use it. For example, the sale of a kitchen knife comes with an implied warranty that the knife will work in ordinary kitchen uses. If the buyer asked the retailer to help pick out a knife that would cut through heavy beef bones, then whatever knife the retailer sold would come with a warranty that it would work for cutting heavy beef bones. This is true regardless of whether or not the knife came with an express, written warranty that it could be used for heavy butcher work.

Be aware of the existence of implied warranties when drafting your contracts. Even if you don't make specific promises in your contracts, you will still be legally bound by the two kinds of implied warranties described above: fitness for ordinary use and fitness for a particular purpose. The law regarding warranties can be complex. You may want to consult an attorney for more detailed information about your obligations as a seller.

EXAMPLE: Printer warrants that the completed newspapers shall be free from printing defects or errors attributable to Printer. In case such errors do occur, Printer and Client may negotiate a discount not to exceed actual damages suffered by Client.

- **A statement of whether either party may transfer the contract to an outside party.** Transferring contract rights is also called assigning. If you have chosen a company to provide products or services because of particular characteristics, such as good personal service or artistic detail, you may not want that company to be able to hand off the job to someone else, who may not do as good a job.

  EXAMPLE: Neither Printer nor Client may assign this contract or any part of it to another party.

- **The contract term.** This section, usually only one sentence, establishes how long the contract will be in effect.

  EXAMPLE: This contract will remain in effect for a period of one year, or until it is terminated by one of the parties, whichever is first.

- **A description of any conditions under which either party may terminate the agreement.** For some types of contracts (for example, contracts to provide an ongoing service), a termination clause often states that either party must give a written termination notice in order to end the contract, often 30 or 60 days in advance.

  EXAMPLE: On written notice of at least 30 days to the other party, either Printer or Client may terminate this agreement.

But you may not want the parties to be able to terminate the contract, even with advance notice, just any old time they feel like it. In this case, you can specify a limited number of certain events that might allow a party to end a contract. For instance, if you want to be able to rely on using your website hosting service for at least a year, you can include a clause in your contract that neither party can terminate the contract for the next 12 months unless either party goes bankrupt, in which case either party would have the right to terminate the contract.

On the other hand, there may be situations in which you want to be able to terminate a contract yourself. For instance, say you own a rock shop that sells lots of agate, so you contract with a supplier to sell you a half-ton of agate each month for a year. To protect yourself, you could include a clause in your contract stating that if you resell less than a quarter-ton of agate in any calendar month, you may terminate the agreement.

- **An outline of how you will deal with a breach-of-contract situation.** Though signing a contract may not head off a subsequent dispute, it can channel the dispute in ways that will allow it to be resolved as quickly and cheaply as possible. There are a number of different approaches you can take.

You can decide, in advance, the amount of damages (financial compensation) a breaching party will have to pay to avoid the often lengthy and contentious process of calculating a party's damages after the other party breaches the contract. When damages are preset in a contract, they are called liquidated damages. In order for a liquidated damages clause to be valid, the dollar amount of damages that you set must be a reasonable estimate of what actual damages would be, not merely a preset penalty for breaking the contract.

Another option is for both parties to agree in the contract to try mediation and, if that fails, arbitration to settle a dispute as an alternative to going to court.

EXAMPLE: If any dispute arises under the terms of this agreement, the parties agree to select a mutually agreeable, neutral third party to help them mediate it. The costs of mediation will be shared equally. If the dispute is not resolved after 30 days in mediation, the parties agree to choose a mutually agreeable arbitrator who will arbitrate the dispute. The costs of arbitration will be assigned to the parties by the arbitrator. The results of any arbitration will be binding and final.

If one or both of you prefers going to court, you can provide in the contract that the losing party in a dispute must pay the other party's legal fees, or you can establish that each party is responsible for individual legal fees regardless of who prevails. Note that, for some commercial transactions, neither party in a lawsuit can collect attorney's fees from the other unless it is provided for in a written contract.

- **For contracts with out-of-state entities, a statement of which state's laws apply to the transaction.** Although contract law in all states is very similar, using the law in your state will generally be the simplest for you, since you'll have more resources at your disposal, including law libraries and local attorneys.

EXAMPLE: This contract is governed by and interpreted under the laws of New Mexico.

- **Signatures, dates, and addresses.** Your signature section should always include room for the date the contract was signed, as well as the addresses of the parties.

Jennifer F. Mahoney, owner of an illustration service in Northern California:

My creativity is exercised just as much by drawing up a good agreement with a client as it is by the way I create art for that client.

2. Putting Your Contract Together

In addition to making sure your contract includes all the necessary information, you'll need to present it in an easy-to-follow, professional format. Generally, contract clauses are organized in numbered paragraphs for easy reference to specific terms.

If your agreement includes any hard-to-articulate details, such as the specifications of a software product, drawing a company logo, or architectural blueprints, you can include them as attachments to the main contract. If you do include an attachment, be sure to label it and refer to it in the main contract. To officially make it a part of the contract, state somewhere in the main contract that you "include the Attachment in the contract" or that you "incorporate the Attachment into the contract."

> **EXAMPLE 1:** Company agrees to pay artist $100 for use of logo. Logo is attached to this contract as Attachment A and is included in this contract.

> **EXAMPLE 2:** Contractor agrees to complete remodeling within one year. The final plans are attached to this contract as Exhibit B and are incorporated into this contract.

D. Reading and Revising a Contract

If you don't like certain terms of a contract that's presented to you, you can propose changes. By doing this, you are technically making a counteroffer. Contracts are commonly negotiated back and forth (offer and counteroffer) this way until all the terms are accepted by both parties. Remember, if the parties aren't in agreement, there's no contract—oral or otherwise. (See Section A, above, on offers and counteroffers.)

Changes to a contract—whether to a form contract or one drafted from scratch—can be made in a number of ways. You can simply cross out

language and fill in new language directly on the contract itself. Both parties should initial any such changes to show that they approve of them, then sign the contract as a whole.

In today's world, however, it's more than likely that there will be an electronic copy of the contract on someone's computer. If so, it makes much more sense to make the necessary changes on the computer and then print out a clean copy for both parties to sign. However some industries (such as the real estate industry) commonly use a separate document when making a counteroffer that states the desired changes and refers back to the original offer. In that case, both the original offer and the counteroffer together form the contract.

A contract can also be amended at a later date with a separate document called an addendum. The addendum should state that its terms prevail over the terms of the original contract, especially if the terms are in direct conflict, such as when the price or completion time for a job is changed. Both parties should sign the addendum.

E. Electronic Contracts

While the basics covered so far generally apply to any contract regardless of form—whether the contract is printed in a formal document, scratched on a cocktail napkin, or just spoken and sealed with a handshake—there are new and emerging rules that apply specifically to contracts created online. Before you read the very general overview of the special issues involved in electronic contracts, keep in mind that law in this area is rapidly evolving—scrambling, in fact—to catch up with fast-evolving technology.

1. What Is an Electronic Contract?

An "electronic contract" is essentially any agreement that is created and executed in electronic form—in other words, no paper or other hard copies are used. Typically, electronic agreements are created either via email or on interactive Web pages. For instance, many companies use interactive forms at their websites that users must complete to purchase goods or software, join a membership organization, participate in a mail listserver, or do whatever else the company is offering. In addition to asking the user to enter various items of personal information, these forms typically display the terms of the contract between the company and the user, and ask the user to agree to the terms by clicking on a button such as "I Accept."

Here's another example of an electronic contract: A business associate of yours emails you a request to purchase a specified number of items you sell, at a named price, for immediate delivery. If you email back to the associate that you agree to all the proposed terms, you've probably just entered into a legally enforceable electronic contract. Why the "probably"? Because there is no way for you to sign the contract with pen and ink, and states vary in how they treat digital signatures. Read on.

2. Taking Traditional Contract Principles Online

As mentioned above, contract law is only beginning to grapple with the details of these types of paperless agreements. When electronic contracts have been challenged, courts have had a difficult time determining whether an actual binding contract existed, since it can be unclear whether all the traditional elements of contract formation were met.

Shortcut Contracts for E-Commerce

When it comes to small transactions in which you pay for goods by credit card, most sites get around the issue of whether a valid contract has been formed by saying that if you are dissatisfied for any reason, they will give you your money back. This is another way of saying that if you don't want a contract to exist, it doesn't. Or put another way, the company concedes in advance that it won't try to enforce the contract. This trust-the-customer approach works well for small transactions but has obvious limitations when it comes to major purchases—a car, for example, or significant business-to-business transactions. In these situations, a real signature on an enforceable contract is needed.

a. Clickwrap Agreements

Businesses have traditionally used standard contracts that aren't open to negotiation; customers have to either accept the contract as is or not complete the transaction. Examples might include a car purchase contract or an agreement to rent a moving truck, in which a consumer who insisted on changing any of the terms of the company's standard contract would not be able to buy the car or rent the truck. Over the years, these types of contracts have been challenged on the grounds that they are not fair to the consumer, since they are typically presented in a take-it-or-leave-it manner, giving the consumer little or no power to amend a contract that is often highly favorable to the seller. Whether or not these types of contracts (sometimes called contracts of adhesion, because consumers are forced to "adhere" to the contract) are valid has long been a contentious area of contract law. Generally, adhesion contracts are held to be valid, as long as the terms are clear to the consumer and not grossly unreasonable.

Today, Internet click-to-agree contracts—often called clickwrap, webwrap, or browsewrap agreements—are facing similar challenges. So are other nonnegotiated agreements, such as the software licenses included with packaged software, sometimes called shrinkwrap agreements. While these types of agreements have generally been found valid, courts have refused to enforce certain terms that are deemed too burdensome or unfair to the consumer. A federal case decided in 2002 sheds some light on the question of when a clickwrap agreement may be deemed invalid. In that case, an Internet user who downloaded software from a website operated by the Netscape company later sued Netscape, claiming that the software license was not binding. To download the software, the user had simply clicked a "Download" button and was not required to view the software license or click any button such as "I Agree" to indicate consent to license terms. To view the license, the user would have had to scroll below the Download button and click on another link to a separate page where the license terms were posted.

The U.S. Court of Appeals for the Second Circuit ruled in favor of the user, based on the principle that for a contract to be binding, both parties must assent to be bound. The court found that the structure of Netscape's software download page "with license terms on a submerged screen" and no button to clearly indicate consent was not sufficient to create a binding contract with the user. *(Specht v. Netscape Communications Corp.*, 306 F.3d 17 (2d Cir. 2002).)

The *Netscape* case establishes that downloading alone does not indicate acceptance of license terms. To make sure a clickwrap agreement is binding, the site must be set up to ensure that a user can clearly indicate consent to the license terms of any downloads. Keep this in mind if you plan to use any clickwrap agreements with your business.

Legislative Attempts to Solve Clickwrap Issues

Over the past few years, there have been a number of state legislative efforts to deal with the issues and problems raised by clickwrap agreements. However, the state laws governing electronic contracts are not consistent, which has actually done more harm than good. And the state courts that have heard and ruled on electronic contract cases have come up with different decisions, with the result that checking an "I accept" box may create a contract in one state, but not in another. No question, this lack of uniformity has been a real thorn in the side of e-commerce, which of course recognizes no state boundaries.

In response, the National Conference of Commissioners on Uniform State Laws (NCCUSL) decided to tackle the problem by drafting model legislation for adoption by the states. One of these proposed laws, the Uniform Computer Information Transactions Act (UCITA), addresses the issue of clickwrap and shrinkwrap agreements, essentially making these types of contracts valid and binding.

But in the several years since the UCITA was drafted, hardly any states have adopted it. One reason may be that many consumer advocates, as well as over 25 state attorneys general, have argued that the UCITA is biased in favor of software vendors and information services providers, leaving consumers with significantly less protection than they have under current law. An online search of the term "UCITA" will lead you to many sites with updated information on the act—and an almost universally negative take on it.

b. Electronic and Digital Signatures

One of the stickier issues involving electronic contracts has to do with whether agreements executed in a purely online environment have been "signed" (outside of clickwrap agreements, discussed above). For many centuries, the traditional way to indicate your acceptance of contracts (and most other binding documents) has been to sign with your unique signature. But electronic contracts can't be signed this way. Instead, people use other means to indicate they accept the terms of a contract, such as simply typing their names into the signature areas of the documents. But, increasingly, better technological approaches to the problem of signing contracts online are being developed, such as fingerprint or iris scanning, or a cryptographic technology known as Public Key Infrastructure (PKI). These methods are collectively known as electronic signatures. The term "digital signature" refers specifically to cryptographic signature methods such as PKI.

What Is PKI?

Security experts currently favor the cryptographic signature method known as Public Key Infrastructure (PKI) as the most secure and reliable method of signing contracts online. Without going too deep into the technical details, PKI involves using an algorithm to encrypt the document so that only the parties will be able to modify it or "sign" it. The process of encrypting the document is known as creating a digital signature. Each party will have a "key" allowing it to read and sign the document, thus ensuring that no one else will be able to sign it fraudulently. PKI standards are still evolving, but the technology is already widely accepted as the best electronic signature method currently available.

Until relatively recently, most states didn't have any laws stating which of these ways to "sign" an electronic document was legally acceptable. In response, the National Conference of Commissioners on Uniform State Laws (NCCUSL) drafted another model law, the Uniform Electronic Transactions Act (UETA), which specifically addresses electronic signatures. In a nutshell, the UETA provides that electronic signatures (in all their forms) and contracts are just as valid and legally binding as their paper counterparts. As of late 2005, all states except Georgia, Illinois, New York, and Washington had enacted the UETA.

c. Federal Law on Electronic Signatures

Fortunately, as the states were mulling over whether to adopt the UETA, the UCITA, or both, the U.S. Congress forged ahead and passed federal legislation establishing the validity of electronic signatures nationwide. This bill, known as the Electronic Signatures in Global and National Commerce Act, was signed into law in June 2000 and became effective on October 1, 2000. The law applies to all states that had not already adopted the UETA or a similar electronic signature law by mid-2000. In this way, the law finally gave some much-needed consistency to the way states treat electronic signatures in online transactions.

This law is similar to the model UETA in that it makes electronic signatures and contracts (including clickwrap agreements) just as valid as paper ones. While certain transactions are exempted from this law and must still be completed on paper (wills, cancellation of utility services, court orders, and other official court documents, among others), the law allows an enormous range of business and consumer transactions to be completed totally online. In essence, it throws the door wide open for all types of e-commerce, allowing businesses and consumers to create (in theory, at least) reliable, binding contracts online, without the inconvenience of shuttling paper documents back and forth.

3. Tips for Creating Contracts Online

While the new federal e-signature law, along with the UETA, creates a solid legal framework for online contracts, electronic signature technology is still evolving, which means the reality of online contracts still falls somewhat short of its promise. Like the UETA, the e-signature law does not specify any particular technology for electronic signatures, leaving that up to software companies and the free market to establish. As mentioned above, Public Key Infrastructure (PKI) technology is currently favored by security experts, though its standards aren't completely nailed down or ready for common use. As developments in PKI and other electronic signature methods create solid, worldwide standards, e-commerce will only become more efficient and widespread.

While waiting for reliable standards to develop, it will be important to approach online contracts carefully. Of particular concern is the possibility for fraud, especially since there is no set standard for what constitutes an electronic signature. Until the technology is airtight, make sure that you trust the other party and are comfortable with the type of electronic signature that you're using. If you're not comfortable creating a contract online, you may want to stay lower-tech and stick with paper contracts, either faxed back and forth or sent by overnight mail.

The nonprofit Consumers Union, which publishes *Consumer Reports* magazine, has issued a set of tips to follow when using electronic signatures and creating online contracts.

- Don't consent to using an online contract if you are uncomfortable using a computer or do not understand how to use email.
- Don't agree to use an online contract or to receive electronic documents until you are sure that your computer's software and hardware will be able to read and use the documents provided.

- Remember that the electronic signatures law allows you to opt to receive documents on paper instead of electronically if you prefer.
- Keep back-up paper copies of the electronic documents you receive, and keep a list of the businesses with which you agree to exchange electronic documents.
- Notify the businesses of any changes that may affect your ability to receive and read email and attachments, such as changing your email address, your hardware, or your software.
- Close any unused email accounts.
- Don't give out your email address to any business if you don't want to receive email notices from it.
- Notify the business right away if you have any problems receiving its emails or opening its documents.

You can find these tips and other information about online contracts at the Consumers Union website at www.consumersunion.org.

Beware of E-Viruses. Never open attachments to email if you aren't expecting the email or don't know who it's from. Nasty viruses are often spread through email attachments, so it's good policy to just throw away suspicious mail as soon as you see it. Even when you know the sender of the email, you need to be cautious. Some viruses use a computer user's email address book to replicate themselves, by sending themselves out to everyone in the book. This means that if you get an email with an attachment from your friend Steve Smith, there's a chance that Steve Smith didn't actually send the email. For this reason, you shouldn't open attachments unless you're expecting them.

More information on digital signatures. The American Bar Association has published a helpful tutorial on digital signature guidelines. You can read it online at www.abanet.org. Search for "digital signatures" to access the tutorial.

☑ Chapter 11 Checklist

☐ Become familiar with the legal basics of contracts.

☐ Put all your contracts into writing whenever possible. (Contracts created online or by email are considered to be "in writing.")

☐ Try to respond to offers promptly, and, when making an offer, include an expiration date.

☐ When you need to draft a contract from scratch, try using standard form contracts to get started.

☐ Be thorough in your contracts. Make sure that any points of potential conflict are clearly spelled out.

☐ Use caution when entering into electronic contracts (also sometimes called online contracts or digital contracts). If you're uncomfortable creating a contract online or by email, don't do it—opt for a paper contract.

CHAPTER 12

Bookkeeping, Accounting, and Financial Management

Perhaps the hardest part of accounting is getting over the psychological hang-up that most people seem to have about it. Many of us hate to balance our checkbooks on a regular basis, much less keep detailed accounts of how our money comes and goes. In truth, you don't need to be a financial wizard to start a small business; you just need a comfortable working knowledge of the basics.

If you read Chapter 5, "Drafting an Effective Business Plan," some of this material may be a review. That chapter explained how to generate financial projections using sales and expense estimates to see if your business is likely to turn a profit. The financial tools used in business planning—particularly profit/loss analysis and cash flow projection—are the same tools used in accounting, just employed slightly differently. This chapter focuses on how to use these and other tools to keep track of current financial data (as opposed to projections) for your business.

This chapter will give you an idea of what records your business should keep and will describe simple ways to keep them. It also explains how to use the information in your financial records to calculate how much profit your business is making and to ensure that enough cash is regularly flowing through your business to pay your important bills on time.

Fortunately for today's entrepreneurs, inexpensive, powerful, and easy-to-use software is available that will help simplify the accounting process. Programs such as *Quickbooks, Quicken Home & Business,* and *MYOB Accounting* make this once-unsavory task much more palatable. Once your income and expenses are entered into the system, you're only a few mouse clicks away from sophisticated financial reports that would have taken many hours and considerable skill to generate just a decade ago. In fact, these programs are so affordable (typically under $200) and user-friendly, it makes little sense not to use one of them.

Don't expect software to do your accounting. You shouldn't simply rely on the numbers that your software program spits out if you don't fully understand them. The accounting concepts and processes described in this chapter are the same whether done manually or by computer—and you should take the time to learn them. While accounting software makes it much easier to manipulate the numbers you've entered and to generate informative financial reports, you still need to understand what all the numbers mean to make them work for your business.

It often pays to get help. The basic information provided in this chapter will be valuable for all business owners who are unfamiliar with accounting basics. But, depending on the size and nature of your business, you may eventually want to do additional reading or hire experienced help. The approach here is to provide enough information to get a new businessperson sensibly started and help you understand what your future accountant is talking about. But even early on in the start-up process, the owner of a small, relatively simple business can almost always benefit from an hour or two with an experienced small business accountant, who can often offer creative strategies for keeping records, selecting and configuring a computerized accounting system, and managing money.

Accounting Glossary

A big part of understanding the financial side of your business consists of nothing more than learning the language of accounting. Once you're familiar with some common terms, you'll be better able to make sense of basic written reports and better able to communicate with others about important financial information. And you'll also be well positioned to cope with a common business problem: people who use key financial terms imprecisely or even incorrectly, needlessly confusing themselves and others.

- **Accounting** is a general term that refers to the overall process of tracking your business's income and expenses, then using these numbers in various calculations and formulas to answer specific questions about the financial and tax status of the business.
- **Bookkeeping** refers to the task of recording the amount, date, and source of all business revenues and expenses. Bookkeeping is essentially the starting point of the accounting process. Only with accurate bookkeeping can there be meaningful accounting.
- An **invoice** is a written record of a transaction, often submitted to a customer or client when requesting payment. Invoices are sometimes called **bills** or **statements**, though the term statement has its own technical meaning (see below).
- A **statement** is a formal written summary of an account. Unlike an invoice, a statement is not generally used as a formal request for payment, but is more of a reminder to a customer or client that payment is due.
- A **ledger** is a physical collection of related financial information, such as revenues, expenditures, accounts receivable, and accounts payable. Ledgers used to be kept in books preprinted with lined ledger paper (which explains why a business's financial info is often referred to as the "books") but are now commonly kept in computer files.
- An **account** is a collection of financial information grouped according to customer or purpose. For example, if you have a regular customer, your information regarding that customer's purchases, payments, and debts would be called his or her "account." A written record of an account is called a **statement**.
- A **receipt** is a written record of a transaction. A buyer receives a receipt to show that he or she paid for an item. The seller keeps a copy of the receipt to show that he or she received payment for the item. Receipts are sometimes called **sales slips**.
- **Accounts payable** are amounts that your business owes. For example, unpaid utility bills and purchases your business makes on credit are included in your accounts payable.
- **Accounts receivable** are amounts owed to your business that you expect to receive, including sales your business makes on credit.

Avoid money laundering. Someone in a trade or business has 15 days to report receiving more than $10,000 in cash in one transaction or related transactions. A "transaction" includes the purchase of property or services, the payment of debt, and even holding cash for someone for more than 15 days as part of a deal. "Cash" includes any combination of U.S. and foreign coins and bills and a cashier's check, money order, bank draft, or travelers' check (but not a personal check) with a face amount of $10,000 or less—unless it comes from a bank loan. To report, the business owner must file Form 8300 with the IRS and the Financial Crimes Enforcement Network (FinCEN). Breaking up one transaction into many little ones to avoid this reporting requirement can lead to prison and heavy fines. Check with your accountant or lawyer if you are in this league.

A. Accounting Basics

Accounting has two basic goals:

- to keep track of your income and expenses, thereby improving your chances of making a profit, and
- to collect the necessary financial information about your business to file your various tax returns and local tax registration papers.

Sounds pretty simple. And it can be, especially if you remind yourself of these two goals whenever you feel overwhelmed by the details of keeping your financial records. You should also be reassured to know that there is no requirement that your records be kept in any specific organizational system. There is a requirement, however, that some businesses use a certain method of crediting their accounts. (See Section B, below, on cash vs. accrual accounting.) In other words, there's no official system or format to organize your books. As long as your records accurately reflect your business's income and expenses, the IRS will find them acceptable.

Organization is everything. One thing that all good bookkeeping systems have in common is organization. A well-organized system with accessible, reasonably neat files not only will be a godsend in the event of an audit, but will help you keep track of your business as well.

The actual process of accounting can be broken down into three steps.

1. Keep receipts or other acceptable records of every payment to, and every expenditure from, your business.
2. Summarize your income and expense records on some periodic basis (generally daily, weekly, or monthly).
3. Use these summaries to create financial reports that will tell you specific information about your business, such as how much monthly profit you're making or how much your business is worth at a specific time.

Whether you do your accounting by hand on ledger sheets or with accounting software, these principles are exactly the same.

Are you beginning to believe that you don't need to be afraid of accounting? Good, because it's something you absolutely need to embrace as part of running any business. Failing to keep track of income and expenses is one of the surest ways to run any business off a cliff. Here are a few more ways that a simple set of books will help your business.

- **You'll be able to price your goods and services more competitively.** Only by staying on top of your business's income and expenses will you know how much money you'll need to bring in each week, month, or year to make a profit. This knowledge is essential to allow you to price your goods and services appropriately. For instance, if you don't know your break-even point, you will only be able to guess at how much you should charge your customers for products or services, with the likely result that you'll charge too little (and make an inadequate profit) or too much (and alienate customers).
- **You'll be able to pace your growth more effectively.** A good set of books will give you the information you need to decide when and how to expand your business. If your numbers tell you that sales and profits have been growing consistently for several months, that may be a signal that it's time to hire additional employees or enter into a new market—or both. Without meaningful financial numbers, making any decisions about growth can be a gamble. For example, just because your business has a lot of money in its checking account doesn't necessarily mean you're making good money. (You might have received several big payments from past sales, while current sales are actually slowing down.)
- **You may be able to reduce taxes.** Knowing your company's finances inside and out will help you save money when tax time comes

around. For example, if the end of the year is nearing and your up-to-date records clearly show the year to be profitable, you can purchase needed supplies or equipment before the end of the year and write off these expenses, reducing your taxable income. Also, keeping careful track of your expenses will remind you to claim them as deductions at year end. Businesses that are sloppy about bookkeeping often miss opportunities for saving tax dollars. Don't be one of them.

- **You'll avoid tax penalties.** In addition to helping you legally save tax dollars, responsible bookkeeping will help you avoid errors in your tax returns that can subject you to fines and other penalties. If your business is audited, the IRS can be really nasty if it finds your books in bad shape. In extreme situations, it may even refuse to recognize perfectly legitimate expenses. In short, neglecting your responsibility to maintain basic, accurate records is likely to result in the kind of trouble with the IRS that you might not wish on even your worst enemy.

B. Cash vs. Accrual Accounting

Before turning to several simple systems for keeping your records, you need to understand the two principal methods of keeping track of a business's income and expenses: cash method and accrual method accounting (sometimes called cash basis and accrual basis accounting). In a nutshell, these methods differ only in the timing of when transactions—both sales and purchases—are credited to or debited from your accounts.

1. How Each Method Works

If you use the cash method, income is counted when cash (or a check) is actually received, and expenses are counted when they are actually paid. But under the more common accrual method, transactions are counted when they happen—regardless of when the money is actually received or paid. In other words, with the accrual method, income is counted when the sale occurs, and expenses are counted when you receive goods or services. You don't have to wait until you see the money, or until you actually pay money out of your checking account, to record the transaction.

Say you purchase a new laser printer on credit in May and pay $2,000 for it in July, two months later. Using cash method accounting, you would record a $2,000 expense for the month of July, the month when the money was actually paid. But under the accrual method, the $2,000 payment would be recorded in May, when you took the laser printer and became obligated to pay for it. Similarly, if your computer installation business finished a job on November 30, 2006 and didn't get paid until January 10, 2007, you'd record the payment in January 2007 if you used the cash method. Under the accrual method, the income would be recorded in your books in November of 2005.

Timing can be tricky. Some sales aren't completed all at once. If you use accrual accounting, you may sometimes wonder exactly when you can enter the transaction into your books. For instance, say someone buys two CDs from your record store but also makes a special order for another CD, and pays for all three at once. Or, say your landscaping company finishes a large project, except for the last step of applying a final lawn fertilizing treatment two weeks after laying the sod. The key date here is the job completion date. Not until you deliver all of the goods, finish all parts of a service, or otherwise meet all terms of a contract can you put the income down in your books. If a job is mostly completed but will take another few days to add the finishing touches, it doesn't go on your books until it is completely done.

Both methods can produce the same results. As you can readily see, the results produced by the cash and accrual accounting methods will only be different if you do some transactions on credit. If all your transactions are paid in cash as soon as completed, including your sales and purchases, then your books will look the same regardless of the method you use.

2. Accounting Methods and Taxes

The most significant way your business is affected by the accounting method you choose involves the tax year in which income and expense items will be counted. (See "Tax Years and Accounting Periods," below.) For instance, if you use the cash method, and you incur expenses in the 2006 tax year but don't pay them until the 2007 tax year, you won't be able to claim them on your 2006 tax return. But you would be able to claim them if you use the accrual method, since that system records transactions when they occur, not when money actually changes hands.

EXAMPLE 1: Zara runs a small flower shop called ZuZu's Petals. On December 22, 2005, Zara buys a number of office supplies for which she will be billed $400. She takes the supplies that day but, according to the terms of the purchase, doesn't pay for them for 30 days. Under her accrual system of accounting, she counts the $400 expense during the December 2005 accounting period, even though she didn't actually write the check until January of the next year. This means that Zara can deduct the $400 from her taxable income of 2005, which is usually a desirable result.

EXAMPLE 2: Scott and Lisa operate A Stitch in Hide, a leather repair shop. They're hired to repair an antique leather couch, and they finish their job on December 15, 2005. They bill the customer $750, which they receive on January 20, 2006. Since they use the accrual

method of accounting, Scott and Lisa count the $750 income in December 2005, because that's when they earned the money by finishing the job. This income must be reported on their 2005 tax return, even though they didn't receive the money that year.

Tax Years and Accounting Periods

Income and expenses must be reported to the IRS for a specific period of time, alternately called your "tax year," "accounting period," or "fiscal year." Unless you have a valid business reason to use a different period, or unless your business is a corporation, you'll have to use the calendar year, beginning on January 1 and ending on December 31. Most business owners do use the calendar year for their tax years, simply because they find it easy and natural to use. But if you want to use a different period, you must request permission from the IRS by filing Form 8716, *Election To Have a Tax Year Other Than a Required Tax Year.* Also, your fiscal year can't begin and end on just any day of the month; it must begin on the first day of a month and end on the last day of the previous month one year later.

3. Which Method to Use

Most businesses that have sales of less than $5 million per year are free to adopt either accounting method, with one big exception: If your business stocks an inventory of items that you will sell to the public, the IRS requires you to use the accrual accounting method. Inventory includes any merchandise you sell as well as supplies you will incorporate into products you intend to sell.

Whichever method you use, it's important to realize that either one only gives you a partial picture of the financial status of your business. While the accrual method shows the ebb and flow of business income and debts more accurately, it may leave you in the dark as to what cash reserves are actually available—and not knowing this information could result in a serious cash flow problem. For instance, your income ledger may show thousands of dollars in sales, while in reality your bank account is empty because your customers haven't paid you yet.

And though the cash method will give you a truer idea of how much actual cash your business has, it may offer a misleading picture of longer-term profitability. Under the cash method, for instance, your books may show one month to be spectacularly profitable because a lot of credit customers paid their bills in that month, when actually sales have been slow. To have a true understanding of your business's finances, you need more than just a collection of monthly totals; you need to understand what your numbers mean and how to use them to answer specific financial questions, as discussed in the rest of this chapter.

C. Keeping Receipts

Comprehensive summaries of your business's income and expenses are the heart of the accounting process. But unless you want to flirt with tax fraud, you can't just make up the information in your books. Each of your business's sales and expenditures must be backed up by some type of record containing the amount, the date, and other relevant information about that transaction. This is true whether your accounting is done by computer or on hand-posted ledgers.

From a legal point of view, your method of keeping receipts can range from slips kept in a cigar box to a sophisticated cash register hooked into a computer system. Practically, you'll want to choose a system that fits your business needs. For example, a small service business that handles only relatively few jobs may get by with a bare-bones approach. But the more sales and expenditures your business makes, the better your receipt filing system needs to be. This section discusses common ways of keeping your receipts. The bottom line is to choose or adapt one to suit your needs.

1. Receipts of Income

Every time your business brings in money, you need a record of it. Most of your revenue will come from sales of your products or services. How you keep track of sales will vary a great deal, depending on what type of business you run and how many sales you make.

a. Keeping Sales Records

Businesses such as grocery stores that make hundreds or even thousands of sales a day will likely need a cash register to produce a record of each sale. Other businesses with slower sales, such as hair salons or auto shops, can get by simply writing out a receipt for each sale from a receipt book. Handwritten receipts should include the date and a brief description of the goods or services sold. If some of your sales are made on credit, your receipts should indicate whether the customer paid and, if not, when payment is due.

Whether you use a cash register tape or hand-written receipts, make sure that you and your employees know the system and use it consistently. If your income records aren't accurate, the ledgers or financial statements you make from them won't be, either.

💡 **Receipts are most important for you.** While it's good business practice to give receipts to customers who purchase goods or services, it's a legal requirement that you keep a copy for yourself. Therefore, if you write out your own receipts, you'll need to make two copies—one for you, and one for the customer. Cash registers and most receipt books make each record in duplicate.

b. Distinguishing Taxable From Nontaxable Sales

Your income records must reflect whether a sale is taxable for state sales tax purposes. This distinction will be essential when you compute and file your state sales taxes. (See "Taxable Sales vs. Taxable Income," below.) If you use a cash register, this distinction can be made by the push of a button at the time of each sale. If you write out a receipt of each sale by hand, be sure to show any sales tax separately, not just as part of a total. If the sale is nontaxable, make that clear by writing "no tax," "nontaxable," or the like.

Assuming you follow the advice to keep your receipts of taxable sales separate from receipts of nontaxable sales, posting them to your accounting system (discussed in Section D, below) should be easy. If you plan to post daily, a simple method involves keeping your receipts for the day in two envelopes or two sections of an accordion folder (one for taxable sales, one for nontaxable) and adding them up at the end of the day. If you use a cash register, the process is simplified, because you can simply run totals at the end of the day for taxable sales and nontaxable sales. Depending on your machine, you may also be able to print out totals for other periods of time, such as one week or a specified number of days.

Taxable Sales vs. Taxable Income

As discussed above (and in more detail in Chapter 9, Section G), many sales of goods are subject to sales tax, which retailers must pay to the state. But other large categories of sales are often exempt from sales tax, such as sales of services, sales to out-of-state residents, or sales to resellers. So some sales income is taxable, and some is not.

However, whether a sale is taxable for *sales tax* purposes is a different issue from whether income is taxable or not for *income tax* purposes. Generally, taxable income—that is, money you take in that is subject to income taxes at the end of the year—includes any money earned by your business, minus certain deductions. All of this income must be reported on your year-end income tax return, whether or not it is subject to state sales tax.

Jennifer F. Mahoney, owner of an illustration service in Northern California:

It's helpful to learn about the accounts payable process for each client and to understand who in the company releases checks. It's often an entirely different person or department from the one who calls you to offer work. You don't necessarily want to strain your relationship with the person who calls offering you work just because a different department of their business doesn't pay on time. Pave the way for timely payments as much as possible by getting to know the correct procedure, and, when it's time to press for payment, you'll know the right person to call.

You should also document any income your business receives from sources other than sales and keep these receipts separate from your sales receipts. If you get a loan or contribute your own personal money to the business, record this fact with some sort of receipt or promissory note. Be sure your written records adequately describe the source of income so you'll know whether to count it as taxable income or not. Most sales income, for example, will be taxed at the end of the year, while income that you personally contribute to the business will not.

2. Expenditure Receipts

Ever hear the business wisdom that the key to small business success is to keep your costs down? While this isn't the only thing a successful business owner needs to do, watching those pennies is always a good idea. The first step in keeping costs down is keeping accurate track of what they are. Just as you keep a record of each individual sale, you need to keep a record each time you spend money for your business. Business expenditures include paychecks to employees, money spent on supplies, and payments on loans, as well as all other costs associated with your business. Legally and practically, each and every one of these expenses must be recorded.

First of all, be sure to get a written receipt for every transaction in which you spend money for the business. Not only is keeping and tallying these receipts an easy way to keep track of your expenses, but receipts also come in handy if there's a problem with any of the goods or services you purchased or a dispute over whether you paid a particular bill.

Many businesspeople like to use their checkbook registers to keep track of expenses. This is fine, but there are two pitfalls to watch out for if you choose this method. Since you will pay for many of your expenditures by check, you may have two records of the same transaction: the notation in your checkbook, and the receipt from the seller. Make sure you don't count that transaction twice. And don't forget to record cash purchases—they won't show up in your checkbook register. There are several easy ways to avoid counting some expenses twice and forgetting others. One is to use

your receipts as the sole record of expenditures, and not to count the amounts in your checkbook. Since most businesspeople don't want to sort through a pile of odd-sized bits of paper, another way is to rely solely on your checkbook for expenditure records, instead of on receipts. Fine, as long as you make sure to include the receipts of cash transactions in your checkbook register.

Don't let multiple receipts muddle you.
Sometimes, you'll receive a number of sales slips for just one purchase: a credit card slip, a register receipt, and an itemized statement, for example. If you throw all three receipts into your files to be posted later, you run the risk of counting all three separately. You might think that you'll remember the transaction, or that it will be obvious to you as you're posting your ledger that the three receipts correspond to a single transaction, but when dealing with dozens of receipts at the end of a long day, it's all too easy for mistakes to creep into your paperwork. To avoid counting transactions more than once, either discard multiple copies of receipts immediately after the transaction or staple them all together.

Each record of an expenditure should include the date, the amount, the method of payment, who was paid and—most important—a description of what type of expense it was, such as rent, supplies, or utilities. The description is important because later, when you post (enter) your expenses to your ledgers, you'll need to assign them into categories such as rent, advertising, supplies, utilities, and taxes. These categories are important for tax purposes, because different types of expenses have different rules for deductibility. To make your bookkeeping job easier, make sure your expense receipts contain enough information to allow you to assign the expense to the appropriate category when you post it in your ledger. Also, it's best to keep your expense receipts separated by category during the month prior to posting them. In other words, keep all of your utilities receipts in one box or envelope, your supplies receipts in another, and so on. (Various expense categories are discussed in Section D2, below.)

D. Step 2: Setting Up and Posting to Ledgers

A completed ledger is really nothing more than a summary of revenues and expenditures, as well as whatever else you're tracking, entered from your receipts according to category and date. Later, you'll use these summaries to answer specific financial questions about your business—such as whether you're making a profit and, if so, how much.

You'll start with a blank ledger page (a sheet with lines) or, more often these days, a computer file of empty rows and columns. On some regular basis—every day, once a week, or once a month—you should transfer ("post") the amounts from your receipts for sales and expenditures into your ledger. How often you do this depends on how many sales and expenditures your business makes and how detailed you want your books to be.

Generally speaking, the more sales you make, the more often you should post to your ledger. A retail store that does hundreds of sales amounting to thousands or tens of thousands of dollars every day should probably post daily. With that volume of sales, it's important to see what's happening every day and not to fall behind with the paperwork. To do this, the busy retailer should use a cash register that totals and posts the day's sales to a computerized bookkeeping system at the push of a button. A slower business, however, or one with just a few large transactions per month, such as a small website design shop, a dog-sitting service, or a swimming-pool repair company, would probably be fine if it posted weekly or even monthly.

To get started on a hand-entry system, get ledger pads from any office supply store. Or, as is more practical these days, purchase an accounting software program that will generate its own ledgers as you enter your information. All but the tiniest new businesses are well advised to use an accounting software package to help keep their books; microbusinesses can often get by with personal finance software such as *Quicken*. Once you've entered your daily, weekly, or monthly numbers, accounting software makes preparing monthly and yearly financial reports incredibly easy.

Learn bookkeeping by hand. Even though a computerized accounting system allows you to generate sophisticated financial reports with a few mouse clicks, you should still take the time to understand how the numbers fit together and what they mean. A good way to do this is to learn how financial reports are done by hand, as explained below, even if you plan to use a computer to generate them. The more you know about your numbers and the relationships between various figures, the better able you'll be to make positive and profitable business decisions.

Every business should have both an income ledger and an expenditure ledger into which its transactions are posted. The sections below will walk you through each of these ledgers, and offer samples of each type. Section 3 will also introduce you to some other types of ledgers that you may want to use, depending on your business.

1. Income Ledger

Despite its name, an income ledger should include only money earned in the course of business—your sales income—not income from every source. For example, income from a loan or transfer of personal money into the business should not be included with sales income on this ledger.

Check out the following example.

Income for May 20xx							
1	2	3	4	5 Nontaxable Sales			6
Date	Sales Period	Taxable Sales	Sales Tax	Sales to Retailers	Nontaxable Services	Other	Total Sales
1		$452.58	$38.47	$96.50	$75.00	$45.00	$707.55
2	closed						
3							
4	(May 3-4)	$765.50	$65.07	$143.50	$125.00	$65.75	$1,164.82
5 ...		$407.88	$34.67	$76.25	$60.00	$45.00	$623.80
... 31		$502.45	$42.71	$105.00	$90.00	$53.50	$793.66
Totals		$9,456.82	$803.83	$1,845.50	$1,365.50	$854.00	$14,325.65

Most income ledgers—whether on paper or part of your accounting software—are set up like the above sample, covering a one-month period and allowing space for daily entries. Your income should be divided into taxable sales, sales tax, and nontaxable sales. Also, your state may require your nontaxable sales to be broken down into certain categories, such as wholesale sales, services, sales to out-of-state customers, or freight charges. Check with your state sales tax agency to find out which, if any, nontaxable subcategories you must use in your record keeping.

When you're ready to post your sales income, however often you decide to do it, go through your receipts for that period and enter the totals into the appropriate columns. Mark each receipt or cash register tape "posted" (stamping is often easiest) once you've recorded it in your ledger. If you post daily, you'll have entries on each line except for days your business is closed, in which case you should enter "closed" in the Sales Period column. If you don't post daily, indicate in the Sales Period column which days are included for the totals you're entering (for example, "June 3 to June 6").

At the end of each month, total the entries in each column. Voila! You now have an income ledger for one month of business. As you can see, even without the help of a computer, creating one is easy. When you've finished a ledger for one month, start a new income ledger for the next month.

After you've completed an income ledger each month for a year, it's easy to add the monthly totals to arrive at your yearly sales income, broken down into taxable and nontaxable sales and sales tax amounts. Simply use a separate ledger sheet or computer file to post your monthly totals into a year-end income ledger. It will look very similar to your monthly income ledgers.

Remember, however, that businesses using the cash method of accounting can only count transactions actually paid during the year. If your business uses the cash method and did any sales on credit, you may need to do a year-end adjustment. If you never recorded unpaid sales in your monthly ledgers, then you're all set—no adjustment is necessary. If, however, you included your total sales figures in your monthly ledgers, including unpaid credit sales, then you'll need to account for these in your year-end totals. Simply add an Accounts Receivable row at the bottom of the year-end ledger, with the totals of any unpaid sales, and subtract them from your yearly totals.

Here's a sample year-end ledger.

Income for 20xx

1	2	3	4			5
			Nontaxable Sales			
Month	**Taxable Sales**	**Sales Tax**	**Sales to Retailers**	**Nontaxable Services**	**Other**	**Monthly Total**
January	$7,873.46	$669.24	$1,595.75	$1,310.75	$749.50	$12,198.70
February	$8,567.45	$728.23	$1,787.25	$1,280.75	$683.00	$13,046.68
March	$8,349.05	$709.67	$1,640.50	$1,150.50	$745.50	$12,595.22
April	$8,995.65	$764.63	$1,788.00	$1,335.75	$823.70	$13,707.73
December	$10,483.88	$891.13	$1,825.25	$1,458.50	$880.50	$15,539.26
Total for Year	$100,468.48	$9,108.72	$20,364.50	$14,076.25	$9,539.90	$153,557.85
Accounts Receivable	$10,345.15	$724.16	$1,565.45	$986.90	$450.55	$14,072.21
Adjusted Year-End Totals	**$90,123.33**	**$8,384.56**	**$18,799.05**	**$13,089.35**	**$9,089.35**	**$139,485.64**

Keep your completed ledgers in a safe place—whether they're hard copies or computer files. For hard copies, keep them in a well-organized file, preferably in a fireproof file cabinet. For computer files, be sure to make regular printouts and backups. Your ledgers will be essential to create financial reports that will give you a picture of your business's financial health (explained in Section E, below), and to complete your local, state, and federal tax returns. Losing your ledgers can be an expensive disaster—dealing with an IRS audit without your records is just one nightmare scenario—so be sure to treat them as the important business documents that they are.

2. Expenditure Ledger

The process of creating an expenditure ledger is quite similar to the income ledger process, but there are some key differences. Most important, the categories into which you'll divide your expenses are different. Here you won't use the "taxable sales," "sales tax," and "nontaxable sales" categories; instead, you'll divide your expenses into categories such as rent, utilities, computer equipment, employee wages, legal fees, postage, or travel, to name a few. Categorizing your expenses is important, because different types of expenses have different rules for deductibility for tax purposes. Some expenditures can be deducted right away in full, others may be deducted only over several years (referred to as "depreciating expenses"), while other costs may not be deductible at all.

The IRS has oceans of rules. For more information on different types of business expenses and their deductibility, read *Tax Savvy for Small Business,* by Frederick W. Daily (Nolo). Reading the rules issued by the IRS isn't a bad idea, either. IRS Publication 334, *Tax Guide for Small Businesses*, is a good place to start. It's available at www.irs.gov/formspubs/index.html.

Another reason for categorizing your expenses is so you'll be able to separate them into fixed costs versus variable costs when you use your ledger information to generate financial reports. Variable costs, you may remember from Chapter 5, are the ones tied to your products or services, while fixed costs (overhead) are the ones that more or less stay the same regardless of your production and sales volume. Since the distinction between variable and fixed costs will be important when generating your profit and loss forecast, be sure to keep track of them separately in your expenditure ledger. For instance, if you run a Web development business and give your work to clients on a Zip disk, make sure to keep track of Zip disks for clients (a variable cost) separately from the Zip disks you use within your office (a fixed cost). One way to do this is to create a Zip disk category for client disks and to simply count your office Zip disks in a general "office supplies" category.

The sample expenditure ledger below is a very simplified one, showing just a few common expense categories. Your business will almost certainly have several more categories of expenses. In defining your categories, keep in mind the distinction between variable and fixed expenses, and do your best to keep your categories tightly defined—but not so narrow that you end up with dozens of tiny groups. As a general reference, here's a list of common expense categories:

- advertising
- automobile
- bank charges
- copying
- delivery/freight/shipping
- dues & fees
- education (classes, workshops, and so on)
- employee wages
- equipment/furniture/computers
- equipment rental
- insurance
- interest on business debt
- legal & professional fees
- meals (business-related)
- office expenses/supplies
- office rent
- online services
- postage
- publications (books, magazines, and so on)
- software
- tax preparation fees
- taxes
- telephone
- travel, and
- utilities (gas, electric).

Expenditures for February 20xx

1	2	3	4	5	6	7	8	9
Date	Payment Method	Transaction	Payee	Office Supplies	Rent	Utilities	Misc.	Monthly Totals
2-1	ck. 1204	Rent	landlord		$1,000.00			
2-5	Visa	Stationery	Office Depot	$78.00				
2-13	cash	Business lunch	Monte Vista café				$32.00	
2-22	ck. 1206	Electric bill	electric co.			$65.00		
Feb. Totals				$78.00	$1,000.00	$65.00	$32.00	$1,175.00

An accountant can help you set up ledgers.
It's a good idea for every small business to use at least a minimal amount of help from an accountant, particularly in the early days when you're figuring out your accounting system. An accountant may be of particular help in figuring out which expense categories your business should use. For example, a carpenter will undoubtedly want to use different categories (such as a category for wood and another for hardware like nails and screws) from a Web designer (who might have a category for printing costs and another for storage media like Zip disks). An accountant, particularly one who's familiar with your type of business, has the expertise to know which expenses are important to group together.

Just as with your income receipts, you must periodically transfer or post the information from your expenditure receipts to your expense ledger. Ideally, you should do this reasonably promptly after you incur the expense. In the Payment Method/Check # column, enter "cash" if you paid in cash, the name of the credit card if you paid with plastic, or the check number if you paid by check. Remember, if you use the cash method of accounting, you will only record expenditures when they are paid—not when you incur them—so for credit card purchases, you'll only record them when you pay your bill. (See Section B, above, for a review of cash versus accrual accounting.) In the Transaction column, enter a brief description of the purchase, and in the Payee column, enter whom you paid. Then enter the amount of the purchase in the appropriate category column.

Unlike your income ledgers, a new expenditure ledger isn't started each month—you'll have one running expense ledger. At the end of the month, simply add up the expenses for that month in each category, and enter each category's total in the next empty row. Then add up all the totals for each category and enter the result in the Monthly Totals column. Draw a double line under the monthly totals, and then continue entering expenses for the next month on the same sheet. Use a new sheet when you run out of room.

At year end, you'll summarize your monthly expenditure totals on a separate ledger in much the same way that you summarized your monthly

Year-end Expenditure Summary					
1	**2**	**3**	**4**	**5**	**6**
Month	**Rent**	**Office Supplies**	**Utilities**	**Misc.**	**Totals**
January	$1,100	$120	$254	$154	$1,628
February	$1,100	$75	$236	$209	$1,620
March	$1,100	$56	$244	$130	$1,530
April	$1,100	$90	$197	$104	$1,491
December	$1,100	$62	$230	$185	$1,577
Year Totals	$13,200	$1,082	$2,164	$1,845	$18,366
Accounts Payable	0	$210	$62	$347	$619
Adjusted Year-End Totals		**$1,292**	**$2,226**	**$2,192**	**$18,985**

income totals. Remember that if you use the accrual accounting method, you'll need to include all expenses for the year, even if you haven't paid them yet. For those using accrual accounting, you'll be all caught up if, every month, you posted all expenses into your expenditure ledger as they became due, even if you didn't pay them. But, if you only posted the expenses that you actually paid (as is common for ease of posting), then you'll need to account for your unpaid bills. Do this by including the totals of any unpaid bills in an Accounts Payable row, categorized like your other expenses, and add it to your yearly total.

3. Designing a Ledger System

The two ledgers just described help you keep track of your most basic business functions: earning and spending money. Depending on how you conduct your business, you may also need to use one or more additional ledgers. If you sell products or services on credit, keep track of these sales (the amount you are owed) using an *accounts receivable* ledger. Similarly, if you make purchases on credit, you can keep track of what you owe with an *accounts payable* ledger. And, if your business has assets such as machinery, computers, or vehicles, you'll need to keep track of their depreciation with an *equipment* ledger. (Depreciation is explained in Chapter 9, Section A.) You'll find prototypes of various types of ledgers at office supply stores, or as a component of any accounting software product.

E. Creating Financial Reports

Financial reports are important, because they bring together several key pieces of financial information about your business in one place. Think of it this way: While your income ledger may tell you that your business brought in a lot of money during the

year, you have no way of knowing whether you turned a profit without measuring your income against your expenses. And even comparing your monthly totals of income and expenses won't tell you whether your credit customers are paying fast enough to keep adequate cash flowing through your business to pay your bills on time. That's why you need financial reports: to combine data from your ledgers and sculpt it into a shape that shows you the big picture of your business.

The financial reports discussed in this section are nothing to freak out about—they're really just the income and expense numbers from your ledgers, tweaked a bit to help you answer questions about how your business is doing. As long as you've been consistent and thorough in keeping your ledgers, you'll be able to generate all the reports you need easily and quickly.

1. Profit and Loss Statement

If the typical owners of a small business start-up got a nickel for every time they asked themselves, "Will my business make a profit?," they'd probably be rich enough to retire before the doors were even open. A profit and loss statement (also called a P & L, or an income statement) is designed to answer this very question. Chapter 5, "Drafting an Effective Business Plan," discussed creating a profit and loss statement with projected numbers. This section explains how to do it after you've opened your doors and have actual numbers to work with.

A P & L is made by totaling your revenues and then subtracting your expenses from that total for a specific period of time, usually each month. If you use accounting software, it will generate a P & L automatically with the data you enter from your sales and expense records. For each month, you'll be able to see whether your revenues are higher or lower than your expenses and by how much. At year end, you can total the monthly results to obtain your annual profit or loss.

To create a profit and loss statement, you'll need to subtract your "fixed costs" and your "variable costs" from your sales revenue—but first you'll need to understand the difference between the two. Fixed costs (also called overhead) are the costs associated with running your business in general, not with individual products or services themselves. Variable costs (also called costs of sale, or product or labor costs) are the expenses that are directly tied to the product or service that you're selling.

For example, say your business produces and sells greeting cards. Your variable costs would include the costs of the paper and printing the cards and the labor cost for the workers that make, package, and distribute them. As the name implies, these costs will vary depending on the amount and type of product you make and sell or service you perform. For example, if you produce more or less of a particular greeting card or if you emboss or use a heavier grade of card stock, your variable expenses will be affected.

Labor costs: sometimes variable, sometimes fixed. If you ask a group of accountants whether the labor costs associated with making a product are fixed or variable, you're likely to get conflicting answers. Some argue that, as long as the workers will get paid regardless of whether they're working on that product, their salaries should be considered fixed, like rent or utilities. Others say that, to have accurate financial records, you need to reflect the cost of the labor that goes into a product. You or your accountant can decide how your business will categorize labor costs for making a product. Labor costs for providing services, on the other hand, are almost always treated as variable costs.

But other costs—your fixed costs—will not go up or down depending on the products you make

or the services you perform. These costs, such as your rent, office utility bills, and insurance for your company vehicles, will be more or less the same, regardless of the amount or type of greeting cards you make. This is exactly why age-old business wisdom says to keep your overhead costs as low as you can. In times of slow sales, you want to be saddled with as few fixed costs as possible.

Now that you know the distinction between variable and fixed costs, you need to understand how they're each subtracted from your revenue on a typical profit and loss statement.

- A profit and loss statement starts with your total sales revenues (remember, you enter that information on your income ledger), then subtracts your variable costs (recorded in one or more columns of your expenditure ledger). The result is called your *gross profit*—how much money you've earned from sales of your products or services over and above their cost to you.

- Next you subtract your fixed costs (again, from your expenditure ledger) from your gross profit. Any money you're left with is your *real profit*—also called net income, net profit, or pretax profit. Other than the various taxes you'll need to pay on this income, this is your (and any other business owners') money.

To sum up, the formula used in a profit and loss statement is basically as follows:

> Sales revenue
> – Variable costs (or costs of sale)
> = Gross profit (or gross margin)
> – Fixed costs
> = Net profit

Here's a typical P & L.

20xx Profit/Loss Statement							December	Year Total
	January	**February**	**March**	**April**	**May**		**December**	**Year Total**
Sales Revenues	$1,900	$1,950	$2,000	$1,850	$2,000		$2,100	$23,550
Variable Costs	$300	$310	$350	$300	$325		$350	$3,840
Gross Profit	**$1,600**	**$1,640**	**$1,650**	**$1,550**	**$1,675**		**$1,750**	**$19,180**
Fixed Expenses Rent	$700	$700	$700	$700	$700		$700	$8,400
Supplies	$150	$100	$75	$90	$125		$100	$1,220
Utilities	$200	$200	$200	$200	$200		$200	$2,400
Advertising	$150	$150	$150	$150	$150		$150	$1,800
Misc.	$75	$80	$65	$70	$75		$85	$830
Total Fixed Expenses	**$1,275**	**$1,230**	**$1,190**	**$1,210**	**$1,250**		**$1,235**	**$14,650**
Net Income (Loss)	**$ 325**	**$410**	**$460**	**$340**	**$425**		**$515**	**$4,530**

The P & L not only will tell you whether you're making or losing money, but also will help you identify which aspects of your business need adjusting in order to boost profits. Often, a profitability problem can be found in your expenses. Being able to see the totals of each of your various expense categories over the course of several months, all on one sheet, can help you pinpoint areas in which you're spending too much money (and help give you the courage to do something about it). And, of course, accurately tracking income totals month by month will help you quickly spot a downturn in revenue and prompt you to take action to boost sales.

2. Cash Flow Projection

Chapter 5 discussed cash flow projections as a way to find out if your business would be able to pay its bills once it got started. A cash flow projection is also a crucial tool to use in your ongoing business. It's essential for your business to have enough cash available at any given time to pay its operating costs. Having lots of customers and thriving sales isn't enough, especially if you sell on credit. If your customers pay you in 90 days, but you must pay your expenses in 30 days or even immediately, you may face a situation where, even though your financial statement says you are making a profit, you can't pay your rent, utilities, delivery services, or other key bills. Unless you make some changes, you may have to take out a line of credit or even close up shop.

Helping you understand why you may not be able to pay your bills despite being profitable—and how to take steps to avoid this—is the role of a cash flow projection. A cash flow projection focuses on the actual cash payments made to and by your business. These payments are called cash-ins and cash-outs (or inflows and outflows) to differentiate them from sales and expenses, which may not be paid right away. Estimating your cash-ins and cash-outs for upcoming months can help you predict when you might run short, allowing you to take action early by tightening up on your credit terms, raising more capital, getting a loan or line of credit, or putting more effort into collecting accounts receivable. Without a prediction of when a cash shortage might happen, by the time it does, it may be too late to do anything about it other than lock your doors.

Your cash flow projection will use most of the same numbers as your profit and loss statement, along with a few new ones. The big difference is that your cash flow projection will include all of your sources of income—not just sales income—and only income that's paid in cash (not credit). In other words, while your profit and loss statement is concerned with how much revenue your business is earning through sales of its products or services, your cash flow projection is designed to show you how much cash you will have on hand from all sources, including paid sales, loans, interest from investments, transfers from your personal accounts, lottery winnings, whatever. That's because when it comes to paying bills, the bottom line is whether you have enough money, period. Similarly, your cash flow projection will include all money you pay out of the business, whether for supplies, taxes (including any estimated taxes you owe; see Chapter 9, Section E), loan repayments, or any other expenditure.

The basic formula for cash flow analysis is:

> Cash in bank at beginning of month
> + Cash receipts for the month
> − Cash disbursements for the month
> = Cash in bank at end of month

In a cash flow projection, each month starts with the amount of money you have in the bank. (This will generally be the same amount that's left over from the previous month.) Next, you'll add any cash that came in during the month in all relevant categories, such as sales income, loans, interest earned, and any personal money you put into the business—your total cash-ins for the month. Next,

subtract the money you spent during the month: your cash-outs. The result is the cash left at the end of the month. Enter that figure into the beginning of the next month's column, and do the same process for the next month. If you use accounting software, a cash flow spreadsheet can be generated automatically once you've entered figures for income and expenses.

Now that you see the basic formula behind cash flow analysis, you need to understand that the real power of this tool is not in tracking actual cash-ins and cash-outs, but in predicting future cash flows. Periodically, say once a month or every couple of months, you should use your actual figures to help make estimates for upcoming months and complete a cash flow projection for the future, generally up to one year. Hopefully, you'll see that you will have enough cash to cover your expenses each month. If not, don't panic. First, pat yourself on the back for doing a cash flow analysis and figuring out ahead of time that you won't be able to cover all your expenses. Then come up with a plan—either put off some expenses that can wait; get more money (perhaps through collecting accounts receivable or getting a short-term loan or line of credit); or sell, sell, sell more product, or services.

Especially when you're in the early stages of a business and don't have much of a business history, predicting cash-ins and cash-outs for future months isn't easy (though cash-outs are often easier to predict than cash-ins, because you have more control over them and many costs recur each month). You'll need to make estimates of how much income will come in and what expenses must be covered—a task that may seem only slightly easier than reading tea leaves.

The key is to do your best—with an emphasis on "do." Accept the fact that your estimates won't be close to 100% accurate, but make them anyway. As the months tick by and the flow of cash into and out from your business settles into daily, weekly, and monthly patterns, making estimates will inevitably become easier, and you'll find them increasingly more accurate.

An example of a cash flow projection you can do on a simple spreadsheet is shown below.

As you can see, arranging income and expense information into a cash flow projection reveals a lot about the financial workings of a business. For example, the sample cash flow forecast shows that cash is tight each and every month (look at the "Cash at End of Month" row), so the business owner might consider ways to cut costs or to tighten credit terms.

Of more pressing importance is the projected cash shortfall starting in June. Knowing a few months in advance that a shortage is likely will help a business owner figure out what to do while there's still time to take action. The owner could contribute some personal money to the business (note that the cash flow didn't include any loans or personal transfers to the business) or could try to cut some nonessential expenses, at least until later in the year when there will be a bit (but only a small bit) more cash available.

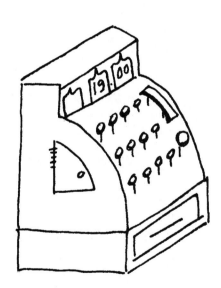

Cash Flow Projection, Completed April, 20xx

	Jan	Feb	Mar	April	May
Cash at Beginning of Month	$2,000	$1,250	$600	$700	$350
Cash-ins					
Sales Paid	$15,000	$14,750	$15,500	$14,750	$15,500
Loans and Transfers	$0	$0	$0	$0	$0
Total Cash-ins	**$15,000**	**$14,750**	**$15,500**	**$14,750**	**$15,500**
Cash-outs					
Variable Costs	$3,000	$3,100	$3,500	$3,000	$3,250
Rent	$7,000	$7,000	$7,000	$7,000	$7,000
Supplies	$1,500	$1,000	$750	$900	$1,250
Utilities	$2,000	$2,000	$2,000	$2,000	$2,000
Loan Payments	$1,500	$1,500	$1,500	$1,500	$1,500
Misc.	$750	$800	$650	$700	$750
Total Cash-outs	**$15,750**	**$15,400**	**$15,400**	**$15,100**	**$15,750**
Cash at End of Month	**$1,250**	**$600**	**$700**	**$350**	**$100**

June	July	Aug	Sept	Oct	Nov	Dec
$100	($300)	$150	$0	$0	($550)	$300
$15,000	$16,100	$16,250	$15,500	$15,250	$16,750	$16,900
$0	$0	$0	$0	$0	$0	$0
$15,000	**$16,100**	**$16,250**	**$15,500**	**$15,250**	**$16,750**	**$16,900**
$3,150	$3,450	$3,500	$3,250	$3,300	$3,400	$3,550
$7,000	$7,000	$7,000	$7,000	$7,000	$7,000	$7,000
$900	$1,100	$850	$1,000	$1,100	$950	$900
$2,000	$2,000	$2,000	$2,000	$2,000	$2,000	$2,000
$1,500	$1,500	$1,500	$1,500	$1,500	$1,500	$1,500
$4,850	$600	$1,550	$750	$900	$1,050	$850
$15,400	**$15,650**	**$16,400**	**$15,500**	**$15,800**	**$15,900**	**$15,800**
($300)	**$150**	**$0**	**$0**	**($550)**	**$300**	**$1,400**

Credit lines provide flexibility and cash flow.
One good strategy for a small business owner who expects seasonal fluctuations in cash flow is to apply for a revolving line of credit from the bank. A line of credit works on the same principle as a credit card. The business can borrow funds up to the credit line limit on an as-needed basis and has to pay interest only on the outstanding balance (not the entire credit line). The business can choose to pay funds back and reborrow them as necessary during the time the credit line is open—credit lines can be open for a specified period, such as five or ten years, or can be open-ended (like a credit card).

Compare your projection to reality. Each month, replace your projections with actual results from your accounting system. It's a great way to see how good a job of projecting you're doing.

Who Needs to Do a Cash Flow Analysis?

David Rothenberg, a CPA and Chief Financial Officer at Nolo, gives the following advice: "If your business is wildly profitable, you have little or no debt, you are not planning on expanding your business anytime soon, and you don't grant your customers a long time to pay, you probably don't need to do a cash flow analysis—you already know you'll have plenty of cash to meet your needs. But if this doesn't sound like your business, then you probably will benefit from keeping a close eye on your cash flow. Remember, the cash flow statement isn't for the IRS, and it isn't for the bank; it's for you! That's right, YOU! You're the one who won't sleep at night if your bank account is empty. So what are you waiting for? Get out there and start projecting!"

Chapter 12 Checklist

☐ Decide whether to use the cash or accrual system of accounting.

☐ Keep records of all payments to and from your business. Create an organized system for keeping your receipts.

☐ Summarize your income and expense records into ledgers on a regular basis. Businesses with high volumes of sales or expenses should do this frequently—daily or weekly.

☐ Use your income and expense ledgers to create financial reports such as a profit/loss statement and a cash flow analysis.

☐ Consult with an accountant or tax professional at least once a year to keep your system on track.

Websites and E-Business

Websites mean many different things to different businesses. For some business owners, having a website is essential because a major part of sales and other business operations will take place completely online. For others, a website is a valuable marketing tool, used to generate business that is done primarily offline. And for still others, a website is an afterthought, something the business owner isn't quite sure he or she needs.

In addition, as discussed in this chapter, the world of e-business can involve more than just maintaining a website. There are other ways businesses can promote themselves and conduct business online—for example, by posting to online bulletin boards or publishing an email newsletter. In this chapter, the term "e-business" refers to the broad range of ways your business can exist online—beyond simply maintaining a website.

What's true for all businesses is that launching a website or engaging in other forms of e-business needs to be approached strategically. You need to establish how your e-business activities will fit into your overall business strategy. And figuring this out before you start developing your site or other online ventures is a critical step. For example, without giving careful thought to your business's e-business strategy before creating a website, you might end up with a site that is ineffective—or worse, one that unexpectedly drains your business's valuable resources.

Even when your strategy is clear, creating a website can be tricky. Some business owners are tempted to do the job themselves to save money, but quickly discover they're out of their depth. Others decide to hire outside Web developers, but find they're at the mercy of programmers who push technologies the business doesn't need or who lack business savvy, resulting in sites that don't achieve business goals.

This chapter demystifies the process of creating a website—starting by helping you clarify your strategy and moving into the specifics of how to find and work with Web developers. It discusses how different types of businesses can strategically use the Web and other electronic communications technologies most appropriately and effectively. And it walks you through a methodical process of developing a website, from strategy and concept to programming and testing.

A. Getting Started

The key to developing a successful e-business is to approach the process strategically, solidly assessing:

- how a website fits into your overall business plan
- other types of electronic communications you may want to include, such as e-newsletters, and
- your specific goals.

Without carefully considering these issues, you're almost assured of running into problems. For example, poorly planned websites tend to do a bad job of communicating effectively with the desired audience. And even worse, a site developed without regard to your larger business plan can seriously sidetrack your core efforts and drain your business's valuable resources.

This section walks you through the initial steps of venturing into e-business, from deciding whether to create a website and incorporate other electronic methods to defining your strategy.

1. Decide Whether You Need a Website

While the rest of this chapter presumes that you do want to create a website, you may be wondering whether you need one at all. Today's conventional wisdom is that every business should have at least a simple website with basic information about what the business does, and contact information. In some cases, this might be nothing more than a one-page site, similar to a listing in the Yellow Pages. Whether to create a more extensive site will depend on the specifics of your business.

Generally, even an ultrabasic site will offer several benefits to your business.

Web Jargon: Defined

In addition to the often bewildering technical jargon that's so often used by Web developers and consultants, even nontechnical terms can be confusing, since the language of the Web is still evolving. To help stay clear about what's what, some of the most common terms are defined below. Keep in mind that since the e-world is relatively new, definitions are still fluid and other people might use these terms somewhat differently.

- **Blog** is short for "weblog," a relatively new form of website that is perhaps most analogous to an online journal. Blogs are websites that are regularly updated—often several times daily—with new information by one or more contributors, called bloggers. Blog entries tend to be short, and almost always link to external information such as articles in online newspapers or other electronic publications. While blogs started out as largely personal communication vehicles, an increasing number of reputable business and political publications are using the blog format. (See Section A2d for more on blogs.)

- **E-business** is a very general term referring to the full range of ways a business can operate in the online world, from using simple marketing emails to complex e-commerce sites, and everything in between. A website is generally—but not always—the focal point of e-business.

- **E-commerce** refers to an online sales operation, generally via a website that is set up to allow online orders and process credit card or other types of payments.

- **Email lists** are simply compilations of email addresses of people who have expressed interest in receiving emails from a specific sender or about a certain topic. For example, your business could send emails about special promotions or events to an email list—which should be composed of people who have clearly expressed interest in receiving your emails. As you're probably aware, unsolicited marketing emails are known as spam and frowned upon by savvy businesspeople and their recipients alike. Recipients of an email list cannot usually post their own messages to the entire group; communications are typically one-way from the administrator to the list. (See Section A2a for more details about email lists.)

- **Marketing websites** refer to basic websites that feature marketing-type information about a company, such as what its products or services are, pricing, and contact information. While an e-commerce site will usually include marketing information, a marketing website by definition does not include an e-commerce component. Very basic marketing websites are sometimes called brochure-ware, since they are analogous to a company brochure.

- **Listservs** are essentially email discussion groups about a specific topic that allow people who have signed up to them to share information with each other. Any subscriber can send an email to the listserv, and that email will automatically be sent to all other listserv subscribers.

- **Online presence** refers to the broad collection of ways a business is represented in the electronic world. For instance, in addition to having a website, you could be listed in numerous online directories; be a regular contributor to online forums; have a regular email newsletter; supply informative articles to other websites; and moderate a listserv. The sum of all these is often called your online presence.

- **Web developers** specialize in all the aspects of creating websites, including organization of the information, graphic design, and programming. Avoid the term Web designer when referring to these individuals, since graphic design is only one aspect of creating a website. Another acceptable term for Web developer is Web builder. Although some Web developers work alone as independent contractors, they typically involve teams to create a website: information architects, graphic designers, content developers, and programmers. (Section C discusses how to choose and work with Web developers.)

- It projects a professional image. Some customers consider businesses that don't have websites to be less serious or less stable than businesses than have them

- It helps you reach the ever-growing number of consumers who look for businesses online. This is true for all kinds of businesses, not just Web-related ones. In our increasingly Web-reliant population, a growing number of people start their searches for a local plumber, a café, a clothing store, or any other type of business on the Web.

- It allows you to communicate more information than you can typically fit on a business card or brochure. When you include the Web address, called the URL for "uniform resource locator," on your business cards, brochures, or other printed materials, potential customers can go to your site for more in-depth information such as product details or portfolio pieces.

- It creates a permanent place where you can post information that potential customers can always refer to, unlike brochures or business cards that often get thrown away or lost. This can be helpful to current customers or clients who may need to look up your phone number or payment mailing address.

- It facilitates word-of-mouth marketing, because your happy customers will easily be able to share information about your business to their friends and family simply by sharing your URL.

- It allows you to market your business without paying print costs. This can save you a lot of money if the information you want to communicate is lengthy or changes frequently such as sales, specials, and new product arrivals. And of course, your website can use full color, which can be quite expensive to print.

- It allows you to develop and refine your marketing messages before committing them to print. For example, you could create a simple three-page site with information about your services, your professional biog-

raphy and contact information—and refine these pieces of content for a month or two until you're satisfied with them; then create a print brochure with the information from the website.

Keep in mind that a website might offer even more opportunities for your particular business, such as the potential for profits from e-commerce and improved customer services. The bottom line is that even the simplest website will be an asset to your business.

Of course, another consideration is what a website will cost. (See Section C3 for a complete discussion of typical costs.)

2. Consider Other Electronic Methods

While a website is generally the centerpiece of a business's online presence, it's smart to consider other online methods of communicating with potential customers when beginning to develop a website.

There are a number of possibilities to consider.

a. Email lists and E-newsletters

Your business can email different kinds of information to customers who have signed up for such communications. Broadly speaking, you can either send marketing information or more substantive information. When you send just marketing information, it's usually called an email list, while substantive information is usually called an e-newsletter. Of course, the line between marketing and substantive information can get awfully blurry, so here are some tips on how to communicate both types most effectively.

When emailing any type of information to your customers who have signed up for it, make sure that they receive the type of information they expected when they gave you their email address. In particular, don't send purely marketing information to customers who are expecting a more substantive newsletter with topic-based articles. Send marketing emails only to customers who have willingly signed up for that information.

Along these same lines, make sure anything that you call a "newsletter" actually lives up to its name. A newsletter—either in print or via email—does not have to be lengthy. In fact, short blurbs of useful information are generally more popular and reader-friendly than lengthy articles. But a so-called newsletter that is little more than promotional copy for products and services will be sure to disappoint any customers expecting more substantive information. Considering how little tolerance people have for marketing emails, also known as "spam," be particularly careful not to send e-newsletters unless they contain truly useful information and are not just thinly disguised marketing copy. Some marketing information is fine in a newsletter, as long as substantive information is the focus. The best way to include marketing information in a newsletter is at the end of the more substantive information that offers some information of value to your readers.

What is appropriate content for a newsletter will vary significantly from one business to the next. It will largely depend on the expectations of your audience. While newsletters traditionally contain topic-based articles, for some businesses it may be sufficient simply to announce upcoming events. For example, an e-newsletter for an independent cinema may send out a monthly newsletter with descriptions of upcoming screenings. Considering that the film screening schedules are the customers' primary interest, they would likely find that content valuable and happily accept that as an e-newsletter. But a monthly "e-newsletter" from a clothing store that had no content other than sales and specials would likely seem like just another marketing email and irritate its recipients. Instead, a short article or two each month about current fashion trends might be more appealing to interested readers. Or, the clothing store might reasonably conclude that an e-newsletter just isn't a good fit for its business, and simply be clear with customers that its email list will receive sales, specials, and other marketing information from the business.

True newsletters, particularly when they are done well, can take a fair amount of time to create. While email newsletters may be simpler to create than print newsletters, don't underestimate the hours it will take you to write, edit, proofread, and send them. Similarly, don't underestimate the importance of well-written text that is free from errors and typos. In addition, when you commit to publishing a newsletter, it means that you commit to putting one out regularly, usually once a month or at least once a quarter. Make a realistic evaluation of whether you or a staffer has the writing skills and the time to be able to reliably create a quality newsletter. If not, then it's best to put off your newsletter plans until you have the resources in place.

When sending out any type of email to your customers, keep in mind the following tips.

- **Use the blind copy function to keep email addresses private.** By putting all the addresses in your email list in the blind copy, or Bcc fields, the recipients will not be able to see all the other recipients' email addresses. Failing to do this risks irritating the members of your lists and making your business appear unprofessional.

- **Use plain text emails instead of HTML-formatted emails.** While HTML emails may look more attractive than plain text emails, they may not be readable by some of your readers and may be filtered by antispam software. Other reasons such as the higher bandwidth used by HTML emails and the possibility of viruses lurking in them has made using plain-text emails one of the rules of proper netiquette.

⚠ Avoid spam at all costs. To avoid being perceived as a spammer, send mass emails only to customers who have requested to be included on your list. Even better, use a "double opt-in" system. In it, customers opt in the first time by indicating a willingness to receive your email communications—perhaps they signed up for your list at your website or signed a sheet at a tradeshow event. Then, you send an email to individual recipients asking them to confirm that they want to be included on your list. A double opt-in system shows your commitment not to send spam—and ensures that the folks receiving your emails actually want them.

b. Bulletin Boards or Forums

Many businesses contribute their expertise and perspective by posting comments to online bulletin boards on topics related to the business. The key is to share information as an expert, not hustle for business. Including your business name and contact info in your signature is okay; actively soliciting business is generally a no-no.

Your business can also include an interactive forum at its website, where people can post messages and interact with each other on topics you choose. Your role is generally to moderate the discussion and remove posts that are off-topic or offensive.

c. Listservs

A listserv is similar to an email list, in that people who have signed up for the listserv receive emails. However, with a listserv, the emails can be sent by anyone who is part of the listserv, not just by the manager of the listserv. For example, someone who reads a listserv email could respond to the whole group by sending an email to the listserv, which would be distributed to all recipients of the listserv. In contrast, email lists are one-directional, from the business to the list.

While listservs are most common in nonprofit organizations and schools, some businesses also have customers who want to engage in an ongoing email discussion group. Business listservs tend to be appropriate only when a business's customer base has a compelling desire to interact, such as software companies whose customers like to share user tips with each other.

d. Blogs

Blogs have been around for a few years, but really hit their stride between 2003 and 2005 as an easy, effective way to communicate late-breaking information. A blog is basically just a website composed of chronologically ordered posts with the most recent entries at the top, much like an online journal. Photos or images are often included with individual posts. Posts tend to be short and almost always include one or more links to related information at other websites. In addition, many blogs allow readers to post comments. Inexpensive blog software makes it easy to add new posts—much easier than it typically is to add content to traditional websites.

While early blogs tended to be more like personal journals, blogs have been embraced by many media outlets and issue-oriented websites seeking new ways to connect with audiences. A number of characteristics have made blogs attractive to the mainstream media. They are easy to update. They allow an informal, friendly voice and more flexible coverage of topics. And perhaps most compelling, readers can easily comment, helping forge a connection between the blog and its readership. With the widespread success of many blogs, it's not surprising that the business world is jumping on board.

The idea with a business blog is that one or more people at your company—quite possibly you, the business owner—add regular posts to the blog on topics related to your business. For example, General Motors started a blog called the FastLane Blog offering posts from the GM Vice Chairman Bob Lutz and other company executives on emerging automotive technologies, design, safety issues, and other related topics. The goal is to draw readers interested in cars with conversational posts from top auto executives who know the latest and greatest innovations being developed.

The trick to a successful business blog is to offer information that's interesting to your potential customers and that favorably inclines them toward your business and products or services, without being too self-serving or marketing heavy. For example, if all your business blog posts are about how great your business is—and even worse, if it's all in marketing-speak—you'll quickly turn off readers. But if you present interesting topics to your readers in a sincerely helpful, information-sharing way, you'll be more likely to attract regular readers who develop a favorable impression of your business. This may even mean occasionally linking to competitors, if appropriate.

Also, blogs that allow users to post comments tend to develop a more loyal readership. Keep in mind, however, that allowing reader posts means you will have to monitor those comments for offensive, libelous, off-topic, or otherwise unacceptable material. It's up to you what line to draw, but inevitably you won't please everyone. If you leave offensive posts untouched, visitors will likely be turned off; while if you edit posts, people are sure to complain that you're censoring them. Still, allowing user posts is a great way to connect with your audience. Just strive to be fair in your policies in editing the posts.

A few examples of business blogging that could be done successfully include:

- a bakery's blog about baking techniques and tips, allowing comments from readers and encouraging readers to submit photos of their results
- a yoga studio's blog about the health benefits of yoga, linking to external articles and studies about yoga's role in healthful living, and
- a bead shop's blog about the history and origin of trade beads, linking to other online sources of historical information on beads.

However, be aware that it's still an open question to what degree businesses will directly benefit from a quality blog. Remember, for a blog to be interesting and useful it shouldn't exclusively focus on the business itself. Most often, the tips that readers find most valuable have nothing to do with the business hosting the blog. For example, consider a software company blog written by the company's chief technical officer. If she mentions how much she loves her new X brand hybrid car,

that fact will likely spread like online wildfire, and may even boost sales of that hybrid brand. But if the same CTO mentions her company's latest software product, people will tend not to get so excited about that, considering the CFO's likely bias in favor of the company's products.

In other words, blogs can offer invaluable tips and tidbits for readers—but the most compelling tidbits are often not directly related to the blogging company, and may not boost sales at all. Blogging is more likely to yield indirectly the benefit of developing your brand as a reputable company that's in the know regarding industry developments. Keep this in mind when evaluating your expected results from a planned business blog.

Even more important are some fundamental rules to understand when considering a business blog. At a minimum, don't overlook the following realities.

- **The blog needs to be regularly updated, ideally a couple of times per week or more.** Don't start a blog unless you're sure you or someone at your business has the time to keep it updated.
- **The blogger needs to be well-informed on the topic and Web-savvy.** While the blogger doesn't have to be the world's top authority on your topic, he or she needs to know enough to create posts that are interesting and helpful to others seeking information on that topic. Part of this is being able to ferret out useful information online and provide links to that info.
- **The blogger needs to have some basic writing skills.** An informal, lively writing style is best on blogs. Avoid dry, academic writing and, at the other end of the spectrum, copy that sounds like a sales pitch.

For more information on online publishing. Cheryl Woodard's *Starting & Running a Successful Newsletter or Magazine* (Nolo) includes a helpful, in-depth chapter on electronic publishing and establishing an online presence. It also offers the latest online communication methods and effective e-publishing strategies.

3. Define Your Strategy

In the broadest strokes, websites tend to focus on one or more of the following functions:

- **marketing**—promoting an offline business
- **e-commerce**—conducting sales online, and
- **publishing**—communicating information that is regularly updated.

⚠ **Look before you leap into publishing.**
Publishing-oriented websites differ from marketing websites in that they focus on substantive information such as articles or reports, not promotional copy. Be careful if you're considering an online newsletter or other publishing activities; they will require a higher commitment and more frequent updating.

Way before you start thinking about the stories you want to write for your email newsletter or all the cool features you want to include on your website, put careful thought into your broad strategy for e-business and how it all fits into your overall business strategy. In broad strokes, this means figuring out whether your e-business activities will mainly promote your offline business—launching a basic marketing site, perhaps—or whether a good portion of your business will actually be conducted online, through an e-commerce or e-publishing operation. Oftentimes, a website performs both functions. The key is to be clear about what you intend your site to achieve.

If your business was originally conceived as an online business—for example, a Web-based dating service, or an electronic publication—you probably already have a clear idea that your online activities will be the focus of your business. But if you are planning a website for a traditional offline business such as a bakery or remodeling service, it's important to take the time to be clear about how your website or other online activities fits into your bigger business plan. Bricks-and-mortar businesses are vulnerable to stumbling into bigger e-business activities than they can handle. If you will be conducting business online, then you need to make sure that you have adequately accounted for these online operations in your business plan. If not, you'll need either to scale back your e-business plans or revise your business plan accordingly.

It's all too easy to be seduced by the latest interactive features and other Web-based applications—online sales and publishing are common examples—and to lose focus of your core business operations. Online sales in particular tend to involve a whole new set of details you'll need to handle, such as shipping and online customer service. If these activities weren't included in your original business plan, you might quickly find yourself overwhelmed and unable to keep customers happy—a bad situation for any business. With careful strategic thinking before launching a website or other e-business activities, you can plan for the resources you'll need and avoid this mistake.

EXAMPLE: Lydia is planning to open a store selling handmade jewelry. She wants to create a website and starts talking to Web developers to get an idea of what a site would cost. Many of the developers she talks with encourage her to create an online store to help increase sales. Without having put much thought into the website, Lydia initially likes the idea. She figures that if the site generates even a few sales per month, it would be welcome additional income.

When Lydia takes the time to think more about an online jewelry store, though, she realizes she has several questions about how it would work. She calls back some of the developers she's talked to and asks about details such as how the site would be updated with photos of current pieces, and how other tasks would be handled, such as shipping, billing, inventory control, and customer service. She learns that indeed, while some tasks such as billing can be somewhat automated, other tasks would have to be handled either by her, an employee, or a subcontractor such as the Web developer.

Lydia realizes that her business plan did not account for the logistics involved in online sales, and that she'd rather stick with her original plan and make sure to run her shop well, as she originally planned. In keeping with this, she decides to keep her website strategy simple, with a basic marketing website used to promote her business, not for online sales.

4. Define Your Goals

Beyond identifying an overall strategy for how your site and other electronic communications will fit within your business, you also need to define specific goals for your online efforts. All too often, business owners fail to do this with any specificity; many think the goal is simply to "increase business." However, goals can and should be more specific so that the content and features at your site are well-tailored to them.

Typical goals for many small business owners would include:

- establishing a basic online presence
- building recognition of the business and its brand
- attracting new clients and customers, either to come to a physical business or to call the business
- collecting email addresses or other contact information for marketing efforts
- showing work samples and portfolio items
- selling products—the very definition of e-commerce
- answering common customer questions to decrease customer service phone calls
- attracting investors, and
- publishing late-breaking information, such as the latest bathroom fixtures or recent technology releases.

By clearly defining goals, you'll be better able to decide what information is important to communicate to your audience. (See Section B6 for a discussion of choosing the content to feature at your site.) In addition, your specific goals will play a big part in determining how information is organized at your site. Content that is closely tied to high-priority goals should be featured prominently.

For example, if you rush to put together your website and fail to provide a prominent link to your "Customer Service" page, you probably won't get too much traffic to that area. If, on the other hand, you outline your goals for the site and identify online customer service as a priority, you would be less likely to make that blunder. This advice may sound obvious, but an unbelievable number of websites are poorly designed to the point of uselessness. Don't join their ranks.

B. Planning and Preparing

Once you are clear about what role your site will play in your overall business and have defined some specific goals for the site and other electronic communications you might use, it's time to make some specific plans—before you contact a Web developer.

If you take the time and effort to consider the issues discussed below before your first meeting, it will help create an efficient workflow, and help you clearly convey to the developer what you want. Of course, it's normal to have some unresolved questions when you initially contact a Web developer and perhaps to work with him or her in refining your overall goals. (See Section D1.) The point is to do at least some planning and preparation in advance to get the most out of the working relationship.

1. Identify Participants

Define early on which people in your company will be involved in the website project—in particular, who will have the authority to make decisions about the site. With small start-ups, this is usually pretty straightforward: The business owners typically are involved, meaning they help to set goals, review the site in various stages of development, and have approval authority. However, if there are several business owners and one or more are not involved from the beginning, the possibility exists that they may raise objections down the line, after significant time and resources have already been spent on the site. To avoid this, make sure all business owners agree from the beginning who will have decision-making authority and what approval process will be followed.

If you outsource your site, retain control of strategic decisions. Unless someone involved with your business has experience creating websites, it's generally best to outsource most aspects of the website creation process. (See Section D for details.) Do not, however, give a consultant or Web development company complete discretion over your site—particularly over identifying your overall strategy for e-business. Even if you know and trust the developer you hire, you and any other business owners must be involved in these important strategic questions.

2. Research Other Sites

One of the best ways to educate yourself about the world of possibilities online and to generate specific ideas for features, designs, content, and other elements to include at your site is to browse the Web and look for examples of sites you like and don't like. Even if a site is very different from how you envision yours, there may be elements that could work for your site—for example, the color scheme, fonts, graphic images, or the organization of the information. Most Web developers will ask you for such examples, so it's a good idea to do this research before meeting with a developer.

3. Decide on a Static or Dynamic Site

Early in the Web development process, you should make the extra effort to understand the difference between a static and a dynamic site. Here's a quick explanation.

- In a **static** website, each Web page at the site generally corresponds to an HTML or Hypertext Markup Language file—a file that contains text content, links to images and other Web pages, HTML code, and other features. To add new information to a page, you must make changes to that HTML file and upload it to the server.

- In a **dynamic** site, also called a database-driven site, all the Web pages for the site are actually templates that display content that is stored in a database. To make changes the content, the information is edited in the database—much like doing data entry in any kind of database—and it will be displayed in the template, which remains unchanged. The database interface is often called the site's back-end. With some sophisticated websites, the back-end is designed to be especially user-friendly and to allow extensive modification of the website content, even for users who don't know how to do website programming. These interfaces are sometimes called content management systems.

Choosing between a static and a dynamic site is one of the fundamental early decisions you'll have to make when working with a Web developer. While your developer will likely have advice for you depending on the specifics of your strategy and goals, here are some general rules to guide your decision.

- **Static sites are easier and cheaper to create, but more difficult to update.** To make changes to static sites—for example, to add a new article or edit your staff biographies—you'll need to understand how to use website creation software or how to edit HTML code. You'll need to either learn how to do this yourself or hire someone to do it. . Updating static sites can be relatively simple, but many business owners decide it's a better use of their time to outsource this task. So, if you plan to change your site content often or to use outside help, this can become a significant cost factor.

- **Dynamic sites are more costly to create, but easier to update.** Instead of using website creation software or editing HTML code, you'll make changes to the content in a database, accessing the database via the site's back-end. If you're familiar with using database software, you'll likely be equipped to do site maintenance of a dynamic, database-driven site. However, keep in mind that some back-ends are quite complicated and may require training and a significant learning curve, even for those familiar with databases. And if no one at your business is comfortable using databases, you'll likely need to outsource maintenance anyway, reducing the value of the site.

In a nutshell, dynamic sites may be the wisest choice if you plan to update your site's content regularly and if you have little tolerance for learning how to format HTML documents. In that case, your goal is to find a developer who will create a clean, easy-to-use back-end that allows you to do maintenance in-house, rather than having to pay someone else to do it. If, on the other hand, you don't plan to change your site often, a static website is likely the best route. If and when you need to make changes to a static site, you can hire a contractor to do it—or take the time to learn Web creation software such as Macromedia Dreamweaver or Adobe GoLive, which really are not that difficult to use at a basic level.

If you're not sure how often you'll be changing site content, it's probably best to start with a simple static site, then convert it to a dynamic site if you find yourself needing to update it regularly.

4. Set a Realistic Budget

While you don't need to spend a fortune creating a website, you certainly can—and you can do so either by choice, or by letting costs spiral out of control. An essential step in preventing costs from smothering your best intentions is to set a budget for what your business can realistically afford for website creation and maintenance. It's best to do this before you start talking to Web developers to get a clear answer from those you contact about whether they can do what you want within your budget. You'll likely get quite a wide range of fees and rates from different developers, which often are affected by how many years they've been in business and what technologies they use. As long as your budget is realistic to begin with, you'll likely be able to find someone who can create something close to the site you want within your budget.

When attempting to set a realistic budget, keep a few parameters in mind. Very generally speaking, a static marketing website—that is, one without e-commerce functions—will cost somewhere between $1,500 and $2,500 to build. For a dynamic or database-driven marketing site, costs start at around $4,000. E-commerce sites are more expensive—generally ranging from $4,000 for a static e-commerce site to $5,000 and higher for dynamic, database-driven e-commerce sites. And there are often third-party fees beyond what the Web developer charges, such as payment processing and security certificate fees for e-commerce sites, and domain name and hosting fees.

The bottom line is that the more features and functionality a site has, the more it will cost. Major, complex websites can cost in the tens or hundreds of thousands of dollars to create.

You get what you pay for. Even simple websites require several components: information architecture, graphic design, content creation, and programming. To have all these done well, you'll generally need a bare minimum budget of $1,000. You are not likely to get a quality, professional site—even a simple one—for $500. Sites in this low price range are often based on website templates which tend not to look professional or to meet specific business needs. It's better to pay a bit more for a site that is customized for you and that has a professional look and feel.

Another cost that you must consider is the cost of maintaining your site after it has been created. As discussed above, updating a static site requires some technical knowledge, so you may need to outsource even the smallest updates. With Web developer fees ranging from $50 to $100 an hour, outsourcing maintenance can get expensive. Dynamic sites are designed to allow the site owner to update the site independently. So to a large degree, the question of how much it will cost to keep your site current will depend on how often updates are necessary, and whether your site is static or dynamic. If you are able to take care of maintenance in-house, be sure to factor in the time commitment required.

Also keep in mind that some updating tasks are independent of whether the site is static or dynamic. The following tasks may be involved in updating any type of site:

- writing new content
- taking new photographs—particularly for e-commerce operations when new products are added
- responding to emails from site visitors
- generating traffic or sales reports, and
- promoting and marketing the website.

5. Establish a Schedule

For some business owners, the timing of the launch of their website is crucial—say, it absolutely needs to go live before an important trade show, or before a Grand Opening. For others, it may not matter very much at all. The point is to consider whether the timing of your website project is an important issue, and if so, schedule accordingly.

It typically takes at least one month from the start of the website project until the site's launch, and usually longer—for complex sites, considerably longer. If holiday online sales are a big part of your business strategy, get the ball rolling in time to get your site up and running by mid-October; this means at a bare minimum getting a contract signed with a developer by September, which means starting your search for a developer and other preparations in early summer. Of course, even this is cutting it close, considering the time it takes to market a site and gain exposure for it. The essential thing is to start the process well before you need your site to be launched.

Also, consider your own busy schedule when planning a Web project. Web developers typically need a fair amount of input from you during the development process, which may require several meetings. For example, you'll likely need to review and approve several demos and provide guidance on site content. Don't assume that once you start the project, the Web developer will just run with it and finish it off; account for the time you'll need to spend reviewing progress and providing information to the developer.

Finally, your cash flow can be an issue in timing your Web project. Make sure you'll have the necessary cash or credit for any advance deposits and other payments.

6. Draft an Outline of Site Content

Drafting at least a rough outline of the content you want to feature at your site is a good idea for a few reasons. The most compelling reason is that your site content should be closely related to your site strategy and goals—and since you know these best, it's wise not to turn this task over entirely to a developer. In addition, drafting the initial content outline may help to reduce costs by reducing the work that a Web developer will have to do. Finally, it generally makes sense for you to take the first stab at outlining content since you know best what kind of content exists or can easily be created for your business. Your Web developer can—and likely will—help you refine a content outline, but you are in the best position to make the first draft.

a. What to Include

A content outline is pretty much what it sounds like. It's not the content itself, but an organized list of topics and subsections that you envision for the site.

When deciding on what to include, focus on the content that will directly help you achieve your goals for the website. For example, if you are creating a simple marketing site with a goal of motivating clients to call you, effective content might include a well-presented portfolio and testimonials from customers, which will impress site visitors about the quality of your work. If your goal is to attract investors, a downloadable PDF of your business plan would be an obvious piece of valuable content, as would your business history and resumes of the owners.

In addition to your substantive content, always include easy-to-find contact information including your phone number, email address, and location. Or, if a site goal is to reduce customer service calls, then only include an email address. Again, think strategically and include content that fits with your strategy.

b. Tips on Drafting

In drafting your conten t outline, just use the same approach you learned in school: list sections and subsections, and possibly third-level or fourth-level subsections. For example, a website for a photography studio might look something like this:

1. Home page
2. Services
3. About the Studio
   a. History
   b. Photographer bios
4. Location & Map
5. Portfolio
   a. Weddings
   b. Graduation photos
   c. Professional head shots
6. Tips for Great Photos
7. Links

Keep in mind that each section may or may not correspond to its own separate Web page. At this stage of the game, don't worry too much about the specifics of each section or the details of whether

certain information will be grouped on one page or on separate pages. Instead, focus on the overall scope of the site and which sections will be offered. Later, as you work with your Web developer, you'll refine your outline into a more detailed blueprint for the website.

C. Choosing and Working With a Web Developer

Ironically, lots of Web developers are poor communicators and tend to drown potential clients in tech-speak, making it hard to discern whether they understand what you want or what they're offering. Obviously, you want a developer who is easy to communicate with and who clearly understands your vision, and who does quality, professional work.

This section offers advice on how to find a Web developer—and gives tips on what to consider when choosing one.

1. Starting Your Search

Just as when you are looking for any professional, the best way to find a Web developer is to ask other business owners for recommendations. In addition, look for examples of good local websites and find out who built them. Sometimes a website will include a credit saying who built it; other times you may have to ask the business owner.

Keep in mind that in the last few years, Web developers have multiplied like little tech-savvy rabbits. Lots of talented developers—and plenty not so talented—operate under the radar, often with no Yellow Pages listing or other advertising presence. Because of this, traditional approaches such as searching the phone book or other listings are likely to miss a significant number of prospects. It's much better to talk with plenty of other business owners to get the word on the street about who does great work, at a reasonable price.

Clare Zurawski, Albuquerque Regional Manager for WESST Corp., a New Mexico nonprofit dedicated to helping people start or grow their own businesses:

WesstArtisans.com is an e-commerce site show-casing handcrafted gifts and housewares made by New Mexican artisans. The steepest learning curve related to developing and maintaining WesstArtisans.com was my role as Project Manager. In the Web development industry, it seems there are few generalists and many specialists. So I had to become the generalist and negotiate contracts with several consultants at once, including a professional product photographer, a graphic designer, an HTML programmer, and a search engine specialist.

To make sure the site reflects our regional flavor, we include a black-and-white photo of each artisan at the top of their product pages. We also provide a link to their biographies and artists' statements. This way a personal connection can be made, and there is no mistaking their work as being mass-produced in a factory somewhere.

At the time we launched WesstArtisans.com in late 2000, we weren't sure how large the site would eventually be. To reduce our expenses, we opted for a static website with 200 items programmed for sale. At its height a few years later, the site had more than 1,000 items for sale, and it is now clear that we should have spent the extra money up front to make it dynamic (database driven) from the start. We are now spending more than we'd like to on HTML programming to add or update product content to the shopping cart. Converting the site to a database is always possible, but costly.

2. What to Look for in a Web Developer

Before you consider hiring any Web developer, visit other sites that he or she has created. Web developers' own websites will usually have online portfolios showing websites they've done. Visit those sites and poke around to make sure they

work well. Ideally, the developer will have experience with sites and features that are similar to what you want. Even better, the developer has experience working with businesses similar to yours. As discussed earlier in this chapter, strategic considerations are critical in website projects, so the more your developer understands your business and the strategies driving it, the better.

a. Professional Skills

Web development involves several different components and skills. Unless you plan to handle certain aspects of the project on your own, your aim should be to find a developer who can perform a number of tasks professionally, including:

- designing the organization of the information at your site, also called information architecture
- designing the graphical elements of your site, including choosing a color palette, fonts, and images
- programming the site, and
- creating and finalizing necessary content, including text and images.

While some individual Web developers may handle all these tasks on their own, you'll usually get a better result from a firm that employs or contracts with specialists such as information architects, graphic designers, programmers, and content developers. This isn't to say that each task absolutely needs to be handled by a separate person, just that it's important that the folks handling the variety of tasks have the right specific skills. For example, many graphic designers sell themselves as Web developers, often calling themselves "Web designers," even if they have minimal skills in information architecture or programming.

Ask directly about whether professional information architects, graphic designers, programmers, and writers will be used. If the person or firm pitching services to you has loads of expertise in one element such as graphic design or programming, but not in other important aspects of Web development such as information architecture or content development, it may be wise to keep looking.

If you do plan to handle certain aspects of Web development in-house, another consideration is to find a Web developer who can work collaboratively with you. For example, if you are certain you want to maintain absolute control over the content and updating of your static site, but want the developer to handle other technical issues, make this fact clear to the prospective developer and evaluate whether you will be a good fit working together.

b. Use of Technologies and Standards

Some Web developers use specialized development platforms and other technologies that are proprietary or difficult for others to use. If you end up parting ways with your developer, however, you might get stuck with a website that is difficult or nearly impossible for others to maintain and update.

When considering Web developers, ask them what technologies they use, whether they are widely supported, and what difficulties might arise for other developers in maintaining the site. You may feel uncomfortable asking this, but it's a perfectly legitimate question that the developer should answer clearly.

In addition, ask whether the developer conforms to Web standards—specifically, the standards established by the World Wide Web Consortium, otherwise known as W3C. Generally, think of Web standards as guidelines that help ensure the best accessibility and compatibility for websites that conform to them. The benefits of conforming to W3C standards are multifold: the website will be compatible with more browsers; it will be easier and cheaper to modify; it will be accessible on other devices such as cell phones and handheld devices; and people with disabilities such as vision limitations will be able to access your content.

c. Project Management Approach

An important but often overlooked issue is how well a Web developer manages and coordinates all the various aspects of the project—such as defining the information organization, doing the graphic design, creating the content, and programming the site—to ensure a smooth process.

Web developers should have a clear process in which you, the business owner, are asked to approve the Web developer's progress at various stages. For example, if a Web developer does not follow a methodical process, and does not obtain your approval of early stages of site development, you may find yourself presented with a nearly finished site that has no resemblance to what you envisioned. If this happens, the developer may virtually have to start all over again—a situation that could have been averted if approvals had been requested along the way.

Don't find out the hard way how time-consuming —and sometimes, costly—a poorly managed website project can be. Make sure your developer uses a systematic, methodical approach with a clear review and approval process. If you get the sense that a developer's approach is to "wing it," it's not a good sign.

Section D offers a broad-strokes outline of a sensible process for Web development. While it's not intended to be a definitive, end-all approach, it should give you a general idea of how the process should go. Use it as a general model when asking Web developers about their processes and approaches.

3. Proposals, Quotes, and Contracts

When you have met with a few potential developers and have narrowed your list down to a few prospects, ask each of them to give you a proposal and quote in writing. Generally speaking, it's best to get at least two or three proposals or quotes to compare. Some developers might give a barebones quote focused on numbers; others will give more of a proposal that outlines their planned approach. While an exhaustive, novel-length proposal isn't necessary, a proposal is better than a strictly numbers-oriented quote, since it will demonstrate whether the developer understands your specific needs and whether he or she has put some thought into finding the right solution for you.

Also, watch out for developers who balk at putting a quote or proposal in writing, or who merely want to give you a total quote without a breakdown of services and fees. At the very least, a quote should show what specific services will be offered; ideally the cost will be broken down into an itemized list.

Once you choose a developer, it's essential that you write and sign a contract clearly outlining the project. At a minimum, that contract should include:

- **an overview of the scope of services.** In particular, make sure that you and the Web developer are on the same page regarding who will be responsible for creating and finalizing content. Web developers typically will work with your text and photographs, but will not write text from scratch or take photographs without charging extra.
- **a list of deliverables**—in other words, anything the developer will deliver to you, such as a site map, a color mock-up, an HTML template, or anything else that he or she promises to deliver as the project progresses and at the end of the project.
- **a clear schedule** giving deadlines for various aspects of the project, often tied to deliverables.
- **intellectual property provisions,** detailing who will own the materials developed in the project—including graphic designs, templates, written content, photographs, software programming, and any other material subject to intellectual property protection. (See Section F for more on intellectual property concerns.)
- **compensation and payment terms**—including specifics on how fees will be calculated if work goes beyond the scope originally anticipated.

- **termination provisions,** detailing what will happen if the working relationship falls apart or either party wants to end the project.

Get it in writing. This advice cannot be overstated: Do not work with a Web developer without a contract. If the developer is reluctant to create or sign a written contract, it's a clear sign that he or she lacks the professional standards that you want.

For more help with Web issues. This chapter focuses on helping you understand the most important considerations when starting a website for your business. For in-depth information on the process itself, you should consult other resources. Here is a short list of some particularly helpful sources.

- *How to Build a Website and Stay Sane,* by Jonathan Oxer (Oft Press), focuses on how to find a Web developer who's a good match, and how to build an effective working relationship in which you retain control of the end result. The Australia-specific information does not detract from its helpful focus on the process of website creation. You can download it free from www .stay-sane.com.
- *How to Get Your Business on the Web: A Legal Guide to e-Commerce,* by Fred Steingold (Nolo), covers every aspect of taking a business online.
- *HTML for the World Wide Web With XHTML and CSS: Visual QuickStart Guide,* by Elizabeth Castro (Peachpit Press), demystifies HTML code with lots of illustrations and screen shots. Beginners and experienced Web developers alike will find it a useful reference.
- *The Non-Designer's Web Book: An Easy Guide to Creating, Designing, and Posting Your Own Web Site,* by Robin Williams and John Tollett (Peachpit Press), is especially helpful for beginners. It offers a solid introduction to technical concepts and principles of effective design.

- *Web and Software Development: A Legal Guide,* by Stephen Fishman (Nolo), discusses the specific intellectual property issues that relate to Web and technology projects.

D. Creating Your Website

As has been mentioned previously, an efficient, methodical process will go a long way toward making your website a success. This is true whether you create a website on your own or hire a Web developer to help you. This section outlines a simple, generalized approach that will help ensure an efficient workflow between the Web developer and your business, including all the participants you've included. (See Section B1 for more on identifying project participants.) Keep in mind these steps aren't written in stone; there's always a certain amount of fluidity in Web development projects.

In particular, be aware that it's common for Web projects to get a bit circular at times and that you may need to revisit earlier steps to make modifications. For example, you may need to refine your site's information architecture after you create content, if some of that content does not fit into your original design. This is normal, as long as it's not chronic and extensive. The reality is that following a methodical process will improve efficiency. Even if you're planning a small, simple site, following a process similar to the one described here will help increase your chances of success.

The planning process will generally involve the following steps, many of which have been discussed earlier in this chapter—and each of which are outlined below. Those steps include:

- defining strategy and goals
- defining content and organization, or information architecture
- defining design elements or the look and feel of the site
- creating content, including text and graphics
- building the website, including any necessary HTML coding, database creation, or programming, and

- testing the site to ensure it functions smoothly before being unleashed on the public.

1. Clarify Your Strategy and Goals

All website projects should start by clearly identifying strategy and goals. (See Sections A3 and A4 for more detail on this.) It's crucial in this early stage that you and your Web developer have open and clear communication about these issues.

Workshop-type meetings in which your business's Web project participants and possibly other staffers or associates contribute ideas are often helpful. And it's often a good idea to solicit comments from a wide range of people in the early stage, even if those people won't be involved in the project as it progresses. Soliciting feedback from people who will be affected by the website— such as your customer service team, or some trusted potential customers—helps ensure that you will include a wide range of perspectives and avoid tunnel vision.

2. Define Information Architecture

The term "information architecture" may sound like tech-speak, but it's actually an accurate description of an important, fundamental aspect of all websites: how the information is organized. This is also sometimes called information design or content mapping. In all websites, defining the information architecture is the first step in actually starting to build the site.

A basic tool in defining information architecture is called a site map. Closely related to a simple content outline, a site map is a visual representation of content modules and how they are related to one other.

Another fundamental tool is called a user interface diagram, or UI diagram, which is a mock layout of how content and other elements such as links and images will be organized on the site pages, which is another way of saying how the pages will look to users. A UI diagram is nearly analogous to an architectural blueprint for a building. Since it's dealing with information rather than building materials, however, a UI will be based in logic rather than mechanical physics.

To help understand the difference between a site map and a UI diagram, bear in mind that a site map shows what content will be at a site, and a UI diagram shows how it will be displayed to site users.

Web developers will generally ask you to approve the site map before creating UI diagrams —and to approve the UI diagrams before moving to next steps.

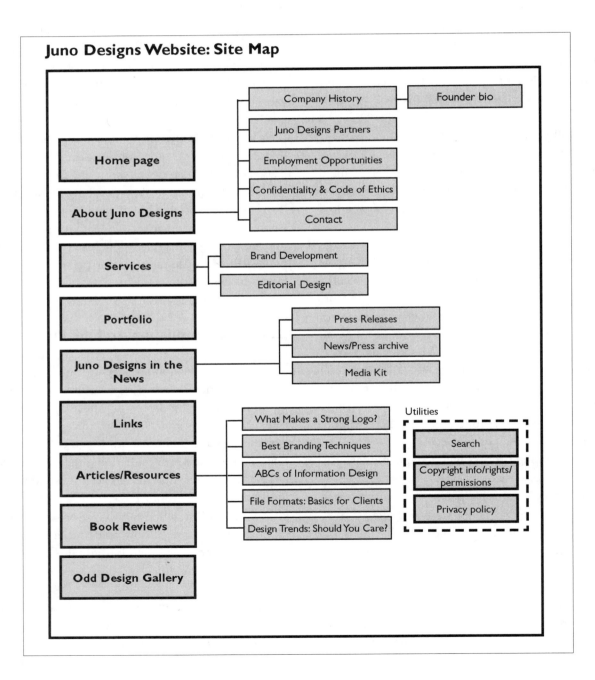

Juno Designs Website: Site Map

- Home page
- About Juno Designs
  - Company History
    - Founder bio
  - Juno Designs Partners
  - Employment Opportunities
  - Confidentiality & Code of Ethics
  - Contact
- Services
  - Brand Development
  - Editorial Design
- Portfolio
- Juno Designs in the News
  - Press Releases
  - News/Press archive
  - Media Kit
- Links
- Articles/Resources
  - What Makes a Strong Logo?
  - Best Branding Techniques
  - ABCs of Information Design
  - File Formats: Basics for Clients
  - Design Trends: Should You Care?
- Book Reviews
- Odd Design Gallery

Utilities
- Search
- Copyright info/rights/permissions
- Privacy policy

Juno Designs logo

image

Search site

Company Information

Home

About

Services

Portfolio

News

Links

Juno Designs
555 Main St.
Springville, NM 12345
info@junodesigns.com

Partner Sites

Spitz Software

Smart Dog Printing

Main Street Independent Business Alliance

Welcome to Juno Designs.
Juno Designs is a graphic design firm specializing in brand development and editorial design. We have helped businesses, nonprofits, trade associations, and others define their brands, develop a compelling company image, and produce award-winning marketing collateral.

The links at the left offer information about our company and services. The links at the right offer a wide range of informational resources on graphic design issues. Please feel free to contact us directly at 555-987-6543 or drop an email to info@junodesigns.com.

Featured Article:
What Makes a Strong Logo?
A strong logo helps develop your brand and ingrain your business in the minds of customers. This short article outlines some principles driving effective logo design.
More...

Featured Projects

image

Annual Report Design. *Client: AAA Corp.*
Juno Designs recently completed a project designing a 150-page report for AAA Corp.
More...

Books

Reviews of the best art and design titles.

image

Articles

Informative articles on design strategies.

Odd Design Gallery

Old ads, trademarks and other odd designs of today and yesteryear.

image

Home | About | Services | Portfolio | News & Events | Press | Contact
Books | Articles | Odd Design Gallery | Design News
Search | Site Map

3. Define the Website's Look and Feel

Once a site map and UI diagrams are approved, the developer will usually start working on the graphic design and other visual elements of the website, which as a whole is generally called the site's look and feel. Color palettes and typefaces are major elements to consider, as well as images and composition. Web developers will typically ask you for some initial direction, such as whether you want your site to appear traditional, modern, funky, high-tech, or whimsical. You'll also usually be asked about what colors you envision at the site. Your input at this stage is important so that the site conveys the right message and strikes the right tone for your business. Then, based on your guidance, the developer will usually make mock Web pages, sometimes called color comprehensives, for you to review and approve.

4. Create Content

With information architecture and visual elements approved, you can get started on creating the content that will populate the website's pages. You may have already spent some time developing brochures, flyers, or other written information about your business. Don't reinvent the wheel: Use what you have as a basis for your website's content. You may need to rework the existing content to make it shorter and more concise for the Web, but it's still much easier to adapt something that's already written than to start from scratch.

If you don't have any written materials, someone will need to start writing. Generally speaking, less is more when it comes to online content. Due to the space constraints of computer screens and the ever-shortening attention spans of most computer users, nothing will turn visitors away from your website faster than dense, lengthy paragraphs. The best Web content is concise and easy to digest, so don't be afraid to get right to the point and condense information into lists, bullet points, and short blurbs.

If you decide to publish longer material—for example, a user manual or an industry report—either break it up into sections or provide the document in a downloadable format, such as a PDF, or Portable Document Format, file. Better yet, offer both an HTML version searchable and navigable by section and a downloadable version, so that your visitors can read the document in whatever manner they prefer.

Finally, make sure that at least two people are involved in creating the website's content to make sure that it is clear, concise, and free from errors. At a minimum, one person should write the material and another person should review and edit it. Even if the writer is experienced, a second set of eyes can really make a difference. A little bit of care in these areas will go a long way toward giving a professional tone to your site and enhancing the credibility of your business.

When you're done creating and formatting your content, you'll provide it to the Web developer to be incorporated into the site pages. Make sure the content is formatted so that the developer can easily see which information belongs in a header, where paragraphs should break, which information belongs in bullet points, and so on. You'll need to review the content again once it's on the site to be sure it formats and flows well and logically.

Banish bad clip art from your site. In addition to lack of planning, another major fault of too many websites is an unprofessional appearance. While a discussion of design aesthetics is beyond the scope of this chapter, one thing to watch out for is bad clip art. If you're new to this term, "clip art" refers to small illustrations and graphics—sometimes animated—that are widely available online, often for free. While some clip art is of high quality, the vast majority tends to be very amateur-looking and will make your site look amateur as well. Don't pepper your site with angels, teddy bears, or animated dragons because you think they look cute. An unprofessional-looking website is simply bad business.

5. Build the Website

Building the website may consist of different approaches, depending on whether your site will be static or dynamic. In either case, this is the stage at which you should make sure someone with professional Web development skills is involved. If your site will be static, the developer will create HTML files with your content and images, as well as links and other elements. If your site will be dynamic, the developer will create HTML templates and a database, and do the necessary programming so that the Web templates communicate with the database and display content contained in the database.

Keep in mind that you'll need to do an extra step if your site is dynamic: When the database has been created, you'll need to enter your content into the database, including both text and images.

One other note: While your Web developer may build the site on a test server, he or she may prefer to build the site on the Web server where it will ultimately have its home. If so, you'll need to tackle domain name registration and Web hosting at this point, before the site is finished. (See Section E for an explanation of these tasks.)

6. Test the Website

When your site is complete, it should be thoroughly and methodically tested, and all glitches—or bugs—fixed. It's normal and not a bad reflection on the Web developer if the site contains some bugs. What's important is to find them and fix them before launching your site to the public. Professional Web developers should include a testing phase. Once it is completed and all bugs reported and corrected, the site is ready to be launched.

E. Domain Names and Hosting

Before you can post your Web pages for the world to see, you must register a domain name and sign up with a Web hosting company. Your domain name is part of the address visitors will use to access your site, such as nolo.com or amazon.com. Your Web host is the company that keeps your site pages on computer servers that are connected to the Internet 24 hours a day, so they're always available for visitors to view.

1. Choosing and Registering a Domain Name

Your first task is to choose an available domain name—that is, a name that is not currently registered to, or being used by, another group. (Choosing a domain name that's both available and that does not pose a trademark conflict is discussed in Chapter 3, Section D.)

As mentioned in Chapter 3, your domain name has tremendous potential marketing value, so you should take the time to choose one carefully. Remember that it may not be just your business name that attracts customers; names of your popular products and services are also good candidates for domain names. Considering how inexpensive domain name registration is—roughly $10 per year—it makes little sense not to register multiple names if they are appropriate for your business.

In addition, it often makes sense to register your domain name in multiple domains in addition to the .com domain in order to establish the widest presence possible for your domain name. Beyond the most common .com domain, the .biz and .net domains are appropriate for for-profit businesses. However, don't make the mistake of registering a .org address for a for-profit business. The .org domain is intended for nonprofit organizations only. Even though this rule is not enforced by the .org registry, it's misleading and inappropriate to use a .org address for your for-profit business. At the very least, using a .org address will make your business look ignorant of domain name rules; at worst, customers will think you are trying to mislead them into believing you are a nonprofit.

Once you select an available name, register it online at a domain name registrar. There are hundreds of options out there. If you'd like to do some comparison shopping, you can find a list of approved registrars at www.internic.org.

How one online registrar works. One popular online registrar is GoDaddy at www.godaddy.com. Here's how it works: At the GoDaddy website, you will first be prompted to enter your proposed domain name to see if it has already been registered. If not, you will be allowed to proceed and register the name yourself.

Fees vary depending on the options you choose; all are generally affordable. Registering one name for one year through GoDaddy costs under $10. Once you've chosen your options, simply enter information about your business and provide credit card information. Or, if you prefer, call GoDaddy at 480-505-8899 and do it by phone.

Although registering a domain name is pretty simple, there are a few potential pitfalls. In particular, if you allow your Web host to take care of domain name registration or renewal—a common practice—you must make sure it lists your business or an authorized representative as the domain name registrant and administrative contact. If anyone but an authorized representative of your business is listed as the domain name registrant, you might find that your control over your domain name is seriously compromised. Web host companies have developed a nasty habit of registering their clients' domain names under the host company's name, rather than the name of the client. This creates serious domain name ownership and control issues.

For example, if your Web host handles the domain name registration process for your business and lists itself as the registrant of the domain name you've chosen, you might not be able to make any changes to your host account or even your domain name account, because you are not listed as the registrant. In this way, the Web host company can hold your domain name hostage, preventing you

from switching hosts or otherwise managing this crucial part of your business's identity.

Your domain name is an asset, and the people or organizations listed in the domain name registration have varying degrees of authority over the asset. Be particularly careful about whom you list as:

- **registrant.** The registrant is the legal owner of the domain name. Use your business's legal name, not your Web host company's name.
- **administrative contact.** The administrative contact should be someone in your business who has authority to make policy decisions, particularly with regard to the domain name. Again, you should not list your Web host company here.
- **technical contact.** This is the person the registrar may contact with technical issues. You may list your Web host company here.

If your Web host handles domain name registration or renewal, make sure it uses the names you want. Otherwise, it may cost you many times the original registration fee to get the registration back in your rightful name. Register.com, for instance, charges a $200 fee to transfer the registrant from one name to another, even if you never intended to list your Web host or someone else as the registrant in the first place. One way to avoid this fee is to transfer the domain name from the registrar where it is currently registered under the wrong name to another registrar, making sure to use the correct names when you transfer the registration.

Clare Zurawski, Albuquerque Regional Manager for WESST Corp., a New Mexico nonprofit dedicated to helping people start or grow their own businesses:

Because WESST Corp. is the parent nonprofit to our e-commerce site WesstArtisans.com, it was important we used the same spelling of the nonprofit name in our domain name. But if somebody heard "WesstArtisans.com" without seeing it, they would probably not be aware of the unusual spelling. So we also bought the domain

"WestArtisans.com" which, sure enough, attracts some customers. Visitors to the misspelled domain name are automatically sent to the correct address.

2. Choosing a Web Host

Once your Web pages are created, you need to post them—that is, upload them to a Web host's server. A server is simply a high-performance computer that's connected to the Internet continuously, serving the Web pages stored on it to the world. A Web host is the company that maintains the servers. When your Web pages are on the host's server and your Web host has configured your domain name correctly, your website will be live and all the information it offers will be available to visitors around the globe, 24 hours a day, 365 days a year.

Searching online for a Web host will yield plenty of results—too many, in fact, to be very useful. It's better to get recommendations from other business owners to find a Web host that offers reliable servers and good customer service.

Selecting a website host is pretty straightforward, but there are a few issues of which you should beware. An important one is that if you or your Web developer used any specialized technologies, you may need to choose a Web host that is compatible with that technology. For example, some dynamic sites that are based on databases use special technologies that the host servers must support. Ask your Web developer for advice and assistance in finding a host that offers any such necessary support.

Web hosts may charge by the month or by the year. Fees are based on how much data you need the server to store—that is, the size of your website in disk space—or how much data you transfer to and from your website each month.

There are countless Web hosts out there with varying rates, so it shouldn't be hard to find one that's in your price range. Of course, the cheapest isn't always the best: Pay attention to the host's customer service practices, the ability to speak with a live tech support person, and any other features you feel are important.

F. Intellectual Property: Who Owns What?

Intellectual property laws establish ownership rights and other rules for various types of works such as text and artwork protected by copyright, marks used in business protected by trademark, and inventions protected by patents. Copyright is of particular importance in Web development projects, as many of the components of websites are protected by copyright. As mentioned earlier, it's crucial that your contract with a Web developer includes clear, detailed terms on ownership and permissions for any materials developed for the website protected by copyright. Other intellectual property laws such as trademark or patent also may come into play, though not as often.

Copyrightable materials include text, photos, artwork, and designs, as well as technology developed for your site, such as databases and programming. As you can imagine, serious troubles can arise if ownership of any aspect of your website is in dispute. The way to avoid this is by including clear copyright terms in your contract with the Web developer. This section gives a quick overview of copyright basics and the specific issues that arise in Web development projects, to help you head off any copyright conflict.

In-depth resources on copyright and intellectual property issues. For the full treatment on copyright and the permissions process, see *Getting Permission: How to License & Clear Copyrighted Materials Online & Off,* by Richard Stim (Nolo). In addition, Nolo's *Web & Software Development: A Legal Guide,* by Stephen Fishman, discusses the specific intellectual property issues that relate to Web and technology projects.

1. Copyright Basics

When someone owns copyright to certain works, it means that others may not reproduce, modify, distribute, or sell the works without the copyright owner's permission. In legal terms, permission to use someone else's copyrighted content is known as a license. When you license content, you do not own it; you simply obtain the right to use it in specific circumstances. In contrast, buying the copyrights to a creative work, known in legal terms as an assignment, gives you all the rights to the work as if you were the original copyright owner.

The general rule is that the person who creates content owns the copyright. However, if the work qualifies as a "work for hire," then the hiring party, not the creator, legally owns the copyright to it. The rules regarding what constitutes a work for hire vary depending on whether the work is created by an employee or an independent contractor.

Employee or Independent Contractor?

A number of laws govern whether a worker is an independent contractor (IC) or an employee, and each of these laws has a different way of looking at the issue. For example, the IRS has one method of determining whether a person is an independent contractor, but your state workers' compensation board may use a different test. Because of all these different laws, often referred to as "worker classification" rules, the issue of whether a worker is an IC is not always straightforward.

The IRS is probably the most important agency to satisfy when it comes to classifying a worker as an IC. Under the IRS's test, workers are considered employees if the company they work for has the right to direct and control the way they work—including the details of when, where, and how the job is accomplished. In contrast, the IRS will consider workers independent contractors if the company they work for does not manage how they work, except to accept or reject their final result. (See Chapter 15, Section A, for a more complete discussion of distinguishing between employees and ICs.)

a. Rules for Employees

When an employee creates any work in the course of employment, the work is considered a work for hire, so that the employer—not the employee—owns the copyright to that work. Having your website created by employees, not contractors, is the simplest and most straightforward way for your business to make sure that it owns copyright in all aspects of the site.

Unfortunately, this isn't an option for many start-up businesses. But fortunately, there are other ways to make the work a work for hire, even if it is created by an independent contractor, not an employee.

b. Rules for Independent Contractors

When an independent contractor creates certain types of content, the hiring party owns the copyright in the work if the contractor and hiring party have made a written agreement stating that the work is a work for hire. The written agreement is essential: Work-for-hire agreements are necessary whenever a nonemployee creates the work. Without a written work-for-hire agreement, the non-employee Web developer owns copyright to the materials he or she develops for the website.

But there's an important wrinkle: You cannot turn every kind of creative work into a work for hire using a written agreement. According to copyright law, a work-for-hire agreement will give copyright to the hiring party only if the content is:

- part of a larger literary work, such as an article in a magazine or a poem or story in an anthology
- part of a motion picture or other audiovisual work, such as a screenplay
- a translation
- a supplementary work, such as an afterword, introduction, chart, editorial note, bibliography, appendix, or index
- a compilation
- an instructional text
- a test or answer material for a test, or
- an atlas.

Without trying to puzzle through how on earth lawyers came up with these categories, it's important to understand that depending on whom you ask, the categories may not include the components of websites. This naturally raises the question: If website materials cannot be the subject of work-for-hire agreements, how can you obtain ownership from a Web development contractor? The answer is that you'll need to have a written and signed copyright assignment—an outright sale of all copyright from the contractor to your business. While it's possible that website materials might legally fall into one of the work-for-hire categories, the safest route is to assume they do not,

and to handle ownership transfer with a copyright assignment.

To sum up, to obtain ownership of materials created by a Web developer for your website, you'll need to:

- hire the creator as an employee—which usually is not a practical option, unless you already planned to hire a Web developer on staff, or
- have a written copyright assignment, signed by both you and the developer, usually within your website development contract.

For more on intellectual property contracts for Web debelopment projects. Both *How to Get Your Business on the Web,* by Fred Steingold (Nolo), and *Web and Software Development: A Legal Guide,* by Stephen Fishman (Nolo) include a standard Web Development Agreement and information on intellectual property issues related to Web and technology projects.

2. Protecting Your Interests

It's obviously in your interest to own all aspects of your website so that you have the legal right to do anything you want with the site. For example, if you fail to obtain a copyright to the site's text content from the Web developer, the developer could potentially prevent you from making any changes to the text on the site. The same is true for images, graphic designs, and technologies created by the Web developer for the website. This may sound far-fetched to you now, but consider what might happen if you and the developer ever got into a conflict and decided to part ways. A developer with a bone to pick who owns any rights to your site could deal a serious blow to your online business.

Be aware that sometimes, a Web developer will not want to assign copyright ownership to your company for certain aspects of the site. As discussed below, this may be perfectly legitimate. What's crucial in this situation is for you to get permission—legally, a license—from the Web developer to use his or her copyrighted work as necessary for you to get the full benefits of your website. Without such permission, you'll be at the mercy of your Web developer when you want to edit content or make changes to technology owned by the developer—a situation you definitely want to avoid.

There are a number of situations in which it might make sense for a Web developer to retain ownership. For example, your business might be able to save money by allowing the developer to retain copyright ownership of things such as photographs taken for the site. And developers sometimes will not transfer ownership of technology they develop for your site, since that technology is the lifeblood of their business. Instead, they'll give your business permission, or a license, to use the technology in specified ways.

EXAMPLE: Marina is negotiating contract terms with the Web developer she chose to create her pottery store's website. To keep costs down, Marina and the developer agree that Marina will be responsible for taking photos. However they also agree that the developer may take photos for the site, and that he would retain the copyright to those photographs. To make sure she retains control over the website, Marina gets a provision in the contract granting her business a license to display any of the developer's photos at her website indefinitely. In addition, Marina asks the developer if he would be willing to include a license allowing her to modify the size and the brightness of the photos in case they ever need such adjustments. The developer agrees to a license to modify that is limited to size and brightness, but no other modifications.

In deciding what ownership or licensing arrangements will work for your business, keep in mind the following rule: The more important content or technology is to your site, the more crucial it is that you either get ownership or a broad license to use and possibly modify those materials. This is true whether or not the Web developer has a valid reason to retain ownership. If it's essential that you own copyright ownership in a database or other technology, don't enter into an agreement that won't confer the rights you need.

☑ Chapter 13 Checklist

☐ Assess your strategy and goals for your site and any other e-business activities, and how they fit into your overall business plan.

☐ Consider other electronic communication methods such as email lists, e-newsletters, listservs, and others when crafting an e-business plan.

☐ Research other sites to get examples of organization, design, content, and features that might work well for your site.

☐ Identify specific goals for your website and e-business activities, and choose content that will directly help achieve those goals.

☐ Choose a Web developer who has strong project management skills.

☐ Insist upon a written contract with your Web developer, and make sure your business will obtain copyright ownership of most, if not all, content and technology developed for the site.

■

Planning for Changes in Ownership

As discussed in Chapter 2, choosing a legal structure is a fundamental task for every new business owner. Whether you operate as a sole proprietorship, partnership, LLC, or corporation has important implications for liability issues and taxes—two areas definitely worthy of your close attention.

For businesses with more than one owner, there's another important and related concern: how to handle any future changes in business ownership. It probably won't be top-of-mind in your early, exciting start-up days, but the fact is that businesses commonly face situations that raise serious—and often unexpected—ownership questions. An incapacitating illness or untimely death are just two of the more extreme situations that call the business's ownership into question. What if an incapacitated owner wants to sell to someone the other owners don't like? Will a deceased owner's child inherit the ownership interest and become an active owner of the business? Plenty of other situations can also have an impact on the ownership of the business; they're discussed later in this chapter.

The best way to handle all these situations is to make an agreement about how the business will deal with them. This type of agreement is known as a buy-sell agreement; the phrase "buy-sell" refers to the rules it outlines for how a company's ownership shares may be bought or sold. By anticipating certain events and defining what will happen if they arise, a buy-sell agreement can lessen the chaos that ownership changes can inflict on a business.

Busy as you may be with the details and concerns of starting up your business, it makes the best sense to address these issues even before you get up and running. Since buy-sell provisions generally limit what owners can and cannot do with their ownership interests, it's crucial to create fair, impartial rules while everyone is on equal footing. If you wait until something happens that puts ownership on the brink of change—for example, one owner becomes incapacitated and desperate

to sell out—you'll have a much harder time imposing rules that are comfortable for everyone involved. And addressing buy-sell provisions early on is one of the best ways to build and maintain harmonious relationships among business co-owners.

This chapter starts by explaining who should consider drafting a buy-sell agreement and why. Then it defines buy-sell agreements, explaining the essential provisions you'll typically find. Finally, it offers sample buy-sell provisions to help you get started in drafting your own agreement.

For more in-depth information. While you'll learn the basic, essential elements of buy-sell agreements in this chapter, *Business Buyout Agreements: A Step-by-Step Guide for Co-Owners*, by Anthony Mancuso and Bethany Laurence (Nolo), covers much more ground. It walks you through the process of drafting a comprehensive buy-sell agreement that addresses a wide range of issues such as structuring and funding buyouts and tax and estate planning concerns.

A. When You Need a Written Agreement

If your business—whether a partnership, LLC, or corporation—has more than one owner, you would be wise to have a written buy-sell agreement in place. Although hopeful co-owners of a new business usually want to think their alliance will last forever, this attitude is unrealistic. Even the most compatible, fair-minded business owners commonly face all sorts of life events that can bring ownership into question: death, divorce, illness, bankruptcy, or simply a decision to change life's direction. Rather than let ownership changes sneak up on you and wreak havoc on your company, it's much smarter to accept that the ownership will likely change at some point, and plan for that day.

If you still need convincing, consider some common situations and how they can impact a business.

1. An Owner Leaves or Retires

It's often said that being a co-owner of a business is like being in a marriage—and the pressures of running the business can lead to bitter break-ups. But even when co-owners get along famously, one of them may simply want to retire or do something different. Perhaps the business didn't provide an owner with the satisfaction anticipated, prompting a decision to change course and leave the business.

Whatever the circumstances, the potential departure of an owner raises serious questions. What if an owner decides to stop working for the company but refuses to sell the share in the business, hoping to earn income without contributing to it? Assuming an owner does plan to sell the interest in the business, can the sale be to anyone at all? Clearly, the remaining co-owners would not be happy to learn the departing owner sold out to someone they all detest. How will the price of the departing owner's interest be determined if offered for sale? Valuing the company and determining share price can be quite contentious, particularly when continuing owners want to purchase the share.

On the flip side, consider what would happen if you wanted to retire. What if you couldn't find someone to buy your interest, and your co-owners didn't want or couldn't afford to buy your share? Would you be stuck, unable to cash out? Failing to address these issues early in the life of your company can result in a real quagmire if they arise in real life.

2. An Owner Becomes Disabled

If one owner has a debilitating stroke, is paralyzed in a car accident, or suffers some other incapacitating illness, the remaining owners face some big questions: Can they force the disabled owner to sell out? Can the departing owner sell to whomever he or she pleases? If the sale is to the continuing owners, what price must they pay for that share?

Again, the issues shift a bit for the person who becomes disabled and wants—or, more likely, needs—to sell. If you find yourself in this situation, you'd likely be concerned about being able to sell your ownership interest for cash to help pay medical bills and get through the tough time. Truth is, it's often difficult for small business owners to find outside buyers, especially for a minority ownership interest. If your co-owners are uninterested or unable to buy you out and you have no buy-sell agreement in place, you could find yourself in a really tight spot.

3. An Owner Dies

The death of a co-owner is sure to be traumatic for everyone in the business. In the midst of it, the co-owners will be faced with the burden of figuring out who will own the deceased owner's share. For example, will they be forced to accept anyone who inherits the ownership interest as a new, active owner? What if the person who inherits the share wants to sell it for cash to the current owners, or to an outside buyer?

Similarly, if you die, these questions will be dropped into the minds of your grieving family members or the people who may take over your ownership share. They may need money for funeral expenses, not to mention living expenses once you aren't earning any income.

A buy-sell agreement can anticipate and provide a clear plan for these emotionally laden situations. Without an agreement, the trauma of losing an owner can go from bad to worse if the current owners and the deceased owner's successors can't agree.

4. An Owner Divorces

You don't need to be reminded that divorce is a possibility, even when marital harmony and bliss seem certain. Roughly half of all marriages end in divorce, so you absolutely must deal with the question of how a marital split might affect your business.

The most glaring possibility is that when a co-owner gets divorced, the ex can become a new owner of the business. Except when a premarital agreement or "prenup" prevents it—and, in reality, many prenups are hard to enforce—spouses of business partners often have a legal interest in the business. This legal right is most clear in community property states—including Arizona, California, Idaho, Nevada, New Mexico, Texas, and Wisconsin—in which each spouse owns half of the couple's community property, usually most of the property gained during the marriage. But even in noncommunity property states, laws often require that a couple's property be divided fairly during divorce.

Having an ex suddenly on board can, of course, be a true disaster, especially if former spouses each have an ownership share and must run the business together. Even if the original co-owner sells out of the business and the ex remains an owner, there's a huge potential for drama and trouble—particularly if the divorce was a nasty one. If the divorce was friendly, an ex who has no business experience or is just plain incompetent may still be unwelcome as an owner. In short, there are ample and compelling reasons to preemptively avoid these situations by implementing a sound buy-sell agreement.

Specific contract language is discussed below in Section G. For now, keep in mind that to avoid the situations outlined above, all the spouses of current business owners should read and sign the buy-sell agreement.

5. An Owner Becomes a Liability

Sometimes conflict with a business owner goes beyond the occasional squabbling and sniping typical of many business relationships. In extreme cases, the conflict crosses the line and some of the owners agree that it's time to push out one of the other owners. This situation can arise for all kinds of reasons: The owner may be inherently unreasonable and difficult, suffering from alcoholism or substance abuse, mentally ill, or engaged in criminal behavior.

Whatever the root cause, once things have deteriorated to an intolerable level, it's important to have a mechanism in place to expel an owner. Having rules—for instance, outlining the situations that call for expulsion—will help make this nasty situation a little less nasty.

To sum up, when any of these often-painful situations occur, you can depend on a buy-sell agreement to dictate an orderly transfer of ownership interests according to rules all have consented to beforehand. As discussed in more detail below, a buy-sell agreement can outline straightforward rules about when ownership shares can or must be sold, to whom they may be sold, and how to determine the share's selling price.

B. Buy-Sell Agreement Basics

A buy-sell agreement is a contract among a business's owners that spells out, in varying degrees of detail, some or all of the following issues:

- who can buy a departing owner's interest
- when the owners can force another owner to sell a share of the business
- when one owner can force the other owners to buy a share
- what price will be paid for a departing owner's share, and
- how a buyout will actually happen, including specific payment terms.

In practice, a buy-sell agreement typically has a few standard provisions to handle these issues. Buy-sell provisions can either be assembled into their own stand-alone agreement or inserted into other business documents such as your partnership agreement, LLC operating agreement, or corporate bylaws. The term buy-sell agreement in this chapter includes any buy-sell provisions your company has adopted, whether they're in a separate agreement or included in another business document.

The three provisions at the heart of buy-sell agreements establish:

- transfer of ownership interests with the right of first refusal
- the right to force buyouts, and
- a set price or a formula to determine share price.

C. Limiting Ownership Transfers

When an owner wants to leave a business and sell an ownership interest, it can create real and lasting chaos if the share is sold to someone the other owners don't want as a co-owner. But if there is a buy-sell agreement that establishes limits on the transfers of ownership shares, this possibility can be avoided.

The best way to avoid unwanted outsiders gaining ownership of your business is with a provision known as a "right of first refusal." This provision gives the company or the remaining co-owners the right to buy a departing owner's interest before it's transferred—that is, sold or given—to an outsider.

It works like this: A departing owner who receives an offer to purchase his or her interest from an outsider may not accept it outright. Instead, the right of first refusal requires the departing owner to give written notice to the company stating the intention to sell the shares and describing the terms of the proposed sale. At that point, the company and the continuing owners have the option to buy the departing owner's interest. Depending on how you structure your right of first refusal, the company and continuing owners will be entitled to

purchase the shares either at the same price as the outsider offered or at a price previously agreed upon and included in the agreement. If the co-owners don't want to buy the ownership interest at those terms, then the departing owner has 60 days to sell it to the outsider according to the terms outlined in the notice.

The right of first refusal focuses on preventing unwanted outsiders from gaining ownership interest in your company. Since this is a fundamental issue, it is important for all business owners to put this provision in place.

But you can also include solutions such as the following for dealing with related issues in the right of first refusal.

- **Extend the right to potential sales to current owners.** If the right of first refusal is structured this way, when a departing owner offers a share to another current owner, all the co-owners must be given the option to buy it. The main reason to use this arrangement is to prevent one or more co-owners from seizing control of the business by buying a departing owner's share.
- **Create different rules for gifts or transfers to trusts.** It's possible to have the right of first refusal apply to sales of ownership shares, as described above, but not to other types of transfers, such as gifts or transfers to trusts. Generally, giving ownership shares to family members or putting them in a trust is done for estate planning purposes—to save estate taxes and avoid probate. If you and your co-owners want more freedom to engage in estate planning techniques with your ownership shares, you may not want the right of first refusal provisions to apply to gifts and transfers to trusts.
- **Prohibit all transfers.** Current owners may keep the tightest grip on control of company ownership by banning all ownership transfers outright. However, since this approach is so rigid and unhelpful to owners who may really need to sell out of a business, it is generally not a good idea.

You can find suggested language for a right of first refusal in Section 2 of the sample agreement in Section G of this chapter, below, and on the CD-ROM in the back of this book.

D. Forcing Buyouts

In addition to controlling who owns a business, an important function of a buy-sell agreement is to provide answers to the questions that can arise when the ownership setup is thrown into question. What if one of your co-owners dies? Will the heirs become co-owners in your business? What if a co-owner slides into crippling alcoholism or substance abuse? Will you be stuck with an inebriated business partner? What if your co-owner gets divorced and the dreaded ex-spouse gets an ownership share as part of the divorce settlement? Is there anything you can do?

You can remove the uncertainty from all of these situations by taking preventive action. By adopting forced buyout provisions in a buy-sell agreement, you'll establish rules for different scenarios such as death, divorce, bankruptcy, retirement, and other business-disrupting events. When the rules are triggered by specific events, an owner can be forced to sell shares, or continuing owners can be forced to buy out a departing owner's share. Forced buyout rules help keep the business stable during difficult times and make ownership transitions as smooth as possible.

As you can imagine, a crucial fact about forced buyout provisions is that they must be agreed to well in advance of any situation that will trigger them. It goes without saying that the situations that trigger these provisions—such as death, disease, and divorce—often cause emotions to run high. You and your co-owners should discuss the possible scenarios and come to a consensus on what rules will apply in those situations before any owner is personally affected.

In a nutshell, there are two different kinds of forced buyouts: Either an owner can be forced to sell out, or a departing owner can force the other owners to buy the departing owner's share.

1. Forcing Owners to Sell

Business owners can force an owner or other person who has obtained an interest in the business to sell out of it—and sell the shares back to the company or the continuing owners at a specified price. They do it by including an option-to-purchase provision in the buy-sell agreement.

This provision can force any of the following people to sell back to the continuing owners:

- any one of the owners—for specified reasons such as retirement, disability, bankruptcy, loss of professional license, or misconduct
- the executor or administrator of a deceased owner's estate, and
- an owner's ex-spouse who gains an interest in the business through a divorce settlement.

The rules vary depending on which situation triggers the forced buyout, but the overall goal is the same: to keep control over the company's ownership and keep out anyone unacceptable to the continuing owners. This includes people who stand to gain ownership through inheritance, divorce, or bankruptcy—as well as current owners whom other owners want to push out.

All options to purchase should also address the price at which the shares will be sold. Usually this is accomplished by referring to the "Agreement Price" outlined in a separate buy-sell provision. (Price provisions are discussed in Section E, below.)

2. Forcing Owners to Buy

The flip side of an option-to-purchase provision is the right to force a sale. Without a right-to-force-a-sale provision, an owner who wants to sell out might be stuck if the current owners don't want—or don't have the funds—to purchase his or her share. But with a forced buyout provision, anyone with an ownership interest in the business can force the other owners to buy that interest at a specified price. Common scenarios include an owner who's retiring or becomes disabled who wants to sell out of the business, or a deceased owner's survivors who want to cash out the ownership interest they got in a will.

Beware that while a forced buyout provision protects owners from being stuck in a business, it also has the potential to seriously damage a company that doesn't have the means to pay out departing owners, particularly when business isn't so hot.

But there is a way to both protect business owners who don't want to be chained to the business forever and to protect the business from bleeding money from cashing out owners. Your right to force a sale clause can allow owners to cash out of the business only after a certain time, by which you expect your business to be stable and profitable enough to pay out a departing owner. Anyone who chooses to cash out before that time—for example, three or five years—will only receive a fraction of the value of ownership share—say, 50%. This creates a disincentive for any owner to leave early in the life of the business, when cash reserves may be crucial.

You can find suggested language for a right of forced buyouts in Section 3 of the sample agreement in Section G of this chapter, below, and on the CD-ROM in the back of this book.

Negotiations can easily get tangled up on price issues, so it's important that the right to force a sale provision addresses the price at which the shares will be sold. Generally it will refer to a separate pricing provision, which is discussed next.

⚠ Wrinkles for co-owners with unequal shares. If your company has one controlling owner and one or more owners with small minority shares, the controlling owner may not want to be subject to the same rules as the minority owners.

For example, say a company has a majority owner who is very identified with the company and who has played the primary role in building it over many years. The majority owner may balk at the idea that the minority owners could force his or her children to sell their shares, elevating the minority owners to control the company. Majority owners should consider consulting an experienced business lawyer before signing a buy-sell agreement. Before doing that, it's a good idea to read *Business Buyout Agreements: A Step-by-Step Guide for Co-Owners,* by Anthony Mancuso and Bethany Laurence (Nolo), which explains the subtleties of buy-sell agreements in much greater detail than this chapter.

E. Establishing the Price for Sales

In addition to spelling out ownership transfer rules for specific situations, a buy-sell agreement should outline how to set the price for shares being sold. In essence, this determines how to value the company. It's all too common for departing and continuing owners to have significantly different ideas about a company's value. Without a consensus as to how to determine the company's value and the price of its shares, negotiations can be stymied or sunk.

In addition, a buy-sell agreement can define details of the ownership transfer such as how it will be funded, payment terms, and other specifics.

Equipment, property, and accounts receivable are simple enough to total, but it's much harder to put a price tag on intangibles such as business reputation or customer lists. When owners don't agree on how to establish a company's value, the haggling involved in an ownership transfer can get gnarly. If the ownership transfer is due to death, divorce, or some other wrenching event, you can count on the negotiations being even tougher.

To avoid these conflicts, a buy-sell agreement establishes in advance a value for the company or a formula that will be used to determine it. Any owner's share can then be calculated by multiplying the ownership percentage by the overall company value.

There are several different ways to value a business, and you can include any of them in your buy-sell agreement.

One approach is to establish a preset value for the company. While the simplicity of this approach may be attractive, the obvious weakness is that the fixed price is likely to become outdated and may not accurately reflect the current value of the business—particularly if the business is growing or shrinking rapidly. One way to remedy this is to update the fixed price periodically, say, every year.

A better approach is to use a valuation formula in your agreement. With a formula, you and your co-owners will have a clearly defined way to figure out the value of the business and, by extension, the ownership shares up for sale. Even better, the value generated by a formula will be more meaningful than a fixed value, since the formula will be based on up-to-date data such as current assets or income.

There are a few different valuation formulas and methods possible. Here is a look at the most common ones.

1. Book Value

A company's book value is simply its assets minus its liabilities, the same as the information on a balance sheet. Since the figures used to calculate book value are readily available from various financial statements, this is an easy formula to use and to understand. While book value does not include intangibles such as reputation, earnings potential, or customer goodwill, this may not be a big issue for new businesses that haven't had the time or luck to develop much of a reputation or goodwill. Another issue is that this method uses the depreciated value of assets, which typically results in a low value overall. As your business grows, you may be wise to switch to a valuation method that reflects more and provides a higher buyout price.

2. Multiple of Book Value

This method is based on the book value approach, but goes further and includes intangible assets such as customer goodwill, a solid client base, a desirable location, a recently implemented marketing campaign, and intellectual property owned by the business. The overall value is reached by taking the business's book value and multiplying it by a predetermined number, aptly called a multiplier. The co-owners will need to choose a multiplier to include in the buy-sell agreement—and choosing is more of an art than a science. You'll find a wide range of multipliers used, from just over one to six or more. Do some research into your particular industry before choosing a multiplier.

3. Capitalization of Earnings

Also called "multiple of earnings," the capitalization of earnings method bases a company's value on its record of profits. Since brand-new businesses won't have a profit record, do not use this method until you develop an earnings history. The valuation begins with the company's annual profit (gross revenues minus costs) multiplied by a predetermined number—a multiplier, sometimes called a capitalization rate. Co-owners will choose a multiplier based on several factors, including general economic conditions, type of business, business age, risk involved in business, or multipliers of similar businesses. Multipliers for the capitalization of earnings method can go as high as ten in some cases.

4. Appraisal Value

Rather than doing it yourselves, you can hire a professional business appraiser to determine a business's value once an ownership transfer is imminent. That certainly makes things easier for the co-owners, but it's not without drawbacks. One is cost: Appraisers don't come cheap. Expect to pay at least $1,000 for an appraisal of a small company, and up to $10,000 for large businesses with annual sales into the millions. Appraisals can also take valuable time, which may be an issue when an owner is eager to sell.

At the end of the day, you'll need to choose the valuation method that works best for your company. As a general rule, methods based on book value tend not to be good choices for service businesses that may have few assets. For such businesses, basing valuation on earnings history makes more sense.

Address other issues such as payment terms and the funding source. Since ownership shares can involve big sums of money, it's not always reasonable to expect that a buyout can be paid for all at once. It's a good idea to outline specific payment terms in your agreement—for instance, monthly payments of principal and interest, or some other arrangement. It's also wise to address where the money will come from in the case of a buyout. Businesses commonly need to take out a loan to pay departing owners, or to use proceeds from life or disability insurance. If you don't plan in advance how you'll fund buyouts, you might find there's not enough time to scramble the money together once something triggers a buyout. For more detail on funding buyouts, see *Business Buyout Agreements: A Step-by-Step Guide for Co-Owners,* by Anthony Mancuso and Bethany Laurence (Nolo).

You can find suggested language for agreement prices in Section 4 of the sample agreement in Section G of this chapter, below, and on the CD-ROM in the back of this book.

F. Implementing Buy-Sell Provisions

In general, buy-sell provisions either can be assembled into their own document, or can be added to your existing business governing document. For corporations, this is the bylaws; for LLCs, it's the operating agreement; for partnerships, it's the partnership agreement. If you want to use the sample provisions provided in Section G, below, it is best that you insert them into your existing business governing document, because only the basic clauses are provided in the template included here.

To insert clauses into the existing document that governs your business, either type or cut and paste the clauses into your document file, preferably near the end. Be sure to renumber the sections as needed to conform with the existing numbering of your document.

Note that many of the standard clauses in the sample agreement have multiple options with checkboxes. Feel free either to copy and paste all the possible options and use the checkboxes to indicate your choices, or to copy and paste only the clauses you choose to use. However, it is not a good idea to select partial language; instead, choose among the clearly defined alternative options.

Before finalizing your agreement, you must tackle an important legal task: a consistency check. This requires scrutinizing whether any of the buy-sell provisions conflict with any existing business documents. Essentially, you need to make sure that your existing documents don't contain any language contradicting any of the buy-sell provisions. Generally, if there are no clauses in your existing document that explicitly contradict the buy-sell provisions, then you may be in the clear. Still, analyzing the provisions for conflict can be confusing, and you may want simply to pay a lawyer to review the existing document and the buy-sell provisions.

⚠ Consistency checks are important business. Often, inconsistencies in documents will be obvious, even to a nonlawyer. For example, say your existing LLC operating agreement states that any person who is at the receiving end of an ownership transfer will have economic rights only—as in, no voting rights or management authority. Your buy-sell provisions, on the other hand, are based on the assumption that full ownership rights are being transferred, including voting and management rights. This should trigger alarm bells. One option is to delete the limited-ownership-rights provision from your existing operating agreement. Or, if you'd prefer, see a lawyer who can make the necessary changes for you.

G. Sample Buy-Sell Provisions

Sample buy-sell clauses are provided below for you to use as a starting point when drafting your own agreement. The sample clauses are also included on the CD-ROM in the back of this book.

The sample agreement begins with one basic provision that may be necessary in some states: a statement that the company does not terminate when an owner transfers an interest, dies, withdraws, files for bankruptcy, is expelled, or otherwise leaves the company. Under some state laws, the legal default is that a partnership or LLC automatically dissolves once an owner is "dissociated"—in other words, when an owner sells an interest, dies, withdraws, or otherwise no longer holds an ownership interest—unless the remaining owners vote to continue the business. The introductory provision included here ensures that your business won't legally dissolve whenever an ownership transfer is triggered under your buy-sell provisions. As mentioned, make sure there is no state-

ment to the contrary elsewhere in your partnership or operating agreement.

Moving on to the real meat of the buy-sell agreement, you'll find samples of the three most important clauses:

- a limitation on the transfer of ownership interests or right of first refusal
- a right to force buyouts, and
- a method to determine share price.

You'll also find a fourth provision: payment terms, which outlines a few alternatives for how a buyout will be paid.

Keep in mind that these sample provisions stick to the basics and should be seen as a skeletal version of a full buy-sell agreement. There are many other details and issues you should consider once you're serious about putting your agreement together. While all business owners would be wise to take these issues seriously from the get-go, it's especially important for businesses that have accumulated significant assets, and for business owners who are concerned about estate planning.

📖 Getting help with the details. For a more detailed agreement that anticipates a comprehensive range of issues and potential situations, consult *Business Buyout Agreements: A Step-by-Step Guide for Co-Owners,* by Anthony Mancuso and Bethany Laurence (Nolo).

💼 Running your buy-sell agreement by an expert. While buy-sell basics aren't hard to understand, it may be a good idea to have an attorney or business consultant review yours once you've drafted it. The expert may be able to point out potential additional issues that are not covered in any depth in this chapter, such as tax and estate planning considerations.

☑ Chapter 14 Checklist

☐ If your business will have more than one owner, consider the various situations that may raise ownership questions: retirement, illness, disability, death, divorce, or conflict among business owners.

☐ To control the transfer of ownership shares in your business, include buy-sell provisions in your business formation document such as your partnership agreement or LLC operating agreement, or in a separate agreement. (The sample clauses in this chapter are to be used in your existing business formation document.)

☐ To limit the ability of a business owner to sell a business interest to an outsider, use a right of first refusal clause.

☐ To force an owner or someone who has acquired an interest in the business to sell the interest to the current owners, use an option to purchase clause.

☐ To force the other owners of the business to purchase a departing owner's share, include a forced buyout clause.

☐ Remember to include provisions for how the price will be set for ownership shares being sold, and payment terms.

Sample Buy-Sell Agreement Provisions

Section 1: Introduction

The legal existence of the company shall not terminate upon the addition of a new owner or the transfer of an owner's interest under this agreement, or the death, withdrawal, bankruptcy, or expulsion of an owner.

Section 2: Limiting the Transfer of Ownership Interests

Right of First Refusal

(a) No owner ("transferring owner") shall have the right to sell, transfer, or dispose of any or all of an ownership interest, for consideration or otherwise, unless he or she delivers to the company written Notice of Intent to Transfer the interest stating the name and the address of the proposed transferee and the terms and conditions of the proposed transfer. Delivery of this notice shall be deemed an offer by the transferring owner to sell to the company and the continuing owners the interest proposed to be transferred.

   If the proposed transfer is a sale of the owner's interest, these terms shall include the price to be paid for the interest by the proposed transferee, and a copy of the offer to purchase the interest on these terms, dated and signed by the proposed transferee, shall be attached to the notice.

(b) The company and the nontransferring owners then have an option, but not an obligation (unless otherwise stated in this agreement), to purchase the interest proposed for transfer, and may do so within 60 days after the date on which the company receives notice or becomes aware of the event triggering the Option to Purchase.

   If the company and the nontransferring owners do not elect to purchase all of the interest stated in the notice, the transferring owner may then transfer his or her interest to the proposed transferee stated in the notice within 60 days after the nontransferring owners' purchase option ends.

(c) Price and terms:

   [Check either Option 1a or Option 1b below.]

   ☐ **Option 1a: Price and terms in offer**

   The company and the nontransferring owners shall have the right to purchase the interest of the transferring owner only at the purchase price and payment terms stated in the Notice of Intent to Transfer submitted to the company by the transferring owner. The price and terms in this notice override the general Agreement Price selected in the "Agreement Price" and "Payment Terms" sections of this agreement.

☐ **Option 1b: Price and terms in agreement**

The company and the nontransferring owners shall have the right to purchase the interest of the transferring owner at the Agreement Price and payment terms selected in the "Agreement Price" and "Payment Terms" sections of this agreement.

Section 3: Providing the Right to Force Buyouts

Scenario 1. When an Active Owner Retires or Quits the Company's Employ

[You may check Option 1, Option 2, both, or neither below.

Check Option 1 if you want the company and continuing owners to have the option to buy a retiring owner's interest.]

☐ **Option 1: Option of Company and Continuing Owners to Purchase a Retiring Owner's Interest**

An owner who voluntarily retires or quits the company's employ is deemed to have offered his or her ownership interest to the company and the continuing owners for sale. The company and the continuing owners shall then have an option, but not an obligation (unless otherwise stated in this agreement), to purchase all or part of the ownership interest within 60 days after the date on which the company receives notice or becomes aware of the event triggering the Option to Purchase. The price to be paid, the manner of payments, and other terms of the purchase shall be according to the "Agreement Price" and "Payment Terms" sections of this agreement. An owner who stops working for the company is referred to as a "retiring owner" below.

[Check Option 2 if you want a retiring owner to be able to force the company to buy his or her interest. This right can be in addition to Option 1 (company and continuing owners' option to purchase) above.]

☐ **Option 2: Right of Retiring Owner to Force a Sale**

An owner who voluntarily retires or quits the company's employ can require the company and the continuing owners to buy all, but not less than all, of his or her ownership interest by delivering to the company at least 60 days before departing a notice of intention to force a sale ("Notice of Intent to Force a Sale"). The notice shall include the date of departure, the name and address of the owner, a description and amount of the owner's interest in the company, and a statement that the owner wishes to force a sale due to the owner's retirement as provided in this provision. The price to be paid, the manner of payments, and other terms of the purchase shall be according to this section and the "Agreement Price" and "Payment Terms" sections of this agreement. An owner who requests that an interest be purchased is referred to as a "retiring owner" below.

Scenario 2. When an Owner Becomes Disabled

[You may check Option 1, Option 2, both, or neither below.

Check Option 1 if you want the company and continuing owners to have the option to buy a disabled owner's interest. If you check Option 1, insert the amount of time an owner must be disabled before the company or the continuing owners can purchase the available interest.]

☐ **Option 1: Option of Company and Continuing Owners to Purchase a Disabled Owner's Interest**

An owner who becomes permanently and totally disabled, and such disability lasts at least ____ months (the "waiting period"), either consecutively or cumulatively, is deemed to have offered his or her ownership interest to the company and the continuing owners for sale. The company and the continuing owners shall then have an option, but not an obligation (unless otherwise stated in this agreement), to purchase all or part of the ownership interest within 60 days after the date on which the company receives notice or becomes aware of the event triggering the Option to Purchase. The price to be paid, the manner of payments, and other terms of the purchase shall be according to this section and the "Agreement Price" and "Payment Terms" sections of this agreement.

An owner who is unable to perform his or her regular duties is considered disabled. If disability insurance is used to fund a buyout under this provision, the insurance company shall establish whether an owner is disabled; without disability insurance, the owner's doctor will establish whether an owner is disabled. An owner who becomes disabled according to this section is referred to as a "disabled owner" below.

[Check Option 2 if you want a disabled owner to be able to force the company to buy his or her interest. This right can be in addition to Option 1 (company and continuing owners' option to purchase) above. If you check Option 2, insert the amount of time an owner must be disabled before forcing the company to purchase an interest.]

☐ **Option 2: Right of Disabled Owner to Force a Sale**

An owner who becomes permanently and totally disabled, and such disability lasts at least ____ months (the "waiting period"), either consecutively or cumulatively, can require the company and the continuing owners to buy all, but not less than all, of his or her ownership interest by delivering to the company, within 30 days of the expiration of the waiting period, a notice of intention to force a sale ("Notice of Intent to Force a Sale") in writing. The notice shall include the name and address of the owner, a description and amount of the owner's interest in the company, and a statement that the owner wishes to force a sale due to disability as provided in this provision. The price to be paid, the manner of payments, and other terms of the purchase shall be according to this section and the "Agreement Price" and "Payment Terms" sections of this agreement.

An owner is who is unable to perform his regular duties is considered disabled. If disability insurance is used to fund a buyout under this provision, the insurance company shall establish whether an owner is disabled; without disability insurance, the owner's doctor will establish whether an owner is disabled. An owner who becomes disabled according to this section is referred to as a "disabled owner" below.

Scenario 3. When an Owner Dies

[You may check Option 1, Option 2, both, or neither below.

Check Option 1 if you want the company and continuing owners to have the right to buy a deceased owner's interest.]

☐ **Option 1: Option of Company and Continuing Owners to Purchase a Deceased Owner's Interest**

An owner who dies and the executor or administrator of the estate or the trustee of a trust holding the ownership interest are deemed to have offered the deceased owner's interest to the company and the continuing owners for sale as of the date of the notice of death received orally or in writing by the company. The company and the continuing owners shall then have an option, but not an obligation (unless otherwise stated in this agreement), to purchase all or part of the ownership interest within 60 days after the date on which the company receives notice or becomes aware of the death. The price to be paid, the manner of payments, and other terms of the purchase shall be according to the "Agreement Price" and "Payment Terms" sections of this agreement. An owner who has died is referred to as a "deceased owner" below.

[Check Option 2 below if you want the estate, trust, or inheritors of a deceased owner to be able to force the company to buy his or her interest. This right can be in addition to Option 1 (company and continuing owners' right to purchase) above.]

☐ **Option 2: Right of Estate, Trust, or Inheritors to Force a Sale**

When an owner dies, the executor or administrator of the deceased owner's estate, the trustee of a trust holding the deceased owner's ownership interest, or the deceased owner's inheritors can require the company and the continuing owners to buy all, but not less than all, of the deceased owner's interest by delivering to the company within 60 days a notice of intention to force a sale ("Notice of Intent to Force a Sale") in writing. The notice shall include the name and address of the deceased owner, the date of death, a description and amount of the owner's interest in the company, the name and address of the person exercising the right to force the sale, and a statement that this person wishes to force a sale of the interest due to the owner's death as provided in this provision. The price to be paid, the manner of payments, and other terms of the purchase shall be according to the "Agreement Price" and "Payment Terms" sections of this agreement. An owner who has died is referred to as a "deceased owner" below.

Scenario 4. When an Owner's Interest Is Transferred to His or Her Former Spouse

[Check Option 1 if you want the company and owners to have the right to buy a divorced owner's interest from his or her former spouse.]

☐ **Option 1: Option of Company and Continuing Owners to Purchase Former Spouse's Interest**

(a) If, in connection with the divorce or dissolution of the marriage of an owner, a court issues a decree or order that transfers, confirms, or awards part or all of an ownership interest to a divorced owner's former spouse, the former spouse is deemed to have offered the newly acquired ownership interest to the divorced owner for purchase on the date of the court award or settlement, according to the terms of this agreement. If the divorced owner does not elect to make such purchase within 30 days of the date of the court award or settlement, the former spouse of the divorced owner is deemed to have offered the newly acquired ownership interest to the company and the co-owners (including the divorced owner) for purchase, according to the terms of this agreement. The divorced owner must send notice to the company, in writing, that his or her former spouse now owns an ownership interest in the company. The notice shall state the name and address of the owner, the name and address of the divorced owner's former spouse, a description and amount of the interest awarded to the former spouse, and the date of the court award. If the company does not receive notice from the divorced owner, an offer to the company and the co-owners is deemed to have occurred when the company actually receives notice orally or in writing of the court award or settlement transferring the divorced owner's interest to the owner's former spouse. The company and the co-owners (including the divorced owner) shall then have an option, but not an obligation (unless otherwise stated in this agreement), to purchase all or part of the ownership interest within 60 days after the date on which the company receives notice or becomes aware of the event triggering the Option to Purchase. The price to be paid, the manner of payments, and other terms of the purchase shall be according to the "Agreement Price" and "Payment Terms" sections of this agreement.

(b) A former spouse who sells an ownership interest back to the company or continuing owners agrees to be responsible for any taxes owed on those sales proceeds.

Scenario 5. Expulsion of Owner

[Check Option 1 below if you want to give the company and the continuing owners the option to purchase an expelled owner's interest. If you check Option 1, also check and fill in Options 1a through 1f.]

☐ **Option 1: Option of Company and Continuing Owners to Purchase an Expelled Owner's Interest**

(a) When the company has three or more owners, situations may arise in which a group of owners wish to expel another owner. An owner may be expelled upon a unanimous vote of all other owners for adequate cause. Upon such expulsion, the expelled owner is deemed to have offered to sell all of his or her interest to the company and the continuing owners. The company and the continuing owners shall then have an option, but not an obligation (unless otherwise stated in this agreement), to purchase all or part of the ownership interest within 30 days after the vote to expel the owner. The price to be paid shall be as specified in this section; if not so specified, then according to the "Agreement Price" section of this agreement. The manner of payments and other terms of the purchase shall be according to the "Payment Terms" section of this agreement. An owner who has been expelled is referred to as an "expelled owner" below.

(b) Adequate cause includes, but is not limited to:

☐ **Option 1a: Any criminal conduct against the company (such as embezzlement)**

☐ **Option 1b: A serious breach of the owner's duties or of any written policy of the company**

☐ **Option 1c: _____**

(c) If an owner is expelled for a reason listed in subsection (b), the price that the company or the continuing owners will pay for the expelled owner's ownership interest will be:

☐ **Option 1d: The full Agreement Price according to the "Agreement Price" section of this agreement**

☐ **Option 1e: Decided by an independent appraisal, according to the Appraised Value Method in the "Agreement Price" section of this agreement**

☐ **Option 1f: The Agreement Price as established in the "Agreement Price" section of this agreement, decreased by __%**

Section 4: Agreement Price

Unless otherwise provided in this agreement, the undersigned agree that the method checked below for valuing the company shall be used to determine a price for ownership interests under this agreement.

[You must check one and only one of the valuation methods below:]

☐ **Valuation Method 1: Agreed Value**

The agreed value of the company shall be $____, or such other amount as fixed by all owners of the company after the date this agreement is adopted as specified in a written statement signed by each owner of the company. If more than one such statement is signed by the owners after this agreement is adopted, the statement with the latest date shall control for purposes of fixing a price for the purchase of ownership interests under this agreement. The value of an individual owner's interest shall be the entire value for the company as determined under this paragraph, multiplied by his or her ownership percentage.

☐ **Valuation Method 2: Book Value**

The value of the company shall be its book value (its assets minus its liabilities as shown on the balance sheet of the company) as of the end of the most recent fiscal year prior to the purchase of an ownership interest under this agreement. The value of an individual owner's interest shall be the entire value for the company as determined under this paragraph, multiplied by his or her ownership percentage.

☐ **Valuation Method 3: Multiple of Book Value**

The value of the company shall be _____ times its book value (its assets minus its liabilities as shown on the balance sheet of the company) as of the end of the most recent fiscal year prior to the purchase of an ownership interest under this agreement. The value of an individual owner's interest shall be the entire value for the company as determined under this paragraph, multiplied by his or her ownership percentage.

☐ **Valuation Method 4: Capitalization of Earnings (Adjusted for Income Taxes)**

The value of the company shall be determined on the basis of _____ times the average net earnings (annual gross revenues of the company minus annual expenses and minus any annual federal, state, and local income taxes payable by the company) for the _____ fiscal years of the company (or the number of fiscal years the company has been in existence, if fewer) that have occurred prior to the purchase of an ownership interest under this agreement. The value of an individual owner's interest shall be the entire value for the company as determined under this paragraph, multiplied by his or her ownership percentage.

☐ **Valuation Method 5: Appraised Value**

The value of the company shall be its fair market value as determined by an independent appraiser mutually selected by the Buyer(s) and Seller of the ownership interest subject to purchase under this agreement. If the Buyer(s) and Seller are unable to agree upon an independent appraiser within 30 days, within the next 10 days, each shall select an independent appraiser. If the selected appraisers are unable, within 60 days, to agree on the fair market value of the company, then the appraisers shall select an additional independent appraiser within the next 10 days, who shall, within 30 days, determine the fair market value of the company. The Buyer(s) and Sellers shall equally share all costs of an appraiser mutually selected by the Buyer(s) and Seller or of an additional appraiser. All costs of an individually selected appraiser shall be paid by the party selecting the appraiser. The value of an individual owner's interest shall be the entire value for the company as determined under this paragraph, multiplied by his or her ownership percentage.

Section 5: Payment Terms

Unless otherwise provided in this agreement, the undersigned agree that the payment terms checked below shall be used for the purchase of ownership interests.

[You must check one and only one of the payment terms alternatives below.]

☐ **Payment Terms Alternative 1: Full Cash Payment**

Cash payment for the Seller's ownership interest shall be made by the Buyer(s) to the Seller within _____ days of the date the company provides a Notice of Intent to Purchase to the Seller under this agreement.

☐ **Payment Terms Alternative 2: Monthly Installments of Principal and Interest**

The Buyer(s) shall pay the Seller the purchase price for an ownership interest in equal installments over a term of _____ months, with interest added to the amount of each installment computed at an annual rate of _____ and compounded annually on the unpaid continuing balance of the purchase price of the ownership interest. The buyer shall make the first installment payment to the Seller by _____, and the continuing payments shall be made on the _____ of every month, until the full purchase price, together with any interest owed, is paid in full.

☐ **Payment Terms Alternative 3: Customized Schedule for Payment for Ownership Interest**

The Buyer(s) shall pay the Seller the purchase price for the ownership interest according to the schedule and other terms included below:

_____

_____

_____

_____

_____

_____

_____

_____

_____

_____

_____

CHAPTER

15

Building Your Business and Hiring Workers

If all your careful planning, hard work, and good karma pay off, you may soon find yourself needing help to handle your thriving business. While part of you will surely be happy that your business is taking off, another, more practical side of you may worry about what's involved in hiring help. This chapter offers a broad overview of the many legal requirements that apply to businesses that have one or more employees. If you're thinking about hiring an employee but aren't sure about how or whether to do it, the information here should help you understand what you're getting into—and help you figure out if there's a better way to go.

In addition to the practical and financial concerns involved in hiring one or more people to work for your business, you need to be aware of several legal rules that apply to businesses with outside workers. First of all, you'll need to understand the difference between the two types of workers: employees and independent contractors. This distinction is crucial, because different rules will apply to your business depending on what kind of workers you hire. If the government considers your workers to be employees, you'll have to follow a number of state and federal laws and pay employment-related taxes. If, on the other

hand, your workers can be characterized as independent contractors, you'll be spared many—but not all—of these financial and legal requirements.

A. Employees vs. Independent Contractors

Anyone who works for your business (other than a business owner) is either an employee or an independent contractor. In a nutshell, an employee is someone who works for you, on your site, with your tools and equipment, and according to your rules and procedures. Independent contractors, on the other hand, are in business for themselves; they work on their own time and with their own tools, and perform services for a number of different clients.

This is not a distinction to be taken lightly. Businesspeople who hire employees owe a number of employment taxes, such as payroll tax and unemployment tax, while those who hire only independent contractors do not owe these taxes. If you treat an employee as an independent contractor and fail to pay employment taxes, you risk subjecting yourself to a huge back-tax bill, plus interest and other state and federal penalties. More than a few businesses have been torpedoed and sunk into bankruptcy after making this mistake.

With that warning in mind, here's the lowdown on classifying your workers.

1. The Agencies That Matter

Since paying taxes is the main drawback to classifying workers as employees, it shouldn't surprise you to learn that the IRS takes a great interest in whether your workers are classified properly. At the federal level, the IRS will take swift and severe action if it finds out that you're treating a worker as an independent contractor when in fact that worker meets the criteria of an being an employee. At the state level, there are rules for classifying workers that may be stricter than or otherwise different from the IRS rules. Since the penalties at

the state level can be at least as harsh as those imposed by the IRS, be sure you understand the rules in your state. The state agency in charge of worker status rules and enforcement is generally an employment agency, tax department, unemployment office, or other employment-related bureau. (A list of the state agencies in charge of worker classification—the unemployment compensation agencies—is included in Appendix A.)

2. IRS Criteria

The IRS's Publication 15-A, *Employer's Supplemental Tax Guide*, offers information and examples to help you determine whether a worker is in fact an independent contractor or an employee. It is available online at www.irs.gov/formspubs/index.html.

A worker should normally be considered an employee, not an independent contractor, when he or she:

- works only for you and not for any other business
- works on your premises
- uses your tools and equipment
- follows work hours you set
- follows your instructions on how to complete a job
- receives reimbursement for expenses incurred in doing a job
- supervises any of your other workers, or
- receives any employee benefits, such as holiday pay, vacation time, or health insurance.

On the flip side, a worker should probably be considered an independent contractor if he or she:

- works for a number of different businesses or clients
- has a personal office, studio, garage, or other permanent place to work
- owns equipment and tools used for the work
- sets his or her own hours
- uses independent judgment as to how best to complete a job
- doesn't get reimbursed for expenses incurred in doing a job, or

- advertises services to the public.

Of course, a worker you hire might display some characteristics of both categories, which makes it harder to say for sure how that worker should be classified. Ultimately, you'll need to consider these factors all together and weigh them against each other to decide whether a worker should be classified as an employee or as an independent contractor.

EXAMPLE 1: Bob does a lot of freelance proofreading for a publisher of books on alternative health, Wholeness Press. He often works for Wholeness Press (about ten projects per year), but he also does four or five jobs per year for other publishers. He always works at home, receives minimal instructions as to how to do his work, and does his proofreading whenever he feels like it. Bob can probably be categorized as an independent contractor.

EXAMPLE 2: Susan programs almost exclusively for one software developer, Fizz Games, but she also does approximately one outside project per year. She sometimes works from home but often uses a computer at Fizz Games' office. She works closely with the software development team at Fizz Games, following instructions from some of the developers while training some of the newer workers in programming techniques. The government is likely to see Susan as an employee. It would be risky to try to treat her as an independent contractor.

In borderline situations, it's safer to treat a worker as an employee than risk the penalties that may result if the IRS or your state decides you've misclassified an employee as an independent contractor. Keep in mind that the IRS and most state authorities tend to disfavor independent contractor status. They'd much rather see borderline workers classified as employees so that they can collect taxes on them.

If you can't decide how one of your workers should be classified, there are a few ways you can proceed. One is to consult a lawyer or an accountant who understands business tax laws. Another option is to go straight to the horse's mouth and ask the IRS or your state agency to tell you how they would classify a certain worker. You can file Form SS-8, *Determination of Worker Status,* to request a formal ruling from the IRS on a worker's status. You can get this form from an IRS office or from the agency's website at www.irs.gov. As mentioned, however, don't be surprised if the IRS classifies your worker as an employee.

For a state determination, contact your state employment or other agency that governs worker classification and find out what procedure it uses. (See Appendix A for contact information for the agency that classifies workers in your state.) Like the IRS, it's common for states to classify workers as employees rather than independent contractors.

Classifying Workers: Don't Make the Same Mistake Microsoft Did

Who would think that lowly temporary workers would be able to beat one of the world's mightiest economic juggernauts, Microsoft? But they did, which should be a lesson to all businesses that hire independent contractors (ICs). Like many software companies, Microsoft supplemented its regular core of employees with a pool of workers whom it classified as independent "freelancers," paying them cash compensation (sometimes more than its employees) but providing them with none of the fringe benefits. Microsoft had the workers sign agreements specifying that they were ICs, which meant Microsoft wouldn't give them fringe benefits available to regular employees or withhold or pay any taxes for them.

The problem with Microsoft's designation of these workers as ICs was that it failed to treat them like ICs—that is, people running their own independent businesses. Instead, Microsoft integrated the workers into its workforce: They often worked on teams along with regular employees, sharing the same supervisors, performing identical functions, and working the same core hours. And because Microsoft required that they work onsite, they received admittance card keys, office equipment, and supplies from the company. Microsoft's treatment of the workers clearly spelled out "employee," not IC.

When the IRS audited the company's payroll tax accounts in 1989 and 1990, it determined that Microsoft treated the workers as employees—not ICs who control the manner and means of how their services are performed—and therefore owed taxes for them. Microsoft agreed with the IRS and admitted that the workers should have been classified as employees for tax purposes. The company paid back payroll taxes and overtime for the workers and moved some of them to permanent employee status.

On learning of the IRS's decision, eight of the formerly misclassified workers sued Microsoft for full employee benefits for the time they worked as independent contractors. The workers finally won their lawsuit, and Microsoft had to pay a small fortune to its misclassified workers. *(Vizcaino v. Microsoft Corp.,* 120 F.3d 1006 (9th Cir. 1997).)

This case demonstrates that merely having a worker sign an agreement that he or she is an IC will not change the worker's status in the eyes of the law. Rather, the worker must be treated like an IC on the job. Since the penalties for misclassification can be severe, make sure that everyone who deals with ICs in your company understands that they can't be supervised or otherwise controlled in the same way as employees.

You'll have to decide for yourself whether it makes sense to leave the determination up to these agencies, or whether you feel confident enough to classify your workers on your own.

For businesses with ICs only. If you decide that all of your workers will be independent contractors, the rest of the rules in this chapter won't apply to you. You may still want to read on, however, if you'd like to get an overview of the regulations that apply to businesses with employees.

Hiring ICs triggers some requirements. For instance, if you pay any independent contractor over $600 in a year, you need to report those payments on Form 1099-MISC, then send it to the worker and to the IRS. For in-depth information about hiring independent contractors, see *Working With Independent Contractors,* by Stephen Fishman (Nolo).

B. Special Hurdles for Employers

As soon as you hire your first employee, you unleash a swarm of legal requirements that apply specifically to employers. Not only will you have to pay a number of employment taxes, but you'll also need to register with certain government agencies, pay for certain types of insurance, and comply with various laws, such as those requiring you to keep a smoke-free workplace and to post certain notices at your business premises.

While the many laws that apply to employers are beyond the scope of this book, here's an overview of the major requirements that apply to businesses with employees. If you can't meet your needs by hiring an independent contractor and you must hire an employee, you'll need to consult additional resources to make sure you comply with the many state and federal laws governing employers. (Some additional resources are included at the end of this chapter.)

In general, owners of businesses with one or more employees are required to take a number of steps.

- Report all new hires to your state's employment department within 20 days of the employee's first day of work.
- Obtain workers' compensation insurance, and follow the rules on notifying employees of their rights to workers' compensation benefits. You may purchase this insurance from a state fund or, in most states, from a private insurance company.
- Comply with state and federal job safety laws, administered by the federal Occupational Safety and Health Administration (OSHA) and the agency in your state that governs workplace safety. This includes filing an illness and injury prevention plan, reporting work-related injuries and illnesses that result in lost work-time, and keeping a log of all work-related injuries and illnesses. For more information about OSHA regulations, visit the OSHA website at www.osha.gov, or contact OSHA at U.S. Department of Labor, Occupational Safety & Health Administration, 200 Constitution Avenue, Washington, DC 20210, 800-321-6742.
- Withhold federal income taxes and FICA taxes (which basically consist of Social Security and Medicare taxes) from employees' paychecks, and periodically report and send these withheld taxes to the IRS.
- Report wages and withholding to each employee and to the IRS with Form W-2.
- Pay the employer's portion of Social Security and Medicare tax for each employee, based on the employee's wages. The employer's portion is the same amount as the employee's share: 7.65% of the employee's wages up to $90,000, and 1.45% of wages in excess of that amount, according to rates for the year 2005.
- Withhold state income taxes from employees' paychecks, and periodically deposit them with your state income tax agency.

- Pay federal unemployment taxes. It's the sole responsibility of the employer to pay the Federal Unemployment Tax (FUTA) directly to the IRS; you may not deduct it from employees' paychecks. The general rule is that you must pay FUTA taxes if you paid a total of $1,500 or more in wages in any calendar quarter or if you had one or more employees for at least some part of a day in each of 20 or more calendar weeks (not necessarily consecutive) during the year. The FUTA tax is reported annually on IRS Form 940, *Employer's Annual Federal Unemployment Tax Return,* available online at www.irs.gov/formspubs/index.html.

- Pay state unemployment taxes in many states. Most states require employers to pay unemployment taxes, which go toward a state unemployment insurance fund. Generally, you can take a credit against the federal unemployment tax for amounts you paid on time into state unemployment funds. A list of state unemployment tax agencies is available in IRS Publication 926, *Household Employer's Tax Guide,* available from the IRS's website at www.irs.gov/formspubs/index.html.

- Pay or withhold other employment-related taxes that may be required by your state, such as disability insurance.

Make payroll taxes a top priority expense. The owner of a cash-strapped small business might be tempted to put off paying payroll taxes for a quarter, or a year. "This happens all the time, but it is a huge mistake. It can lead to jail time," says David Rothenberg, an accountant and the CFO of Nolo. You must include payroll taxes in your cash flow planning and then pay those taxes regularly.

Thinking twice about becoming an employer? There's no way around it: Adding employees to your business will greatly complicate your life.

(And this is even without considering many other possibilities, such as providing optional benefits, including health insurance and 401(k) plans.) If there's a way to meet your needs with independent contractors rather than employees, it may be a much more practical road to take. At the very least, you shouldn't jump into hiring employees without having a clear reason to do so.

For more information on being an employer. *The Employer's Legal Handbook,* by Fred S. Steingold, is an indispensable, comprehensive reference for employers that covers the legal rules on hiring, firing, taxes, workplace safety, and much more. For information on hiring independent contractors, be sure to read *Working With Independent Contractors,* by Stephen Fishman. See also *Tax Savvy for Small Business,* by Frederick W. Daily (all published by Nolo).

☑ Chapter 15 Checklist

☐ Become familiar with the legal differences between employees and independent contractors.

☐ Before hiring help, determine whether you need to hire employees or whether you could hire independent contractors instead.

☐ Don't avoid the obligations of having employees by misclassifying your workers as independent contractors. If the IRS decides your workers are really employees, you can face serious penalties, including payment of back payroll taxes.

☐ Make sure you're ready to take care of all the legal, bureaucratic, and tax requirements that apply to businesses with employees before hiring your first one.

Getting Professional Help

Most business owners, especially sole proprietors and partners in general partnerships, won't need to rely on professional help for the vast majority of their day-to-day business affairs. As the chapters in this book have shown, the legal tasks required to start a business, as well as many of those relating to its ongoing operation, involve nothing more than complying with simple bureaucratic requirements, filling out standard forms, and paying fees.

But life's not always so simple, of course. From time to time, you may find yourself feeling like you're in over your head. Maybe you're struggling to decide whether it's a good time, financially speaking, to expand your business. Or perhaps there's a dispute brewing between you and a business partner. These are just a couple of examples of the types of situations where an expert can come in handy.

Even when things are running smoothly, virtually every business should at least occasionally consult an accountant or other tax expert for help in preparing tax returns. A tax professional can also help you manage your business's finances in order to minimize your taxes. Making contact with a lawyer and a tax professional early in your business life is often a sensible step. As your business grows, you'll be able to consult these experts for help with ongoing questions.

Once you decide you want to hire a professional, your next question very likely will be, "How do I find someone I can trust?" This chapter offers strategies that will help you find and hire a professional such as a lawyer or an accountant who's competent and aboveboard.

A. Working With Lawyers

Despite the fact that the attorney section of the Yellow Pages is often the biggest section of the phone book, a good lawyer can be hard to find. This section explains how to find a lawyer who meets your needs and how to make sure you're getting the most for your hard-earned money.

1. What to Look for in a Lawyer

First, you want to make sure to find an attorney who has some experience with small business issues, preferably for your type of small business. Plus, you want someone who's intelligent and competent—two qualities that don't necessarily go hand in hand with having a law degree. And, of course, you want a lawyer whom you can trust.

In today's world of ever-increasing specialization, lawyers often focus their areas of expertise rather narrowly. For example, an expert negotiator may not be an effective courtroom lawyer, and vice versa. Make sure that your lawyer can handle the particular type of problem you're facing, in terms of both its subject matter and the type of work involved.

In addition to finding a lawyer with the skills and experience relevant to your situation, it's important that you and the lawyer get along on a personal level. If an otherwise perfect lawyer—smart, experienced, and trustworthy—is condescending or rude, you should keep looking for someone with better personal skills. This general rule is especially true for small business owners, who will ideally develop a long-term relationship with a lawyer. The better an attorney knows you and your business, the better equipped he or she will be to provide the best advice and assistance for your specific situation.

Finally, you may want to make a special effort to find a lawyer who is willing to work with you collaboratively on certain matters that you can handle at least partially on your own. Handling some routine legal issues, such as amending your partnership agreement or executing a contract for services, may be well within your abilities, though you may be more comfortable having a lawyer review your work or give you limited advice. A trend has recently emerged where lawyers act as coaches for their clients, giving only as much service as the client wants. If you'd like to be more involved with your business's legal matters and minimize the attorney's fees you'll owe, be sure to ask the lawyer directly whether he or she is willing to have this kind of working relationship with you. (Legal coaching is discussed in more detail in Section 3, below.)

For more on hiring and working with lawyers. See *The Lawsuit Survival Guide: A Client's Companion to Litigation*, by Joseph Matthews (Nolo).

2. How to Find a Lawyer

Unfortunately, the easiest and quickest ways to find a lawyer are usually the least effective. Sure, you'll find hundreds of lawyers' names in the Yellow Pages, but how will you choose among them? You'll have the same problem if you look in legal newspapers for attorney ads. By the way, flashy, aggressive advertising is not necessarily a good indicator of quality legal services. Also, watch out for commercial referral services that collect fees from lawyers who are in their referral database. To filter out the lawyers who are wrong for you, you'll need to do more research.

The best way to find a good lawyer is to get a personal referral, preferably from someone who runs a small business. Even better is a referral from an owner of a business that's similar to yours. Book publishers, for instance, face different types of legal issues than do auto repair shops, and would be best served by a lawyer familiar with legal areas such as copyright and freedom of speech.

If you just can't find anyone who can give you a personal referral, try investigating lawyers who work in your industry. One good way to do this is to keep your eyes and ears open for names of attorneys who have worked on cases in your field. For example, a trade magazine might have an article about a current lawsuit involving a business similar to yours that mentions the names of the attorneys working on it. You can also contact organizations and visit websites that focus on your type of business. They can often direct you to lawyers who have worked in your industry. Once you get some names, try calling these lawyers and asking if they're available. If not, there's a good chance they will know someone else who might be able to help you.

Speak with the lawyer personally. You can probably get a good idea of how an attorney operates by paying close attention to the way your call is handled. Is the lawyer available right away, and, if not, is your call promptly returned? Is the lawyer willing to spend at least a few minutes talking with you to determine whether the two of you are good fits? Do you get a good feeling from your conversation? How you're treated during your initial call can be a good indicator of how the lawyer treats clients in general.

3. Using a Lawyer as a Coach

In a traditional attorney/client relationship, a client hires an attorney to take care of a legal problem and then hands over all responsibility for—and control over—the matter to the lawyer. While some clients like it this way, many would rather be more involved in their cases, both to maintain some control and to save money on legal fees. But, until recently, limited legal help from a lawyer wasn't much of an option. Most lawyers wouldn't take cases unless they could handle them fully on their own.

A new model of legal services has finally emerged. In this approach, sometimes called "legal coaching" or "unbundled legal services," a lawyer provides only the services that a client wants, and nothing more. For example, a client who wants legal help in drafting a contract can arrange a short consultation with a lawyer to get answers to general questions, go home and draft the contract, then fax it to the lawyer, who will review it and suggest changes. Or, a client who wants to represent himself or herself in small claims court can use a lawyer to help draft motions and prepare for hearings but otherwise pursue the case alone.

For a small business owner, using a lawyer as a coach can be especially useful. More often than not, the legal issues that arise in the course of business are relatively simple, and—with a bit of good legal advice—most businesspeople can handle them. Many times, a business owner needs nothing more than some guidance through the bureaucratic maze that small businesses need to navigate. For instance, a businessperson facing a zoning conflict may be perfectly served by a five-minute explanation from a legal coach on the process of appealing a planning commission's decision. Rather than hiring an attorney for upwards of $1,000 to deal with the problem, using a coach might cost $50 and enable the business owner to proceed alone.

Despite the good sense to this approach, it still can take some effort to find a lawyer who is willing to be just a coach. To find a legal coach, use the same strategies discussed above (personal referrals, for example), but take the extra step of asking the lawyer directly whether he or she is willing to help you in your efforts to solve your own legal problems. If you don't find one right away, be persistent. In today's increasingly competitive legal marketplace, it's becoming easier to find lawyers who are willing to be flexible in the services they offer.

4. Dealing With Bills and Payments

Before you hire any lawyer, be sure you fully understand how your fees will be calculated. All too often, clients are unpleasantly surprised by their bills, because they didn't pay enough attention to the billing terms when they hired the lawyer. For instance, make sure you understand who's responsible for paying for things such as court fees, copy fees, transcription costs, and phone bills. These costs aren't trivial and can quickly send your otherwise affordable bill into the keep-you-awake-at-night range.

Lawyers generally use one of the following methods of calculating fees for their services.

- **Hourly fees.** This arrangement works just like it sounds: You pay the attorney's hourly rate for the number of hours the attorney spends on your case. Simple as this system is, there are some details to consider. First, find out what hourly increments the lawyer uses for billing. For instance, if an attorney bills in half-hour increments, you'll be charged for a full half-hour even if you talk for just five minutes. That can easily total $100 or more for a five-minute phone call—a rate that would make even AT&T blush. You'd be better off if your lawyer uses ten- or 15-minute periods, though not all attorneys break down their time into such small increments.

    Another issue to ask about is whether all time spent on the case—even if the attorney isn't doing the work—is billed at the attorney's regular rate. For example, it's reasonable to expect a discounted rate for time spent by the attorney's administrative staff on making copies or organizing paperwork. Make sure that the hourly fee for the attorney applies only to the work of the actual attorney.

    Hourly fees for attorneys range from $100 or so to over $400 per hour. High rates may reflect a lawyer's extensive experience—or they might simply reflect a need to pay for a swank office. Don't pay the highest rates unless you feel the lawyer's expertise—not that Armani suit—is worth it.

- **Flat fees.** For some types of cases, attorneys will charge a flat fee for a specific task, such as negotiating a contract or filing Articles of Incorporation. As long as the job goes as expected, you'll pay only the agreed price, regardless of how many hours the lawyer spent on the job. If the lawyer hits a snag, however, or if the case becomes convoluted for some reason, the price may go up. Be sure you and the lawyer are on the same page regarding the situations that may result in a higher fee. Also, find out if any expenses, such as court costs or copy fees, are charged in addition to the flat fee.

- **Contingency fees.** In a contingency fee arrangement, you pay an attorney's fee only if the lawyer wins money for you through a court judgment or a negotiated settlement. In that case, the fee you'd pay would be a percentage of the monetary award, usually one-third to one-half. In contingency fee arrangements, you need to be especially careful of costs such as travel expenses, transcription fees, and phone bills. If you lose your case, you won't owe attorneys' fees (because your lawyer didn't recover any money). But you will often be responsible for the lawyer's out-of-pocket expenses while working on your case.

  Small business matters don't typically require contingency fee arrangements. This payment method is usually used in personal injury cases and others in which a plaintiff sues someone in hopes of winning a large money award.

- **Retainers.** Sometimes you can hire a lawyer to be more or less "on call" by paying a regular fee (usually monthly) called a retainer. This type of arrangement is useful when you have regular, ongoing legal needs such as contract review or negotiation. Based on your expected needs, you and the lawyer settle on a mutually accept-

able monthly fee. Then you simply have the lawyer take care of any routine legal matters that arise. If you run into a sudden, complex legal dispute, or if your problems escalate greatly, you'll likely have to make additional payments. For this type of arrangement to work, it's important that you and the lawyer have a clear understanding of the routine services that you expect. Unless your legal needs are regular and predictable, a retainer arrangement is probably not your best option.

State laws may require a fee agreement to be in writing in some cases, such as if your lawyer estimates the total cost of legal services to be more than $1,000, or if you have a contingency fee arrangement. Even if it's not legally required, it's always a good idea to get your fee agreement in writing. A written agreement will help prevent disputes over billing and is the best way to avoid getting gouged.

B. Working With Accountants and Others

Many of the issues that small business owners face can be solved by professionals other than lawyers. In particular, tax professionals are often indispensable in helping you deal with tax laws, which have a huge impact on your business both financially and legally. In fact, tax advice is so essential to a successful small business that we recommend that every small business owner consult with a tax expert at least occasionally, say, once a year.

Obviously, you want to manage your business and the money flowing through it so as to minimize your tax bill. But you also need to be extremely careful not to violate any tax laws—which are insanely complex—and to avoid making simple mistakes that can result in costly penalties. While complicated tax troubles may indeed call for a tax attorney, many other more common questions can usually be answered by an accountant.

1. Matching People to Your Needs

For routine maintenance of your books, you probably don't need the experience—or expense—of an accountant (certified or otherwise). An experienced bookkeeper will be able to put in place an effective system of tracking your income and expenses and staying on top of your important bills, including the various taxes your business will owe. Depending on the complexity of your business, you may even decide to do your own bookkeeping—a job that's undoubtedly easier these days with the availability of accounting software. As your business grows, however, an experienced bookkeeper will likely become a valuable investment.

If you find yourself seeking specific tax advice or encountering a tricky financial problem, you may need to go up a step on the professional ladder and hire an accountant who's intimate with tax laws. The top dogs of accountants are called certified public accountants (CPAs), who are licensed and regulated by the state. Uncertified accountants, called public accountants, also may be licensed by your state. Since the licensing requirements for CPAs are more stringent, they are considered to be the most experienced and knowledgeable type of accountants and, accordingly, will be the most expensive.

In addition to bookkeepers and accountants, there are other professionals out there who specialize in tax preparation. The main thing to keep in mind is that some are licensed and some are not. An enrolled agent (EA) is a tax professional, licensed by the IRS, who can answer tax questions and help you prepare your returns. Others who simply use the title "tax preparer" or "tax return preparer" may not be licensed at all. If a tax professional doesn't have a license as an enrolled agent or as a public or certified public accountant, it may mean that the "professional" has no official qualifications whatsoever.

The bottom line is that you should hire the person who is best equipped to meet your needs. Obviously, you shouldn't pay a CPA to do simple bookkeeping, nor should you use a bookkeeper for preparing complex tax returns. You'll need to decide for yourself what kind of professional to hire for your financial tasks.

2. Finding Good Professional Help

Finding a tax professional is a lot like finding a lawyer: Your goal is to find someone both competent and trustworthy. The strategies discussed above for finding a lawyer are equally useful in finding other professionals. Getting a personal referral is the best way to find someone you can trust. Referrals from businesspeople in your field are particularly valuable. Since virtually every business has consulted a tax pro at one point or another, it shouldn't be too hard to get a decent list of names.

As with attorneys, choose a tax professional carefully, with an eye to developing a long-term relationship. Don't be shy about asking questions. Find out about the person's experience with small businesses similar to yours, and about his or her knowledge of bookkeeping methods, the tax code, the IRS, or anything else that's relevant to the work you want the professional to do for you.

Also be sure you understand the professional's fee structure up front, before any work is done. Most charge hourly fees, which vary a great deal depending on what kind of qualifications the professional has. Like your attorney fee agreement, your fee agreement with a tax professional should be in writing. Written fee agreements reduce the possibility of disputes over the bill.

C. Internet Legal Research

Some of the legal questions you may run into won't warrant an expensive consultation with an attorney but may be beyond the scope of a self-help book. For instance, you may need to look up specific consumer protection regulations on warranties and advertising, or find out what your state's rules are on hiring and firing practices. If you don't want to call your lawyer every time you have a question, you might consider doing a little legal research yourself.

Finding basic small business law is usually not difficult—much of the information you'll need can be found on the Internet. Start by visiting Nolo's website at www.nolo.com and checking under the Business & Human Resources tab to see if your question has already been answered, or to get some background information in the area of the law that interests you.

Here are some other websites that offer helpful information on small business and tax law:

- National Federation of Independent Business at www.nfib.com. Here you can find small business news and practical information.
- Internal Revenue Service at www.irs.gov. You can download forms and instructions as well as a wide range of publications that do a fairly good job of explaining the tax laws.
- U.S. Small Business Administration at www.sba.gov. This site has a lot of good information on starting and financing your own business. The SBA also offers links to state websites related to business issues.
- SCORE (Service Corps of Retired Executives) at www.score.org. SCORE's association of retired executives and business owners offers email counseling and mentoring and an excellent directory of small business resources on the Web.
- The Thomas Legislative Information site at http://thomas.loc.gov. Here you can read small business bills pending in Congress, as well as laws that have recently been adopted.

Help with legalese. If, during your legal meandering, you come across strange phrases like "blue sky," "naked option," or "commercial frustration" and you just know there's got to be a legal meaning behind them, try looking them up in Nolo's online glossary at www.nolo .com under the Business & Human Resources tab.

In addition to Nolo.com and other business-oriented sites, you should become familiar with your state's official website. These sites often offer valuable information for small businesses such as start-up registration requirements, state tax rules, laws on corporations and LLCs, and much more. Keep in mind that there's a lot of variation from state to state in how much info you'll find but, in general, the states have been rapidly improving their online information systems and making their sites more useful and accessible for citizens. (On the CD-ROM that comes with this book, you'll find computer files that contain links to state websites, including business-related sites and tax sites. These files are simple to use with your Web browser; Appendix B explains how to use them.)

More help with legal research. There may be times when you'll need more guidance in researching a particular business problem. One resource that teaches you how to find answers to your legal questions is Nolo's *Legal Research: How to Find & Understand the Law,* by Stephen R. Elias and Susan Levinkind. Learning how to use legal resources online or at the law library will teach you to take care of a wide range of simple, everyday matters yourself rather than paying someone else to handle them.

Chapter 16 Checklist

☐ Ask business associates and friends for recommendations for lawyers, as well as accountants or other tax professionals. Also check trade magazines and other industry sources.

☐ Try to find a lawyer who will work as a legal coach, if that approach appeals to you.

☐ Get your fee agreements in writing.

☐ Become familiar with online sources of legal information such as Nolo.com, the IRS website, and your official state website.

State Contact Information

This appendix offers contact information for various agencies that deal with businesses and taxes for each state. While every attempt has been made to direct you to the most appropriate agency or office for each topic, please keep in mind that governmental agencies often overlap and may not be organized in any logical structure. One state agency may have several offices or programs under its umbrella, and it may be under the administration of yet another office. Often, a governmental agency may provide information or laws—at its website, for instance—that are actually administered by a different agency. And, of course, addresses, phone numbers, and websites are subject to change. In other words, when it comes to state government offices, it's a jungle out there.

The goal with this appendix is to direct you to the office that not only provides the best information on the subject, but that also has some actual authority over the matter. For example, the preference is to provide contact information to an official state licensing office rather than the state's chamber of commerce, because even if the chamber offered helpful business licensing information, it wouldn't have authority over licensing matters. This appendix also directs you to specific divisions within larger agencies, such as the sales tax division within a state's tax and revenue agency where that information is available.

A couple of other things to keep in mind: As much as possible, walk-in addresses are provided for the agencies listed here, though sometimes only a mailing address was available. Be sure to call before going to the office in person to make sure that office has a service center open to the public. Finally, while many state offices offer toll-free phone numbers, some of them are only for calls within the state.

Using the Charts From the CD-ROM

Electronic copies of the charts in this appendix are included on the CD-ROM disk in Adobe Acrobat PDF format. You must have the Adobe Acrobat Reader installed on your computer to use these forms.

For your convenience, these charts have been included on the CD with "hot" URLs. If you want to go to a website listed on one of the charts in this appendix, you can open the appropriate file and simply click on the URL. Clicking on the link will launch your Web browser and take you to the indicated website. Linked URLs will be green.

The URL links have been provided for your convenience. However, things change rapidly and without warning on the Internet, so there's a chance that not all the links will remain live.

For more detailed instructions on how to use the CD-ROM, follow the instructions in Appendix B.

List of Charts Included on the CD-ROM

The following charts—included in this appendix—are also included on the CD-ROM:

File Name	Chart Name
Information.pdf	Small Business Start-Up Information
TaxAgency.pdf	State Tax Agencies
SalesTax.pdf	State Sales Tax or Seller's Permit Agencies
LLCOffices.pdf	LLC Offices
Unemployment.pdf	State Unemployment Compensation Agencies

Small Business Start-Up Information

Alabama

Department of Revenue
Sales, Use, & Business Tax Division, Severance
  & License Section
Gordon Persons Building
50 N. Ripley Street, Room 3103
Montgomery, AL 36104
334-353-7827
www.revenue.alabama.gov

Alaska

Department of Community and Economic
  Development
Division of Occupational Licensing
333 Willoughby Avenue, 9th Floor
State Office Building
Juneau, AK 99801
907-465-2534
www.commerce.state.ak.us/occ

Arizona

Department of Commerce
Small Business Services
1700 W. Washington Street
Phoenix, AZ 85007
602-771-1196
www.azcommerce.com/smallbus/default.asp

Arkansas

Department of Economic Development
One Capitol Mall
Little Rock, AR 72201
800-ARKANSAS
501-682-1121
www.1800arkansas.com

California

Small Business Loan Guarantee Program
980 9th Street, Suite 1500
Sacramento, CA 95814
916-323-5825
www.commerce.ca.gov

Colorado

Small Business Development Center
Business Assistance Center
1625 Broadway, Suite 1700
Denver, CO 80202
303-892-3840
www.coloradosbdc.org

Connecticut

Connecticut Business Response Center
805 Brook Street, Building #4
Rocky Hill, CT 06067
800-392-2122
860-571-7136
www.cerc.com

Delaware

Division of Revenue
Carvel Street Office Building
820 N. French Street
Wilmington, DE 19899
800-292-7826
302-577-8200
www.state.de.us/revenue

District of Columbia

Department of Consumer and Regulatory Affairs
941 N. Capitol Street, NE
Washington, DC 20002
202-442-4400
http://dcra.dc.gov

Florida

Enterprise Florida, Inc.
390 N. Orange Avenue, Suite 1300
Orlando, FL 32801
407-316-4600
www.eflorida.com

Georgia

Secretary of State
First Stop Business Information Center
Suite 315, West Tower
2 Martin Luther King, Jr. Drive
Atlanta, GA 30334
404-656-2817
www.gacorporations.org

Hawaii

Department of Commerce and Consumer Affairs
Business Registration Division
335 Merchant Street, Room 203
Honolulu, HI 96813
808-586-2744
www.businessregistrations.com

Idaho

Department of Commerce
700 W. State Street
P.O. Box 83720-0093
Boise, ID 83720
208-334-2470
www.cl.idaho.gov

Illinois

Department of Commerce and Community
   Affairs
First Stop Business Information Center
100 W. Randolph Street, Suite 3-400
Chicago, IL 60601
312-814-7179
www.commerce.state.il.us

Indiana

Department of Commerce
One N. Capitol, Suite 700
Indianapolis, IN 46204
317-232-8800
www.iedc.in.gov

Iowa

Department of Economic Development
Small Business Resource Office
200 E. Grand
Des Moines, IA 50309
515-242-4700
www.iowa.gov/state/main/business_portal/
   index.html

Kansas

Department of Commerce and Housing
KSBusiness Center
1000 SW Jackson, Suite 100
Topeka, KS 66612
785-296-3481
http://kansascommerce.com

Kentucky

Kentucky Cabinet for Economic Development
300 W. Broadway
Frankfort, KY 40601
800-626-2930
502-564-7140
www.thinkkentucky.com/kyedc/busstart.asp

Louisiana

Secretary of State
First Stop Shop Division
8549 United Plaza Boulevard
P.O. Box 44279
Baton Rouge, LA 70804
225-342-4479
www.sec.state.la.us/comm/fss/fss-index.htm

Maine

Department of Economic and Community
   Development
Office of Business Development
59 State House Station
Augusta, ME 04333
207-624-9804
www.econdevmaine.com

Maryland

Department of Business and Economic
   Development
217 E. Redwood Street, 12th Floor
Baltimore, MD 21202
888-Choosemd
www.blis.state.md.us

Massachusetts

Office of Business Development
Department of Economic Development
10 Park Plaza, Suite 3730
Boston, MA 02116
617-973-8600
www.mass.gov

Michigan

Economic Development Corporation
300 N. Washington Square
Lansing, MI 48913
517-373-9808
http://medc.michigan.org

Minnesota

Department of Employment and Economic
   Development
Small Business Assistance Office
1st National Bank Building
332 Minnesota Street, Suite E200
St. Paul, MN 55101
651-297-5770
www.mnsbdc.com

Mississippi

Development Authority
501 N. West Street
Jackson, MS 39201
601-359-3155
www.mississippi.org

Missouri

Missouri Small Business Development Center
410 S. Sixth Street
Columbia, MO 65211
573-882-0344
www.missouribusiness.net/sbdc/centers.asp

Montana

Department of Commerce
Small Business Development Center
301 S. Park Avenue
Helena, MT 59620
406-841-2700
www.commerce.mt.gov/BRD_SBDC.asp

Nebraska

Department of Economic Development
301 Centennial Mall S
Lincoln, NE 68509
800-426-6505
www.neded.org

Nevada

Department of Business and Industry
555 E. Washington Avenue, Suite 4900
Las Vegas, NV 89101
702-486-2750
http://dbi.state.nv.us

New Hampshire

University of New Hampshire
The Whittemore School of Business
108 McConnell Hall
Durham, NH 03824
603-862-2200
www.nhsbdc.org

New Jersey

Division of Revenue
Business Gateway Services
225 W. State Street
Trenton, NJ 08608
609-292-9292
www.state.nj.us/njbgs

New Mexico

Economic Development Department
1100 St. Francis Drive
Santa Fe, NM 87503
800-374-3061
505-827-0300
www.nmbiz.com

New York

Governor's Office of Regulatory Reform
Empire State Plaza
Agency Building, 1-4th Floor
P.O. Box 2107
Albany, NY 12220
800-342-3464
518-474-8275
www.gorr.state.ny.us/gorr/startbus.html

North Carolina

North Carolina Department of Commerce
Business License Information Office
4344 Mail Service Center
Raleigh, NC 27699
800-228-8443
919-715-2864
www.secretary.state.nc.us/blio/default.asp

North Dakota

U.S. Small Business Administration
700 E. Main, 2nd Floor
P.O. Box 5509
Bismarck, ND 58506
701-328-5850
www.sba.gov

Ohio

Greater Columbus Chamber of Commerce
37 N. High Street
Columbus, OH 43215
614-221-1321
www.columbus.org

Oklahoma

Tax Commission
2501 N. Lincoln Boulevard
Connors Building, Capitol Complex
Oklahoma City, OK 73194
405-521-3160
www.oktax.state.ok.us

Oregon

Secretary of State
Business Information Center
255 Capitol Street NE, Suite 151
Salem, OR 97310
503-986-2200
www.filinginoregon.com/contactus/index/htm

Pennsylvania

Department of Community and Economic
    Development
Center for Entrepreneurial Assistance
Commonwealth Keystone Building
400 North Street, 4th Floor
Harrisburg, PA 17120
800-280-3801
717-783-5700
www.newpa.com/default.aspx?id=25

Rhode Island

Economic Development Corporation
One W. Exchange Street
Providence, RI 02903
401-222-2601
www.riedc.com

South Carolina

Small Business Development Center
1705 College Street
Columbia, SC 29208
803-777-4907
http://scsbdc.moore.sc.edu

South Dakota

Governor's Office of Economic Development
711 E. Wells Avenue
Pierre, SD 57501
800-872-6190
605-773-3301
www.sdgreatprofits.com

Tennessee

Department of Economic and Community
  Development
Business Services
312 8th Avenue N, 10th Floor
Nashville, TN 37243
615-741-2626
www.state.tn.us/ecd

Texas

Department of Economic Development
221 E. 11th Street, 4th Floor
Austin, TX 78701
512-936-0101
www.governor.state.tx.us

Utah

Department of Community and Economic
  Development
324 S. State Street, Suite 500
Salt Lake City, UT 84111
801-538-8700
http://community.utah.gov

Vermont

Department of Economic Development
109 State Street
Montpelier, VT 05609
800-341-2211
802-828-3221
www.gmpvt.com/vtecdev.htm

Virginia

Economic Development Partnership
901 E. Byrd Street
P.O. Box 798
Richmond, VA 23218
804-371-8100
http://yesvirginia.org

Washington

Department of Licensing
Master License Service
1125 Washington Street, SE
P.O. Box 9034
Olympia, WA 98507
360-664-1400
www.dol.wa.gov

West Virginia

Secretary of State
Bldg. 1, Suite 157-K
1900 Kanawha Boulevard E
Charleston, WV 25305
304-558-8000
www.wvsos.com/common/startbusiness.htm

Wisconsin

Department of Commerce
201 W. Washington Avenue
P.O. Box 7970
Madison, WI 53707
800-HELPBUS
608-266-1018
www.commerce.state.wi.us

Wyoming

Small Business Development Center
1000 E. University, Dept. 3922
Laramie, WY 82071
800-348-5194
307-766-3505
http://uwyo.edu/sbdc

State Tax Agencies

Alabama

Department of Revenue
Gordon Persons Building
50 N. Ripley Street
Montgomery, AL 36132
334-242-1170
www.ador.state.al.us

Alaska

Department of Revenue—Tax Division
333 W. Willoughby Avenue, 11th Floor Side B
P.O. Box 110420
Juneau, AK 99811
907-465-2320
www.tax.state.ak.us

Arizona

Department of Revenue
1600 W. Monroe
Phoenix, AZ 85007
800-352-4090
602-255-3381
www.revenue.state.az.us

Arkansas

Department of Finance and Administration
1509 W. 7th, Suite 401
P.O. Box 3278
Little Rock, AR 72203
501-682-2242
www.arkansas.gov/dfa

California

Franchise Tax Board
3321 Power Inn Road, Suite 250
P.O. Box 942840
Sacramento, CA 94240
800-852-5711
www.ftb.ca.gov

Colorado

Department of Revenue
1375 Sherman Street, Room 204
Denver, CO 80261
303-238-7378
www.taxcolorado.com

Connecticut

Department of Revenue Services
Taxpayer Services Division
25 Sigourney Street
Hartford, CT 06106
800-382-9463 (within the state)
860-297-5962
www.ct.gov/drs

Delaware

Department of Finance—Division of Revenue
Carvel State Office Building
820 N. French Street
Wilmington, DE 19801
302-577-8205
www.state.de.us/revenue/default.shtml

District of Columbia

Office of Tax and Revenue
Customer Service Center
941 N. Capitol Street NE, 1st Floor
Washington, DC 20002
202-727-4829
http://brc.dc.gov/tax/tax.asp

Florida

Department of Revenue
Tax Information Services
1379 Blountstown Highway
Tallahassee, FL 32304
800-352-3671
850-488-6800
http://sun6.dms.state.fl.us/dor/taxes

Georgia

Department of Revenue
1800 Century Center Boulevard, NE
Atlanta, GA 30345
404-417-4857
www.georgia.gov/00/channel_title/
  0,2094,4802_4971,00.html

Hawaii

Department of Taxation
Taxpayer Services
830 Punchbowl Street
P.O. Box 259
Honolulu, HI 96809
800-222-3229
808-587-4242
808-587-6515 (Jan.–Apr. 20)
www.state.hi.us/tax/tax.html

Idaho

State Tax Commission
800 Park Boulevard, Plaza IV
Boise, ID 83712
800-972-7660
208-334-7660
http://tax.idaho.gov/index.html

Illinois

Department of Revenue
James R. Thompson Center
Concourse Level
100 W. Randolph Street
Chicago, IL 60601
217-782-3336
www.revenue.state.il.us

Indiana

Department of Revenue
100 N. Senate Avenue
202 State Office Building
Indianapolis, IN 46204
317-233-4018
www.in.gov/dor

Iowa

Department of Revenue and Finance
Taxpayer Services
Hoover Building
1305 Walnut, 4th Floor
Des Moines, IA 50319
800-367-3388
515-281-3114
www.state.ia.us/tax/business/business.html

Kansas

Department of Revenue
Taxpayer Assistance Center
Docking State Office Building
915 SW Harrison Street, Room 150
Topeka, KS 66612
785-368-8222
www.ksrevenue.org

Kentucky

Revenue Cabinet
200 Fair Oaks Lane
Frankfort, KY 40620
502-564-4581
http://revenue.ky.gov

Louisiana

Department of Revenue
617 N. Third Street
Baton Rouge, LA 70802
225-219-7318
www.rev.state.la.us

Maine

Revenue Services
24 State House Station
Augusta, ME 04333
207-287-2076
www.state.me.us/revenue

Maryland

State Comptroller
Taxpayer Registration Assistance Center
301 W. Preston Street, Room 206
Baltimore, MD 21201
800-492-1751
410-767-1313
http://business.marylandtaxes.com

Massachusetts

Department of Revenue
Customer Service Bureau
200 Arlington Street
Chelsea, MA 02150
800-392-6089
617-887-6367
www.dor.state.ma.us

Michigan

Department of Treasury
Lansing, MI 48922
517-373-3200
www.michigan.gov/treasury

Minnesota

Department of Revenue
Harold Stassen Building
600 N. Robert Street
St. Paul, MN 55146
651-296-3781
www.taxes.state.mn.us

Mississippi

State Tax Commission
1577 Springridge Road
Raymond, MS 39154
601-923-7390
www.mstc.state.ms.us/regist.htm

Missouri

Department of Revenue
Division of Taxation & Collection
301 W. High Street, Room 330
Jefferson City, MO 65101
800-877-6881
http://dor.mo.gov

Montana

Department of Revenue
Attn: Business Tax
P.O. Box 5805
Helena, MT 59604
406-444-6900
www.discoveringmontana.com/revenue

Nebraska

Department of Revenue
301 Centennial Mall S
P.O. Box 94818
Lincoln, NE 68509
800-742-7474
402-471-5729
www.revenue.state.ne.us

Nevada

Department of Taxation
1550 E. College Parkway, Suite 115
Carson City, NV 89706
775-684-2000
http://tax.state.nv.us

New Hampshire

Department of Revenue Administration
45 Chenell Drive
P.O. Box 457
Concord, NH 03302
603-271-2191
www.nh.gov/revenue

New Jersey

Division of Taxation
Taxation Building
50 Barrack Street, 1st Floor
Trenton, NJ 08695
609-292-6400
www.state.nj.us/treasury/taxation

New Mexico

Taxation & Revenue Department
1100 S. St. Francis Drive
P.O. Box 630
Santa Fe, NM 87504
505-827-0700
www.state.nm.us/tax

New York

Department of Taxation & Finance
W. Averill Harriman Campus
Albany, NY 12227
800-972-1233
www.tax.state.ny.us/sbc/default.htm

North Carolina

Department of Revenue
501 N. Wilmington Street
Raleigh, NC 27604
877-252-3052
www.dor.state.nc.us

North Dakota

Office of State Tax Commissioner
State Capitol
600 E. Boulevard Avenue
Bismarck, ND 58505
701-328-2770
www.dor.state.nc.us

Ohio

Department of Taxation
Taxpayer Services Division
800 Freeway Drive N
Columbus, OH 43229
614-387-1801
www.state.oh.us/tax

Oklahoma

Tax Commission
2501 N. Lincoln Boulevard
Connors Building, Capitol Complex
Oklahoma City, OK 73194
405-521-3160
www.oktax.state.ok.us/oktax/busreg.html

Oregon

Department of Revenue
955 Center Street NE
Salem, OR 97301
800-356-4222
503-378-4988
www.dor.state.or.us

Pennsylvania

Department of Revenue
Strawberry Square
Fourth and Walnut Streets Lobby
Harrisburg, PA 17128
717-787-1064
www.revenue.state.pa.us

Rhode Island

Division of Taxation
One Capitol Hill
Providence, RI 02908
401-222-3050
www.tax.state.ri.us

South Carolina

Department of Revenue
Columbia Main Office
301 Gervais Street
P.O. Box 125
Columbia, SC 29214
803-898-5000
www.sctax.org

South Dakota

Department of Revenue
445 E. Capitol Avenue
Pierre, SD 57501
605-773-3311
800-829-9188
www.state.sd.us/revenue

Tennessee

Department of Revenue
500 Deaderick Street
Nashville, TN 37242
800-342-1003
615-253-0600
www.state.tn.us/revenue

Texas

Comptroller of Public Accounts
Lyndon B. Johnson State Office Building
111 E. 17th Street
Austin, TX 78774
877-662-8375
512-463-4865
www.cpa.state.tx.us

Utah

State Tax Commission
210 N. 1950 West
Salt Lake City, UT 84134
800-662-4335
801-297-2200
http://tax.utah.gov

Vermont

Department of Taxes
Taxpayer Services Division
109 State Street
Pavilion Office Building
Montpelier, VT 05601
802-828-2505
www.state.vt.us/tax/index.htm

Virginia

Department of Taxation
3600 W. Broad, Suite 160
Richmond, VA 23230
804-367-8037
www.tax.virginia.gov

Washington

Department of Revenue
2101 4th Avenue, Suite 1400
Seattle, WA 98121
800-647-7706
206-956-3000
http://dor.wa.gov

West Virginia

State Tax Department
1206 Quarrier Street
Charleston, WV 25301
304-558-3333
800-982-8297
www.state.wv.us/taxdiv

Wisconsin

Department of Revenue
2135 Rimrock Road
Madison, WI 53713
608-266-2772
www.dor.state.wi.us

Wyoming

Department of Revenue
Herschler Building, 2nd Floor W
122 W. 25th Street
Cheyenne, WY 82002
307-777-7961
http://revenue.state.wy.us

State Sales Tax or Seller's Permit Agencies

Alabama

Department of Revenue
Sales, Use, and Business Tax Section
Taxpayer Service Center
1021 Madison Avenue
Montgomery, AL 36104
334-242-1490
www.ador.state.al.us/salestax/index.html

Alaska

No state sales tax.

Arizona

Department of Revenue
Transaction Privilege (Sales) and Use Tax
1600 W. Monroe
Phoenix, AZ 85007
800-843-7196
602-255-2060
www.revenue.state.az.us

Arkansas

Sales and Use Tax
Department of Finance and Administration
Joel Ledbetter Building, Room 1340
1800 7th Street
Little Rock, AR 72201
501-682-7104
www.arkansas.gov/dfa

California

Board of Equalization
3321 Power Inn Road, Suite 210
Sacramento, CA 95826
800-400-7115
916-227-6700
www.boe.ca.gov

Colorado

Department of Revenue
1375 Sherman Street, Room 204
Denver, CO 80261
303-238-7378
www.revenue.state.co.us

Connecticut

Department of Revenue Services
Taxpayer Services Division
25 Sigourney Street
Hartford, CT 06106
800-382-9463
860-297-5962
www.ct.gov/drs

Delaware

(No state sales tax, but state gross receipts tax.)
Department of Finance—Division of Revenue
820 N. French Street
Wilmington, DE 19801
302-577-8200
www.state.de.us/revenue

District of Columbia

Office of Tax and Revenue
Customer Service Center
941 N. Capitol Street NE, 1st Floor
Washington, DC 20002
202-727-4829
http://cfo.dc.gov

Florida

Department of Revenue
Registration Information
5050 W. Tennessee Street
Tallahassee, FL 32399
800-352-3671
850-488-6800
http://sun6.dms.state.fl.us/dor/taxes/
    sales_tax.html

Georgia

Department of Revenue
Sales and Use Tax Division
1800 Century Center Boulevard NE, Suite 8214
Atlanta, GA 30345
404-417-4477
www.etax.dor.ga.gov

Hawaii

Taxpayer Services Branch
830 Punchbowl Street
Honolulu, HI 96813
800-222-3229
808-587-4242
www.state.hi.us/tax/tax.html

Idaho

State Tax Commission
800 Park Boulevard, Plaza IV
Boise, ID 83712
800-972-7660
208-334-7660
http://revenue.ky.gov

Illinois

Department of Revenue
James R. Thompson Center
Concourse Level
100 W. Randolph Street
Chicago, IL 60601
217-782-3336
www.revenue.state.il.us

Indiana

Department of Revenue
100 N. Senate Avenue
Indiana Government Center N, Room N105
Indianapolis, IN 46204
317-233-4015
www.in.gov/dor

Iowa

Department of Revenue
Taxpayer Services
1305 E. Walnut
Des Moines, IA 50319
800-367-3388
515-281-3114
www.state.ia.us/tax

Kansas

Department of Revenue
Docking State Office Building, 1st Floor
915 SW Harrison Street
Topeka, KS 66626
785-368-8222
www.ksrevenue.org

Kentucky

Revenue Cabinet
200 Fair Oaks Lane
Frankfort, KY 40620
502-564-4581
http://revenue.ky.gov

Louisiana

Department of Revenue
617 N. Third Street
Baton Rouge, LA 70802
Sales Tax Division Taxpayer
Assistance Section:
225-219-7318
www.rev.state.la.us

Maine

Revenue Services
Sales and Use Tax Division
P.O. Box 1065
Augusta, ME 04332
207-624-9693
www.state.me.us/revenue/salesuse/
   homepage.html

Maryland

State Comptroller
Taxpayer Registration Assistance Center
State Office Building
301 W. Preston Street, Room 206
Baltimore, MD 21201
800-492-1751
410-767-1300 (within the state)
http://business.marylandtaxes.com/taxinfo/
   salesanduse/default.asp

Massachusetts

Department of Revenue
Customer Service Bureau
200 Arlington Street
Chelsea, MA 02150
800-392-6089
617-887-6367
www.dor.state.ma.us

Michigan

Department of Treasury
Sales, Use, and Withholding Taxes Section
Treasury Building
Lansing, MI 48922
517-373-3200
www.michigan.gov/treasury

Minnesota

Department of Revenue
600 N. Robert Street
St. Paul, MN 55101
651-296-6181
www.taxes.state.mn.us/taxes/sales/forms.shtml

Mississippi

State Tax Commission
1577 Springridge Road
Raymond, MS 39154
601-923-7015
www.mstc.state.ms.us

Missouri

Department of Revenue
Taxation and Collection
301 W. High Street, Room 330
Jefferson City, MO 65101
573-751-2836
http://dor.mo.gov

Montana

No general sales tax.

Nebraska

Department of Revenue
301 Centennial Mall S
P.O. Box 94818
Lincoln, NE 68509
800-742-7474
www.revenue.state.ne.us

Nevada

Department of Taxation
1550 E. College Parkway, Suite 115
Carson City, NV 89706
775-684-2000
http://tax.state.nv.us

New Hampshire

No state sales tax.

New Jersey

Division of Taxation
Taxation Building
50 Barrack Street, 1st Floor
Trenton, NJ 08695
609-292-6400
www.state.nj.us/treasury/taxation

New Mexico

Taxation & Revenue Department
1100 S. St. Francis Drive
P.O. Box 630
Santa Fe, NM 87504
505-827-0700
www.state.nm.us/tax

New York

Department of Taxation & Finance
Sales Tax Registration
W. Averill Harriman Campus
Albany, NY 12227
800-972-1233
www.tax.state.ny.us/nyshome/stidx.htm

North Carolina

Department of Revenue
Sales and Use Tax Division
501 N. Wilmington Street
Raleigh, NC 27604
919-733-2151
www.dor.state.nc.us/taxes/sales

North Dakota

Office of State Tax Commissioner
State Capitol
600 E. Boulevard Avenue
Bismarck, ND 58505
701-328-2770
www.nd.gov/tax

Ohio

Department of Taxation
Sales and Use Tax Division
30 E. Broad Street, 20th Floor
Columbus, OH 43215
888-405-4039
http://tax.ohio.gov

Oklahoma

Tax Commission
2501 N. Lincoln Boulevard
Connors Building, Capitol Complex
Oklahoma City, OK 73194
405-521-4321
www.oktax.state.ok.us/oktax/busreg.html

Oregon

No state sales tax.

Pennsylvania

Department of Revenue
Strawberry Square
Fourth and Walnut Streets Lobby
Harrisburg, PA 17128
717-787-1064
www.revenue.state.pa.us

Rhode Island

Division of Taxation
One Capitol Hill
Providence, RI 02908
401-222-2950
www.tax.state.ri.us/info/synopsis/1.htm

South Carolina

Department of Revenue
P.O. Box 125
Columbia, SC 29214
803-898-5000
www.sctax.org

South Dakota

Department of Revenue
445 E. Capitol Avenue
Pierre, SD 57501
800-829-9188
605-773-3311
www.state.sd.us/revenue/businesstax/
  bustax.htm

Tennessee

Department of Revenue
500 Deaderick Street
Nashville, TN 37242
800-342-1003
615-253-0600
www.state.tn.us/revenue

Texas

Comptroller of Public Accounts
Lyndon B. Johnson State Office Building
111 E. 17th Street
Austin, TX 78774
877-662-8375
512-463-4865
www.window.state.tx.us/taxinfo/sales/
  new_business.html

Utah

State Tax Commission
210 N. 1950 West
Salt Lake City, UT 84134
800-662-4335
801-297-2200
www.tax.utah.gov

Vermont

Department of Taxes
Taxpayer Services Division
109 State Street
Pavilion Office Building
Montpelier, VT 05601
802-828-2551
www.state.vt.us/tax/index.htm

Virginia

Department of Taxation
3610 W. Broad
Richmond, VA 23230
804-367-8031
www.tax.virginia.gov

Washington

Department of Revenue
2101 4th Avenue, Suite 1400
Seattle, WA 98121
800-647-7706
206-956-3002
http://dor.wa.gov

West Virginia

State Tax Department
1206 Quarrier Street
Charleston, WV 25301
800-982-8297
304-558-3333
www.state.wv.us/taxdiv

Wisconsin

Department of Revenue
2135 Rimrock Road
Madison, WI 53713
608-266-2772
www.dor.state.wi.us

Wyoming

Department of Revenue
122 W. 25th Street
Cheyenne, WY 82002
307-777-5200
http://revenue.state.wy.us

LLC Offices

Alabama

Secretary of State
Corporate Section
11 S. Union Street, Room 208
Box 5616
Montgomery, AL 36103
334-242-5324
www.sos.state.al.us

Alaska

Department of Community & Economic
  Development
Division of Banking, Securities, & Corporations
Corporations Section
150 Third Street, Suite 217
Juneau, AK 99803
907-465-2530
www.dced.state.ak.us

Arizona

Arizona Corporation Commission
Corporation Filing Section
1300 W. Washington
Phoenix, AZ 85007
800-345-5819 (within the state)
602-542-3135
www.cc.state.az.us/corp

Arkansas

Arkansas Secretary of State
Victory Building
Corporations Division
1401 W. Capital, Suite 250
Little Rock, AR 72201
501-682-3409
888-233-0325
www.sosweb.state.ar.us/corp_ucc_fees.html

California

California Secretary of State
Limited Liability Company Unit
1500 11th Street, Suite 345
Sacramento, CA 95814
916-653-3795
www.ss.ca.gov

Colorado

Secretary of State
1700 Broadway, 2nd and 3rd Floors
Denver, CO 80290
303-894-2200
www.sos.state.co.us

Connecticut

Connecticut Secretary of State
30 Trinity Street
Hartford, CT 06106
860-509-6002
www.sots.state.ct.us

Delaware

Department of State
Division of Corporations
Townsend Building
401 Federal Street, Suite 4
Dover, DE 19901
302-739-3073
www.state.de.us/corp

District of Columbia

Department of Consumer & Regulatory Affairs
Business Regulation Administration
Corporations Division
941 N. Capitol Street, NE
Washington, DC 20002
202-442-4432
http://dcra.dc.gov

Florida

Florida Department of State
Registration Section
Division of Corporations
P.O. Box 6327
Tallahassee, FL 32314
850-245-6051
800-755-5111
www.dos.state.fl.us

Georgia

Secretary of State
Corporations Division
Suite 315, West Tower
2 Martin Luther King, Jr. Drive
Atlanta, GA 30334
404-656-2817
www.georgiacorporations.org

Hawaii

Department of Commerce and Consumer Affairs
Business Registration Division
335 Merchant Street
P.O. Box 40
Honolulu, HI 96813
808-586-2744
www.businessregistrations.com

Idaho

Idaho Secretary of State
Corporations Division
700 W. Jefferson, Capital Building
Boise, ID 83720
208-334-2300
www.idsos.state.id.us

Illinois

Illinois Secretary of State
Department of Business Services
69 W. Washington, Suite 1240
Chicago, IL 60602
312-793-3380
www.sos.state.il.us

Indiana

Indiana Secretary of State
Corporations Division
302 W. Washington, Room E018
Indianapolis, IN 46204
317-232-6576
www.in.gov/sos

Iowa

Iowa Secretary of State
Lucas Building, 1st Floor
321 E. 12th Street
Des Moines, IA 50319
515-281-5204
www.sos.state.ia.us

Kansas

Kansas Secretary of State
Corporation Division
First Floor, Memorial Hall
120 SW 10th Avenue
Topeka, KS 66612
785-296-4564
www.kssos.org

Kentucky

Kentucky Secretary of State
Business Filings
700 Capitol Avenue, Suite 152
Frankfort, KY 40601
502-564-3490
www.sos.state.ky.us

Louisiana

Louisiana Secretary of State
Corporations Division
P.O. Box 94125
Baton Rouge, LA 70804
225-342-4471
www.sec.state.la.us

Maine

Secretary of State
Bureau of Corporations, Elections, &
  Commissions
101 State House Station
Augusta, ME 04333
207-624-7736
www.state.me.us/sos

Maryland

Maryland Department of Assessments &
  Taxation
Corporate Charter Division
Room 801
301 W. Preston Street
Baltimore, MD 21201
410-767-1184
888-246-5941
www.dat.state.md.us

Massachusetts

Commonwealth of Massachusetts
Corporations Division
One Ashburton Place, 17th Floor
Boston, MA 02108
617-727-9640
www.sec.state.ma.us/cor

Michigan

Michigan Department of Consumer
  and Industry Services
Corporation Division
2501 Woodlake Circle
Okemos, MI 48864
517-241-6470
www.michigan.gov/cis

Minnesota

Minnesota Secretary of State
Business Services Division
180 State Office Building
100 Rev. Dr. Martin Luther King Jr. Boulevard
St. Paul, MN 55155
651-296-2803
877-551-6767
www.sos.state.mn.us

Mississippi

Mississippi Secretary of State
Corporate Division
700 North Street
Jackson, MS 39202
601-359-1633
800-256-3494
www.sos.state.ms.us

Missouri

Secretary of State
Corporation Division
600 W. Main Street
Missouri State Information Center
Room 322
P.O. Box 778
Jefferson City, MO 65101
573-751-4153
www.sos.mo.gov

Montana

Montana Secretary of State
Corporation Bureau
Room 260, Capitol
P.O. Box 202801
Helena, MT 59620
406-444-2034
http://sos.state.mt.us

Nebraska

Nebraska Secretary of State
Corporate Division
Room 1301, State Capitol
P.O. Box 94608
Lincoln, NE 68509
402-471-4079
www.sos.state.ne.us

Nevada

Secretary of State
New Filings Section
101 N. Carson Street, Suite 3
Carson City, NV 89701
775-684-5708
http://sos.state.nv.us
Filings may also be made at the Secretary of
  State Satellite Office in Las Vegas:
  702-486-2880.

New Hampshire

New Hampshire Secretary of State
State House Annex, Room 341
25 Capitol Street
Concord, NH 03301
603-271-3244
www.state.nh.us/sos

New Jersey

New Jersey Department of Treasury
Division of Revenue
Corporate Filings Unit
225 W. State Street, 3rd Floor
Trenton, NJ 08608
609-292-9292
www.state.nj.us/treasury/revenue

New Mexico

State Corporation Commission
Corporation Department
1120 Paseo de Peralta
P.O. Drawer 1269
Santa Fe, NM 87504
505-827-4508
800-947-4722
www.nmprc.state.nm.us

New York

Department of State
Division of Corporations, State Records, and
   Uniform Commercial Code
41 State Street
Albany, NY 12231
518-473-2492
www.dos.state.ny.us

North Carolina

North Carolina Department of the
   Secretary of State
Corporations Division
2 S. Salisbury Street
Raleigh, NC 27601
919-807-2225
888-246-7636
www.secstate.state.nc.us

North Dakota

North Dakota Secretary of State
Corporations Division
600 E. Boulevard Avenue
Bismarck, ND 58505
701-328-4284
www.nd.gov/sos

Ohio

Ohio Secretary of State
Client Service Center
30 E. Broad Street, Lower Level
Columbus, OH 43215
877-767-3453
www.state.oh.us/sos

Oklahoma

Oklahoma Secretary of State
2300 N. Lincoln Boulevard, Room 101
State Capitol Building
Oklahoma City, OK 73105
405-521-3912
www.sos.state.ok.us/business
   /business_filing.htm

Oregon

Oregon Secretary of State
Corporation Division
Public Service Building, Suite 151
255 Capitol Street NE
Salem, OR 97310
503-986-2200
www.sos.state.or.us

Pennsylvania

Department of State
Corporation Bureau
206 North Office Building
Harrisburg, PA 17120
717-787-1057
www.dos.state.pa.us

Rhode Island

Rhode Island Secretary of State
Corporations Division
100 N. Main Street, 1st Floor
Providence, RI 02903
401-222-3040
www.state.ri.us

South Carolina

South Carolina Secretary of State
Corporations Department
Edgar Brown Building
1205 Pendleton Street, Suite 525
Columbia, SC 29201
803-734-2158
www.scsos.com

South Dakota

South Dakota Secretary of State
State Capitol
500 E. Capitol Avenue, Suite 204
Pierre, SD 57501
605-773-4845
www.sdsos.gov

Tennessee

Tennessee Department of State
Division of Business Services
312 Eighth Avenue N, 6th Floor
William R. Snodgrass Tower
Nashville, TN 37243
615-741-2286
www.state.tn.us/sos

Texas

Texas Secretary of State
Corporations Section
1019 Brazos
Austin, TX 78701
512-463-5555
www.sos.state.tx.us

Utah

Utah Division of Corporations
  & Commercial Code
160 E. 300 South, 2nd Floor
Box 146705
Salt Lake City, UT 84114
801-530-4849
877-526-3994
www.commerce.utah.gov/cor

Vermont

Vermont Secretary of State
81 River Street, Drawer 09
Montpelier, VT 05609
802-828-2386
www.sec.state.vt.us

Virginia

Clerk of the State Corporation Commission
1300 E. Main Street
Richmond, VA 23219
804-371-9967
800-552-7945 (within the state)
www.state.va.us/scc

Washington

Washington Secretary of State
Corporations Division
Dolliver Building
801 Capital Way South
P.O. Box 40234
Olympia, WA 98504
360-753-7115
www.secstate.wa.gov/corps

West Virginia

West Virginia Secretary of State
Corporations Division
Bldg. 1, Suite 157-K
1900 Kanawha Boulevard E
Charleston, WV 25305
304-558-8000
www.wvsos.com

Wisconsin

Department of Financial Institutions
Corporations Section, 3rd Floor
P.O. Box 7846
Madison, WI 53707
608-261-7577
www.wdfi.org

Wyoming

Secretary of State's Office
Corporations Division
State Capitol Building, Room 110
200 W. 24th Street
Cheyenne, WY 82002
307-777-7311
http://soswy.state.wy.us

State Unemployment Compensation Agencies

Alabama

Department of Industrial Relations
649 Monroe Street
Montgomery, AL 36131
334-242-8025
www.dir.state.al.us

Alaska

Division of Employment Security
1111 W. 8th Street
P.O. Box 25509
Juneau, AK 99802
907-465-2712
www.labor.state.ak.us

Arizona

Unemployment Tax Registration
1789 W. Jefferson Street
Phoenix, AZ 85007
602-248-9396
www.de.state.az.us

Arkansas

Employment Security Department
1 Pershing Circle N
Little Rock, AR 72114
501-682-2033
www.accessarkansas.org/esd

California

Employment Development Department
800 Capitol Mall, MIC 83
Sacramento, CA 95814
800-815-9387
www.edd.cahwnet.gov

Colorado

Department of Labor and Employment
633 17th Street
Denver, CO 80202
303-318-8000
www.coworkforce.com

Connecticut

Department of Labor
200 Folly Brook Boulevard
Wethersfield, CT 06109
860-263-6000
www.ctdol.state.ct.us

Delaware

Department of Labor
4425 N. Market Street
Wilmington, DE 19802
302-761-8085
www.delawareworks.com

District of Columbia

Department of Employment Services
609 H Street, NE
Washington, DC 20002
202-724-7000
http://does.ci.washington.dc.us

Florida

Agency for Workforce Innovation
107 E. Madison Street, Caldwell Building
Tallahassee, FL 32399
850-245-7105
www.floridajobs.org

Georgia

Department of Labor
Andrew Young International Boulevard NE,
  Suite 600
Atlanta, GA 30303
404-232-3990
www.dol.state.ga.us

Hawaii

Department of Labor and Industrial Relations
830 Punchbowl Street
Room 437
Honolulu, HI 96813
808-586-8865
http://hawaii.gov/labor

Idaho

Department of Labor
317 W. Main Street
Boise, ID 83735
208-334-6300
http://cl.idaho.gov

Illinois

Department of Employment Security
33 S. State Street
Chicago, IL 60603
312-793-5700
www.ides.state.il.us

Indiana

Department of Workforce Development
Indiana Government Center S
10 N. Senate Avenue
Indianapolis, IN 46204
888-967-5663
www.in.gov/dwd

Iowa

Workforce Development
1000 E. Grand Avenue
Des Moines, IA 50319
515-281-5387
www.state.ia.us/government/des

Kansas

Department of Human Resources
401 SW Topeka Boulevard
Topeka, KS 66603
785-296-5025
www.hr.state.ks.us

Kentucky

Department for Employment Services
275 E. Main Street
Frankfort, KY 40621
502-564-5331
http://oet.ky.gov

Louisiana

Department of Labor
Office of Workers Compensation Administration
P.O. Box 94040
Baton Rouge, LA 70804
225-342-7555
www.ldol.state.la.us

Maine

Department of Labor
P.O. Box 259
Augusta, ME 04332
207-624-6400
www.state.me.us/labor

Maryland

Department of Labor, Licensing, & Regulation
1100 N. Eutaw Street
Baltimore, MD 21201
800-492-5524
www.dllr.state.md.us/employment

Massachusetts

Division of Employment and Training
19 Staniford Street
Boston, MA 02114
617-626-6535
www.detma.org

Michigan

Workers Compensation Agency
7150 Harris Drive
P.O. Box 30016
Detroit, MI 48909
888-396-5041
www.michigan.gov/wca

Minnesota

Department of Employment & Economic
  Development
332 Minnesota Street, Suite E200
St. Paul, MN 55101
651-297-1291
800-657-3858
www.mnwfc.org

Mississippi

Employment Security Commission
1235 Echelon Parkway
P.O. Box 1699
Jackson, MS 39215
601-321-6000
www.mesc.state.ms.us/tax

Missouri

Division of Employment Security
421 E. Dunklin Street
P.O. Box 59
Jefferson City, MO 65102
573-751-3215
www.dolir.mo.gov/es

Montana

Department of Labor and Industry
1327 Lockey
P.O. Box 1728
Helena, MT 59624
406-444-2840
http://dli.state.mt.us

Nebraska

Workforce Development
Department of Labor
550 S. 16th Street
P.O. Box 94600
Lincoln, NE 68509
402-471-2600
www.dol.state.ne.us

Nevada

Department of Employment Training and
  Rehabilitation
500 E. Third Street
Carson City, NV 89713
775-684-3849
http://detr.state.nv.us

New Hampshire

Department of Employment Security
32 S. Main Street
Concord, NH 03301
603-224-3311
www.nhes.state.nh.us

New Jersey

Department of Labor and Workforce
  Development
P.O. Box 947
Trenton, NJ 08625
609-292-2811
www.state.nj.us/labor

New Mexico

Department of Labor
Workforce Development Center
501 Mountain Road NE
Albuquerque, NM 87102
505-222-4600
www.dol.state.nm.us

New York

Department of Labor
W. Averell Harriman State Office Campus,
  Building 12
Albany, NY 12240
518-447-3992
www.labor.state.ny.us

North Carolina

Employment Security Commission
Business Services
700 Wade Avenue
Raleigh, NC 27605
919-733-7506
www.ncesc.com

North Dakota

Job Service of North Dakota
1000 E. Divide
P.O. Box 5507
Bismarck, ND 58506
701-328-2868
800-366-6888
www.state.nd.us/jsnd

Ohio

Department of Job and Family Services
30 E. Broad Street, 32nd Floor
Columbus, OH 43215
614-466-6282
http://jfs.ohio.gov

Oklahoma

Employment Security Commission
2401 N. Lincoln Boulevard
P.O. Box 52003
Oklahoma City, OK 73152
405-557-7100
888-980-9675
www.oesc.state.ok.us

Oregon

Employment Department
Central Administration Office
875 Union Street, NE
Salem, OR 97311
800-237-3710
www.emp.state.or.us

Pennsylvania

Department of Labor and Industry
7th and Forster Street, Room 1700
Harrisburg, PA 17120
717-787-5279
www.dli.state.pa.us

Rhode Island

Dept of Labor and Training
Central General Complex
1511 Pontiac Avenue
Cranston, RI 02920
401-462-8000
www.det.state.ri.us

South Carolina

Employment Security Commission
1550 Gadsden Street
P.O. Box 995
Columbia, SC 29202
803-737-3070
www.sces.org/ui

South Dakota

Department of Employment Security
700 Governors Drive
Pierre, SD 57501
605-773-3101
www.state.sd.us/dol

Tennessee

Department of Employment Security
500 James Robertson Parkway
8th Floor, Davy Crocket Tower
Nashville, TN 37245
615-741-2486
www.state.tn.us/labor-wfd

Texas

Workforce Commission
101 E. 15th Street
Austin, TX 78778
512-463-2699
www.twc.state.tx.us

Utah

Department of Workforce Services
140 E. Third South
P.O. Box 45249
Salt Lake City, UT 84145
801-526-9675
http://jobs.utah.gov

Vermont

Department of Employment and Training
5 Green Mountain Drive
P.O. Box 488
Montpelier, VT 05601
802-828-4000
www.det.state.vt.us

Virginia

Employment Commission
703 E. Main Street
Richmond, VA 23219
804-786-1485
www.vec.state.va.us

Washington

Employment Security Department
212 Maple Park
P.O. Box 9046
Olympia, WA 98507
360-902-9360
www.wa.gov/esd

West Virginia

Workforce West Virginia
Capitol Complex Building 4
Room 609
112 California Avenue
Charleston, WV 25305
304-558-7024
877-967-5498
www.wvbep.org/bep/default.htm

Wisconsin

Department of Workforce Development
201 E. Washington Avenue
Madison, WI 53702
608-266-3131
www.dwd.state.wi.us

Wyoming

Employment Tax Division
Unemployment Insurance
Employment Services
100 W. Midwest
P.O. Box 2760
Casper, WY 82602
307-235-3217
http://wydoe.state.wy.us

How to Use the CD-ROM

The charts in Appendix A, the tear-out forms in Appendix C, and some useful business planning spreadsheets are included on a CD-ROM in the back of the book. This CD-ROM, which can be used with Windows computers, installs files that you use with software programs that are already installed on your computer. It is *not* a stand-alone software program. Please read this appendix and the README.TXT file included on the CD-ROM for instructions on using the Forms CD.

Note to Mac users: This CD-ROM and its files should also work on Macintosh computers. Please note, however, that Nolo cannot provide technical support for non-Windows users.

How to View the README File

If you do not know how to view the file README.TXT, insert the Forms CD-ROM into your computer's CD-ROM drive and follow these instructions:

- Windows 9x, 2000, Me, and XP: (1) On your PC's desktop, double click the My Computer icon; (2) double click the icon for the CD-ROM drive into which the CD-ROM was inserted; (3) double click the file README.TXT.
- Macintosh: (1) On your Mac desktop, double click the icon for the CD-ROM that you inserted; (2) double click on the file README.TXT.

While the README file is open, print it out by using the Print command in the File menu.

Four different kinds of files are contained on the CD-ROM:

- Word processing (RTF) forms that you can open, complete, print, and save with your word processing program (see Section B, below), and

- Forms from the IRS (PDF) that can be viewed only with Adobe Acrobat Reader 4.0 or higher (see Section C, below). Some of these forms have "fill-in" text fields and can be completed using your computer. You will not, however, be able to save the completed forms with the filled-in data. PDF forms without fill-in text fields must be printed out and filled in by hand or with a typewriter.
- Business planning spreadsheets in Microsoft Excel format (XLS), which you can use with Microsoft's Excel or another spreadsheet program that can read XLS files (see Section D, below), and
- Charts from Appendix A that can be viewed only with Adobe Acrobat Reader 4.0 or higher. These charts contain contact information as well as linked URLs for various states' agencies. See Appendix A for more information.

See Section E below for the complete list of files and forms included on the disc.

A. Installing the Form Files Onto Your Computer

Before you can do anything with the files on the CD-ROM, you need to install them onto your hard disk. In accordance with U.S. copyright laws, remember that copies of the CD-ROM and its files are for your personal use only.

Insert the Forms CD and do the following.

1. Windows 9x, 2000, Me, and XP Users

Follow the instructions that appear on the screen. (If nothing happens when you insert the Forms CD-ROM, then: (1) double click the My Computer icon; (2) double click the icon for the CD-ROM drive into which the Forms CD-ROM was inserted; and (3) double click the file WELCOME.EXE.)

By default, all the files are installed to the \Small Business Start-Up Forms folder in the \Program Files folder of your computer. A folder called "Small Business Start-Up Forms" is added to the "Programs" folder of the Start menu.

2. Macintosh Users

Step 1: If the "Small Business Start-Up CD" window is not open, open it by double clicking the "Small Business Start-Up CD" icon.

Step 2: Select the "Small Business Start-Up Forms" folder icon.

Step 3: Drag and drop the folder icon onto the icon of your hard disk.

B. Using the Word Processing Files

This section concerns the files for forms that can be opened and edited with your word processing program.

All word processing forms come in rich text format. These files have the extension ".rtf." For example, the form for the Partnership Agreement discussed in Chapter 2 is on the file Partnership.rtf. A list of all forms can be found in Appendix C.

RTF files can be read by most recent word processing programs including all versions of MS Word for Windows and Macintosh, WordPad for Windows, and recent versions of WordPerfect for Windows and Macintosh.

To use a form from the CD to create your documents you must: (1) open a file in your word processor or text editor; (2) edit the form by filling in the required information; (3) print it out; (4) rename and save your revised file.

The following are general instructions. However, each word processor uses different commands to open, format, save, and print documents. Please read your word processor's manual for specific instructions on performing these tasks.

Do not call Nolo's technical support if you have questions on how to use your word processor.

Step 1: Opening a File

There are three ways to open the word processing file included on the CD-ROM after you have installed them onto your computer:

- Windows users can open a file by selecting its "shortcut" as follows: (1) click the Windows "Start" button; (2) open the "Programs" folder; (3) open the "Small Business Start-Up Forms" subfolder; and (4) click on the shortcut to the form you want to work with.

- Both Windows and Macintosh users can open a file directly by double clicking on it. Use My Computer or Windows Explorer (Windows 98, 2000, Me, or XP) or the Finder (Macintosh) to go to the folder you installed or copied the CD-ROM's files to. Then, double click on the specific file you want to open.

- You can also open a file from within your word processor. To do this, you must first start your word processor. Then, go to the File menu and choose the Open command. This opens a dialog box where you will tell the program (1) the type of file you want to open (*.RTF); and (2) the location and name of the file (you will need to navigate through the directory tree to get to the folder on your hard disk where the CD's files have been installed). If these directions are unclear, you will need to look through the manual for your word processing program—Nolo's technical support department will *not* be able to help you with the use of your word processing program.

Where Are the Files Installed?

Windows Users
- RTF files are installed by default to a folder named \Small Business Start-Up Forms in the \Program Files folder of your computer.

Macintosh Users
- RTF files are located in the "Small Business Start-Up Forms" folder.

Step 2: Editing Your Document

Fill in the appropriate information according to the instructions and sample agreements in the book. Underlines are used to indicate where you need to enter your information, frequently followed by instructions in brackets. Be sure to delete the underlines and instructions from your edited document. You will also want to make sure that any signature lines in your completed documents appear on a page with at least some text from the document itself. If you do not know how to use your word processor to edit a document, you will need to look through the manual for your word processing program—Nolo's technical support department will *not* be able to help you with the use of your word processing program.

Editing Forms That Have Optional or Alternative Text

Some of the forms have check boxes before text. The check boxes indicate:
- Optional text, where you choose whether to include or exclude the given text.
- Alternative text, where you select one alternative to include and exclude the other alternatives.

If you are using the Forms CD, however, we recommend that instead of marking the check boxes, you do the following:

Optional text

If you don't want to include optional text, just delete it from your document.

If you do want to include optional text, just leave it in your document.

In either case, delete the check box itself as well as the italicized instructions that the text is optional.

Alternative text

First delete all the alternatives that you do not want to include.

Then delete the remaining check boxes, as well as the italicized instructions that you need to select one of the alternatives provided.

Step 3: Printing Out the Document

Use your word processor's or text editor's "Print" command to print out your document. If you do not know how to use your word processor to print a document, you will need to look through the manual for your word processing program—Nolo's technical support department will *not* be able to help you with the use of your word processing program.

Step 4: Saving Your Document

After filling in the form, use the "Save As" command to save and rename the file. Because all the files are "read-only," you will not be able to use the "Save" command. This is for your protection. *If you save the file without renaming it, the underlines that indicate where you need to enter your information will be lost, and you will not be able to create a new document with this file without re-copying the original file from the CD-ROM.*

If you do not know how to use your word processor to save a document, you will need to look through the manual for your word processing program—Nolo's technical support department will *not* be able to help you with the use of your word processing program.

C. Using IRS Forms

Electronic copies of useful forms from the IRS are included on the CD-ROM in Adobe Acrobat PDF format. You must have the Adobe Reader installed on your computer to use these forms. Adobe Reader is available for all types of Windows and Macintosh systems. If you don't already have this software, you can download it for free at www.adobe.com.

All IRS forms are listed in Appendix C. These form files were created by the IRS, not by Nolo.

Some of these forms have fill-in text fields. To create your document using these files, you must: (1) open a file; (2) fill in the text fields using either your mouse or the tab key on your keyboard to navigate from field to field; and (3) print it out.

Forms without fill-in text fields cannot be filled out using your computer. To create your document using these files, you must: (1) open the file; (2) print it out; and (3) complete it by hand or type-writer.

Step 1: Opening a Form

PDF files, like the word processing files, can be opened one of three ways.

- Windows users can open a file by selecting its "shortcut" as follows: (1) click the Windows "Start" button; (2) open the "Programs" folder; (3) open the "Small Business Start-Up Forms" subfolder; (4) open the "Tax Forms" subfolder; and (5) click on the shortcut to the form you want to work with.

- Both Windows and Macintosh users can open a file directly by double clicking on it. Use My Computer or Windows Explorer (Windows 98, 2000, Me, or XP) or the Finder (Macintosh) to go to the folder you created and copied the CD-ROM's files to. Then, double click on the specific file you want to open.

- You can also open a PDF file from within Acrobat Reader. To do this, you must first start Reader. Then, go to the File menu and choose the Open command. This opens a dialog box where you will tell the program the location and name of the file (you will need to navigate through the directory tree to get to the folder on your hard disk where the CD's files have been installed). If these directions are unclear, you will need to look through Acrobat Reader's help—Nolo's technical support department will *not* be able to help you with the use of Acrobat Reader.

> ## Where Are the IRS Forms Installed?
>
> **Windows Users**
> - IRS forms are installed by default to a folder named \Small Business Start-Up Forms\Tax Forms in the \Program Files folder of your computer.
>
> **Macintosh Users**
> - IRS forms are located in the "Tax Forms" folder within the "Small Business Start-Up Forms" folder.

Step 2: Filling in a Form

Use your mouse or the Tab key on your keyboard to navigate from field to field within these forms. Be sure to have all the information you will need to complete a form on hand, because you will not be able to save a copy of the filled-in form to disk. You can, however, print out a completed version.

Step 3: Printing a Form

Choose Print from the Acrobat Reader File menu. This will open the Print dialog box. In the "Print Range" section of the Print dialog box, select the appropriate print range, then click OK.

D. Using the Business Planning Spreadsheets

This section concerns the files for the business planning spreadsheets that can be opened and completed with Microsoft's Excel or another spreadsheet program that "understands" XLS files.

These spreadsheets are in Microsoft's Excel format. These files have the extension ".XLS." For example, the Billable Rate Worksheet discussed in Chapter 6 is on the file BillableRate.xls. All spreadsheets and their filenames are listed in Section E, below.

To complete a business planning spreadsheet you must: (1) open the file in a spreadsheet program that is compatible with XLS files; (2) fill in the needed fields; (3) print it out; (4) rename and save your revised file.

The following are general instructions. However, each spreadsheet program uses different commands to open, format, save, and print documents. Please read your spreadsheet program's manual for specific instructions on performing these tasks.

Do not call Nolo's technical support if you have questions on how to use your spreadsheet program.

Step 1: Opening a File

There are three ways to open the spreadsheet files included on the CD-ROM after you have installed them onto your computer.

- Windows users can open a file by selecting its "shortcut" as follows: (1) Click the Windows "Start" button; (2) open the "Programs" folder; (3) open the "Small Business Start-Up Forms" subfolder; (4) open the "Business Planning Spreadsheets" subfolder; and (5) click on the shortcut to the spreadsheet you want to work with.
- Both Windows and Macintosh users can open a file directly by double clicking on it. Use My Computer or Windows Explorer (Windows 9x, 2000, Me, or XP) or the Finder (Macintosh) to go to the folder you installed or copied the CD-ROM's files to. Then, double click on the specific file you want to open.
- You can also open a file from within your spreadsheet program. To do this, you must first start your spreadsheet program. Then, go to the File menu and choose the Open command. This opens a dialog box where you will tell the program (1) the type of file you want to open (*.XLS); and (2) the location and name of the file (you will need to navigate through the directory tree to get to the folder on your hard disk where the CD's files have been installed). If these directions are unclear

you will need to look through the manual for your spreadsheet program—Nolo's technical support department will not be able to help you with the use of your spreadsheet program.

Where Are the XLS Forms Installed?

Windows Users
- XLS files are installed by default to a folder named \Small Business Start-Up Forms \Business Planning Spreadsheets in the \Program Files folder of your computer.

Macintosh Users
- XLS files are located in the "Business Planning Spreadsheets" folder within the "Small Business Start-Up Forms" folder.

Step 2: Entering Information Into the Spreadsheet

Fill in the appropriate information according to the instructions and sample spreadsheets in the book. As you fill in these spreadsheets, numeric calculations are performed automatically. If you do not know how to use your spreadsheet program to enter information into an XLS file, you will need to look through the manual for your spreadsheet program—Nolo's technical support department will *not* be able to help you with the use of your spreadsheet program.

Step 3: Printing Out the Spreadsheet

Use your spreadsheet program's "Print" command to print out your document. If you do not know how to use your spreadsheet program to print a document, you will need to look through the manual for your spreadsheet program—Nolo's technical support department will not be able to help you with the use of your spreadsheet program.

Step 4: Saving Your Spreadsheet

After filling in the form, use the "Save As" command to save and rename the file. Because all the files are "read-only," you will not be able to use the "Save" command. This is for your protection. *If you save the file without renaming it, you will overwrite the original business planning spreadsheet, and you will not be able to create a new document with this file without recopying the original file from the CD-ROM.*

If you do not know how to use your spreadsheet program to save a document, you will need to look through the manual for your spreadsheet program—Nolo's technical support department will not be able to help you with the use of your spreadsheet program.

E. List of Forms Included on the Forms CD-ROM

The following word processing files are in rich text format (RTF):

File Name	Form Name
Partnership.rtf	Partnership Agreement
BuySellSample.rtf	Sample Buy-Sell Agreement Provisions

The following IRS forms are in Adobe Reader format (PDF):

File Name	Form Name
f8716.pdf	IRS Form 8716
f8832.pdf	IRS Form 8832
fss4.pdf	IRS Form SS-4
fss8.pdf	IRS Form SS-8
iss4.pdf	IRS Instructions for Form SS-4

The following state contact charts are in Adobe Reader format (PDF):

File Name	Form Name
Information.pdf	Small Business Start-Up Information
LLCOffices.pdf	LLC Offices
SalesTax.pdf	State Sales Tax or Seller's Permit Agencies
TaxAgency.pdf	State Tax Agencies
Unemployment.pdf	State Unemployment Compensation Agencies

The following spreadsheets are in Microsoft's Excel format (XLS):

File Name	Form Name
BillableRate.xls	Billable Rate Worksheet
CashFlow.xls	Cash Flow Projection Worksheet
BreakEven .xls	Break-Even Analysis Worksheet
ProfitLoss.xls	Profit/Loss Forecast Worksheet
Warranty.xls	Warranty Track Worksheet

■

Tear-Out Forms

Partnership Agreement

Application for Employer Identification Number (Form SS-4)

Determination of Worker Status for Purposes of Federal Employment Taxes and Income Tax Withholding (Form SS-8)

Election To Have a Tax Year Other Than a Required Tax Year (Form 8716)

Entity Classification Election (Form 8832)

Partnership Agreement

1. Partners

_____ (Partners) make

the following Partnership Agreement.

2. Creation of Partnership

As of _____, the Partners agree to enter into a Partnership for

the purpose of operating a business known as: _____

_____ (Partnership Business).

The name of the Partnership (if different from name of Partnership Business) shall be: _____

_____ (Partnership Name).

3. Nature of Partnership Business

The Partnership Business will consist of the following business activities: _____

_____ .

4. Contributions to the Partnership

The Partners will make the following contributions to the Partnership:

Partner Name	Cash Contribution	Other Contribution (describe property and/or work; give cash value)	Total Contribution Value
	$	Total cash value:	$
	$	Total cash value:	$
	$	Total cash value:	$
	$	Total cash value:	$

5. Profit and Loss Allocation

The Partners will share business profits and losses as follows:

☐ in the same proportions as their contributions to the business.

☐ as follows:_____ .

6. Management of Partnership Business

The Partners will have the following management powers and responsibilities:

☐ The Partners will have equal management powers and responsibilities.

☐ The Partners will share management powers and responsibilities as follows: _____ .

7. Addition of a Partner

A new Partner may be added to the Partnership under the following conditions:

☐ unanimous vote of all Partners.

☐ majority vote of Partners.

☐ other conditions: _____.

8. Departure of a Partner

A Partner can be expelled by:

☐ unanimous vote of the other Partners.

☐ majority vote of the other Partners.

Any Partner who leaves voluntarily will give at least 30 days' written notice.

If any Partner leaves the Partnership for any reason, including voluntary withdrawal, expulsion, or death, the Partnership will ☐ survive. ☐ dissolve.

If the Partnership survives, the remaining Partner(s) will pay, within a reasonable time, the departing Partner, or the deceased Partner's estate, the fair market value of the departing Partner's share of the business as of the date of his or her departure. The Partnership's accountant will determine the fair market value of the departing Partner's share of the business according to the following method: _____

_____.

9. Dispute Resolution

If a dispute arises under this Agreement, the Partners agree to first try to resolve the dispute with the help of a mutually agreed-on mediator. Any costs and fees other than attorney fees will be shared equally by the Partners. If it is impossible to arrive at a mutually satisfactory solution, the Partners agree to submit the dispute to binding arbitration in the same city or region, conducted on a confidential basis pursuant to the Commercial Arbitration Rules of the American Arbitration Association.

10. Amendment of Agreement

This agreement cannot be amended without the written consent of all Partners.

11. Partner Signatures

Name: _____ Date:_____

Address: _____

Signature:_____ SSN: _____

Name: _____ Date:_____

Address: _____

Signature:_____ SSN: _____

Form **SS-4**
(Rev. December 2001)
Department of the Treasury
Internal Revenue Service

Application for Employer Identification Number

(For use by employers, corporations, partnerships, trusts, estates, churches, government agencies, Indian tribal entities, certain individuals, and others.)

▶ See separate instructions for each line.   ▶ Keep a copy for your records.

EIN

OMB No. 1545-0003

Type or print clearly.

1 Legal name of entity (or individual) for whom the EIN is being requested

2 Trade name of business (if different from name on line 1)

3 Executor, trustee, "care of" name

4a Mailing address (room, apt., suite no. and street, or P.O. box)

5a Street address (if different) (Do not enter a P.O. box.)

4b City, state, and ZIP code

5b City, state, and ZIP code

6 County and state where principal business is located

7a Name of principal officer, general partner, grantor, owner, or trustor

7b SSN, ITIN, or EIN

8a **Type of entity** (check only one box)
- ☐ Sole proprietor (SSN) _____
- ☐ Partnership
- ☐ Corporation (enter form number to be filed) ▶ _____
- ☐ Personal service corp.
- ☐ Church or church-controlled organization
- ☐ Other nonprofit organization (specify) ▶ _____
- ☐ Other (specify) ▶

- ☐ Estate (SSN of decedent) _____
- ☐ Plan administrator (SSN) _____
- ☐ Trust (SSN of grantor) _____
- ☐ National Guard   ☐ State/local government
- ☐ Farmers' cooperative   ☐ Federal government/military
- ☐ REMIC   ☐ Indian tribal governments/enterprises
- Group Exemption Number (GEN) ▶ _____

8b If a corporation, name the state or foreign country (if applicable) where incorporated

State

Foreign country

9 **Reason for applying** (check only one box)
- ☐ Started new business (specify type) ▶ _____
- ☐ Hired employees (Check the box and see line 12.)
- ☐ Compliance with IRS withholding regulations
- ☐ Other (specify) ▶

- ☐ Banking purpose (specify purpose) ▶ _____
- ☐ Changed type of organization (specify new type) ▶ _____
- ☐ Purchased going business
- ☐ Created a trust (specify type) ▶ _____
- ☐ Created a pension plan (specify type) ▶ _____

10 Date business started or acquired (month, day, year)

11 Closing month of accounting year

12 First date wages or annuities were paid or will be paid (month, day, year). **Note:** *If applicant is a withholding agent, enter date income will first be paid to nonresident alien. (month, day, year)* . . . . ▶

13 Highest number of employees expected in the next 12 months. **Note:** *If the applicant does not expect to have any employees during the period, enter "-0-."* . . . . ▶

Agricultural	Household	Other

14 Check **one** box that best describes the principal activity of your business.
- ☐ Construction ☐ Rental & leasing ☐ Transportation & warehousing
- ☐ Real estate   ☐ Manufacturing   ☐ Finance & insurance
- ☐ Health care & social assistance   ☐ Wholesale–agent/broker
- ☐ Accommodation & food service   ☐ Wholesale–other   ☐ Retail
- ☐ Other (specify)

15 Indicate principal line of merchandise sold; specific construction work done; products produced; or services provided.

16a Has the applicant ever applied for an employer identification number for this or any other business? . . . . . ☐ **Yes**   ☐ **No**
Note: *If "Yes," please complete lines 16b and 16c.*

16b If you checked "Yes" on line 16a, give applicant's legal name and trade name shown on prior application if different from line 1 or 2 above.
Legal name ▶   Trade name ▶

16c Approximate date when, and city and state where, the application was filed. Enter previous employer identification number if known.
Approximate date when filed (mo., day, year) | City and state where filed | Previous EIN

Third Party Designee

Complete this section **only** if you want to authorize the named individual to receive the entity's EIN and answer questions about the completion of this form.

Designee's name

Designee's telephone number (include area code)
( )

Address and ZIP code

Designee's fax number (include area code)
( )

Under penalties of perjury, I declare that I have examined this application, and to the best of my knowledge and belief, it is true, correct, and complete.

Applicant's telephone number (include area code)
( )

Name and title (type or print clearly) ▶

Applicant's fax number (include area code)
( )

Signature ▶   Date ▶

For Privacy Act and Paperwork Reduction Act Notice, see separate instructions.   Cat. No. 16055N   Form **SS-4** (Rev. 12-2001)

Do I Need an EIN?

File Form SS-4 if the applicant entity does not already have an EIN but is required to show an EIN on any return, statement, or other document.[1] **See also the separate instructions for each line on Form SS-4.**

IF the applicant...	AND...	THEN...
Started a new business	Does not currently have (nor expect to have) employees	Complete lines 1, 2, 4a- 6, 8a, and 9- 16c.
Hired (or will hire) employees, including household employees	Does not already have an EIN	Complete lines 1, 2, 4a- 6, 7a- b (if applicable), 8a, 8b (if applicable), and 9- 16c.
Opened a bank account	Needs an EIN for banking purposes only	Complete lines 1- 5b, 7a- b (if applicable), 8a, 9, and 16a- c.
Changed type of organization	Either the legal character of the organization or its ownership changed (e.g., you incorporate a sole proprietorship or form a partnership)[2]	Complete lines 1- 16c (as applicable).
Purchased a going business[3]	Does not already have an EIN	Complete lines 1- 16c (as applicable).
Created a trust	The trust is other than a grantor trust or an IRA trust[4]	Complete lines 1- 16c (as applicable).
Created a pension plan as a plan administrator[5]	Needs an EIN for reporting purposes	Complete lines 1, 2, 4a- 6, 8a, 9, and 16a- c.
Is a foreign person needing an EIN to comply with IRS withholding regulations	Needs an EIN to complete a Form W-8 (other than Form W-8ECI), avoid withholding on portfolio assets, or claim tax treaty benefits[6]	Complete lines 1- 5b, 7a- b (SSN or ITIN optional), 8a- 9, and 16a- c.
Is administering an estate	Needs an EIN to report estate income on Form 1041	Complete lines 1, 3, 4a- b, 8a, 9, and 16a- c.
Is a withholding agent for taxes on non-wage income paid to an alien (i.e., individual, corporation, or partnership, etc.)	Is an agent, broker, fiduciary, manager, tenant, or spouse who is required to file **Form 1042,** Annual Withholding Tax Return for U.S. Source Income of Foreign Persons	Complete lines 1, 2, 3 (if applicable), 4a- 5b, 7a- b (if applicable), 8a, 9, and 16a- c.
Is a state or local agency	Serves as a tax reporting agent for public assistance recipients under Rev. Proc. 80-4, 1980-1 C.B. 581[7]	Complete lines 1, 2, 4a- 5b, 8a, 9, and 16a- c.
Is a single-member LLC	Needs an EIN to file **Form 8832,** Classification Election, for filing employment tax returns, **or** for state reporting purposes[8]	Complete lines 1- 16c (as applicable).
Is an S corporation	Needs an EIN to file **Form 2553,** Election by a Small Business Corporation[9]	Complete lines 1- 16c (as applicable).

[1] For example, a sole proprietorship or self-employed farmer who establishes a qualified retirement plan, or is required to file excise, employment, alcohol, tobacco, or firearms returns, must have an EIN. **A partnership, corporation, REMIC (real estate mortgage investment conduit), nonprofit organization (church, club, etc.), or farmers' cooperative must use an EIN for any tax-related purpose even if the entity does not have employees.**

[2] However, **do not** apply for a new EIN if the existing entity only **(a)** changed its business name, **(b)** elected on Form 8832 to change the way it is taxed (or is covered by the default rules), or **(c)** terminated its partnership status because at least 50% of the total interests in partnership capital and profits were sold or exchanged within a 12-month period. (The EIN of the terminated partnership should continue to be used. See Regulations section 301.6109-1(d)(2)(iii).)

[3] Do not use the EIN of the prior business unless you became the "owner" of a corporation by acquiring its stock.

[4] However, IRA trusts that are required to file **Form 990-T,** Exempt Organization Business Income Tax Return, must have an EIN.

[5] A plan administrator is the person or group of persons specified as the administrator by the instrument under which the plan is operated.

[6] Entities applying to be a Qualified Intermediary (QI) need a QI-EIN even if they already have an EIN. **See Rev. Proc. 2000-12.**

[7] See also *Household employer* on page 4. (**Note:** State or local agencies may need an EIN for other reasons, e.g., hired employees.)

[8] Most LLCs **do not** need to file Form 8832. See **Limited liability company (LLC)** on page 4 for details on completing Form SS-4 for an LLC.

[9] An existing corporation that is electing or revoking S corporation status should use its previously-assigned EIN.

✪

Instructions for Form SS-4
(Rev. December 2001)

**Department of the Treasury
Internal Revenue Service**

Application for Employer Identification Number

Section references are to the Internal Revenue Code unless otherwise noted.

General Instructions

Use these instructions to complete **Form SS-4,** Application for Employer Identification Number. Also see **Do I Need an EIN?** on page 2 of Form SS-4.

Purpose of Form

Use Form SS-4 to apply for an employer identification number (EIN). An EIN is a nine-digit number (for example, 12-3456789) assigned to sole proprietors, corporations, partnerships, estates, trusts, and other entities for tax filing and reporting purposes. The information you provide on this form will establish your business tax account.

 *An EIN is for use in connection with your business activities only. Do **not** use your EIN in place of your social security number (SSN).*

File only one Form SS-4. Generally, a sole proprietor should file only one Form SS-4 and needs only one EIN, regardless of the number of businesses operated as a sole proprietorship or trade names under which a business operates. However, if the proprietorship incorporates or enters into a partnership, a new EIN is required. Also, each corporation in an affiliated group must have its own EIN.

EIN applied for, but not received. If you do not have an EIN by the time a **return** is due, write "Applied For" and the date you applied in the space shown for the number. **Do not** show your social security number (SSN) as an EIN on returns.

If you do not have an EIN by the time a **tax deposit** is due, send your payment to the Internal Revenue Service Center for your filing area as shown in the instructions for the form that you are are filing. Make your check or money order payable to the **"United States Treasury"** and show your name (as shown on Form SS-4), address, type of tax, period covered, and date you applied for an EIN.

Related Forms and Publications

The following **forms** and **instructions** may be useful to filers of Form SS-4:
- **Form 990-T,** Exempt Organization Business Income Tax Return
- **Instructions for Form 990-T**
- **Schedule C (Form 1040),** Profit or Loss From Business
- **Schedule F (Form 1040),** Profit or Loss From Farming
- **Instructions for Form 1041 and Schedules A, B, D, G, I, J, and K-1,** U.S. Income Tax Return for Estates and Trusts

- **Form 1042,** Annual Withholding Tax Return for U.S. Source Income of Foreign Persons
- **Instructions for Form 1065,** U.S. Return of Partnership Income
- **Instructions for Form 1066,** U.S. Real Estate Mortgage Investment Conduit (REMIC) Income Tax Return
- **Instructions for Forms 1120 and 1120-A**
- **Form 2553,** Election by a Small Business Corporation
- **Form 2848,** Power of Attorney and Declaration of Representative
- **Form 8821,** Tax Information Authorization
- **Form 8832,** Entity Classification Election

For more **information** about filing Form SS-4 and related issues, see:
- **Circular A,** Agricultural Employer's Tax Guide (Pub. 51)
- **Circular E,** Employer's Tax Guide (Pub. 15)
- **Pub. 538,** Accounting Periods and Methods
- **Pub. 542,** Corporations
- **Pub. 557,** Exempt Status for Your Organization
- **Pub. 583,** Starting a Business and Keeping Records
- **Pub. 966,** EFTPS: Now a Full Range of Electronic Choices to Pay All Your Federal Taxes
- **Pub. 1635,** Understanding Your EIN
- **Package 1023,** Application for Recognition of Exemption
- **Package 1024,** Application for Recognition of Exemption Under Section 501(a)

How To Get Forms and Publications

Phone. You can order forms, instructions, and publications by phone 24 hours a day, 7 days a week. Just call 1-800-TAX-FORM (1-800-829-3676). You should receive your order or notification of its status within 10 workdays.

Personal computer. With your personal computer and modem, you can get the forms and information you need using the IRS Web Site at **www.irs.gov** or File Transfer Protocol at **ftp.irs.gov.**

CD-ROM. For small businesses, return preparers, or others who may frequently need tax forms or publications, a CD-ROM containing over 2,000 tax products (including many prior year forms) can be purchased from the National Technical Information Service (NTIS).

To order **Pub. 1796,** Federal Tax Products on CD-ROM, call **1-877-CDFORMS** (1-877-233-6767) toll free or connect to **www.irs.gov/cdorders.**

Tax Help for Your Business

IRS-sponsored Small Business Workshops provide information about your Federal and state tax obligations. For information about workshops in your area, call 1-800-829-1040 and ask for your Taxpayer Education Coordinator.

How To Apply

You can apply for an EIN by telephone, fax, or mail depending on how soon you need to use the EIN.

Application by Tele-TIN. Under the Tele-TIN program, you can receive your EIN by telephone and use it immediately to file a return or make a payment. To receive an EIN by telephone, IRS suggests that you complete Form SS-4 so that you will have all relevant information available. Then call the Tele-TIN number at 1-866-816-2065. (International applicants must call 215-516-6999.) Tele-TIN hours of operation are 7:30 a.m. to 5:30 p.m. The person making the call must be authorized to sign the form or be an authorized designee. See **Signature** and **Third Party Designee** on page 6. Also see the **TIP** below.

An IRS representative will use the information from the Form SS-4 to establish your account and assign you an EIN. Write the number you are given on the upper right corner of the form and sign and date it. Keep this copy for your records.

If requested by an IRS representative, mail or fax (facsimile) the signed Form SS-4 (including any Third Party Designee authorization) **within 24 hours** to the Tele-TIN Unit at the service center address provided by the IRS representative.

TIP *Taxpayer representatives can use Tele-TIN to apply for an EIN on behalf of their client and request that the EIN be faxed to their **client** on the same day. (**Note:** By utilizing this procedure, you are authorizing the IRS to fax the EIN without a cover sheet.)*

Application by Fax-TIN. Under the Fax-TIN program, you can receive your EIN by fax within 4 business days. Complete and fax Form SS-4 to the IRS using the Fax-TIN number listed below for your state. A long-distance charge to callers outside of the local calling area will apply. Fax-TIN numbers can only be used to apply for an EIN. **The numbers may change without notice.** Fax-TIN is available 24 hours a day, 7 days a week.

Be sure to provide your fax number so that IRS can fax the EIN back to you. (**Note:** By utilizing this procedure, you are authorizing the IRS to fax the EIN without a cover sheet.)

Do not call Tele-TIN for the same entity because duplicate EINs may be issued. See **Third Party Designee** on page 6.

Application by mail. Complete Form SS-4 at least 4 to 5 weeks before you will need an EIN. Sign and date the application and mail it to the service center address for your state. You will receive your EIN in the mail in approximately 4 weeks. See also **Third Party Designee** on page 6.

Call 1-800-829-1040 to verify a number or to ask about the status of an application by mail.

If your principal business, office or agency, or legal residence in the case of an individual, is located in:	Call the Tele-TIN or Fax-TIN number shown or file with the "Internal Revenue Service Center" at:
Connecticut, Delaware, District of Columbia, Florida, Georgia, Maine, Maryland, Massachusetts, New Hampshire, New Jersey, New York, North Carolina, Ohio, Pennsylvania, Rhode Island, South Carolina, Vermont, Virginia, West Virginia	Attn: EIN Operation Holtsville, NY 00501 Tele-TIN 866-816-2065 Fax-TIN 631-447-8960
Illinois, Indiana, Kentucky, Michigan	Attn: EIN Operation Cincinnati, OH 45999 Tele-TIN 866-816-2065 Fax-TIN 859-669-5760
Alabama, Alaska, Arizona, Arkansas, California, Colorado, Hawaii, Idaho, Iowa, Kansas, Louisiana, Minnesota, Mississippi, Missouri, Montana, Nebraska, Nevada, New Mexico, North Dakota, Oklahoma, Oregon, Puerto Rico, South Dakota, Tennessee, Texas, Utah, Washington, Wisconsin, Wyoming	Attn: EIN Operation Philadelphia, PA 19255 Tele-TIN 866-816-2065 Fax-TIN 215-516-3990
If you have no legal residence, principal place of business, or principal office or agency in any state:	Attn: EIN Operation Philadelphia, PA 19255 Tele-TIN 215-516-6999 Fax-TIN 215-516-3990

Specific Instructions

Print or type all entries on Form SS-4. Follow the instructions for each line to expedite processing and to avoid unnecessary IRS requests for additional information. Enter "N/A" (nonapplicable) on the lines that do not apply.

Line 1—Legal name of entity (or individual) for whom the EIN is being requested. Enter the legal name of the entity (or individual) applying for the EIN exactly as it appears on the social security card, charter, or other applicable legal document.

Individuals. Enter your first name, middle initial, and last name. If you are a sole proprietor, enter your individual name, not your business name. Enter your business name on line 2. Do not use abbreviations or nicknames on line 1.

Trusts. Enter the name of the trust.

Estate of a decedent. Enter the name of the estate.

Partnerships. Enter the legal name of the partnership as it appears in the partnership agreement.

Corporations. Enter the corporate name as it appears in the corporation charter or other legal document creating it.

Plan administrators. Enter the name of the plan administrator. A plan administrator who already has an EIN should use that number.

Line 2—Trade name of business. Enter the trade name of the business if different from the legal name. The trade name is the "doing business as " (DBA) name.

 *Use the full legal name shown on line 1 on all tax returns filed for the entity. (However, if you enter a trade name on line 2 and choose to use the trade name instead of the legal name, enter the trade name on **all returns** you file.) To prevent processing delays and errors, **always** use the legal name only (or the trade name only) on **all** tax returns.*

Line 3—Executor, trustee, "care of" name. Trusts enter the name of the trustee. Estates enter the name of the executor, administrator, or other fiduciary. If the entity applying has a designated person to receive tax information, enter that person's name as the "care of" person. Enter the individual's first name, middle initial, and last name.

Lines 4a-b—Mailing address. Enter the mailing address for the entity's correspondence. If line 3 is completed, enter the address for the executor, trustee or "care of" person. Generally, this address will be used on all tax returns.

TIP *File **Form 8822**, Change of Address, to report any subsequent changes to the entity's mailing address.*

Lines 5a-b—Street address. Provide the entity's physical address **only** if different from its mailing address shown in lines 4a-b. **Do not** enter a P.O. box number here.

Line 6—County and state where principal business is located. Enter the entity's primary **physical** location.

Lines 7a-b—Name of principal officer, general partner, grantor, owner, or trustor. Enter the first name, middle initial, last name, and SSN of **(a)** the principal officer if the business is a corporation, **(b)** a general partner if a partnership, **(c)** the owner of an entity that is disregarded as separate from its owner (disregarded entities owned by a corporation enter the corporation's name and EIN), or **(d)** a grantor, owner, or trustor if a trust.

If the person in question is an **alien individual** with a previously assigned individual taxpayer identification number (ITIN), enter the ITIN in the space provided and submit a copy of an official identifying document. If necessary, complete **Form W-7,** Application for IRS Individual Taxpayer Identification Number, to obtain an ITIN.

You are **required** to enter an SSN, ITIN, or EIN unless the only reason you are applying for an EIN is to make an entity classification election (see Regulations section 301.7701-1 through 301.7701-3) and you are a nonresident alien with no effectively connected income from sources within the United States.

Line 8a—Type of entity. Check the box that best describes the type of entity applying for the EIN. If you are an alien individual with an ITIN previously assigned to you, enter the ITIN in place of a requested SSN.

 This is not an election for a tax classification of an entity. See "Limited liability company (LLC)" on page 4.

Other. If not specifically mentioned, check the "Other" box, enter the type of entity and the type of return, if any, that will be filed (for example, "Common Trust Fund, Form 1065" or "Created a Pension Plan"). Do not enter "N/A." If you are an alien individual applying for an EIN, see the **Lines 7a-b** instructions above.
- **Household employer.** If you are an individual, check the "Other" box and enter "Household Employer" and your SSN. If you are a state or local agency serving as a tax reporting agent for public assistance recipients who become household employers, check the "Other" box and enter "Household Employer Agent." If you are a trust that qualifies as a household employer, you do not need a separate EIN for reporting tax information relating to household employees; use the EIN of the trust.
- **QSub.** For a qualified subchapter S subsidiary (QSub) check the "Other" box and specify "QSub."
- **Withholding agent.** If you are a withholding agent required to file Form 1042, check the "Other" box and enter "Withholding Agent."

Sole proprietor. Check this box if you file Schedule C, C-EZ, or F (Form 1040) and have a qualified plan, or are required to file excise, employment, or alcohol, tobacco, or firearms returns, or are a payer of gambling winnings. Enter your SSN (or ITIN) in the space provided. If you are a nonresident alien with no effectively connected income from sources within the United States, you do not need to enter an SSN or ITIN.

Corporation. This box is for any corporation **other than a personal service corporation.** If you check this box, enter the income tax form number to be filed by the entity in the space provided.

 *If you entered "1120S" after the "Corporation" checkbox, the corporation **must** file Form 2553 **no later than the 15th day of the 3rd month of the tax year the election is to take effect.** Until Form 2553 has been received and approved, you will be considered a Form 1120 filer. See the Instructions for Form 2553.*

Personal service corp. Check this box if the entity is a personal service corporation. An entity is a personal service corporation for a tax year only if:
- The principal activity of the entity during the testing period (prior tax year) for the tax year is the performance of personal services substantially by employee-owners, and
- The employee-owners own at least 10% of the fair market value of the outstanding stock in the entity on the last day of the testing period.

Personal services include performance of services in such fields as health, law, accounting, or consulting. For more information about personal service corporations, see the Instructions for Forms 1120 and 1120-A and Pub. 542.

Other nonprofit organization. Check this box if the nonprofit organization is other than a church or church-controlled organization and specify the type of nonprofit organization (for example, an educational organization).

 *If the organization also seeks tax-exempt status, you **must** file either Package 1023 or Package 1024. See Pub. 557 for more information.*

If the organization is covered by a group exemption letter, enter the four-digit **group exemption number (GEN).** (Do not confuse the GEN with the nine-digit EIN.) If you do not know the GEN, contact the parent organization. Get Pub. 557 for more information about group exemption numbers.

Plan administrator. If the plan administrator is an individual, enter the plan administrator's SSN in the space provided.

REMIC. Check this box if the entity has elected to be treated as a real estate mortgage investment conduit (REMIC). See the Instructions for Form 1066 for more information.

Limited liability company (LLC). An LLC is an entity organized under the laws of a state or foreign country as a limited liability company. For Federal tax purposes, an LLC may be treated as a partnership or corporation or be disregarded as an entity separate from its owner.

By **default,** a domestic LLC with only one member is **disregarded** as an entity separate from its owner and must include all of its income and expenses on the owner's tax return (e.g., **Schedule C (Form 1040)**). Also by default, a domestic LLC with two or more members is treated as a partnership. A domestic LLC may file Form 8832 to avoid either default classification and elect to be classified as an association taxable as a corporation. For more information on entity classifications (including the rules for foreign entities), see the instructions for Form 8832.

Do not file Form 8832 if the LLC accepts the default classifications above. However, if the LLC will be electing S Corporation status, it must timely file both Form 8832 and Form 2553.

Complete Form SS-4 for LLCs as follows:
• A single-member, domestic LLC that accepts the default classification (above) does not need an EIN and generally should not file Form SS-4. Generally, the LLC should use the name and EIN of its **owner** for all Federal tax purposes. However, the reporting and payment of employment taxes for employees of the LLC may be made using the name and EIN of **either** the owner or the LLC as explained in Notice 99-6, 1999-1 C.B. 321. You can find Notice 99-6 on page 12 of Internal Revenue Bulletin 1999-3 at **www.irs.gov. (Note:** If the LLC-applicant indicates in box 13 that it has employees or expects to have employees, the owner (whether an individual or other entity) of a single-member domestic LLC will also be assigned its own EIN (if it does not

already have one) even if the LLC will be filing the employment tax returns.)
• A single-member, domestic LLC that accepts the default classification (above) and wants an EIN for filing employment tax returns (see above) or non-Federal purposes, such as a state requirement, must check the "Other" box and write "Disregarded Entity" or, when applicable, "Disregarded Entity—Sole Proprietorship" in the space provided.
• A multi-member, domestic LLC that accepts the default classification (above) must check the "Partnership" box.
• A domestic LLC that will be filing Form 8832 to elect corporate status must check the "Corporation" box and write in "Single-Member" or "Multi-Member" immediately below the "form number" entry line.

Line 9—Reason for applying. Check only **one** box. Do not enter "N/A."

Started new business. Check this box if you are starting a new business that requires an EIN. If you check this box, enter the type of business being started. **Do not** apply if you already have an EIN and are only adding another place of business.

Hired employees. Check this box if the existing business is requesting an EIN because it has hired or is hiring employees and is therefore required to file employment tax returns. **Do not** apply if you already have an EIN and are only hiring employees. For information on employment taxes (e.g., for family members), see Circular E.

You may be required to make electronic deposits of all depository taxes (such as employment tax, excise tax, and corporate income tax) using the Electronic Federal Tax Payment System (EFTPS). See section 11, Depositing Taxes, of Circular E and Pub. 966.

Created a pension plan. Check this box if you have created a pension plan and need an EIN for reporting purposes. Also, enter the type of plan in the space provided.

TIP *Check this box if you are applying for a trust EIN when a new pension plan is established. In addition, check the "Other" box in line 8a and write "Created a Pension Plan" in the space provided.*

Banking purpose. Check this box if you are requesting an EIN for banking purposes only, and enter the banking purpose (for example, a bowling league for depositing dues or an investment club for dividend and interest reporting).

Changed type of organization. Check this box if the business is changing its type of organization. For example, the business was a sole proprietorship and has been incorporated or has become a partnership. If you check this box, specify in the space provided (including available space immediately below) the type of change made. For example, "From Sole Proprietorship to Partnership."

Purchased going business. Check this box if you purchased an existing business. **Do not** use the former owner's EIN unless you became the "owner" of a corporation by acquiring its stock.

Created a trust. Check this box if you created a trust, and enter the type of trust created. For example, indicate if the trust is a nonexempt charitable trust or a split-interest trust.

Exception. Do **not** file this form for certain grantor-type trusts. The trustee does not need an EIN for the trust if the trustee furnishes the name and TIN of the grantor/owner and the address of the trust to all payors. See the Instructions for Form 1041 for more information.

 Do not check this box if you are applying for a trust EIN when a new pension plan is established. Check "Created a pension plan."

Other. Check this box if you are requesting an EIN for any other reason; and enter the reason. For example, a newly-formed state government entity should enter "Newly-Formed State Government Entity" in the space provided.

Line 10—Date business started or acquired. If you are starting a new business, enter the starting date of the business. If the business you acquired is already operating, enter the date you acquired the business. Trusts should enter the date the trust was legally created. Estates should enter the date of death of the decedent whose name appears on line 1 or the date when the estate was legally funded.

Line 11—Closing month of accounting year. Enter the last month of your accounting year or tax year. An accounting or tax year is usually 12 consecutive months, either a calendar year or a fiscal year (including a period of 52 or 53 weeks). A calendar year is 12 consecutive months ending on December 31. A fiscal year is either 12 consecutive months ending on the last day of any month other than December or a 52-53 week year. For more information on accounting periods, see Pub. 538.

Individuals. Your tax year generally will be a calendar year.

Partnerships. Partnerships must adopt one of the following tax years:
• The tax year of the majority of its partners,
• The tax year common to all of its principal partners,
• The tax year that results in the least aggregate deferral of income, or
• In certain cases, some other tax year.
See the Instructions for Form 1065 for more information.

REMICs. REMICs must have a calendar year as their tax year.

Personal service corporations. A personal service corporation generally must adopt a calendar year unless:
• It can establish a business purpose for having a different tax year, or
• It elects under section 444 to have a tax year other than a calendar year.

Trusts. Generally, a trust must adopt a calendar year except for the following:
• Tax-exempt trusts,
• Charitable trusts, and
• Grantor-owned trusts.

Line 12—First date wages or annuities were paid or will be paid. If the business has or will have employees, enter the date on which the business began or will begin to pay wages. If the business does not plan to have employees, enter "N/A."

Withholding agent. Enter the date you began or will begin to pay income (including annuities) to a nonresident alien. This also applies to individuals who are required to file Form 1042 to report alimony paid to a nonresident alien.

Line 13—Highest number of employees expected in the next 12 months. Complete each box by entering the number (including zero ("-0-")) of "Agricultural," "Household," or "Other" employees expected by the applicant in the next 12 months. For a definition of agricultural labor (farmwork), see Circular A.

Lines 14 and 15. Check the **one** box in line 14 that best describes the principal activity of the applicant's business. Check the "Other" box (and specify the applicant's principal activity) if none of the listed boxes applies.

Use line 15 to describe the applicant's principal line of business in more detail. For example, if you checked the "Construction" box in line 14, enter additional detail such as "General contractor for residential buildings" in line 15.

 Do not complete lines 14 and 15 if you entered zero "(-0-)" in line 13.

Construction. Check this box if the applicant is engaged in erecting buildings or other structures, (e.g., streets, highways, bridges, tunnels). The term "Construction" also includes special trade contractors, (e.g., plumbing, HVAC, electrical, carpentry, concrete, excavation, etc. contractors).

Real estate. Check this box if the applicant is engaged in renting or leasing real estate to others; managing, selling, buying or renting real estate for others; or providing related real estate services (e.g., appraisal services).

Rental and leasing. Check this box if the applicant is engaged in providing tangible goods such as autos, computers, consumer goods, or industrial machinery and equipment to customers in return for a periodic rental or lease payment.

Manufacturing. Check this box if the applicant is engaged in the mechanical, physical, or chemical transformation of materials, substances, or components into new products. The assembling of component parts of manufactured products is also considered to be manufacturing.

Transportation & warehousing. Check this box if the applicant provides transportation of passengers or cargo; warehousing or storage of goods; scenic or sight-seeing transportation; or support activities related to these modes of transportation.

Finance & insurance. Check this box if the applicant is engaged in transactions involving the creation, liquidation, or change of ownership of financial assets and/or facilitating such financial transactions;

underwriting annuities/insurance policies; facilitating such underwriting by selling insurance policies; or by providing other insurance or employee-benefit related services.

Health care and social assistance. Check this box if the applicant is engaged in providing physical, medical, or psychiatric care using licensed health care professionals or providing social assistance activities such as youth centers, adoption agencies, individual/family services, temporary shelters, etc.

Accommodation & food services. Check this box if the applicant is engaged in providing customers with lodging, meal preparation, snacks, or beverages for immediate consumption.

Wholesale—agent/broker. Check this box if the applicant is engaged in arranging for the purchase or sale of goods owned by others or purchasing goods on a commission basis for goods traded in the wholesale market, usually between businesses.

Wholesale—other. Check this box if the applicant is engaged in selling goods in the wholesale market generally to other businesses for resale on their own account.

Retail. Check this box if the applicant is engaged in selling merchandise to the general public from a fixed store; by direct, mail-order, or electronic sales; or by using vending machines.

Other. Check this box if the applicant is engaged in an activity not described above. Describe the applicant's principal business activity in the space provided.

Lines 16a-c. Check the applicable box in line 16a to indicate whether or not the entity (or individual) applying for an EIN was issued one previously. Complete lines 16b and 16c **only** if the "Yes" box in line 16a is checked. If the applicant previously applied for **more than one** EIN, write "See Attached" in the empty space in line 16a and attach a separate sheet providing the line 16b and 16c information for each EIN previously requested.

Third Party Designee. Complete this section **only** if you want to authorize the named individual to receive the entity's EIN and answer questions about the completion of Form SS-4. The designee's authority terminates at the time the EIN is assigned and released to the designee. **You must complete the signature area for the authorization to be valid.**

Signature. When required, the application must be signed by **(a)** the individual, if the applicant is an individual, **(b)** the president, vice president, or other principal officer, if the applicant is a corporation, **(c)** a responsible and duly authorized member or officer having knowledge of its affairs, if the applicant is a partnership, government entity, or other unincorporated organization, or **(d)** the fiduciary, if the applicant is a trust or an estate. Foreign applicants may have any duly-authorized person, (e.g., division manager), sign Form SS-4.

Privacy Act and Paperwork Reduction Act Notice. We ask for the information on this form to carry out the Internal Revenue laws of the United States. We need it to comply with section 6109 and the regulations thereunder which generally require the inclusion of an employer identification number (EIN) on certain returns, statements, or other documents filed with the Internal Revenue Service. If your entity is required to obtain an EIN, you are required to provide all of the information requested on this form. Information on this form may be used to determine which Federal tax returns you are required to file and to provide you with related forms and publications.

We disclose this form to the Social Security Administration for their use in determining compliance with applicable laws. We may give this information to the Department of Justice for use in civil and criminal litigation, and to the cities, states, and the District of Columbia for use in administering their tax laws. We may also disclose this information to Federal, state, or local agencies that investigate or respond to acts or threats of terrorism or participate in intelligence or counterintelligence activities concerning terrorism.

We will be unable to issue an EIN to you unless you provide all of the requested information which applies to your entity. Providing false information could subject you to penalties.

You are not required to provide the information requested on a form that is subject to the Paperwork Reduction Act unless the form displays a valid OMB control number. Books or records relating to a form or its instructions must be retained as long as their contents may become material in the administration of any Internal Revenue law. Generally, tax returns and return information are confidential, as required by section 6103.

The time needed to complete and file this form will vary depending on individual circumstances. The estimated average time is:

Recordkeeping	6 min.
Learning about the law or the form	22 min.
Preparing the form	46 min.
Copying, assembling, and sending the form to the IRS	20 min.

If you have comments concerning the accuracy of these time estimates or suggestions for making this form simpler, we would be happy to hear from you. You can write to the Tax Forms Committee, Western Area Distribution Center, Rancho Cordova, CA 95743-0001. **Do not** send the form to this address. Instead, see **How To Apply** on page 2.

Form **SS-8**
(Rev. June 2003)
Department of the Treasury
Internal Revenue Service

Determination of Worker Status
for Purposes of Federal Employment Taxes
and Income Tax Withholding

OMB No. 1545-0004

Name of firm (or person) for whom the worker performed services	Worker's name
Firm's address (include street address, apt. or suite no., city, state, and ZIP code)	Worker's address (include street address, apt. or suite no., city, state, and ZIP code)

Trade name	Telephone number (include area code) ( )	Worker's social security number

Telephone number (include area code) ( )	Firm's employer identification number	Worker's employer identification number (if any)

If the worker is paid by a firm other than the one listed on this form for these services, enter the name, address, and employer identification number of the payer.

Important Information Needed To Process Your Request

We must have your permission to disclose your name and the information on this form and any attachments to other parties involved with this request. **Do we have your permission to disclose this information?** . . . . ☐ Yes ☐ No
If you answered "No" or did not mark a box, we will not process your request and will not issue a determination.

You must answer ALL items OR mark them "Unknown" or "Does not apply." If you need more space, attach another sheet.

A This form is being completed by: ☐ Firm ☐ Worker; for services performed _____ to _____ .
(beginning date)   (ending date)

B Explain your reason(s) for filing this form (e.g., you received a bill from the IRS, you believe you received a Form 1099 or Form W-2 erroneously, you are unable to get worker's compensation benefits, you were audited or are being audited by the IRS). ----------------------------
----

C Total number of workers who performed or are performing the same or similar services _____ .

D How did the worker obtain the job? ☐ Application ☐ Bid ☐ Employment Agency ☐ Other (specify) _____ .

E Attach copies of all supporting documentation (contracts, invoices, memos, Forms W-2, Forms 1099, IRS closing agreements, IRS rulings, etc.). In addition, please inform us of any current or past litigation concerning the worker's status. If no income reporting forms (Form 1099-MISC or W-2) were furnished to the worker, enter the amount of income earned for the year(s) at issue $ _____ .

F Describe the firm's business. ----------------------------------
----

G Describe the work done by the worker and provide the worker's job title. ----------------------
----

H Explain why you believe the worker is an employee or an independent contractor. ----------------------
----

I Did the worker perform services for the firm before getting this position? . . . . ☐ Yes ☐ No ☐ N/A
If "Yes," what were the dates of the prior service? ----------------------------------
If "Yes," explain the differences, if any, between the current and prior service. ----------------------
----

J If the work is done under a written agreement between the firm and the worker, attach a copy (preferably signed by both parties). Describe the terms and conditions of the work arrangement. ----------------------------------
----

Part I   Behavioral Control

1   What specific training and/or instruction is the worker given by the firm? _____
    _____

2   How does the worker receive work assignments? _____
    _____

3   Who determines the methods by which the assignments are performed? _____

4   Who is the worker required to contact if problems or complaints arise and who is responsible for their resolution? _____
    _____

5   What types of reports are required from the worker? Attach examples. _____
    _____

6   Describe the worker's daily routine (i.e., schedule, hours, etc.). _____
    _____
    _____

7   At what location(s) does the worker perform services (e.g., firm's premises, own shop or office, home, customer's location, etc.)? _____
    _____

8   Describe any meetings the worker is required to attend and any penalties for not attending (e.g., sales meetings, monthly meetings, staff
    meetings, etc.). _____

9   Is the worker required to provide the services personally?   .   .   .   .   ☐ **Yes**   ☐ **No**

10 If substitutes or helpers are needed, who hires them? _____

11 If the worker hires the substitutes or helpers, is approval required?   .   .   .   .   ☐ **Yes**   ☐ **No**
    If "Yes," by whom? _____

12 Who pays the substitutes or helpers? _____

13 Is the worker reimbursed if the worker pays the substitutes or helpers?   .   .   .   .   ☐ **Yes**   ☐ **No**
    If "Yes," by whom?

Part II   Financial Control

1   List the supplies, equipment, materials, and property provided by each party:
    The firm _____
    The worker _____
    Other party _____

2   Does the worker lease equipment?   .   .   .   .   ☐ **Yes**   ☐ **No**
    If "Yes," what are the terms of the lease? (Attach a copy or explanatory statement.) _____
    _____

3   What expenses are incurred by the worker in the performance of services for the firm? _____
    _____

4   Specify which, if any, expenses are reimbursed by:
    The firm _____
    Other party _____

5   Type of pay the worker receives: ☐ Salary   ☐ Commission   ☐ Hourly Wage   ☐ Piece Work
    ☐ Lump Sum   ☐ Other (specify) _____
    If type of pay is commission, and the firm guarantees a minimum amount of pay, specify amount $ _____ .

6   Is the worker allowed a drawing account for advances?   .   .   .   .   ☐ **Yes**   ☐ **No**
    If "Yes," how often? _____
    Specify any restrictions. _____

7   Whom does the customer pay?   .   .   .   .   ☐ Firm   ☐ Worker
    If worker, does the worker pay the total amount to the firm?   ☐ **Yes**   ☐ **No**   If "No," explain. _____

8   Does the firm carry worker's compensation insurance on the worker?   .   .   .   .   ☐ **Yes**   ☐ **No**

9   What economic loss or financial risk, if any, can the worker incur beyond the normal loss of salary (e.g., loss or damage of equipment,
    material, etc.)? _____
    _____

Part III — Relationship of the Worker and Firm

1 List the benefits available to the worker (e.g., paid vacations, sick pay, pensions, bonuses). ....

2 Can the relationship be terminated by either party without incurring liability or penalty? . . . . ☐ **Yes** ☐ **No**
   If "No," explain your answer. ....

3 Does the worker perform similar services for others? . . . . ☐ **Yes** ☐ **No**
   If "Yes," is the worker required to get approval from the firm? . . . . ☐ **Yes** ☐ **No**

4 Describe any agreements prohibiting competition between the worker and the firm while the worker is performing services or during any later period. Attach any available documentation. ....

5 Is the worker a member of a union? . . . . ☐ **Yes** ☐ **No**

6 What type of advertising, if any, does the worker do (e.g., a business listing in a directory, business cards, etc.)? Provide copies, if applicable. ....

7 If the worker assembles or processes a product at home, who provides the materials and instructions or pattern? ....

8 What does the worker do with the finished product (e.g., return it to the firm, provide it to another party, or sell it)? ....

9 How does the firm represent the worker to its customers (e.g., employee, partner, representative, or contractor)? ....

10 If the worker no longer performs services for the firm, how did the relationship end? ....

Part IV — For Service Providers or Salespersons- Complete this part if the worker provided a service directly to customers or is a salesperson.

1 What are the worker's responsibilities in soliciting new customers? ....

2 Who provides the worker with leads to prospective customers? ....

3 Describe any reporting requirements pertaining to the leads. ....

4 What terms and conditions of sale, if any, are required by the firm? ....

5 Are orders submitted to and subject to approval by the firm? . . . . ☐ **Yes** ☐ **No**

6 Who determines the worker's territory? ....

7 Did the worker pay for the privilege of serving customers on the route or in the territory? . . . . ☐ **Yes** ☐ **No**
   If "Yes," whom did the worker pay? ....
   If "Yes," how much did the worker pay? . . . . $ _____ .

8 Where does the worker sell the product (e.g., in a home, retail establishment, etc.)? ....

9 List the product and/or services distributed by the worker (e.g., meat, vegetables, fruit, bakery products, beverages, or laundry or dry cleaning services). If more than one type of product and/or service is distributed, specify the principal one. ....

10 Does the worker sell life insurance full time? . . . . ☐ **Yes** ☐ **No**

11 Does the worker sell other types of insurance for the firm? . . . . ☐ **Yes** ☐ **No**
   If "Yes," enter the percentage of the worker's total working time spent in selling other types of insurance. . . . . _____ %

12 If the worker solicits orders from wholesalers, retailers, contractors, or operators of hotels, restaurants, or other similar establishments, enter the percentage of the worker's time spent in the solicitation. . . . . _____ %

13 Is the merchandise purchased by the customers for resale or use in their business operations? . . . . . . ☐ **Yes** ☐ **No**
   Describe the merchandise and state whether it is equipment installed on the customers' premises. ....

Part V — Signature (see page 4)

Under penalties of perjury, I declare that I have examined this request, including accompanying documents, and to the best of my knowledge and belief, the facts presented are true, correct, and complete.

Signature ▶ _____   Title ▶ _____   Date ▶ _____
(Type or print name below)

General Instructions

Section references are to the Internal Revenue Code unless otherwise noted.

Purpose

Firms and workers file Form SS-8 to request a determination of the status of a worker for purposes of Federal employment taxes and income tax withholding.

A Form SS-8 determination may be requested only in order to resolve Federal tax matters. If Form SS-8 is submitted for a tax year for which the statute of limitations on the tax return has expired, a determination letter will not be issued. The statute of limitations expires 3 years from the due date of the tax return or the date filed, whichever is later.

The IRS does not issue a determination letter for proposed transactions or on hypothetical situations. We may, however, issue an information letter when it is considered appropriate.

Definition

Firm. For the purposes of this form, the term "firm" means any individual, business enterprise, organization, state, or other entity for which a worker has performed services. The firm may or may not have paid the worker directly for these services. **If the firm was not responsible for payment for services, be sure to enter the name, address, and employer identification number of the payer on the first page of Form SS-8 below the identifying information for the firm and the worker.**

The SS-8 Determination Process

The IRS will acknowledge the receipt of your Form SS-8. Because there are usually two (or more) parties who could be affected by a determination of employment status, the IRS attempts to get information from all parties involved by sending those parties blank Forms SS-8 for completion. The case will be assigned to a technician who will review the facts, apply the law, and render a decision. The technician may ask for additional information from the requestor, from other involved parties, or from third parties that could help clarify the work relationship before rendering a decision. The IRS will generally issue a formal determination to the firm or payer (if that is a different entity), and will send a copy to the worker. A determination letter applies only to a worker (or a class of workers) requesting it, and the decision is binding on the IRS. In certain cases, a formal determination will not be issued. Instead, an information letter may be issued. Although an information letter is advisory only and is not binding on the IRS, it may be used to assist the worker to fulfill his or her Federal tax obligations.

Neither the SS-8 determination process nor the review of any records in connection with the determination constitutes an examination (audit) of any Federal tax return. If the periods under consideration have previously been examined, the SS-8 determination process will not constitute a reexamination under IRS reopening procedures. Because this is not an examination of any Federal tax return, the appeal rights available in connection with an examination do not apply to an SS-8 determination. However, if you disagree with a determination and you have additional information concerning the work relationship that you believe was not previously considered, you may request that the determining office reconsider the determination.

Completing Form SS-8

Answer all questions as completely as possible. Attach additional sheets if you need more space. Provide information for all years the worker provided services for the firm. Determinations are based on the entire relationship between the firm and the worker.

Additional copies of this form may be obtained by calling 1-800-829-4933 or from the IRS website at **www.irs.gov.**

Fee

There is no fee for requesting an SS-8 determination letter.

Signature

Form SS-8 must be signed and dated by the taxpayer. A stamped signature will not be accepted.

The person who signs for a corporation must be an officer of the corporation who has personal knowledge of the facts. If the corporation is a member of an affiliated group filing a consolidated return, it must be signed by an officer of the common parent of the group.

The person signing for a trust, partnership, or limited liability company must be, respectively, a trustee, general partner, or member-manager who has personal knowledge of the facts.

Where To File

Send the completed Form SS-8 to the address listed below for the firm's location. However, for cases involving Federal agencies, send Form SS-8 to the Internal Revenue Service, Attn: CC:CORP:T:C, Ben Franklin Station, P.O. Box 7604, Washington, DC 20044.

Firm's location:	Send to:
Alaska, Arizona, Arkansas, California, Colorado, Hawaii, Idaho, Illinois, Iowa, Kansas, Minnesota, Missouri, Montana, Nebraska, Nevada, New Mexico, North Dakota, Oklahoma, Oregon, South Dakota, Texas, Utah, Washington, Wisconsin, Wyoming, American Samoa, Guam, Puerto Rico, U.S. Virgin Islands	Internal Revenue Service SS-8 Determinations P.O. Box 630 Stop 631 Holtsville, NY 11742-0630
Alabama, Connecticut, Delaware, District of Columbia, Florida, Georgia, Indiana, Kentucky, Louisiana, Maine, Maryland, Massachusetts, Michigan, Mississippi, New Hampshire, New Jersey, New York, North Carolina, Ohio, Pennsylvania, Rhode Island, South Carolina, Tennessee, Vermont, Virginia, West Virginia, all other locations not listed	Internal Revenue Service SS-8 Determinations 40 Lakemont Road Newport, VT 05855-1555

Instructions for Workers

If you are requesting a determination for more than one firm, complete a separate Form SS-8 for each firm.

 Form SS-8 is not a claim for refund of social security and Medicare taxes or Federal income tax withholding.

If the IRS determines that you are an employee, you are responsible for filing an amended return for any corrections related to this decision. A determination that a worker is an employee does not necessarily reduce any current or prior tax liability. For more information, call 1-800-829-1040.

Time for filing a claim for refund. Generally, you must file your claim for a credit or refund within 3 years from the date your original return was filed or within 2 years from the date the tax was paid, whichever is later.

Filing Form SS-8 does not prevent the expiration of the time in which a claim for a refund must be filed. If you are concerned about a refund, and the statute of limitations for filing a claim for refund for the year(s) at issue has not yet expired, you should file **Form 1040X,** Amended U.S. Individual Income Tax Return, to protect your statute of limitations. File a separate Form 1040X for each year.

On the Form 1040X you file, do not complete lines 1 through 24 on the form. Write "Protective Claim" at the top of the form, sign and date it. In addition, you should enter the following statement in Part II, Explanation of Changes to Income, Deductions, and Credits: "Filed Form SS-8 with the Internal Revenue Service Office in (Holtsville, NY; Newport, VT; or Washington, DC; as appropriate). By filing this protective claim, I reserve the right to file a claim for any refund that may be due after a determination of my employment tax status has been completed."

Filing Form SS-8 does not alter the requirement to timely file an income tax return. Do not delay filing your tax return in anticipation of an answer to your SS-8 request. In addition, if applicable, do not delay in responding to a request for payment while waiting for a determination of your worker status.

Instructions for Firms

If a **worker** has requested a determination of his or her status while working for you, you will receive a request from the IRS to complete a Form SS-8. In cases of this type, the IRS usually gives each party an opportunity to present a statement of the facts because any decision will affect the employment tax status of the parties. Failure to respond to this request will not prevent the IRS from issuing a determination letter based on the information he or she has made available so that the worker may fulfill his or her Federal tax obligations. However, the information that you provide is extremely valuable in determining the status of the worker.

If **you** are requesting a determination for a particular class of worker, complete the form for **one** individual who is representative of the class of workers whose status is in question. If you want a written determination for more than one class of workers, complete a separate Form SS-8 for one worker from each class whose status is typical of that class. A written determination for any worker will apply to other workers of the same class if the facts are not materially different for these workers. Please provide a list of names and addresses of all workers potentially affected by this determination.

If you have a reasonable basis for not treating a worker as an employee, you may be relieved from having to pay employment taxes for that worker under section 530 of the 1978 Revenue Act. However, this relief provision cannot be considered in conjunction with a Form SS-8 determination because the determination does not constitute an examination of any tax return. For more information regarding section 530 of the 1978 Revenue Act and to determine if you qualify for relief under this section, you may visit the IRS website at **www.irs.gov.**

Privacy Act and Paperwork Reduction Act Notice. We ask for the information on this form to carry out the Internal Revenue laws of the United States. This information will be used to determine the employment status of the worker(s) described on the form. Subtitle C, Employment Taxes, of the Internal Revenue Code imposes employment taxes on wages. Sections 3121(d), 3306(a), and 3401(c) and (d) and the related regulations define employee and employer for purposes of employment taxes imposed under Subtitle C. Section 6001 authorizes the IRS to request information needed to determine if a worker(s) or firm is subject to these taxes. Section 6109 requires you to provide your taxpayer identification number. Neither workers nor firms are required to request a status determination, but if you choose to do so, you must provide the information requested on this form. Failure to provide the requested information may prevent us from making a status determination. If any worker or the firm has requested a status determination and you are being asked to provide information for use in that determination, you are not required to provide the requested information. However, failure to provide such information will prevent the IRS from considering it in making the status determination. Providing false or fraudulent information may subject you to penalties. Routine uses of this information include providing it to the Department of Justice for use in civil and criminal litigation, to the Social Security Administration for the administration of social security programs, and to cities, states, and the District of Columbia for the administration of their tax laws. We may also disclose this information to Federal and state agencies to enforce Federal nontax criminal laws and to combat terrorism. We may provide this information to the affected worker(s) or the firm as part of the status determination process.

You are not required to provide the information requested on a form that is subject to the Paperwork Reduction Act unless the form displays a valid OMB control number. Books or records relating to a form or its instructions must be retained as long as their contents may become material in the administration of any Internal Revenue law. Generally, tax returns and return information are confidential, as required by section 6103.

The time needed to complete and file this form will vary depending on individual circumstances. The estimated average time is: **Recordkeeping,** 22 hrs.; **Learning about the law or the form,** 47 min.; and **Preparing and sending the form to the IRS,** 1 hr., 11 min. If you have comments concerning the accuracy of these time estimates or suggestions for making this form simpler, we would be happy to hear from you. You can write to the Tax Products Coordinating Committee, Western Area Distribution Center, Rancho Cordova, CA 95743-0001. **Do not** send the tax form to this address. Instead, see **Where To File** on page 4.

Election To Have a Tax Year Other Than a Required Tax Year

OMB No. 1545-1036

Type or Print

Name

Employer identification number

Number, street, and room or suite no. (or P.O. box number if mail is not delivered to street address)

City or town, state, and ZIP code

1 Check applicable box to show type of entity:
- [ ] Partnership
- [ ] S corporation (or C corporation electing to be an S corporation)
- [ ] Personal service corporation (PSC)

2 Name and telephone number (including area code) of person who may be called for information:

3 Enter ending date of the tax year for the entity's last filed return. A new entity should enter the ending date of the tax year it is adopting. . . . .

Month	Day	Year

4 Enter ending date of required tax year determined under section 441(i), 706(b), or 1378 . .

Month	Day

5 Section 444(a) Election. Check the applicable box and enter the ending date of the first tax year for which the election will be effective that the entity is (see instructions):
- [ ] Adopting
- [ ] Retaining
- [ ] Changing to

Month	Day	Year

Under penalties of perjury, I declare that the entity named above has authorized me to make this election under section 444(a), and that the statements made are, to the best of my knowledge and belief, true, correct, and complete.

▶ _____
Signature and title (see instructions)

▶ _____
Date

General Instructions

Section references are to the Internal Revenue Code unless otherwise noted.

Purpose of Form

Form 8716 is filed by partnerships, S corporations, and personal service corporations (as defined in section 441(i)(2)) to elect under section 444 to have a tax year other than a required tax year.

When To File

Form 8716 must be signed and filed by itself by the earlier of:

1. The 15th day of the 5th month following the month that includes the 1st day of the tax year the election will be effective or

2. The due date (not including extensions) of the income tax return for the tax year resulting from the section 444 election.

Items **1** and **2** relate to the tax year, or the return for the tax year, for which the ending date is entered on line 5 above.

Under Regulations section 301.9100-2, the entity is automatically granted a 12-month extension to make an election on Form 8716. To obtain an extension, type or legibly print "Filed Pursuant To Section 301.9100-2" at the top of a properly prepared Form 8716, and file the form within 12 months of the original due date.

Where To File

File Form 8716 with the **Internal Revenue Service Center** at the applicable address shown below.

For . . .	The Address Is:
Partnerships, S corporations, and personal service corporations whose principal business, office, or agency is located in a foreign country or U.S. possession	Philadelphia, PA 19255
Partnerships, S corporations, and personal service corporations whose total assets at the end of the tax year are $10 million or more **or** whose principal business, office, or agency is located in Alabama, Alaska, Arizona, Arkansas, California, Colorado, Florida, Georgia, Hawaii, Idaho, Iowa, Kansas, Louisiana, Minnesota, Mississippi, Missouri, Montana, Nebraska, Nevada, New Mexico, North Dakota, Oklahoma, Oregon, South Dakota, Tennessee, Texas, Utah, Washington, or Wyoming	Ogden, UT 84201
All others not listed above.	Cincinnati, OH 45999

Also file a copy of Form 8716 with your income tax return for the first tax year for which the election is made. To enable electronic filing, you may file an unsigned Form 8716 containing the same information as on the signed Form 8716 you filed by itself.

Effect of Section 444 Election

Partnerships and S corporations. An electing partnership or S corporation must file **Form 8752**, Required Payment or Refund Under Section 7519, for each year the election is in effect. Form 8752 is used to figure and make the payment required under section 7519 or to obtain a refund of net prior year payments. Form 8752 must be filed by May 15 following the calendar year in which each applicable election year begins.

The section 444 election will end if the partnership or S corporation is penalized for willfully failing to make the required payments.

Personal service corporations. An electing personal service corporation (PSC) should not file Form 8752. Instead, it must comply with the minimum distribution requirements of section 280H for each year the election is in effect. If the PSC does not meet these requirements, the applicable amounts it may deduct for payments made to its employee-owners may be limited.

Use **Schedule H (Form 1120),** Section 280H Limitations for a Personal Service Corporation (PSC), to figure the required minimum distribution and the maximum deductible amount. Attach Schedule H to the income tax return of the PSC for each tax year the PSC does not meet the minimum distribution requirements.

The section 444 election will end if the PSC is penalized for willfully failing to comply with the requirements of section 280H.

Members of Certain Tiered Structures May Not Make Election

No election may be made under section 444(a) by an entity that is part of a tiered structure other than a tiered structure that consists entirely of partnerships and/or S corporations all of which have the same tax year. An election previously made will be terminated if an entity later becomes part of a tiered structure that is not allowed to make the election. See Temporary Regulations section 1.444-2T for other details.

Acceptance of Election

After your election is received and accepted by the service center, the center will stamp it "Accepted" and return a copy to you. Be sure to keep a copy of the form marked "Accepted" for your records.

End of Election

The election is made only once. It remains in effect until the entity changes its accounting period to its required tax year or some other permitted year or it is penalized for willfully failing to comply with the requirements of section 280H or 7519. If the election is terminated, the entity may not make another section 444 election.

Signature

Form 8716 is not a valid election unless it is signed. For partnerships, a general partner or a member-manager of a limited liability company must sign and date the election.

For corporations, the election must be signed and dated by the president, vice president, treasurer, assistant treasurer, chief accounting officer, or any other corporate officer (such as tax officer) authorized to sign its tax return.

If a receiver, trustee in bankruptcy, or assignee controls the entity's property or business, that person must sign the election.

Specific Instructions

Line 1

Check the applicable box to indicate whether the entity is classified for federal income tax purposes as a partnership, an S corporation (or a C corporation electing to be an S corporation), or a PSC.

A corporation electing to be an S corporation that wants to make a section 444 election is not required to attach a copy of Form 8716 to its **Form 2553,** Election by a Small Business Corporation. However, the corporation is required to state on Form 2553 its intention to make a section 444 election (or a backup section 444 election). If a corporation is making a backup section 444 election (provided for in item Q, Part II, of Form 2553), it must type or print the words "Backup Election" at the top of the Form 8716 it files. See Temporary Regulations section 1.444-3T for more details.

Line 2

Enter the name and telephone number (including the area code) of a person that the IRS may call for information needed to complete the processing of the election.

Line 4

Required tax year. The required tax year for an S corporation or PSC is a calendar year. Generally, the required tax year for a partnership is the tax year of a majority of its partners (see Regulations section 1.706-1(b) for details).

Line 5

The following limitations and special rules apply in determining the tax year an entity may elect.

New entity adopting a tax year. An entity adopting a tax year may elect a tax year under section 444 only if the deferral period of the tax year is not longer than 3 months. See below for the definition of deferral period.

Existing entity retaining a tax year. In certain cases, an entity may elect to retain its tax year if the deferral period is no longer than 3 months. If the entity does not want to elect to retain its tax year, it may elect to change its tax year as explained below.

Existing entity changing a tax year. An existing entity may elect to change its tax year if the deferral period of the elected tax year is no longer than the shorter of 3 months or the deferral period of the tax year being changed. If the tax year being changed is the entity's required tax year, the deferral period for that year is zero and the entity is not permitted to make a section 444 election.

Example. ABC, a C corporation that historically used a tax year ending October 31, elects S status and wants to make a section 444 election for its tax year beginning November 1. ABC's required tax year under section 1378 is a calendar tax year. In this case, the deferral period of the tax year being changed is 2 months. Thus, ABC may elect to retain its tax year beginning November 1 and ending October 31 or elect a tax year beginning on December 1 (with a deferral period of one month). However, it may not elect a tax year beginning October 1 because the

3-month deferral period would be longer than the 2-month deferral period of the tax year being changed. If ABC elects a tax year beginning on December 1, it must file a short tax year return beginning November 1 and ending November 30.

Deferral period. The term "deferral period" means the number of months that occur between the last day of the elected tax year and the last day of the required tax year. For example, if you elected a tax year that ends on September 30 and your required tax year is the calendar year, the deferral period would be 3 months (the number of months between September 30 and December 31).

Paperwork Reduction Act Notice. We ask for the information on this form to carry out the Internal Revenue laws of the United States. You are required to give us the information. We need it to ensure that you are complying with these laws and to allow us to figure and collect the right amount of tax.

You are not required to provide the information requested on a form that is subject to the Paperwork Reduction Act unless the form displays a valid OMB control number. Books or records relating to a form or its instructions must be retained as long as their contents may become material in the administration of any Internal Revenue law. Generally, tax returns and return information are confidential, as required by section 6103.

The time needed to complete and file this form will vary depending on individual circumstances. The estimated average time is:

Recordkeeping . . . . 2 hr., 37 min.

Learning about the law or the form . . . . 1 hr., 12 min.

Preparing and sending the form to the IRS . . . 1 hr., 16 min.

If you have comments concerning the accuracy of these time estimates or suggestions for making this form simpler, we would be happy to hear from you. You can write to the Tax Products Coordinating Committee, Western Area Distribution Center, Rancho Cordova, CA 95743-0001. **Do not** send the form to this address. Instead, see **Where To File** on page 1.

Form **8832**
(Rev. September 2002)
Department of the Treasury
Internal Revenue Service

Entity Classification Election

OMB No. 1545-1516

Type or Print

Name of entity

EIN ▶

Number, street, and room or suite no. If a P.O. box, see instructions.

City or town, state, and ZIP code. If a foreign address, enter city, province or state, postal code and country.

1 Type of election (see instructions):

a ☐ Initial classification by a newly-formed entity.

b ☐ Change in current classification.

2 Form of entity (see instructions):

a ☐ A domestic eligible entity electing to be classified as an association taxable as a corporation.

b ☐ A domestic eligible entity electing to be classified as a partnership.

c ☐ A domestic eligible entity with a single owner electing to be disregarded as a separate entity.

d ☐ A foreign eligible entity electing to be classified as an association taxable as a corporation.

e ☐ A foreign eligible entity electing to be classified as a partnership.

f ☐ A foreign eligible entity with a single owner electing to be disregarded as a separate entity.

3 Disregarded entity information (see instructions):
a Name of owner ▶ ....
b Identifying number of owner ▶ ....
c Country of organization of entity electing to be disregarded (if foreign) ▶ ....

4 Election is to be effective beginning (month, day, year) (see instructions) . . . . ▶ ____ / ____ / ____

5 Name and title of person whom the IRS may call for more information

6 That person's telephone number
( )

Consent Statement and Signature(s) (see instructions)

Under penalties of perjury, I (we) declare that I (we) consent to the election of the above-named entity to be classified as indicated above, and that I (we) have examined this consent statement, and to the best of my (our) knowledge and belief, it is true, correct, and complete. If I am an officer, manager, or member signing for all members of the entity, I further declare that I am authorized to execute this consent statement on their behalf.

Signature(s)	Date	Title

For Paperwork Reduction Act Notice, see page 4.   Cat. No. 22598R   Form **8832** (Rev. 9-2002)

General Instructions

Section references are to the Internal Revenue Code unless otherwise noted.

Purpose of Form

For Federal tax purposes, certain business entities automatically are classified as corporations. See items **1** and **3** through **8** under the definition of **corporation** on this page. Other business entities may choose how they are classified for Federal tax purposes. Except for a business entity automatically classified as a corporation, a business entity with at least two members can choose to be classified as either an association taxable as a corporation or a partnership, and a business entity with a single member can choose to be classified as either an association taxable as a corporation or disregarded as an entity separate from its owner.

Generally, an eligible entity that does not file this form will be classified under the default rules described below. An eligible entity that chooses not to be classified under the default rules or that wishes to change its current classification must file Form 8832 to elect a classification. The IRS will use the information entered on this form to establish the entity's filing and reporting requirements for Federal tax purposes.

60-month limitation rule. Once an eligible entity makes an election to change its classification, the entity generally cannot change its classification by election again during the 60 months after the effective date of the election. However, the IRS may (**by private letter ruling**) permit the entity to change its classification by election within the 60-month period if more than 50% of the ownership interests in the entity as of the effective date of the election are owned by persons that did not own any interests in the entity on the effective date of the entity's prior election. See Regulations section 301.7701-3(c)(1)(iv) for more details.

Note: *The 60-month limitation does not apply if the previous election was made by a newly formed eligible entity and was effective on the date of formation.*

Default Rules

Existing entity default rule. Certain domestic and foreign entities that were in existence before January 1, 1997, and have an established Federal tax classification generally do not need to make an election to continue that classification. If an existing entity decides to change its classification, it may do so subject to the 60-month limitation rule. See Regulations sections 301.7701-3(b)(3) and 301.7701-3(h)(2) for more details.

Domestic default rule. Unless an election is made on Form 8832, a domestic eligible entity is:

1. A partnership if it has two or more members.

2. Disregarded as an entity separate from its owner if it has a single owner.

A change in the number of members of an eligible entity classified as an association does not affect the entity's classification. However, an eligible entity classified as a partnership will become a disregarded entity when the entity's membership is reduced to one member and a disregarded entity will be classified as a partnership when the entity has more than one member.

Foreign default rule. Unless an election is made on Form 8832, a foreign eligible entity is:

1. A partnership if it has two or more members and **at least** one member does not have limited liability.

2. An association taxable as a corporation if all members have limited liability.

3. Disregarded as an entity separate from its owner if it has a single owner that does not have limited liability.

Definitions

Association. For purposes of this form, an association is an eligible entity that is taxable as a corporation by election or, for foreign eligible entities, under the default rules (see Regulations section 301.7701-3).

Business entity. A business entity is any entity recognized for Federal tax purposes that is not properly classified as a trust under Regulations section 301.7701-4 or otherwise subject to special treatment under the Code. See Regulations section 301.7701-2(a).

Corporation. For Federal tax purposes, a corporation is any of the following:

1. A business entity organized under a Federal or state statute, or under a statute of a federally recognized Indian tribe, if the statute describes or refers to the entity as incorporated or as a corporation, body corporate, or body politic.

2. An association (as determined under Regulations section 301.7701-3).

3. A business entity organized under a state statute, if the statute describes or refers to the entity as a joint-stock company or joint-stock association.

4. An insurance company.

5. A state-chartered business entity conducting banking activities, if any of its deposits are insured under the Federal Deposit Insurance Act, as amended, 12 U.S.C. 1811 et seq., or a similar Federal statute.

6. A business entity wholly owned by a state or any political subdivision thereof, or a business entity wholly owned by a foreign government or any other entity described in Regulations section 1.892-2T.

7. A business entity that is taxable as a corporation under a provision of the Code other than section 7701(a)(3).

8. A foreign business entity listed on page 5. See Regulations section 301.7701-2(b)(8) for any exceptions and inclusions to items on this list and for any revisions made to this list since these instructions were printed.

Disregarded entity. A disregarded entity is an eligible entity that is treated as an entity that is not separate from its single owner. Its separate existence will be ignored for Federal tax purposes unless it elects corporate tax treatment.

Eligible entity. An eligible entity is a business entity that is not included in items **1** or **3** through **8** under the definition of corporation above.

Limited liability. A member of a foreign eligible entity has limited liability if the member has no personal liability for any debts of or claims against the entity by reason of being a member. This determination is based solely on the statute or law under which the entity is organized (and, if relevant, the entity's organizational documents). A member has personal liability if the creditors of the entity may seek satisfaction of all or any part of the debts or claims against the entity from the member as such. A member has personal liability even if the member makes an agreement under which another person (whether or not a member of the entity) assumes that liability or agrees to indemnify that member for that liability.

Partnership. A partnership is a business entity that has **at least** two members and is not a corporation as defined on page 2.

Who Must File

File this form for an **eligible entity** that is one of the following:

● A domestic entity electing to be classified as an association taxable as a corporation.

● A domestic entity electing to change its current classification (even if it is currently classified under the default rule).

● A foreign entity that has more than one owner, all owners having limited liability, electing to be classified as a partnership.

● A foreign entity that has at least one owner that does not have limited liability, electing to be classified as an association taxable as a corporation.

● A foreign entity with a single owner having limited liability, electing to be an entity disregarded as an entity separate from its owner.

● A foreign entity electing to change its current classification (even if it is currently classified under the default rule).

Do not file this form for an eligible entity that is:

● Tax-exempt under section 501(a) or

● A real estate investment trust (REIT), as defined in section 856.

Effect of Election

The Federal tax treatment of elective changes in classification as described in Regulations section 301.7701-3(g)(1) is summarized as follows:

● If an eligible entity classified as a partnership elects to be classified as an association, it is deemed that the

partnership contributes all of its assets and liabilities to the association in exchange for stock in the association, and immediately thereafter, the partnership liquidates by distributing the stock of the association to its partners.

● If an eligible entity classified as an association elects to be classified as a partnership, it is deemed that the association distributes all of its assets and liabilities to its shareholders in liquidation of the association, and immediately thereafter, the shareholders contribute all of the distributed assets and liabilities to a newly formed partnership.

● If an eligible entity classified as an association elects to be disregarded as an entity separate from its owner, it is deemed that the association distributes all of its assets and liabilities to its single owner in liquidation of the association.

● If an eligible entity that is disregarded as an entity separate from its owner elects to be classified as an association, the owner of the eligible entity is deemed to have contributed all of the assets and liabilities of the entity to the association in exchange for the stock of the association.

Note: *For information on the Federal tax treatment of elective changes in classification, see Regulations section 301.7701-3(g).*

When To File

See the instructions for line 4.

A newly formed entity may be eligible for late election relief under Rev. Proc. 2002-59, 2002-39 I.R.B. 615 if:

● The entity failed to obtain its desired classified election solely because Form 8832 was not timely filed,

● The due date for the entity's desired classification tax return (excluding extension) for the tax year beginning with the entity's formation date has not passed, and

● The entity has reasonable cause for its failure to make a timely election.

To obtain relief, a newly formed entity must file Form 8832 on or before the due date of the first Federal tax return (excluding extensions) of the entity's desired classification. The entity must also

write "FILED PURSUANT TO REV. PROC. 2002-59" at the top of the form. The entity must attach a statement to the form explaining why it failed to file a timely election. If Rev. Proc. 2002-59 does not apply, an entity may seek relief for a late entity election by requesting a private letter ruling and paying a user fee in accordance with Rev. Proc. 2002-1, 2002-1 I.R.B. 1 (or its successor).

Where To File

File Form 8832 with the Internal Revenue Service Center, Philadelphia, PA 19255. Also attach a copy of Form 8832 to the entity's Federal income tax or information return for the tax year of the election. If the entity is not required to file a return for that year, a copy of its Form 8832 **must** be attached to the Federal income tax or information returns of **all** direct or indirect owners of the entity for the tax year of the owner that includes the date on which the election took effect. Although failure to attach a copy will not invalidate an otherwise valid election, each member of the entity is required to file returns that are consistent with the entity's election. In addition, penalties may be assessed against persons who are required to, but who do not, attach Form 8832 to their returns. Other penalties may apply for filing Federal income tax or information returns inconsistent with the entity's election.

Specific Instructions

Name. Enter the name of the eligible entity electing to be classified using Form 8832.

Employer identification number (EIN). Show the correct EIN of the eligible entity electing to be classified. Any entity that has an EIN will retain that EIN even if its Federal tax classification changes under Regulations section 301.7701-3.

If a disregarded entity's classification changes so that it is recognized as a partnership or association for Federal tax purposes, and that entity had an EIN, then the entity must use that EIN and not the identifying number of the single owner. If the entity did not already have its own EIN, then the entity must apply for an EIN and not use the identifying number of the single owner.

A foreign person that makes an election under Regulations section 301.7701-3(c) must also use its own taxpayer identifying number. See sections 6721 through 6724 for penalties that may apply for failure to supply taxpayer identifying numbers.

If the entity electing to be classified using Form 8832 does not have an EIN, it must apply for one on **Form SS-4,** Application for Employer Identification Number. If the filing of Form 8832 is the only reason the entity is applying for an EIN, check the "Other" box on line 9 of Form SS-4 and write "Form 8832" to the right of that box. If the entity has not received an EIN by the time Form 8832 is due, write "Applied for" in the space for the EIN. **Do not** apply for a new EIN for an existing entity that is changing its classification if the entity already has an EIN.

Address. Enter the address of the entity electing a classification. Include the suite, room, or other unit number after the street address. If the Post Office does not deliver mail to the street address and the entity has a P.O. box, show the box number instead of the street address.

Line 1. Check box 1a if the entity is choosing a classification for the first time **and** the entity does not want to be classified under the applicable default classification. **Do not** file this form if the entity wants to be classified under the default rules.

Check box 1b if the entity is changing its current classification.

Line 2. Check the appropriate box if you are changing a current classification (no matter how achieved), or are electing out of a default classification. **Do not** file this form if you fall within a default classification that is the desired classification for the new entity.

Line 3. If an eligible entity has checked box 2c or box 2f and is electing to be disregarded as an entity separate from its owner, it must enter the name of its owner on line 3a and the owner's identifying number (social security number, or individual taxpayer identification number, or EIN) on line 3b. If the owner is a foreign person or entity and does not have a U.S. identifying number, enter "none" on line 3b. If the entity making the election is foreign, enter the name of the country in which it was formed on line 3c.

Line 4. Generally, the election will take effect on the date you enter on line 4 of this form or on the date filed if no date is entered on line 4. However, an election specifying an entity's classification for Federal tax purposes can take effect no more than 75 days prior to the date the election is filed, nor can it take effect later than 12 months after the date on which the election is filed. If line 4 shows a date more than 75 days prior to the date on which the election is filed, the election will take effect 75 days before the date it is filed. If line 4 shows an effective date more than 12 months from the filing date, the election will take effect 12 months after the date the election was filed.

Consent statement and signatures. Form 8832 must be signed by:

1. Each member of the electing entity who is an owner at the time the election is filed; or

2. Any officer, manager, or member of the electing entity who is authorized (under local law or the organizational documents) to make the election and who represents to having such authorization under penalties of perjury.

If an election is to be effective for any period prior to the time it is filed, each person who was an owner between the date the election is to be effective and the date the election is filed, and who is not an owner at the time the election is filed, must also sign.

If you need a continuation sheet or use a separate consent statement, attach it to Form 8832. The separate consent statement must contain the same information as shown on Form 8832.

Paperwork Reduction Act Notice

We ask for the information on this form to carry out the Internal Revenue laws of the United States. You are required to give us the information. We need it to ensure that you are complying with these laws and to allow us to figure and collect the right amount of tax.

You are not required to provide the information requested on a form that is subject to the Paperwork Reduction Act unless the form displays a valid OMB control number. Books or records relating to a form or its instructions must be retained as long as their contents may become material in the administration of any Internal Revenue law. Generally, tax returns and return information are confidential, as required by section 6103.

The time needed to complete and file this form will vary depending on individual circumstances. The estimated average time is:

Recordkeeping . . 1 hr., 49 min.

Learning about the law or the form . . 2 hr., 7 min.

Preparing and sending the form to the IRS . . . 23 min.

If you have comments concerning the accuracy of these time estimates or suggestions for making this form simpler, we would be happy to hear from you. You can write to the Tax Forms Committee, Western Area Distribution Center, Rancho Cordova, CA 95743-0001. **Do not** send the form to this address. Instead, see **Where To File** on page 3.

Foreign Entities Classified as Corporations for Federal Tax Purposes:

American Samoa—Corporation
Argentina—Sociedad Anonima
Australia—Public Limited Company
Austria—Aktiengesellschaft
Barbados—Limited Company
Belgium—Societe Anonyme
Belize—Public Limited Company
Bolivia—Sociedad Anonima
Brazil—Sociedade Anonima
Canada—Corporation and Company
Chile—Sociedad Anonima
People's Republic of China—Gufen Youxian Gongsi
Republic of China (Taiwan)—Ku-fen Yu-hsien Kung-szu
Colombia—Sociedad Anonima
Costa Rica—Sociedad Anonima
Cyprus—Public Limited Company
Czech Republic—Akciova Spolecnost
Denmark—Aktieselskab
Ecuador—Sociedad Anonima or Compania Anonima
Egypt—Sharikat Al-Mossahamah
El Salvador—Sociedad Anonima
Finland—Julkinen Osakeyhtio/ Publikt Aktiebolag
France—Societe Anonyme
Germany—Aktiengesellschaft
Greece—Anonymos Etairia
Guam—Corporation
Guatemala—Sociedad Anonima
Guyana—Public Limited Company
Honduras—Sociedad Anonima
Hong Kong—Public Limited Company
Hungary—Reszvenytarsasag

Iceland—Hlutafelag
India—Public Limited Company
Indonesia—Perseroan Terbuka
Ireland—Public Limited Company
Israel—Public Limited Company
Italy—Societa per Azioni
Jamaica—Public Limited Company
Japan—Kabushiki Kaisha
Kazakstan—Ashyk Aktsionerlik Kogham
Republic of Korea—Chusik Hoesa
Liberia—Corporation
Luxembourg—Societe Anonyme
Malaysia—Berhad
Malta—Public Limited Company
Mexico—Sociedad Anonima
Morocco—Societe Anonyme
Netherlands—Naamloze Vennootschap
New Zealand—Limited Company
Nicaragua—Compania Anonima
Nigeria—Public Limited Company
Northern Mariana Islands—Corporation
Norway—Allment Aksjeselskap
Pakistan—Public Limited Company
Panama—Sociedad Anonima
Paraguay—Sociedad Anonima
Peru—Sociedad Anonima
Philippines—Stock Corporation
Poland—Spolka Akcyjna
Portugal—Sociedade Anonima
Puerto Rico—Corporation
Romania—Societe pe Actiuni
Russia—Otkrytoye Aktsionernoy Obshchestvo

Saudi Arabia—Sharikat Al-Mossahamah
Singapore—Public Limited Company
Slovak Republic—Akciova Spolocnost
South Africa—Public Limited Company
Spain—Sociedad Anonima
Surinam—Naamloze Vennootschap
Sweden—Publika Aktiebolag
Switzerland—Aktiengesellschaft
Thailand—Borisat Chamkad (Mahachon)
Trinidad and Tobago—Limited Company
Tunisia—Societe Anonyme
Turkey—Anonim Sirket
Ukraine—Aktsionerne Tovaristvo Vidkritogo Tipu
United Kingdom—Public Limited Company
United States Virgin Islands—Corporation
Uruguay—Sociedad Anonima
Venezuela—Sociedad Anonima or Compania Anonima

 See Regulations section 301.7701-2(b)(8) for any exceptions and inclusions to items on this list and for any revisions made to this list since these instructions were printed.

Index

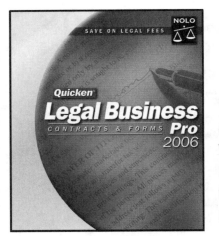

CATALOG

...more from Nolo

	PRICE	CODE

BUSINESS

	PRICE	CODE
Becoming a Mediator: Your Guide to Career Opportunities	$29.99	BECM
Business Buyout Agreements (Book w/CD-ROM)	$49.99	BSAG
The CA Nonprofit Corporation Kit (Binder w/CD-ROM)	$69.99	CNP
California Workers' Comp: How to Take Charge When You're Injured on the Job	$34.99	WORK
The Complete Guide to Buying a Business	$24.99	BUYBU
The Complete Guide to Selling Your Business	$24.99	SELBU
Consultant & Independent Contractor Agreements (Book w/CD-ROM)	$29.99	CICA
The Corporate Records Handbook (Book w/CD-ROM)	$69.99	CORMI
Create Your Own Employee Handbook (Book w/CD-ROM)	$49.99	EMHA
Dealing With Problem Employees	$44.99	PROBM
Deduct It! Lower Your Small Business Taxes	$34.99	DEDU
Effective Fundraising for Nonprofits	$24.99	EFFN
The Employer's Legal Handbook	$39.99	EMPL
Federal Employment Laws	$49.99	FELW
Form Your Own Limited Liability Company (Book w/CD-ROM)	$44.99	LIAB
Home Business Tax Deductions: Keep What You Earn	$34.99	DEHB
How to Create a Noncompete Agreement (Book w/CD-ROM)	$44.95	NOCMP
How to Form a California Professional Corporation (Book w/CD-ROM)	$59.99	PROF
How to Form a Nonprofit Corporation (Book w/CD-ROM)—National Edition	$49.99	NNP
How to Form a Nonprofit Corporation in California (Book w/CD-ROM)	$49.99	NON
How to Form Your Own California Corporation (Binder w/CD-ROM)	$59.99	CACI
How to Form Your Own California Corporation (Book w/CD-ROM)	$34.99	CCOR
How to Get Your Business on the Web	$29.99	WEBS
How to Run a Thriving Business: Strategies for Success & Satisfaction	$19.99	THRV

Prices subject to change.

	PRICE	CODE
How to Write a Business Plan	$34.99	SBS
Incorporate Your Business	$49.99	NIBS
The Independent Paralegal's Handbook	$34.99	PARA
Legal Guide for Starting & Running a Small Business	$34.99	RUNS
Legal Forms for Starting & Running a Small Business (Book w/CD-ROM)	$29.99	RUNSF
LLC or Corporation?	$24.99	CHENT
The Manager's Legal Handbook	$39.99	ELBA
Marketing Without Advertising	$20.00	MWAD
Mediate, Don't Litigate	$24.99	MEDL
Music Law (Book w/CD-ROM)	$34.99	ML
Negotiate the Best Lease for Your Business	$24.99	LESP
Nolo's Guide to Social Security Disability	$29.99	QSS
Nolo's Quick LLC	$29.99	LLCQ
Nondisclosure Agreements (Book w/CD-ROM)	$39.95	NAG
The Partnership Book: How to Write a Partnership Agreement (Book w/CD-ROM)	$39.99	PART
The Performance Appraisal Handbook	$29.99	PERF
The Small Business Start-up Kit (Book w/CD-ROM)	$29.99	SMBU
The Small Business Start-up Kit for California (Book w/CD-ROM)	$24.99	OPEN
Starting & Running a Successful Newsletter or Magazine	$29.99	MAG
Tax Savvy for Small Business	$36.99	SAVVY
Workplace Investigations: A Step by Step Guide	$39.99	CMPLN
Working for Yourself: Law & Taxes for Independent Contractors, Freelancers & Consultants	$39.99	WAGE
Working With Independent Contractors (Book w/CD-ROM)	$29.99	HICI
Your Crafts Business: A Legal Guide (Book w/CD-ROM)	$26.99	VART
Your Limited Liability Company: An Operating Manual (Book w/CD-ROM)	$49.99	LOP
Your Rights in the Workplace	$29.99	YRW

CONSUMER

	PRICE	CODE
How to Win Your Personal Injury Claim	$29.99	PICL
Nolo's Encyclopedia of Everyday Law	$29.99	EVL

	PRICE	CODE

Nolo's Guide to California Law .... $24.99   CLAW

ESTATE PLANNING & PROBATE

8 Ways to Avoid Probate .... $19.99   PRAV

Estate Planning Basics .... $21.99   ESPN

The Executor's Guide: Settling a Loved One's Estate or Trust .... $34.99   EXEC

How to Probate an Estate in California .... $49.99   PAE

Make Your Own Living Trust (Book w/CD-ROM) .... $39.99   LITR

Nolo's Simple Will Book (Book w/CD-ROM) .... $36.99   SWIL

Plan Your Estate .... $44.99   NEST

Quick & Legal Will Book .... $16.99   QUIC

Special Needs Trust: Protect Your Child's Financial Future .... $34.99   SPNT

FAMILY MATTERS

Building a Parenting Agreement That Works .... $24.99   CUST

The Complete IEP Guide .... $34.99   IEP

Divorce & Money: How to Make the Best Financial Decisions During Divorce .... $34.99   DIMO

Do Your Own California Adoption: Nolo's Guide for Stepparents
    and Domestic Partners (Book w/CD-ROM) .... $34.99   ADOP

Every Dog's Legal Guide: A Must-Have for Your Owner .... $19.99   DOG

Get a Life: You Don't Need a Million to Retire Well .... $24.99   LIFE

The Guardianship Book for California .... $39.99   GB

A Legal Guide for Lesbian and Gay Couples .... $34.99   LG

Living Together: A Legal Guide (Book w/CD-ROM) .... $34.99   LTK

Living Wills and Powers of Attorney in California (Book w/CD-ROM) .... $21.99   CPOA

Nolo's IEP Guide: Learning Disabilities .... $29.99   IELD

Prenuptial Agreements: How to Write a Fair & Lasting Contract (Book w/CD-ROM) .... $34.99   PNUP

Using Divorce Mediation: Save Your Money & Your Sanity .... $29.99   UDMD

	PRICE	CODE

GOING TO COURT

	PRICE	CODE
Beat Your Ticket: Go To Court & Win! (National Edition)	$21.99	BEYT
The Criminal Law Handbook: Know Your Rights, Survive the System	$34.99	KYR
Everybody's Guide to Small Claims Court (National Edition)	$26.99	NSCC
Everybody's Guide to Small Claims Court in California	$29.99	CSCC
Fight Your Ticket & Win in California	$29.99	FYT
How to Change Your Name in California	$34.99	NAME
How to Collect When You Win a Lawsuit (California Edition)	$29.99	JUDG
The Lawsuit Survival Guide	$29.99	UNCL
Nolo's Deposition Handbook	$29.99	DEP
Represent Yourself in Court: How to Prepare & Try a Winning Case	$34.99	RYC
Win Your Lawsuit: A Judge's Guide to Representing Yourself in California Superior Court	$29.99	SLWY

HOMEOWNERS, LANDLORDS & TENANTS

	PRICE	CODE
California Tenants' Rights	$27.99	CTEN
Deeds for California Real Estate	$24.99	DEED
Every Landlord's Legal Guide (National Edition, Book w/CD-ROM)	$44.99	ELLI
Every Landlord's Tax Deduction Guide	$34.99	DELL
Every Tenant's Legal Guide	$29.99	EVTEN
For Sale by Owner in California	$29.99	FSBO
How to Buy a House in California	$34.99	BHCA
The California Landlord's Law Book: Rights & Responsibilities (Book w/CD-ROM)	$44.99	LBRT
The California Landlord's Law Book: Evictions (Book w/CD-ROM)	$44.99	LBEV
Leases & Rental Agreements	$29.99	LEAR
Neighbor Law: Fences, Trees, Boundaries & Noise	$26.99	NEI
The New York Landlord's Law Book (Book w/CD-ROM)	$39.99	NYLL
New York Tenants' Rights	$27.99	NYTEN
Renters' Rights (National Edition)	$24.99	RENT

	PRICE	CODE

IMMIGRATION

Becoming A U.S. Citizen: A Guide to the Law, Exam and Interview .... $24.99 — USCIT

Fiancé & Marriage Visas (Book w/CD-ROM) .... $44.99 — IMAR

How to Get a Green Card .... $29.99 — GRN

Student & Tourist Visas .... $29.99 — ISTU

U.S. Immigration Made Easy .... $44.99 — IMEZ

MONEY MATTERS

101 Law Forms for Personal Use (Book w/CD-ROM) .... $29.99 — SPOT

Bankruptcy: Is It the Right Solution to Your Debt Problems? .... $21.99 — BRS

Chapter 13 Bankruptcy: Repay Your Debts .... $36.99 — CHB

Credit Repair (Book w/CD-ROM) .... $24.99 — CREP

Getting Paid: How to Collect From Bankrupt Debtors .... $29.99 — CRBNK

How to File for Chapter 7 Bankruptcy .... $29.99 — HFB

IRAs, 401(k)s & Other Retirement Plans: Taking Your Money Out .... $34.99 — RET

Solve Your Money Troubles .... $19.99 — MT

Stand Up to the IRS .... $29.99 — SIRS

Surviving an IRS Tax Audit .... $24.95 — SAUD

Take Control of Your Student Loan Debt .... $26.95 — SLOAN

PATENTS AND COPYRIGHTS

All I Need is Money: How to Finance Your Invention .... $19.99 — FINA

The Copyright Handbook: How to Protect and Use Written Works (Book w/CD-ROM) .... $39.99 — COHA

Copyright Your Software (Book w/CD-ROM) .... $34.95 — CYS

Getting Permission: How to License and Clear Copyrighted Materials

  Online and Off (Book w/CD-ROM) .... $34.99 — RIPER

How to Make Patent Drawings .... $29.99 — DRAW

	PRICE	CODE
The Inventor's Notebook	$24.99	INOT
License Your Invention (Book w/CD-ROM)	$39.99	LICE
Nolo's Patents for Beginners	$29.99	QPAT
Patent, Copyright & Trademark	$39.99	PCTM
Patent It Yourself	$49.99	PAT
Patent Pending in 24 Hours	$29.99	PEND
Patenting Art & Entertainment: New Strategies for Protecting Creative Ideas	$39.99	PATAE
The Public Domain	$34.99	PUBL
Trademark: Legal Care for Your Business and Product Name	$39.99	TRD
Web and Software Development: A Legal Guide (Book w/ CD-ROM)	$44.99	SFT
What Every Inventor Needs to Know About Business & Taxes (Book w/CD-ROM)	$21.99	ILAX

RESEARCH & REFERENCE

Legal Research: How to Find & Understand the Law	$39.99	LRES

SENIORS

Long-Term Care: How to Plan & Pay for It	$21.99	ELD
Social Security, Medicare & Goverment Pensions	$29.99	SOA

Order Form

Name

Address

City

State, Zip

Daytime Phone

E-mail

Our "No-Hassle" Guarantee

Return anything you buy directly from Nolo for any reason and we'll cheerfully refund your purchase price. No ifs, ands or buts.

☐ Check here if you do not wish to receive mailings from other companies

Item Code	Quantity	Item	Unit Price	Total Price

Method of payment

☐ Check ☐ VISA ☐ MasterCard
☐ Discover Card ☐ American Express

Subtotal	
Add your local sales tax (California only)	
Shipping: RUSH $12, Basic $9 (See below)	
"I bought 3, ship it to me FREE!" (Ground shipping only)	
TOTAL	

Account Number

Expiration Date

Signature

Shipping and Handling

Rush Delivery—Only $12

We'll ship any order to any street address in the U.S. by UPS 2nd Day Air* for only $12!

* Order by noon Pacific Time and get your order in 2 business days. Orders placed after noon Pacific Time will arrive in 3 business days. P.O. boxes and S.F. Bay Area use basic shipping. Alaska and Hawaii use 2nd Day Air or Priority Mail.

Basic Shipping—$9

Use for P.O. Boxes, Northern California and Ground Service.

Allow 1-2 weeks for delivery. U.S. addresses only.

For faster service, use your credit card and our toll-free numbers

Call our customer service group
Monday thru Friday 7am to 7pm PST

Phone	1-800-728-3555
Fax	1-800-645-0895
Mail	Nolo
950 Parker St.
Berkeley, CA 94710

Order 24 hours a day @
www.nolo.com